Estranged

Guns N' Roses & *Use Your Illusion*

Geoff Harkness

Paperback ISBN: 979-8-9887170-7-2

Hardcover ISBN: 979-8-9887170-6-5

First edition February 2026

Cover photo by Kevin Mazur, courtesy Getty Images

Cover design by J. Hurst

Interior design by J. Hurst

Carol Press

Geoff Harkness wrote this book without AI or any other technology besides a basic word processor.

Also by Geoff Harkness

40-Foot Lemon: The Complete Story of U2's Pop & PopMart

Rain King: The Life & Music of Adam Duritz & Counting Crows

DVS Mindz: The Twenty-Year Saga of the Greatest Rap Group to Almost Make it Outta Kansas

Changing Qatar: Culture, Citizenship, & Rapid Modernization

Chicago Hustle & Flow: Gangs, Gangsta Rap, & Social Class

For Ben, Emma, and Laura

Contents

Cast of Characters

Steven Adler First drummer for GNR

Tracey Amos Backup singer for GNR on part of the Illusion tour

Teddy Andreadis Multi-instrumentalist who played with GNR on part of the Illusion tour

West Arkeen Musician who co-wrote several songs with GNR

Sebastian "Bass" Bach Singer for Skid Row

Amy Bailey Axl Rose's sister

Stuart Bailey Axl Rose's brother

Bryn Bridenthal Publicist for Geffen Records

Gilby Clarke Second rhythm guitarist for GNR

Bob Clearmountain Created the original mix for *Use Your Illusion*, which GNR rejected

Mike Clink Producer of *Use Your Illusion*

Kurt Cobain Singer and guitarist for Nirvana

Alice Cooper 1970s hard-rock legend who sang on the *Use Your Illusion* song "The Garden"

Dan Diemer St. Louis County assistant prosecuting attorney

Craig Duswalt Personal assistant to Axl Rose

Erin Everly Ex-wife of Axl, daughter of Don Everly of the Everly Brothers

Roberta Freeman Backup singer for GNR on part of the Illusion tour

Earl Gabbidon Bodyguard for Axl Rose

Doug Goldstein GNR's manager after they fired Alan Niven

Billy Gould Bassist for Faith No More

James Hetfield Singer and rhythm guitarist for Metallica

Kirk Hammett Lead guitarist for Metallica

Shannon Hoon Lafayette, Indiana native and singer for Blind Melon

Ice-T Rapper and vocalist for Body Count

Michael Jackson Singer whose 1991 album *Dangerous* included guitar work from Slash

Mick Jagger Singer for the Rolling Stones

Del James Musician and journalist who befriended Axl Rose in 1985

Robert John Official photographer for GNR since their club days

Gabriella "Gabby" Kantor Axl's next-door neighbor who sued him after an altercation

Anne King Trumpet player for GNR on part of the Illusion tour

Mark Kostabi Artist whose painting *Use Your Illusion* was commissioned by Axl

Lenny Kravitz Musician who collaborated with Slash and performed in concert with GNR

Wendy Laister Tour publicist for GNR

Johann Langlie Electronic musician who worked on *Use Your Illusion*

Elizabeth "Beta" Lebeis Nanny for Stephanie Seymour, who later became Axl's personal assistant

Kurt Loder News reporter for MTV

Suzzy London Therapist for Axl

Courtney Love Singer and guitarist for Hole and wife of Kurt Cobain

Arthur Margulis An attorney for Axl

Lisa Maxwell Saxophonist for GNR on part of the Illusion tour

Brian May Guitarist for Queen

Tom Mayhue Onstage technician and personal roadie for Axl

Sharon Maynard Psychic advisor to Axl

Robert McCulloch St. Louis County prosecuting attorney

Duff McKagan Bassist for GNR

Gerald McMahon An attorney for Axl

Jim Mitchell Engineer of *Use Your Illusion*

Andy Morahan Video director of "Don't Cry," "November Rain," "Estranged" and more

Vince Neil Singer for Mötley Crüe

Jason Newsted Bassist for Metallica

Alan Niven GNR manager who was fired at the beginning of the Illusion tour

Krist Novoselic Bassist for Nirvana

Sabrina Okamoto Masseuse for the Illusion tour

Mike Patton Singer for Faith No More

Tom Petty Musician who invited Axl to sing with him in concert and on television

Bill Price Mixer of *Use Your Illusion*

Riki Rachtman MTV personality and co-owner of the Cathouse nightclub

Dizzy Reed Keyboardist for GNR

John Reese Tour manager for the Illusion tour

Vernon Reid Guitarist for Living Colour

Keith Richards Guitarist for the Rolling Stones

Josh Richman Producer and co-writer of the "Don't Cry" music video

Axl Rose Vocalist for GNR

Arnold Schwarzenegger *Terminator* actor featured in the "You Could Be Mine" music video

Stephanie Seymour Supermodel and one-time girlfriend of Axl Rose

Joe Shanahan Owner of the Chicago nightclubs Metro and Smartbar – GNR rehearsed upstairs

Slash Lead guitarist for GNR

Tabitha Soren News reporter for MTV

Matt Sorum Second drummer for GNR

Izzy Stradlin Original rhythm guitarist for GNR

Bill "Stump" Stephenson Fan who got into an altercation with Axl at a concert in St. Louis

Stephen Thaxton Chiropractor for the Illusion tour

Steven Tyler Singer for Aerosmith

Lars Ulrich Drummer for Metallica

Arlett Vereecke Publicist for GNR from 1987-1992

CeCe Worrall Flute and saxophone player for GNR on part of the Illusion tour

Tom Zutaut A&R executive who signed GNR to Geffen Records

Introduction

Stones N' Roses

Axl Rose never wanted to be called a heavy metal singer even though he fronted what many believed to be the biggest metal band in the world. Guns N' Roses struck gold when they covered Bob Dylan's "Knockin' on Heaven's Door" during their 1988 appearance at the Ritz in New York City, which was broadcast repeatedly on MTV. Choosing Dylan instantly set Guns apart from peers such as Mötley Crüe and Poison, who covered Brownsville Station, Kiss, and Slade. Members of GNR had been interviewed for the 1988 documentary *Decline of the Western Civilization Part II*, which featured notables such as Poison and W.A.S.P., but pulled out at the eleventh hour because they did not want to be associated with the Sunset Strip metal scene. While their peers played at each other's shows, Axl worked to align Guns with a different set of 1970s icons, collaborating with legends such as Don Henley and Sex Pistols guitarist Steve Jones.

So, when GNR got the call to open for the Rolling Stones on the venerable English quintet's *Steel Wheels* tour, it was an opportunity they could not pass up. Pairing with the Stones was a dream come true for everyone in Guns, the highest of honors. The Stones initially offered GNR the opening slot for the entire tour, but the group demurred, eager to headline and in no shape to go on the road. They eventually settled on four dates at the 72,000-capacity Los Angeles Memorial Coliseum. Guns would earn a cool $1 million for hometown shows that required few expenses or personnel and thus would yield significant profit. Industry insiders estimated that GNR accounted for twenty to forty percent of ticket sales at the L.A. stops.[2]

The Stones-Guns matchup generated controversy from the get-go. After GNR passed on opening the entire tour, the Stones offered the slot to Living Colour, an all-black hard-rock quartet from New York City. Stones vocalist Mick Jagger had taken an early interest in Living Colour, producing a couple of demos that helped the act land a deal with Epic Records. Their debut *Vivid*, issued in May 1988, reached number six on the Billboard album chart on the strength of the single "Cult of Personality." *Vivid* would go on to sell more than two million copies.

Living Colour's leader, dexterous guitarist Vernon Reid, was an outspoken social activist who co-founded the Black Rock Coalition in 1985. The Coalition's mission was to combat racism toward blacks in the music industry and support black rock musicians. Reid and the Coalition had publicly denounced "One in a Million," a song from 1988's *G N' R Lies,* whose controversial lyrics confronted immigrants and other groups using loaded terms such as "nigger" and "faggot." The squabble between Living Colour and GNR generated more controversy when it was announced that both acts would play with the Stones in L.A.

That fall, as the dates approached, Living Colour appeared on *The Arsenio Hall Show*, where they were asked about sharing a bill with Axl and company. Bassist Muzz Skillings took the high road, stating, "Ultimately, it's about making music. Everybody has a different way of expressing themselves. Most problems arise out of lack of communication. There's no problem with us; we're having a good time. They're doing their thing, we're doing ours."

Arsenio Hall loved Skillings' strategy. "Kill him with love. Shake his hand and educate my man," the host enthused. But guitarist Vernon Reid wasn't having it. "You gotta let 'em know," he countered. "Black people, gay people, women are not objects to be labeled and to be talked about any which way. We're people with feelings. They gotta understand that and then we can go on and just make music." The audience applauded in agreement.

At the time, many journalists compared Guns to N.W.A, an L.A.-based gangsta rap outfit whose hardcore material and streetwise image had generated every bit as much controversy as GNR. Axl agreed with this analogy and refused to apologize for "One in a Million," defending himself in the press. "This band grew up on the streets of this town and that's where these songs are rooted," he told the *Los Angeles Times* shortly after "One in a Million's" release. "That's what you need if you are going to write about the street. You have to tell it the way it actually happened, including the language. Living on the streets, you go through a lot of hard times and a lot of my hard times were with people of different races or different beliefs. I haven't anything against those people. I'm not a racist. The songs are just an account of what happened to us. If you change the words or soften them, you change the truth."[3]

But that was then. Today, more than anything, Axl wanted to put "One in a Million" behind him and get to work on GNR's second album. There was no need to make "Million" the focus of an ongoing debate. Guns had only performed it three times in concert, years earlier, before it was released. Axl certainly had no intention of playing it now, which he thought would serve as a distraction and slow the group's progress.

Axl believed that if GNR's sophomore record was good enough, an epic awash in generation-defining classics, it could make the controversy go away, silencing the critics and launching Guns into the stratosphere. But they hadn't been into a recording studio in ages, and lead guitarist Slash and drummer Steven Adler were openly using heroin.

The media could not resist a good celebrity scandal, and continued to stoke the flames as the Stones gigs drew near. Around this time, outlets that included *Entertainment Tonight*, the *Today* show, and the *Village Voice* ran negative stories that heavily criticized Axl and "One in a Million." Arsenio Hall called Axl an "ignorant racist" on his late-night talk show.[4] In September, *The New York Times* published a lengthy article that decried bigotry in popular music, supposedly on the rise. The *Times* focused much of its ire on Axl, comparing Guns and their ilk to "cockroaches in a clean kitchen, signaling more trouble to come," and declaring that the group "addresses a white majority and remains unrepentant. Mr. Rose spewed his racism in a song on a Top 10 recording, the two-million-selling *G N' R Lies*, and he considers himself brave and forthright."[5]

Even some of Axl's own bandmates were taking shots at him. In August, rhythm guitarist Izzy Stradlin gave an interview to British music magazine *The Face* that was published a few weeks before the Stones matchup. Asked about "One in a Million," GNR's founding axeman did not mince words. "'One in a Million' is just flat-out racist," he declared. "I have a big problem with that lyric. I was pissed off. I was very against that shit going on our record."[6]

On October 15, just three days before opening night in L.A., *Eyes on the Prize* author Juan Williams penned an op-ed for *The Washington Post* that condemned racism, sexism, and gay bashing in popular music. Williams declared "One in a Million" to be a "racist tirade" and a "hateful song," and dismissed Axl for his supposedly "stunning ignorance of American history."[7]

Closer to home, on the same day, the *Los Angeles Times* published a feature-length screed under the headline "Behind the Guns N' Roses Racism Furor: The Continuing Debate Over Whether the Band's song, 'One in a Million,' Promotes Bigotry."[8] In the piece, Arsenio Hall again blasted Axl's use of the n-word and asserted that, "Guns N' Roses' attitude points out the very danger in using it. Because ignorant white people like Axl Rose are going to get the idea that it's okay to use it, too. The difference is very clear. N.W.A uses it in a figurative way, whereas Guns N' Roses uses it in a negative, derogatory way – as a white slave master would use it."

Axl was furious, but also terrified. The world knew him as the swaggering frontman of the modern-day Led Zeppelin, but Axl had always suffered from paralyzing stage fright. He was a world-class singer and performer, but it took almost every ounce of his mental energy to get on stage. Never was the tightly wound singer more anxious than when he had to perform. And the Stones gigs were the biggest of his career. Axl had hoped to deliver a top-notch show in front of his musical heroes. Instead, he had to walk onstage as the newly crowned king of racism. The singer threatened to cancel the concerts and quit the music industry altogether.

"It was pretty nerve-wracking," recalled Izzy, who received a 6 a.m. "quitting-the-band" phone call from Axl on October 18, the date of the first Stones appearance. "I told the other guys, 'It's gonna be a long four days, fellas.'"9

The Stones arranged it so that the dressing rooms for Guns and Living Colour were located on opposite sides of the vast backstage, doing everything possible to keep the two camps apart. Living Colour went on at 6 p.m., not long after the gates opened, in broad daylight. Only about 5,000 spectators were on hand, growing to about 20,000 during their thirty-minute, ten-song set. Before departing the stage, guitarist Vernon Reid delivered a lecture to "anyone who uses the n-word."10

Meanwhile, Axl was unwilling to leave his hotel room and flat-out refused to perform. GNR's manager, Alan Niven, later claimed to have a SWAT team on short dial, which was dispatched to extract the singer from his hotel room, carried out in handcuffs if necessary. In reality, Niven sent photographer and band friend Robert John, who persuaded Axl to come to the Coliseum.

On this night, Guns were the biggest and most controversial musical act on the planet, and the group's largest-ever hometown audience had gathered to bear witness. Anticipation for the gigs could not be higher and nearly every seat in the house was filled. N.W.A's "Straight Outta Compton" blasted from the sound system at top volume. The lights went out and 72,000 voices screamed in unison, their cries rising into the night sky, high above the outdoor stadium.

"Of all the bands in the world," an announcer bellowed dramatically, before adding the punchline, "This is one of them. Guns! And! Roses!"

The Coliseum was going ballistic, practically shaking with anticipation. This was the moment everyone had all been waiting for.

Steven Adler remembered that he walked on stage and encountered the largest and most adoring audience GNR had ever experienced. "The sound of that crowd was so powerful that it actually gave me an incredible buzz. When the audience caught sight of us, they all bolted upright. It was like one giant wave of energy, intensely stimulating. We were the proud prodigy, the bastard sons of the Rolling Stones."[11]

But Axl wasn't having it. Seething with fury, he stormed onto the stage, heading straight for his microphone stand, where he was lit by a lone spotlight. Every eye and ear in the Los Angeles Coliseum was focused on the singer. "Before we start playing, calm the fuck down!" he ordered, sharply. Axl backed away from the microphone, waiting for a stadium full of rock fans to pipe down. The singer realized it was not going to work. He stepped forward.

"I am sick and fuckin' tired of this publicity *bullshit* about 'One in a Million' with police and niggers, immigrants and faggots, radicals and racists. I don't give a goddamn fuck what color you are, as long as you ain't no goddamn thief, drug-using, crack-selling piece of shit!"

The crowd went crazy at Axl's cursing, and they hollered and jeered in response. This only seemed to embolden the singer. He continued. "I use the word nigger, but that don't mean every black man's a nigger. That means if you go downtown and some asshole's trying to sell you free parking for fifteen bucks, kick him in the nuts." The audience, many of whom had just paid the going rate of $15 to park in one of the numerous small, private lots and driveways that were proximal to the Coliseum, loved this line, giving it a massive response. Axl was on a roll now and had no intention of stopping.

"Faggots? I don't give a shit about gay people either, but I don't need some faggot trying to rape me. Immigrants, I don't care what goddamn country you're from. You're in America, just act like it, that's all." These lines also resulted in loud applause and knowing laughter.

Axl kept going. "I don't give a fuck if you got a problem or what color you are, and you want to call me a racist, shove your head up your fuckin' ass. This is a song called 'It's So fuckin' Easy.'"

GNR launched into the *Appetite* ode to Hollywood hedonism, leaning into the tune like they had something to prove. Axl was determined to cover every inch of the sprawling *Steel Wheels* set's various catwalks, wings, and staircases. The singer whipsawed from one side of the stadium to the other as the musicians pummeled away behind him, putting it all into the music. The so-called world's most dangerous band had played "It's So Easy" a thousand times, at countless rehearsals and hundreds of shows. It always killed and tonight was no exception; even wasted out of their minds, they could hit every note. The number crashed to a close and the audience roared.

Slash struck a power chord on his Les Paul and the crowd hollered, excited for Guns to blast into their next number. But Axl stopped the group cold.

"I hate to do this on stage. But I've tried every other way. And unless certain people in this band get their shit together, these *will be* the last Guns N' Roses shows you'll ever see. 'Cause I'm tired of too many people in this organization dancing with Mr. *goddamn* Brownstone."

Steven kickstarted "Mr. Brownstone's" Bo-Diddley beat, with the other musicians joining in moments later, but everyone seemed puzzled. "The crowd became absolutely quiet," bassist Duff McKagan recalled years later in his memoir. "People in the audience looked at one another; they seemed confused as we were. They really had no idea what Axl was talking about. I shrank. I felt so embarrassed."[12]

Axl defended himself. "I was watching my band mentally and physically fall apart," he said in an interview two years after the concert. "It was a harsh move, talking about it onstage, but we had tried everything else, and nobody would stop. It just kept getting worse."[13]

"It was way over the top," Steven would later recall, joking that, "Disbanding GNR for drug abuse was like grounding a bird for flying."[14] "Brownstone" was a first-person account of rock 'n' roll heroin addiction, set to a rhythm that reeled like a Saturday night bender. *Appetite* was steeped in this type of nonfiction, with material that felt lived in. At the Stones show, the group walked a razor's edge as they plowed through a tune about the same drug that was currently destroying them from within. Guns never sounded more alive, laying into "Brownstone" like it was the last time they would ever perform the song in concert – there was certainly a sense that it could be.

"We killed that night," Steven said. "We were there to show the world that rock was alive and bigger than ever, and we succeeded in every way."[15] But Slash remembered things differently. "It was a disaster," recalled the guitarist, who isolated himself at the far-left side of the vast stadium stage early on. "I spent the better half of the show facing my amps. Nothing was together that night, the band sounded horrible."[16]

With Guns teetering on a tightrope, the concert pressed forward. Axl toppled off the stage during "Out Ta Get Me," but barely missed a word, laughing it off afterward as the result of "bad footwork and bitchin' lighting" before joking, "That ain't exactly what I planned for stage diving."

"Move to the City" was a tune by Hollywood Rose – one of Axl and Izzy's early groups – that was included on GNR's debut EP. The song featured the Suicide Horn Section, a three-piece unit led by trombonist Matt McKagan, Duff's brother, who would go on to become a popular high-school music teacher in Seattle. In their club days, Guns regularly invited the Horns on stage to perform the number live, and they brought them back for the Stones gigs. The trio would later appear on the studio version of "Live and Let Die," which GNR recorded for their next album.

"City" was followed by "Patience," with Axl singing as much to himself and his bandmates as anyone in the crowd. Having unloaded on the audience at the beginning of the show, Axl now threw himself into the performance, crisscrossing the stage as he belted out "My Michelle" and "Rocket Queen."

"I'm gonna dedicate this one to Erin," the singer said, introducing "Sweet Child O' Mine." Erin Everly was Axl's twenty-two-year-old girlfriend, daughter of Don Everly, who co-founded the pioneering vocal-harmony duo the Everly Brothers. Axl and Erin had a tumultuous relationship, and she was said to give every bit as much as she got.

Afterward Axl asked, almost tenderly, "Do you people know where you are?" The audience roared in approval. They knew alright. "Do you know you are?" Axl teased, milking the moment before letting it rip. "I said do you know where the *fuck you are?*"

"Welcome to the Jungle" followed and then Slash played an instrumental version of Alice Cooper's "Only Women Bleed." Guns were nine numbers into an eleven-song set and Axl seemed almost pensive, saying in a soft voice, "We're gonna dedicate this song to trying to get through life the best you can, trying to achieve your dreams, and not lettin' things get in your way." "Knockin' on Heaven's Door" followed, with Axl telling the audience during the singalong, "Since this is the biggest Los Angeles crowd that I've ever personally seen, then that means that you oughta be the loudest crowd I've ever seen. If you can't find a reason to sing, think about somebody you miss, somebody that meant a lot to you, somebody that ain't here today that you wish they were."

Had the show ended there, some of the earlier turmoil might have been forgotten, but when GNR returned to the stage for an encore, Axl stated, "We're gonna do one more song. Before that, I'd like to announce that this is my last gig with Guns N' Roses. This is called 'Paradise City' cause there ain't no such fuckin' place anywhere." With that, Slash strummed the opening chords of what was ostensibly the final number they would ever play. "Have a nice life," Axl sneered as "Paradise" ended, looking over at Slash and throwing his microphone to the stage floor.

"It was both a troubling and fascinating display – one that will probably go down as a storied moment in L.A. rock," opined the *Los Angeles Times* in a review the next morning. "Rose has the potential to be one of the most compelling figures in American rock since the late Jim Morrison."[17] An equally effusive assessment in the *Santa Ana County Register* noted, "There is an air around them that anything can happen."

If the Stones were upstaged by their opener that night, they took it in stride. "I think Axl did a good share of the talking, so I'm going to shut up and just play," Mick Jagger quipped, midway through the Stones set, adding, "We're not the only ones with mixed emotions." The British quintet rattled off their reunion single, "Mixed Emotions," which Jagger and Keith Richards penned about the Stones' own famed inner turmoil.

But some words can never be taken back, and what happened on stage that night changed Guns forever. "Once Axl took his concerns public, the times of being a gang – us against the world – were over," Duff wrote in his memoir. "Afterward, and really for the remainder of our career, we just went our separate ways. That night officially rang the bell for the end of an era of GNR."[18]

Finale

The drama continued on night two as multiple plotlines played out onstage. Living Colour vocalist Corey Glover wore a T-shirt bearing the slogan "Stop Racism," and Vernon Reid continued to wage war against "One in a Million." "Yesterday some things were said on stage that the band has a problem with," he told the crowd. "A certain person was trying to explain himself. Look, if you don't have a problem with gay people, then don't call them faggots. If you don't have a problem with black people, then don't call them niggers. I never met a nigger in my life. Peace."

But Axl and company had moved on, with more pressing matters to contend with. Having announced he was done with GNR, there was genuine concern that the singer would not show up on night two. The group came onstage without their vocalist. Slash approached the microphone, wearing a white T-shirt that said "Betty Ford Clinic" in large black letters. Steven tapped out the beat to "Mr. Brownstone" behind him.

"I just want to make an announcement. I wanted to say that over the years, rock 'n' roll has lost a lot of the great ones, from Elvis and Hendrix and Bonham and Joplin," Slash said, rambling on for a bit about drugs and youth before adding, "A lot of attention's been brought to this band about some of the excesses that we get into. A lot of that press is bullshit, and a lot of stuff is true."

This was all a distraction for Guns, the guitarist insisted. "Last night almost saw the very last gig of this band. Guns N' Roses worked for a long time to get to this point. I mean, me and Steven used to walk down these corridors to see Aerosmith, and Van Halen, and the Stones. And we used to dream about getting up onstage at this place and doing the same thing and we're actually here."

Steven smiled over at Slash as he continued to pound out "Brownstone's" tribal beat. Slash wrapped up with, "Smack and all that crap is just not what it's all about. Guns N' Roses is not gonna be one of those weak bands that falls apart over it. So, this is a song dedicated by me and whoever else wants to stand up and say something against it."

Slash's mea culpa allowed Axl to save face and the singer immediately sashayed onto the stage to a resounding ovation. "I wanna thank Slash for that intro, and I want to apologize for my comments and actions last night," he told the audience. "It's just that I don't want to see my friends slip away."

The singer seemed to have moved past whatever bee was in his bonnet on opening night. "In the fiery set that followed, Rose and company were on their best behavior," wrote the *L.A. Times*, adding, "You've got to hand it to a band that not only throws its tantrums in front of the multitudes, but turns them into high psychodrama and squeezes every possible drop of ink from them."[19]

But others were less impressed. "Has Keith Richards ever apologized?" asked the *Village Voice*. "Has he ever got up in front of 72,000 people and blubbered about how he's messed his life up on drugs? More than any other shows on this Stones tour, which seems to be peaking right now, the concerts in L.A. put things in perspective. It was a battle of the bands, and Guns N' Roses got blown off the stage."[20]

On night three, Axl offered a restrained rant about the press's reaction to "One in a Million." "I can say what I want; this is art, this is how I feel. If you don't like it, turn it off," he told the audience. "I don't understand it, someone hasn't been crucified in rock 'n' roll for a while, so why not Guns N' Roses? Why not Axl? Is that it? They can shove it."

Fabled writer Jonathan Gold described the concert as uneventful: "Routine as the 47th date on an 80-city tour or a bread-and-butter show in Ames, Iowa." Gold jested that Rose did not apologize for "One in a Million," but "in an apparent show of solidarity with the gay community, he performed 'Rocket Queen' clad in nothing but black leather jacket, motorcycle cap and bare-bottom chaps, mooning the audience while Slash soloed on guitar."[21]

By the fourth and final appearance, Axl's psychological storm seemed to have passed. The singer was in what might be called a good mood, joking about the rainy weather, spontaneously calling for "Welcome to the Jungle" early in the setlist, and circling the Coliseum track during "Knockin' on Heaven's Door." He even let the audience vote for the last song, cheering for either "Sweet Child O' Mine" or "Paradise City." (The latter won.)

Slash cut loose with another long, rambling apology, this time for not playing any new tunes. "Next time we grace the stages of L.A. or any stages for that matter, we're gonna play new material," the guitarist promised, adding that he did not want unrecorded tracks leaked to the public by bootleggers. "After all the work that's gone into it, it'd be a real drag if you hear one of the new songs on the radio before we even recorded it. So, you're gonna have to wait but I promise you it's gonna be a good one."

As much press as Axl got for his opening night rants, few wrote about his conciliatory remarks at the closer. Introducing "Out Ta Get Me," Axl said, "This is something that I dedicated to groups collectively when I was pissed off, which was wrong. Not every person you meet in a certain group is an asshole. It's not fair to think of all of them as assholes." Axl thanked the police working the show for helping to keep the audience safe. "So, instead we'll dedicate this to authority figures who just try to stop you from being a human being that you're hoping to become."

Later that night, as "Paradise City" crashed to a close, Axl stood at center stage, shirtless, all the spotlights pointing toward him, every eye in the Coliseum on him. He raised both arms in victory, staring out of the sea of spectators, affirming to himself everything he had achieved. And in that moment, he only had one thought: "Motherfuckers, you ain't seen *nothing* yet."

The five original members of Guns N' Roses congregated at the front of the stage, standing together as a band to take one final bow, before going their separate ways. It would be their last complete concert together. The GNR of *Appetite for Destruction* was finished, and the *Illusion* era had begun.

Chapter 1

Chicago

How do you follow up the best-selling and most critically
acclaimed debut album of all time? That question dominated the
Guns camp in the summer of 1989, as the quintet recovered from the
two-year whirlwind that accompanied the release of their 1987
inauguration, *Appetite for Destruction*.

The media, the band's record label, Geffen, GNR's
management, and their millions of fans had been hounding them
with questions about *Appetite's* follow-up ever since. When was it
coming? What did it sound like? And most importantly, could a
group whose first record overflowed with classics such as "Welcome
to the Jungle," "Paradise City," and "Sweet Child O' Mine," capture
lightning in a bottle twice? Slash recalled that even Aerosmith lead
singer Steven Tyler pulled him aside around this time and asked, "Is
there another 'Jungle' on it?"[22]

"The pressure's kind of on," the top-hatted guitarist admitted to
a reporter in March 1989, when asked about GNR's sophomore
effort. "Still, it's nothing we can't handle. What I try and do is act as
if nothing has really happened. So, we sold a lot of records – big deal.
It's not going to change the way we live or the way we try to make
our music. Surface things will take a different course, sure, but the
important thing for us is to just ignore it."[23]

Axl had been thinking about GNR's sophomore album for years.
Before the band even had a first record, the singer was strategizing,

analyzing, and preparing for the second. In October 1987, just months after *Appetite* hit the shelves, Axl told a reporter, "We have a handful of songs that we deliberately didn't include in the first album, because both the label and us thought that it would've been a big shock for people. We took a big step from the EP to the album, and our second album will be a new step for sure, because we already have many of the songs that will be on it."[24]

During interviews in 1987 and 1988, the singer suggested that forty tunes had been prepped for *Appetite,* and that the quintet was sifting through the remains for its follow-up. He had even earmarked some of them for album number three. "We've already planned a certain progression of style. We introduced it now, we'll go with a stronger sense of it later, and an even stronger one on our third record."[25]

In addition to the *Appetite* leftovers, Guns were also developing new material that would eventually end up on the second album. In late 1988, as the *Appetite* tour was wrapping up, the group were playing around with new riffs at soundchecks, and Axl and Duff began writing "Civil War," the first new piece for what would become GNR's sophomore effort, *Use Your Illusion.*

The end of innocence

In December 1988, Guns returned home after more than a year of touring in support of *Appetite.* They were scrappy street urchins when their debut was released, but now they were rich, famous rock stars. Everyone in the band dove into excesses during the first half of 1989, buying houses and cars and bags of cocaine. Heroin, too. Everyone in the group but Axl was using it.

GNR's lead singer was largely sober, reveling in his newfound wealth and rock stardom instead. Axl had always believed that he would make it and now that he had arrived, he had no intention of going anywhere. "I've toned it all down, because I have other things I have to do. I can't be doing drugs every night because, after selling six million records, the business I have to deal with is a lot more intense than most people's," Axl said during an interview in spring

1989.[26] "All of a sudden, you're dealing with major record executives and businesspeople and MTV and everything else. You start becoming one of those people you thought you were against. You have to work with them. They're there for you and kicking ass, so you have to produce."

This included working with one of his musical heroes, Don Henley, the former Eagles vocalist and drummer who had spent two-and-a-half years honing his third solo album, *The End of Innocence*. Henley was a renowned perfectionist who fastidiously oversaw every detail of his recordings. He was also a notorious crank who disdained most modern music and young musicians. *Innocence's* tunes were recorded by a veritable who's who of 1970s and 1980s rock royalty: Mike Campbell and Stan Lynch from Tom Petty's band, Toto's David Paich and Jeff Porcaro, Danny Kortchmar, Waddy Wachtel, Bruce Hornsby, Melissa Etheridge, and Sheryl Crow.

With that lineup on deck, some were surprised when Henley invited Axl to sing backup on "I Will Not Go Quietly," a mid-tempo rocker. But Henley knew what he was doing. Axl's strident voice pierced through the track, his vocal soaring high above Henley's pleasant-but-workaday singing. Axl's contribution elevated the proceedings, transforming a run-of-the-mill rock tune into a declaration of resistance. Axl was merely returning the favor – Henley had filled in for a rehabbing Steven Adler on drums in January at the 1989 American Music Awards.

The End of Innocence hit retailers in June 1989 and would be among the year's most acclaimed releases, yielding three hits, earning a Grammy, and selling more than six million copies. Axl's high-profile guest appearance enabled him to take another step away from GNR's Sunset Strip metal roots and toward the type of timeless rock he wanted to be known for. Perhaps more significantly, Axl noted how Henley's perfectionism had yielded another megahit in a career that was filled with them.

Axl was eager to apply what he'd learned to his own band but there was little writing or recording taking place. Around the time Henley's album was released, Axl was asked about GNR's sophomore effort, and he replied, "A lot of riffs were going around in the air at soundchecks during the Japanese tour [in December 1988], things I've been hearing Slash and Duff go over. I've had a lot of ideas for words, but I'm going to wait until we get in the studio to see what we put together."[27] The singer reiterated that there was plenty of leftover material to consider recording for the second album. "There were a lot of songs to choose from in the beginning, and there will be a few of those songs on the next album, like 'November Rain' and possibly 'Don't Cry.' We've written new stuff, but nothing is decided yet."[28]

Appetite had been created by five musicians who lived together in a tiny apartment, playing and writing material around the clock. But with success came money and Guns splintered when they returned home at the end of 1988, buying homes and going their separate ways. A quintet that had once been like five fingers of the same hand had drifted apart. Axl was convinced that Guns needed to return to their *Appetite* methodology to recreate the magic on the follow-up.

In summer 1989, the singer declared that the entire group needed to relocate from L.A. to Chicago, rent an apartment, and write songs for the second album. Living together in Chicago, Axl insisted, would enable GNR to work around the clock without distraction, to bond and write organically, as they had when they composed *Appetite*.

Moving a world-famous musical act, their equipment, and personnel halfway across the country was a complicated and expensive proposition, one that would require buy-in from the rest of the band. But everyone enthusiastically agreed to Axl's idea. "We wanted to make Guns music our top priority," Slash recalled. Steven added, "In Chicago, there was a conscious effort to top *Appetite*."[29]

Wrigleyville

Slash, Duff, and Steven arrived in Chicago first, eager to get started. The trio was joined by Slash's technician, Adam Day, and Axl's technician, Tom Mayhue. Their jobs included tasks such as tuning guitars, repairing amplifiers, and testing microphones. Also on hand were GNR's production manager Mike, and Earl Gabbidon, a 6'4"

Jamaican-born former pro football player who served as Axl's security guard.

Doug Goldstein, GNR's road manager, rented a pair of furnished four-bedroom condos at the intersection of Sheffield Avenue and Webster in Lincoln Park. The condos were located on the second and third floors, above Leona's, an Italian restaurant that was popular with the DePaul University students who resided nearby. Steven, Duff, Adam, Tom, and Mike stayed in the second-floor unit, while Slash and Earl took the top, to be joined by Axl, who was due to arrive any day. "What we were doing wasn't business as usual for us, but it was a start," Slash recalled.[30]

Doug Goldstein secured a place for Guns to write and rehearse at Top Note Theatre, on Clark Street in the northwestern shadows of Wrigley Field. Top Note was an abandoned playhouse located three floors above Cabaret Metro, one of the hottest live rock venues in Chicago. In the basement was Smartbar, an über-cool dance club featuring live DJs. "We didn't have a name for it back then. It was just a little theater," Metro/Smartbar owner Joe Shanahan recalled of the space he rented to Guns. "It was a space we would use for rehearsal. It would be like, 'Oh, you're gonna woodshed.' It was a small stage with decent acoustics, and you could work some things out."[31]

Slash, Duff, and Steven would arrive at the Top Note sometime in the mid-afternoon, jamming for a few hours until the bars on Clark Street began to fill. Guns had a handful of leftovers from the early days they planned to revisit in Chicago. "Don't Cry" and Hollywood Rose's "Back Off Bitch" appeared on GNR's first-known recording, a five-track demo tape they laid down at Mystic Sound Studios in August 1985. The hard-charging rockers "Perfect Crime" and "Ain't Goin' Down" cropped up briefly in GNR's 1986 setlists. "You Could Be Mine" was developed and discarded during the *Appetite* sessions; that album's inner sleeve included a printed non sequitur that was later revealed to be a lyric from the song: "With your bitch slap rappin' and your cocaine tongue you get nothin' done." There was also "Civil War," the new tune Duff and Axl started working on a few months earlier, and "Double Talkin' Jive," and "Pretty Tied Up (The Perils of Rock N' Roll Decadence)," two recent contributions from Izzy, the latter of which Guns had worked on in L.A.

"We've just begun pre-production in Chicago, and this will last until the end of July," Duff told a reporter shortly after his arrival. "In August we begin working with producer Mike Clink on actually recording the LP, probably at studios in Los Angeles. And hopefully the record will be out by November."[32]

Duff named several unreleased tracks – "November Rain," "Yesterdays," "Ain't Goin' Down," and "Just Another Sunday" – and said that there was serious talk of issuing a double album. "We've got so many songs together. Slash and I have written some cool shit. And Axl has come up with some great stuff. Including the songs left over from *Appetite*, we've got about forty numbers knocking around at the moment."

Guns had no shortage of material and there was more coming in. While rehearsing at the Top Note, Slash, Duff, and Steven put together the music for what would become "Get in the Ring." But the trio found it hard to get much done without everyone on hand. Axl and Izzy were arguably GNR's most prolific songwriters, and the early Chicago rehearsals mostly yielded riffs and ideas. It didn't help that Slash and Duff had become round-the-clock consumers of vodka, and Steven was ingesting prodigious amounts of cocaine and heroin. As the trio waited with increasing impatience for Axl and Izzy to show up, they began to spend more time in the bars and less time rehearsing. Meanwhile, Guns were never hotter – "Patience" had just reached number four on the Billboard Hot 100 chart.

GNR's rented condos and rehearsal space were located two miles apart, and Slash would sometimes ride his BMX bike to band practice, bunny hopping around the Clark Street sidewalks in his leather jacket as passersby gawked. The guitarist also kept in shape with the occasional trip to the local YMCA, where he and Duff would lift weights in their jeans, as Axl's bemused bodyguard Earl looked on. Afterward, they would cool down with multiple rounds of drinks at a local sports pub. After a couple hours of jamming, it was on to the bars for the night, where the trio were greeted like rock stars and gladly assumed the role.

Smartbar, located beneath Metro, featured techno and hardcore industrial music such as KMFDM, Front 242, and Chicago's own Ministry. Back at the condo, Faith No More's new album *The Real Thing*, released June 20, was in constant rotation. These new sounds were harbingers of things to come – heavy music was changing, moving away from the monsters of rock who dominated the mid-1980s and melding with rap, electronica, and punk to create new subgenres and styles.

When Guns first hit it big with *Appetite*, they instantly made Sunset Strip superstars like Poison and Mötley Crüe look silly and inauthentic. In 1989, genre-blending new acts were creating waves that would ultimately capsize Guns, making their stadium-ready rock seem bloated and passé. L.A.'s Red Hot Chili Peppers had just finished recording their fourth studio effort *Mother's Milk*, an energetic blend of rap, funk metal, and punk. Upon its release, the album would spawn three singles, garner significant MTV airplay, and earn the quartet their first Gold record. On "Punk Rock Classic," the Peppers gleefully made fun of image-conscious musicians who groveled to get on MTV. The number ended with guitarist John Frusciante reproducing Slash's iconic opening lick to "Sweet Child O' Mine."

In exile

While three-fifths of Guns were killing time jamming in Chicago, one of their principal songwriters was adrift in Europe. The success of *Appetite* affected everyone in the band differently. Axl and Slash wholly embraced their newfound fame, stepping into the rock star role like they were hopping into a stretch limousine. Duff and Steven had no problem with the attention, either. But Izzy was a rocker at heart, and he hated fame. Back when he was still a junkie, Izzy was too oblivious to care, but these days he was increasingly interested in the prospect of sobriety, or something like it. That was going to be difficult in a hard-partying outfit like GNR, particularly when he had been the biggest druggie in the quintet for years. Izzy began to distance himself from the group.

He found solace in travel and hit the road. Alone. While venturing through Germany in August 1989, Izzy told a reporter he had "been in exile for seven or eight months. Travel here, travel there. I don't have a really permanent place where I always am. Of course, I spend a lot of time in Los Angeles. In three, maybe four weeks I will go back there and meet with the band."[33]

As for GNR's singer, no one had seen him. This was not unusual. Axl was easily the most famous member of the group, accosted by fans any time he was out in public. When he needed solitude, the singer would go into hiding, keeping his whereabouts to himself. "I'll disappear for a few weeks at a time, and people presume if I'm not in the public's eye, something must have happened," Axl explained a few months earlier. "I'll be right in Hollywood, laying low, not calling or wanting to deal with anybody; so, no one knows exactly what happened to Axl. I just have to get away every so often to digest and understand all that's going on around me."[34]

Axl's delayed arrival began to cause resentment back in Chicago. Slash, Duff, and Steven had uprooted their lives and moved there to write material for the new record. Now they were just sitting around, waiting to get started. And this whole idea was Axl's in the first place.

Everyone's already-prolific drinking increased. Duff discovered that if he snorted cocaine, he could drink more vodka; he became a frequent user of the powder. Steven bought cocaine an ounce at a time, a stash he kept in a butter tray in his refrigerator. The drummer liked to combine it with heroin, getting completely zonked for days on end. "In Chicago, Steven started to become frightening even to us, a couple of guys not accustomed to getting spooked when it came to intoxicants," Duff recalled.[35]

Bored with the lack of action in Chicago, the various Guns members traveled in and out of town constantly, further hindering progress on the songwriting front. On a whim, Steven married his girlfriend in Las Vegas. Slash and Duff attended a Faith No More show at the Roxy in L.A., hopping onstage for a cover of Black Sabbath's "War Pigs."

Five days later, the pair attended a Metallica show in Wisconsin, about ninety miles north of Chicago. The opening act was The Cult, who GNR had toured with in the early days of *Appetite*. This was their first time meeting The Cult's new drummer, Matt Sorum, and the highly intoxicated duo made an impression. "That's when I first met the guys and they were in kind of a state," Sorum recalled, adding that fame "got thrown on them in a major way. They came from out of the clubs to selling millions of records and they didn't have any time to adjust."[36]

Psssssssst

When they were in Chicago, Slash, Duff, and Steven were out partying in the bars every night, frequently making a spectacle of themselves, having sex with random girls in bathroom stalls, wearing sunglasses indoors at night, and openly snorting lines of coke off bars between shots. "Everyone had seen them around town," said Metro owner Joe Shanahan. "They dressed the way they dressed – it was no question who they were. In L.A. they might have been able to blend in a little bit; not in Chicago."[37]

Wanting to maintain a low profile, GNR's road manager Doug Goldstein had ordered Shanahan and the Metro staff to keep quiet about the group's rehearsing in the theater above the bar. But with Slash, Duff, and Steven drawing attention to themselves all over the North Side, word was out.

At Kelly's Pub, a popular Lincoln Park tavern that opened in 1933, the proprietor bought a round of Irish whiskey shots and made an elaborate toast after the trio showed up one night. GNR's long hair and leather jackets initially frightened some of the regulars until the owner's daughter recognized them. "Just the biggest rock band on the planet, Dad," she told him sardonically. "No big deal."[38]

It wasn't long before local reporters started sniffing around. *Chicago Tribune* entertainment writer David Silverman rang up Doug Goldstein, hoping to get the story, and was rebuffed. "Who the fuck do you think you're fucking dealing with?" Goldstein allegedly asked the reporter. "If you fucking print anything that says they're there, you'll never talk to this fucking band. Ever."

The *Tribune* went with the story, running it under the headline "Pssssssst . . ." and opening with, "Guns N' Roses is not in Chicago. Ignore that group of young men with the big hair, sunglasses and bodyguard. Don't listen to the rumors on Clark Street. It's not them. They're simply not here. Never have been. Honest."[39]

Erroneously reporting that all five members were in town, the *Tribune* got the other details right: "Rent a condo on the North Side, hang out at some bars and rehearse upstairs at the Cabaret Metro." The reporter noted that Guns "had been sighted in the shops, bars and restaurants along Clark Street as well as Leona's on Sheffield." The paper wrote that GNR "saved their wilder side for a series of North Side bars, including Sheffield's, Exit and especially the Smartbar, downstairs at the Cabaret Metro." The *Tribune* added that Duff had been seen outside the Metro recently, so drunk he could barely stand. Earl supposedly had to "hail a cab, fold Duff in half and gently place the bassist in the back seat before driving off with him."

In the story, Metro owner Joe Shanahan denied Guns were rehearsing upstairs, but the *Tribune* reported that, "Several Metro employees said practice sessions took place in the empty rooms above Metro." Shanahan admitted, "All I know is that they've been downstairs, having a good time in the bar. They seem to like the atmosphere."

GNR had just sold seven million albums and their videos played in constant rotation on MTV. Immediately after the *Tribune* piece was published, all the locations mentioned in the story were besieged by fans. This included Leona's, the Italian restaurant beneath the condos where the group lived. It didn't take long before devotees were keeping watch around the clock on the steps of St. Vincent de Paul Parish, just across the street from the building.

Duff, who had been reluctant to go to the Midwest in the first place, found the entire situation untenable. "Perhaps the lone advantage Chicago could have offered was anonymity, and now kids came to seek us out from all over the place, with the hope of getting a glimpse of us or even partying with the band."[40]

The spaghetti incident

After nearly six weeks of waiting, Axl finally arrived in Chicago, claiming that he was delayed because he opted to drive from Los Angeles instead of flying. Slash, Duff, and Steven fumed with resentment, but were also afraid to confront the hypersensitive vocalist, lest he pull another one of his frequent disappearing acts.

Axl's presence in Chicago didn't help things much. On the days he actually showed up for rehearsals, he was hours late, keeping the musicians and crew waiting. Then he would arrive and spend his time sitting at a grand piano that had been brought in, tinkering with "November Rain," a ballad he had been working on since 1985. Axl's initial inspiration was Mötley Crüe's "Home Sweet Home." "I saw that video, then shut off the TV and started on 'November Rain,'" the singer recalled. "It made me realize that I could take what I did know about piano and focus it into something simple, but very serious. Because the part that Tommy Lee does is beautiful; it's very simple, but it's the right part."[41] "November Rain" was considered during the *Appetite* sessions, but the number was not finished and Geffen urged them to go with the more developed "Sweet Child O' Mine" instead.[42] "Child" became the biggest hit of GNR's entire career, topping the Billboard pop chart for two weeks in 1988.

"We have a lot of stuff written," Axl told a reporter shortly before his arrival in Chicago. "We have about ten ballads that I feel are more credible than 'Sweet Child O' Mine.' We wanted to save those ballads, because we wanted to wait until we had a bigger audience. We have some songs we've been wanting to spring on people for a long time."[43]

But things were slow to get started in Chicago. Slash pointed out that *Appetite* was created at a time when Guns were "living five similar lives. Now that we'd become a band who had to set up shop, and we were coming from different perspectives, that dynamic was gone."[44]

"We got into fights in Chicago," Axl recalled during an interview in spring 1990. "Everybody's schedules were weird, and we were all showing up at different times. But when I would show up, I was like, 'Okay, let's do this one of yours Slash. Okay, now let's hear that one Duff's got.' And that's when everybody decided I was a dictator."[45]

Despite the tensions, over the next couple weeks, the quartet made progress on three new tunes: "Garden of Eden," a Slash number called "Bad Apples," and an ambitious Axl piano composition titled "Estranged." Like "November Rain," Axl had been toying around with the piano part to "Estranged" for years, slowly developing a mellifluous set of chord changes.

But everyone was so pissed at Axl that the writing sessions were arduous and little progress was made. "We'd lost that communal inspiration to produce," Slash recalled. "The desire to get together and write songs is one thing: that's like a day job. It's quite another to be inspired by a mutual collaboration. That was the hardest reality for us to come to terms with. For the first time, we had to work at it."[46]

For Slash, having to work at it killed the entire thing. This wasn't rock 'n' roll, it was a chore. "The vibe among us was just too dark and not conducive to real creativity," the guitarist remembered. "We had moved our entire operation to the Midwest and come up with nothing but a few complete songs and a handful of rudimentary ideas, many of which we'd brought out there with us."[47]

Axl disagreed: "As far as I was concerned, we were on a roll. Slash is complaining we're getting nothing done and I'm like, 'What do you mean? We just put down six new parts for songs! We've got all this stuff done in a couple of weeks.' And he was like, 'Yeah, but I've been sitting here a month waitin' for you to show up.' So suddenly, everything's a bummer and it's all my fault."[48]

As tensions increased to a boiling point, Axl's everyday demeanor shifted from laid back to rageful. The pressure on Axl – the sheer number of eyes on him at all times – was immense. The singer was accosted by fans everywhere he went, including at the condos, where a growing throng of devotees stood waiting at the church across the street. One night Axl got home and destroyed the place, splintering artwork, smashing glass, and overturning furniture. Hearing the ruckus, some of the fans outside cheered and clapped.

This further enraged Axl, who tossed the entirety of that night's catering meal – an Italian spread from Leona's – onto the sidewalk below.

It was at exactly this time that Izzy finally arrived, having driven 125 miles from Lafayette, Indiana. The guitarist parked his car, got out, took one look at the "spaghetti incident," and immediately turned around and drove home. "His day-to-day involvement with the band pretty much died that day," Duff recalled.[49]

Slash was the next to depart Chicago, having had enough of Axl's tantrums and the lack of progress on the new album. "It's not happening here, and I can't deal with it anymore," the guitarist scrawled on a note that he left for Axl.[50] Duff and Steven followed shortly after.

Axl phoned Izzy in Indiana and asked him to return to Chicago to work on the new album. Reluctantly, the guitarist agreed. "It was a very intense environment," Izzy said of Chicago later that summer. "But that was okay, because our music has always been intense; maybe it needs such a push."

Axl and Izzy had known each other for a decade and had a strong personal connection that was unlike any other friendship in Guns. Everyone else had abandoned ship – the only two men left were GNR's founders.

Axl told Izzy that he needed him to step up, to assume a more central and active role, to be the Keith Richards to his Mick Jagger. Slash, a guitar hero for the ages, had been upheld by the media as Axl's counterpart, but that spot had always been reserved for Izzy. Izzy was spotlight avoidant, partly due to shyness and partly because he had been too wasted most of the time to do much of anything. But he was a great songwriter and exuded coolness at all times. Axl needed him to be more involved.

Axl told Izzy he wanted him to sing lead vocals, live and on the albums, the same way Keith Richards did. The pair could make special guest appearances – just the two of them – at awards shows and other high-profile gigs. Axl and Izzy would be the faces of GNR the same way Led Zeppelin was led by Jimmy Page and Robert Plant and Aerosmith was fronted by Steven Tyler and Joe Perry. Taking on a larger role sounded good to Izzy, although the guitarist doubted things would play out so smoothly. But it was enough to inspire a productive writing session and the two musicians completed work on several half-finished numbers.

"In Chicago we cobbled together nine or ten songs within three nights," Izzy recalled. "After a few start-up problems, things went like clockwork. The songs just needed to be brought into the final form. We had a studio there and – importantly – our guitars. Axl and I sat down and put together a list of over thirty titles. In three nights, we tore it down."

Little did either musician know, this would be one of their final collaborations, and that their decade-long friendship would soon come to an end.

Chapter 2

Free Falling

After things fell apart in Chicago, Slash, Duff, and Steven returned to L.A., but Axl and Izzy headed East, where they met up with West Arkeen. Arkeen was a twenty-nine-year-old guitarist who had been Izzy and Duff's neighbor back in Hollywood, long before GNR were famous. Arkeen was a prolific songwriter and had collaborated with the band on several tunes, most notably "It's So Easy." There were a handful of leftover Arkeen co-writes that hadn't been used on *Appetite,* and Axl was determined to record them for the new album. These included "Bad Obsession," "The Garden," and "Yesterdays."

"The Garden" and "Yesterdays" had been composed by Axl, Arkeen, and Del James, a musician who moved to Hollywood in 1985 and became a friend of Axl's. On July 22, 1989, while in New York, Axl and Arkeen performed parts of the two numbers while being videotaped by MTV. The pair sat atop stools in the Scrap Bar, a Manhattan hard-rock hangout, with Arkeen flailing on an acoustic guitar as Axl crooned between sips of beer and drags on a cigarette.

"The Garden" was a lyrically overwrought ode to isolation and insanity, set to a winding guitar lick. At the Scrap Bar, Axl effortlessly sprinkled the tune with swooping vocal histrionics, following Arkeen's fingers as they descended the guitar neck. But there was nothing especially compelling about "Garden," which Guns had rejected during the *Appetite* sessions. Still, Axl wasn't taking any chances. For GNR's second effort, he was determined to record everything the band had on hand, so "Garden" was resurrected. "We're going to try and make the longest record that we can," the singer told *Kerrang* around this time. "We're going to try and put down as many songs as we can. I don't know if it will be a very, very, long single album or maybe a double album."[51]

"Yesterdays" was an arena-ready singalong that was also on Axl's list for the *Appetite* follow-up. A home demo from the mid-1980s featured Arkeen on guitars, backed by a drum machine. Axl's piercing vocals were largely in place and did not differ substantially from those he would later record for *Illusion*. Guns didn't spend a lot of time rewriting old cuts. They mostly recorded them as they had been originally demoed, and devoted their songwriting energy toward writing and revising new material. At the Scrap Bar, Axl nailed "Yesterdays" with an easy familiarity, as if he'd sung it a thousand times. After a few lines, perhaps wary of having unreleased material leak to the video camera, Axl ordered Arkeen to play something else.

Sometime after midnight, members of The Cult arrived, fresh from a show at New Jersey's Meadowlands. GNR had opened for The Cult in 1987 so everyone knew each other, except for new drummer Matt Sorum, who was quickly introduced. The party eventually moved to a nearby rehearsal space called The Loft, where an hours-long jam session broke out, with everyone switching instruments and taking turns singing. Covers of Aerosmith, Zeppelin, the Stones, Sabbath, and the Sex Pistols were played.

The jam session was mentioned in the press, and a few snippets of the Scrap Bar footage appeared in an MTV "rockumentary" on GNR that aired later that fall. In New York, Axl agreed to sit for a lengthy interview with MTV, where he described the challenges Guns faced in trying to follow *Appetite*. "We found ourselves trying to write the next 'Jungle,' write the next 'Paradise City,'" he admitted. "Lyrics were coming out with lines about our other songs. It took a few months to get past that, to put those to rest."[52]

In late July, two years after its initial release in 1987, *Appetite for Destruction* received its eighth Platinum award in the U.S., denoting sales of eight million. *Appetite* was an astonishing hit that had outsold every peer act, and expectations for its successor could not be higher.

During the interview with MTV, Axl stated he fully intended to top the debut. "I hope this album's more successful because I just want to bury *Appetite*. I like the album but I'm sick of it. I don't want to live my life through that one album. So, rather than throwing a bunch of songs together we think are fun, we're going over it with a fine-tooth comb and work on everything. That's the goal, bury *Appetite*."[53]

Axl's quest to eclipse GNR's debut was not just about outselling it. The singer wanted Guns to be the biggest band on the planet, but also the best, to create works of art that were transformative. Elton John and Queen didn't make records, they altered the culture, and Axl aspired to nothing less. "I have responsibilities to myself and to the music, and things I want to do with it," he declared. "I'm trying to relate to as many people and help open their minds up, at least make them think. I'm not telling them we can save the world, but I can kind of describe the world and at least let them think about it."[54]

Axl conceded that creating an earth-shattering masterpiece was going to be difficult, given the current state of Guns, laid bare by the tensions in Chicago. "We have to work on pulling things together," the singer admitted. "Because we definitely have our own lives and individual personalities and dreams and goals. You try to find a way to make all those things fit together, and it's not necessarily easy. None of us are trained in psychology."[55]

Dead, jail or rock 'n' roll

Among the biggest obstacles to GNR's progress on the second album was the widespread drug use within the band, exacerbated by success. When they were poor and struggling, everyone lived together and looked out for one another, but *Appetite's* triumph meant they never saw each other anymore. "We'd stopped hanging out together – me, Duff, Slash, all of us," Izzy recalled. "Isolated in small apartments somewhere. The drugs and drinking and stuff was a big part of the isolation. It was self-imposed and it became worse. The drugs and all that just got worse."[56]

Izzy spent the late summer traveling across western Europe. The guitarist felt restless; he was searching for something, and it seemed like maybe he could find it out there on the road. He spent time in Germany and Amsterdam, where journalist Nick Kent ran into him. "He was aimlessly traveling through Europe, trying to avoid getting back to L.A. and partaking in the gnarly business of getting to grips with that difficult second album," Kent wrote. "Three months had already been wasted in Chicago. Stradlin talked a lot about how he hoped the recording could be completed without any one of the group's lives being turned into absolute shit."[57]

Slash preferred to shoot speedballs of heroin and cocaine, but the guitarist's voluminous intake did not hinder his playing much or seemingly slow him down. Slash was content to do nothing but get high and play guitar. With his black leather attire, low-slung Les Paul, and top hat over a mane of shaggy curls, Slash was an instant metal icon. On August 3, he and Steven joined Ozzy Osbourne at Irvine Meadows for a cover of Black Sabbath's "Paranoid." A few weeks later Slash hopped onstage in Manhattan with Great White to perform the Stones' "Jumping Jack Flash." (GNR manager Alan Niven also managed Great White.)

Back on the East Coast, Axl was collaborating with some heroes of his own, including ex-Hanoi Rocks frontman Michael Monroe. Hanoi Rocks was a Finnish quintet that had an immense influence on Guns, particularly Izzy, whose fashion sense split the difference between Keith Richards and Hanoi guitarist Andy McCoy. Hanoi's seminal 1984 live LP *All Those Wasted Years* featured a full-throttled cover of Alice Cooper's "Under My Wheels," the same number Guns chose to cover with Cooper in 1988. "Don't Cry," GNR's first real song, borrowed heavily from Hanoi's "Don't You Ever Leave Me," and "Welcome to the Jungle," perhaps GNR's most recognizable tune, lifted its title directly from the chorus of Hanoi's "Underwater World." Guns repaid this debt in 1989 by reissuing Hanoi's entire catalog on Uzi Suicide, their boutique label distributed by Geffen.

Monroe was in New York to shoot a music video for "Dead, Jail or Rock 'n' Roll," the lead single from his second solo effort, *Not Fakin' It*. Axl popped by the set. He did not sing on the recording of "Dead, Jail or Rock 'n' Roll," but benevolently agreed to lip sync next to Monroe in the music video, ensuring more airings than it would receive otherwise. "Dead, Jail or Rock 'n' Roll" featured Monroe's trademark harmonica, a highlight of early Hanoi classics such as "Beer and a Cigarette." Axl thought Monroe's bluesy harp would be perfect for GNR's "Bad Obsession," and promised Monroe he would call when it was time to record.

In late August, Axl partnered with another classic-rock legend, joining Tom Petty and the Heartbreakers on stage at the New York State Fairgrounds in Syracuse. Axl appeared during the encore, guesting on "Free Fallin'," released earlier that April on Petty's album *Full Moon Fever*. This was followed by a powerful rendition of "Knockin' on Heaven's Door," Bob Dylan's signature song Guns had adopted on the *Appetite* tour.

According to Petty, Axl approached him about singing "Free Fallin'" after seeing it performed on *Saturday Night Live*. "I know this girl, and that is her song, that's her story. And I'd really like to sing the song," Axl told Petty.[58] Petty was so impressed with Axl's vocals on "Free Fallin'" in Syracuse, he invited him to play it again two weeks later at the MTV Video Music Awards.

Izzy expresses himself

The day after Axl's appearance with Petty in New York, Izzy and a girlfriend boarded USAir Flight 350 in Indianapolis on its way to Los Angeles. Izzy was returning to L.A. to work on the new record. Bryn Bridenthal, a publicist for Geffen, claimed that earlier in the day, the guitarist had been "bitten in the face by a dog in Indianapolis and was still a little bit shocked."[59]

The flight Izzy was scheduled to take was delayed by several hours, so he and his girlfriend spent that Sunday afternoon drinking in an airport bar. By the time the plane finally took off, the pair were plastered. This was during a time when airplanes still featured smoking sections. Izzy and his girlfriend weren't seated in the smoking section but lit up anyway. According to Scott Rivas, an FBI agent who later took Izzy into federal custody, the guitarist "repeatedly cursed a flight attendant who told him four times he could not smoke in the no-smoking section of the aircraft."[60]

The flight staff relocated Izzy and his girlfriend to the smoking section, which required a downgrade from first class to coach. This upset the two even more. "It was just sort of one bad thing piling up on another," Bridenthal, the Geffen publicist, tried to explain.[61] Izzy continued to use foul language and make obscene gestures.[62]

The guitarist got up to use the restroom, but it was occupied. He stood woozily in the plane's tiny rear galley for what seemed like an eternity. "I'm not waiting any longer," Izzy mumbled.[63] He unzipped his fly, pressed up against a trash can, and quietly relieved himself. Izzy tried to be inconspicuous, but he was completely wasted, and the flight attendants saw the whole thing.

Izzy returned to his seat and passed out as the flight made a scheduled stopover in Arizona at Phoenix Sky Harbor Airport. According to the *L.A. Times*, "After the plane landed in Phoenix, Izzy refused to deplane and two police officers boarded to arrest him for creating a disturbance on an airline flight, a federal offense. The musician was booked in Maricopa County Jail, and the case was turned over to the FBI."[64]

Izzy spent the night in jail. He was charged with interfering with a flight crew, a felony. According to Scott Rivas, the FBI agent, Izzy was polite and cooperative. "He was never a jerk like a lot of people in higher positions," Rivas recalled. "In fact, he was quite the opposite. A real nice guy."[65]

Izzy's airline incident made headlines around the world. *Lies* had just earned its third Platinum award in the U.S., denoting sales of three million, and the tale of the guitarist's drunken arrest was irresistible to the media. Bryn Bridenthal downplayed the incident, joking to the press that "relieving himself in the galley was just his way of expressing himself. He has expressed himself this way before."[66]

But the situation was serious. A prior drug conviction combined with the new federal charge, meant the twenty-seven-year-old guitarist was facing six months in jail. Izzy was released after posting a $5000 cash bond and promising to appear at a preliminary hearing two weeks later in the U.S. District Court in Phoenix.[67]

For Izzy, getting arrested was the beginning of a long journey out of addiction. "I just kept getting in trouble, fucking up, being unhealthy. My lifestyle was really bad. I wasn't having any fun with it at all anymore. It was just a drag, the whole thing," he recalled. "Jail is a great reminder. That's the ultimate sobering effect and that was my – I guess what they call a low point, where you kind of bottom out."[68]

Vince and the VMAs

The week after his arrest, Izzy was back on stage with Axl and Tom Petty, rehearsing "Free Fallin'," which they would perform that night on live television to an audience of millions. The occasion was the MTV Video Music Awards, held at the Universal Amphitheatre in L.A. Guns declined to perform, but the band were up for three prizes that night. "Paradise City" was nominated for Best Stage Performance in a Video and "Sweet Child O' Mine" was competing in the heavy metal and group categories.

The Tom Petty-Guns mashup was slated to play two numbers, "Free Fallin'" and a cover of Elvis Presley's "Heartbreak Hotel," which GNR had performed in their club days. As the musicians worked out the chord changes in rehearsal, an impatient Cher waited in the wings, fuming over the delay.[69]

During the broadcast, the four members of Mötley Crüe presented the award for Best Heavy Metal Video. "Sweet Child O' Mine" was up against entries by Aerosmith, Def Leppard, and Metallica. "By the way, Jethro Tull is not nominated," Crüe drummer Tommy Lee joked, referencing Tull's nationally lampooned win over Metallica in the metal category at the Grammys that year.

After GNR's name was announced, Duff and Steven ambled to the stage to accept the prize. "We want to thank everybody for this," Duff said, before Steven, arms raised to the sky, drowned him out with an enthusiastic scream. Duff glanced over at the drummer briefly before continuing: "Despite the Grammys, the screw up on the Grammys, we're going to take this for Metallica."

Speaking later that night to members of the press, Axl asserted that Metallica should have won and continued to distance Guns from metal. "I don't like winning anything that has the labeling 'heavy metal,'" he said. "I don't like the title 'heavy metal' because it cheapens the art form."[70]

Axl's divestment from metal was apparent in his performance of "Free Fallin'" that night. Petty, backed by Izzy and the Heartbreakers, took the opening verse before Axl serpentine-danced on stage for verse two. The singer was resplendent, every inch the rock star, festooned with jewelry, necklaces, bracelets, rings, earrings, a bandana topped by a backward baseball cap, and three days of stubble. From the moment Axl began singing, he positively dominated Petty's tune, digging into every inch of the lyrics, and mining them for new contours, taking it to previously unimaginable heights.

Axl completely took over the performance, tearing into "Free Fallin's" soaring chorus with everything he had as he danced back and forth at center stage. Petty, laid back and sure of his status as a legend, looked bemused, happy to cede the spotlight to a talented upstart who clearly loved his song. The duet ended dramatically, with the Heartbreakers climaxing as Axl struck a pose.

A few weeks later, Petty's record label released the studio version of "Free Fallin'" as a single. The track did not feature Axl, but the singer's guest appearance clearly made an impression on listeners — "Free Fallin'" shot to number seven on the Billboard singles chart and became one of Petty's most beloved anthems.

As the VMA credits rolled, the band broke into "Heartbreak Hotel." Their version was unpolished, and Axl and Petty were obviously enjoying themselves. Izzy was on hand for both tunes, but the guitarist did little to distinguish himself, standing in the shadows both physically and musically, seemingly there at Axl's behest. Axl earned every inch of his right to not only stand alongside legends like Petty and the Heartbreakers, but to lead them. The singer's triumph was witnessed by millions, including the entirety of the American music industry, and Axl's stature grew in accordance.

As the television broadcast ended, Petty, the Heartbreakers, Axl, and Izzy made their way offstage. Suddenly, Mötley Crüe vocalist Vince Neil came rushing out of the darkness, punching Izzy in the face, then dashing off in a waiting limousine. The whole thing happened within seconds in almost complete darkness, so there was mostly confusion.

The Crüe singer was angry about an altercation between his wife and Izzy that had taken place months earlier. According to Guns manager Alan Niven, Izzy had Neil's wife "ejected from a private room" at a Hollywood nightclub. Through a spokesperson, Neil countered that an inebriated Izzy had attempted to remove Neil's wife's clothing and physically assaulted her that night, leading to charges that were eventually dropped. The Crüe frontman added that he felt justified in punching Izzy at the VMAs. "When I saw him, I did what any man would do."[71]

Niven chided Neil in a statement issued through Geffen Records the day after the VMAs. "Fortunately, Vince is a powder puff and can't do much damage, but it was a chicken thing to do."

Tom Petty, the seen-it-all rock legend, laughed off the incident. "Well, you know us, we manage to get into shit somehow," he told *Musician* magazine. "I don't dig blindsiding somebody, if that's what happened. I didn't see it. I just saw Vince Neil go storming by and a guy running behind him with a walkie talkie. I heard a commotion, but I didn't know what it was. [Heartbreakers lighting designer] Jim Lenahan threw a couple of punches at Vince Neil. Lenahan's great. He's like, 'Izzy's with us – at least for right now.'"[72]

For Izzy, the Neil incident was just one more blow, literally and figuratively. The last thing he needed right now was another punch. GNR's founding guitarist had been addicted to heroin, cocaine, and alcohol for years, but his embarrassing behavior in Hollywood nightclubs, an overdose in New York City that summer, and the prospect of going to jail over the airplane incident scared him. "I wanted to stop," he said. "I figured, at some point your heart's just gonna pop, or your mind's gonna snap. Eventually, that shit will kill ya, and it does. It kills people all the time."[73]

Izzy was convinced that he needed to quit heroin once and for all. He got a prescription for Valium and codeine, drove to his mother's house in Lafayette, Indiana, and went cold turkey. "I probably weighed about 115 pounds," the guitarist recalled. "That was a pretty traumatic experience, kicking in the house I grew up in. Lying there thinking, 'I fucked up somewhere.'"[74]

The prescription medications helped, as did the copious amounts of alcohol Izzy continued to swill on a daily basis. If anything, the guitarist's drinking increased in the wake of his detox. But kicking heroin at his mother's house was the first in a long series of steps that Izzy would take to achieve sobriety.

The best cathouse in town

A month later, on October 10, a newly heroin-free Izzy was back on stage for what was billed as "An Intimate Evening with Guns N' Roses at the Cathouse." With the first Stones appearance just eight days away, an under-rehearsed GNR wanted to get a couple of warmup shows under their belt. The Cathouse was a 400-capacity metal-themed nightclub co-owned by Faster Pussycat vocalist Taime Downe and Riki Rachtman, host of MTV's metal program Headbanger's Ball. It was a high-profile location, regularly promoted by Rachtman on the air and attracting Sunset Strip A-listers such as Tommy Lee, Bret Michaels, and David Lee Roth. The *L.A. Times* described the venue as "a fourteen-year-old's fantasy of what a rock 'n' roll club might be like, a place that features ferocious loud metal, half-clad leather girls in go-go cages, and real-life rock stars who not only hang out, but even jam."[75]

Guns opened their Cathouse appearance with "It's So Easy," the first of three airings that night. The group had decided to shoot a music video for the *Appetite* rocker. "What we're making this for is ourselves," Axl told an adoring crowd of fans and friends. "If we made a nice video for MTV, we could put it out and sell more records, but instead we're gonna spend a hundred-and-fifty grand just to make something we wanna see."

Axl was famous for his distinct look. Even in a band full of colorfully costumed characters, the singer stood out. From the beginning, he sported unique and frequently outrageous stagewear, undergoing numerous changes of attire throughout a given performance. Axl did not want to be seen wearing the same thing in the "It's So Easy" video, so he changed outfits for each take.

First, Axl sported a red plaid kilt, stagewear that dated to his early club days he would revive to become one of the Illusion tour's signature wardrobe pieces. Over this, Axl wore black leather pants and black leather skeleton jacket, his hair teased up in a throwback to GNR's early club days. For the second take of "Easy," Axl donned a sleeveless T-shirt and the bicycle shorts that would also become regular Illusion tourwear. For take number three, the singer appeared shirtless.

In addition to the Cathouse footage, he also shot scenes drinking and making out with two women in the back of a limousine and engaging in a bondage session with a gagged-and-bound Erin Everly. It was supposed to be edgy – in the scenes with Everly, Axl appears wearing black leather and heavy mascara. But there was also footage of scantily clad women gyrating on stage in time with the music, the type of image found in innumerable Sunset Strip metal videos. Perhaps due to these factors, the video for "It's so Easy" was never released to the public, although a re-edited and tamed-down version surfaced decades later.

In attendance at the Cathouse that night was a besotted David Bowie, who made a drunken pass at Erin Everly backstage. Consumed with jealousy, Axl nearly got into blows with the rock legend, chasing him down Sunset Boulevard, allegedly threatening to kill him. (The two later made up over dinner.)[76]

Three nights after this, Guns played another warm-up at the Park Plaza Hotel Ballroom. Hosted by the Cathouse, the gig was billed as *Rip's* third anniversary party, with Faster Pussycat opening. *Rip* was an L.A.-based heavy metal magazine that was owned by notorious *Hustler* publisher Larry Flynt.

The 1,000-capacity Park Plaza could not possibly meet the demand for tickets – hundreds of would-be concertgoers were turned away at the door. It was a higher-profile gig. According to the *L.A. Times*, "The Cathouse show was more a club show, five guys playing the songs they know for a bunch of friends; this was a full-fledged stadium show, million-dollar lighting apparatus, bombast, half-stepping and all."[77]

GNR went on sometime after 1 a.m., playing for nearly two hours, trying out some of the moves they would use at the Coliseum five nights later. "Move to the City" featured the Suicide Horn Section, and Hanoi frontman Michael Monroe was back for a cover of "Heartbreak Hotel," wailing away on harmonica.

Izzy in court

On October 17, the day before the first Stones concert, Izzy appeared before Judge Michael Mignella in the U.S. District Court in Phoenix. The felony charge of interfering with the duties of an airline crew was dropped in exchange for Izzy's pleading guilty to four misdemeanor counts of illegally smoking in a non-smoking section. For this, Izzy was fined $2,000, placed on probation for six months, and ordered to see a psychiatrist to determine whether he had an alcohol-abuse problem. He was also ordered to pay USAir up to $1,000 to clean up the mess he made. If the guitarist did not complete his probation, he would be fined an additional $4,000.

Izzy was described as "subdued" during his thirty-minute court appearance.[78] When Judge Mignella asked the rocker whether he had any comment, Izzy responded in a barely audible voice, "I apologize to the court."

Mignella told Izzy he needed assurances that such antics would not occur again. Izzy stoically replied, "No problem."

Asked about being forced to see a psychiatrist, Izzy said, "This is okay, this is fine. The doctor is very good."

Izzy's attorney, Edward Novak, told Mignella that his client was "remorseful," adding that he was convinced Stradlin did not "intend to act in this manner in the future. He is an individual of few words, but someone who can keep his word and is anxious to find out whether he has a problem with alcohol."[79]

Izzy was put on probation for a year and subjected to random urine tests. Now he really had to stop taking drugs – he was legally prohibited from doing so. It dawned on Izzy right there. "I can't use drugs anymore or I'm going to jail. Wow."[80]

The following night, Izzy performed in front of 72,000 spectators at the Coliseum, his future never more uncertain.

Opium den

Axl's threat to dissolve Guns after the Stones shows seemed to galvanize the quintet, spurring at least some members to change direction. Izzy was avoiding cocaine and heroin while meeting with his probation officer and being subjected to random drug tests. Slash spent a month in rehab and was the second member of GNR to kick heroin. Steven went the opposite direction, diving into an array of vices without regard to the collateral damage. And there were still plenty of party materials going around, even within the newly "cleaned up" version of the group.

On December 6, 1989, four-fifths of Guns gathered at Mates Rehearsal Studios in North Hollywood to work on material for the second album. Axl was not there that night, per custom. The singer almost never attended GNR rehearsals. "I like to go all out," he explained. "If the band's not going at the same intensity – they're concentrating more on getting the music right – I feel like an idiot, jumping around, taking it so serious."[81]

Guns kept a permanent rehearsal room at Mates, described as akin to "stepping into an opium den. The only light in the room was from a couple of lamps in one corner and on the little stage. Almost every surface was covered with a Persian rug, and there was a refrigerator against one wall."[82]

It was a loose session with a casual vibe. Izzy sat on a black leather sofa in the middle of the room, pouring liquor from a pint-sized bottle into a soda cup as various technicians set up the gear. The guitarist had given up hard drugs, but he continued to struggle with addiction when he was around GNR. "I'd come in for rehearsals for *Use Your Illusion* and there's one of the guys with a big line of coke. 'Hey, Iz – you want some coke?' 'Ah, no thanks, I just got back from my probation officer.' To get sober is really tough, to do it like that, in a situation where everybody's still using."[83]

It was only rehearsal, but Guns kept a full complement of instruments and amps on hand, including four Marshall stacks for Slash, eight giant speaker cabinets, piled in pairs, that formed a wall on the left side of the stage. Some of these amps were strictly for the look – Slash only actually used two of them. The other two were purely aesthetic.[84]

The guitarist sported red shorts and a black Gibson T-shirt, a backwards baseball cap keeping his curls under control. Izzy strapped on a black Gibson Les Paul, testing his sound level as Steven pounded away behind him. Slash told Duff and Izzy about a couple of new tunes he'd been working on. "Let's warm up with something," Duff said. The band launched into "It's So Easy."

Steven was GNR's secret weapon, the key, as it turned out, to the quintet's sound. It was the drummer's brilliant bass pedal work and hooky turnarounds that transformed hard rockers like "Welcome to the Jungle" into songs you could dance to. Despite a talented troupe of successors, Guns never sounded the same with any other drummer. "Whenever we've played with other drummers, I mean, these guys can be meter-perfect, but it just has never worked," Izzy had explained a few months earlier.[85] "Stevie's timing is all up and down. It speeds up, then it slows down. It's fucked up but it works."

Never was that more apparent than at the Mates rehearsal, where the four musicians ripped through several rockers that would eventually appear on *Illusion*. The band leaned into "Don't Damn Me," which snorted, stopped, and started with fervor. The number was built upon a ballistic riff that Slash brought in fully formed. They paused to work out the opening of "Garden of Eden," which began with Slash scratching his low guitar string with a pick before bursting into the main riff.

The rawness of the Mates rehearsal – two guitars, bass, and drums live in the room – offered a stark contrast to the polished sound that would dominate *Illusion*. "Locomotive (Complicity)," a tune that never completely came together in the studio, was funkier and grittier here, closer to "Mr. Brownstone" in the hands of the *Appetite* crew. Izzy and Slash effortlessly melded together and weaved around one another, held together by Duff's roving basslines and Steven's deft drum work.

Duff yowled the opening lines of "Dust N' Bones," Izzy's existential ode to futility and acceptance. Early Izzy material such as "Don't Cry," was ripped straight from the pages of the Hanoi Rocks playbook, but his contributions on *Illusion* borrowed heavily from the Rolling Stones circa the early 1970s. "Dust N' Bones" was built on a stomping groove that was perfect for a drummer with Steven's innate sense of swing. More songs followed, including primal passes at "Bad Apples" and "Coma," offering glimpses of what was to come and what might have been.

The music for "Bad Apples" and "Coma" was written by Slash, who brought them to Guns already arranged, sans lyrics. The guitarist wrote "Coma" on an acoustic guitar, playing around with different ideas for several days until it finally came together.[86] Like much of the new material developed for *Illusion*, "Coma" was long and complex, a ten-plus minute tune built around an intricate series of chord progressions and musical movements. Izzy hated this type of thing and loathed Slash and Axl's desire to turn their garage band into a modern-day Pink Floyd. "Left on our own, I'm sure everyone would make very different albums," Slash conceded, describing "Coma" as "ten minutes long and 500 chord changes."[87]

But "Coma" held great personal significance to Slash, whose music he wrote to reflect the estrangement he felt from the group, friends, and larger society as fortune and fame consumed GNR. "It's about how cold and materialistic people really are," the guitarist explained around this time. "Most of the lyrics will be written by Axl, but they'll reflect the thoughts, pain and feelings of the individuals in the band."[88]

As Slash indicated, Axl was given the unenviable task of writing lyrics to Slash's sweeping musical masterpiece. "There's a song called 'Coma' that's like eleven minutes and 45 seconds long with no chorus and only one verse that somewhat repeats itself. It's Slash's baby, it's his monster," the singer said.[89] "I used to curse him, going, 'Man, that son of a bitch has written this thing and I've got to write to it and don't know what to write.' It was so hard."[90]

Axl pondered it for months, frustrated by his inability to put words to Slash's feelings of alienation. Ultimately, the singer decided to write about a near-death experience that took place a few years earlier. In a fit of rage, the singer swallowed an entire bottle of pills and overdosed, awakening in an emergency room. Axl said that he was prepared to die. "I liked that I wasn't in the fight anymore and I was fully conscious that I was leaving. But then I go, 'Okay, you haven't toured enough. The records, it's not gonna last, it's gonna be forgotten. You have work to do, get out of this.' And I woke up and pulled myself out of it. In describing that, some people could take it wrong and think this means go put yourself into a coma. So, it's really tricky. I'm still playing with the words to figure out how to show some hope in there."[91] Axl would spend the next year writing and revising the lyrics to "Coma."

Most of the original material that would comprise *Illusion* finally came together over a two-night acoustic session at Slash's house in Laurel Canyon. Axl, Izzy, Duff, and Slash were there, working out the chord changes and adding final touches. It was the one time *Appetite's* principle writers were all in the same room for the writing of *Illusion*. "It had just been so difficult to get into that groove," Slash recalled. "That acoustic session basically sewed it up."[92]

Salt of the earth

Axl and Slash each joined Michael Monroe for a number at the Whisky a Go Go on December 12. The next night, the pair performed the Velvet Underground's "White Light, White Heat" alongside Mott the Hoople's Ian Hunter and Mick Ronson at the Palace. Axl and Slash had never even heard the song before, but they gave it a quick listen backstage and plowed ahead. Four days later, Axl was on stage again, this time as a guest of the Rolling Stones.

The Guns-Stones matchup in L.A. generated enough media headlines to earn Axl an invite to perform with the Stones in Atlantic City. (Notably, Living Colour received no such request.) The Stones were playing the final three stops of the U.S. leg of the Steel Wheels tour; the second concert, held December 19, would be televised live on pay-per-view, reaching an estimated 13 million viewers.[93] Axl, ever determined to align GNR with classic-rock legends, immediately agreed, insisting Izzy join him.

As usual, the media tried to stir up controversy over the year-old "One in a Million," but the Stones laughed it off. At a press conference, Mick Jagger was asked why he invited Axl, given his "offensive remarks in the past about gays and blacks." Jagger quipped, "Because we want to appeal more to the gay, black market."[94]

When Izzy arrived backstage in Atlantic City, the Stones were there to greet him, but Axl was late. Izzy and Axl had suggested they play "Salt of the Earth," a deep cut from the Stones' 1968 opus *Beggars Banquet.* Nobody in the Stones knew the song – they had never performed it live and could barely even remember recording it. *You guys wrote it, you must remember some of it,* Izzy thought to himself.[95]

He and the Stones sat together in a tiny trailer, a cassette of "Salt of the Earth" playing at top volume. Izzy and Keith Richards strummed along on acoustic guitars, while Mick Jagger read over a sheet of paper with the lyrics written on them. Charlie Watts and Bill Wyman watched and listened, nodding appreciatively. *This is so cool, this is so wild,* Izzy thought. He couldn't believe Axl was missing it.

They finished playing and everyone turned to Izzy, wanting to know when his singer was going to show up. "I had no answer," the guitarist recalled. "Axl was late again. Real late."[96] When the singer finally appeared, seconds before showtime, an irate Keith Richards told him, "I slept in a *chandelier* last night, but I still got here."

Axl's last-second arrival infuriated the Stones, but no one could deny his masterful take on "Salt of the Earth" that night. As with Petty's "Free Fallin'," Axl did not just sing the song, his interpretation elevated it to something greater than the original. The next night, before an audience of millions, Axl repeated the feat, looking every inch the leather-clad rock star as he strode confidently to the stage. Axl was up against one of rock's all-time great frontmen and he more than earned his right to be there, serpentine dancing as he sang to the rafters. It was yet another performance where the rising star outmatched the master on his home turf.

Axl was teaching the old dogs some new tricks, but he was learning a few lessons as well. For "Salt of the Earth," he, Izzy, and the five-piece Stones were augmented by ten additional musicians, including a pianist, keyboard player, saxophonist, a trio of backup singers, and a four-man horn section. This array of instruments and voices enhanced Axl's performance, adding dramatic elements to his crooning vocals. Having a large backing group meant the Stones could permeate venues with sound and reproduce almost anything in their catalog. Axl was also impressed by Jagger's athleticism and inexhaustible energy.

Axl saw what it meant to be a large, professionally managed operation on a megatour that filled massive stadiums with big lighting, big sound, and huge production. This was how a world-class rock band conducted itself. And they made millions doing it. Tickets for the Atlantic City shows ranged from $38.50 to $250, considered outrageous at the time.[97] Stones fans loved merchandise, too, as evidenced by the brisk sales of T-shirts, skateboards, and $450 leather jackets. In a first, concertgoers could pay by credit card, yielding the Stones more than $20 million in merchandise revenues in the U.S. alone.

Axl took it all in, every inch of it. The singer saw everything the Stones were doing with the Steel Wheels megatour and wanted all of it and more for GNR. But that was going to be difficult, given the current state of the band and their incomplete second album.

Civil War

Following the Stones concert, Izzy spent the winter being drug tested and attending meetings with his probation officer every seven days. "Once I got a week of sobriety, actually going a whole week without a drink, I thought, 'Oh god, if I can just keep this up.'"[98] Every inch was a struggle for the guitarist, and he kept his distance from his bandmates.

Duff was faring even worse, drowning himself in booze and arguing with Mandy, his wife of two years. The pair broke up on Christmas Day. "I felt completely lost and heartbroken," Duff recalled, so depressed that one of GNR's roadies removed a shotgun the bassist kept stashed in a bedroom closet. Duff began adding cocaine to an already prodigious vodka habit. "It proved a diabolical cocktail for me," the bassist wrote in his memoir. "Now I could drink until I finally had to sleep – and if you're doing coke, you don't have to sleep for up to four days in my case."[99]

Slash spent the Christmas season hanging out with a new girlfriend and trying to write material for the second album. The guitarist assumed finally having money would make life easier, freeing him to be a creative spirit once and for all. Instead, Slash found the old cliché to be true – more money just meant more headaches. "Instead of sitting around 24-hours-a-day creating music and hanging out with the band, you deal with business problems, mortgage payments, car payments, dealing with accountants, attorneys, divorce. And at the same time, you're supposed to get all your creativity in there somewhere. Some of it gives you inspiration, but most of it doesn't. Most of it is killing the inspiration. It takes away the passion."[100]

While Guns were struggling in L.A., Axl and Erin Everly were on vacation in France, where they ran into some troubles of their own. The couple spent ten days in Paris, where they were attacked by a gang of French thugs, who targeted them for being Americans. Erin ended up with a black eye, while Axl suffered two broken fingers.[101]

The Rumbo sessions

After a year of getting almost nothing done, 1990 arrived and it was time to get to work. The plan was to hit the studio starting in mid-January. The band booked time at Rumbo Recorders, the same Canoga Park studio where they recorded *Appetite*. Rumbo was owned by Daryl Dragon and Toni Tenille, a married couple who found success in the 1970s as pop duo Captain & Tennille. Dragon designed the original studio, which was built in 1979. Artists who had recorded at Rumbo included Tom Petty, Fleetwood Mac, Bob Seger, and Megadeth.

In 1990, Rumbo featured two studios, both about the same size. As they had with *Appetite*, GNR worked from the newer B room. Looking to recreate the debut's magic, they were again working with producer Mike Clink and using much of the same equipment, right down to the Trident recording console and the Otari reel-to-reel tape recorder.

Guns had amassed about thirty tunes they intended to record, spanning their entire career. There was a slew of leftovers from the pre-*Appetite* days ("Ain't Going Down," "Don't Cry," "Back Off Bitch," "You Could Be Mine," "Perfect Crime"), including three numbers that West Arkeen wrote with help from Axl ("Yesterdays," "The Garden," and "Just Another Sunday"). During an interview at Rumbo, Slash explained, "These were songs which could have surfaced on the first album, but we weren't really working on them at the time. We were concentrating on the songs that came on that first album, so we saved them for later."[102]

This included what Duff called the new record's "one piano song," Axl's epic ballad "November Rain," which the singer had intentionally held for GNR's second record. "Dead Horse" was an old Axl number, and the band had worked on several tunes the previous summer in Chicago, including "Civil War," "Get in the Ring," "Double Talkin' Jive," and "Pretty Tied Up." Then there was newer material the group had cooked up in recent months, such as "Garden of Eden" and "Locomotive (Complicity)." There were individual contributions brought in by Slash ("Night Crawler," "Don't Damn Me," "Bad Apples," and "Coma"), Duff ("So Fine"), and Izzy ("Dust N' Bones"). By this point, Guns had also decided to record a cover of Wings' 1973 tune "Live and Let Die," which Axl and Slash felt represented GNR's worldview.

There was easily enough material for a double LP, and they intended to record it all. "If we do this right, we won't have to make another album for five years," Axl said, semi joking.[103] "Our attitude is not, 'Save it for the next record,'" Slash added in an interview around this time. "Hell, there might not *be* a next record. Right now, all that lies in the future for Guns N' Roses is the next LP."[104]

Guns began by working on basic tracks, with Slash, Duff, and Steven playing together to build the foundation for the record. Izzy dropped by the Rumbo sessions from time to time, but his presence was spotty at best. Axl was not there at all – he would record vocals later, once the instrumental tracks were completed.

On January 21, Steven took part in the Rock N' Jock Diamond Derby at the University of Southern California. The event, which was broadcast on MTV, paired famous actors and musicians with professional baseball players. Notables taking part included Keanu Reeves, MC Hammer, Daryl Strawberry, Sammy Hagar, Kevin Costner, Tone Loc, Bret Michaels, and Sam Kinison.

Steven was briefly interviewed by MTV and talked about the second record. "The sound is great, the songs are coming together and we're just really looking forward to getting it out," he said, sounding pretty wasted. Asked when the album would be ready,

Steven demurred. "You know my band. We're unpredictable. God knows what is gonna happen in the studio. But it's coming on really well. We're very pleased."

But things were not going well at Rumbo. Steven was using crack and heroin, and his timing was erratic. He spent many of the sessions asleep or halfway there, nodding off between takes and talking to himself incoherently.

Steven was not the only member of GNR having issues with intoxicants. The day after the baseball game, Slash and Duff appeared at the Shrine Auditorium, where Guns were nominated for two American Music Awards, best heavy metal/hard-rock album and artist. They won both prizes and a barely coherent Slash, drink in hand, offered slurred acceptance speeches from the podium, replete with four-letter words. The guitarist's loutish swearing was so bad during the second speech, the network simply cut him off and went to commercial. ABC, which was broadcasting the show live, was inundated with complaints from viewers, prompting the network to delete both GNR segments from the tape-delayed West Coast airing. The incident made headlines around the world.

The following day, ABC offered a somber apology in an official statement. "We regret that last night's live telecast of the American Music Awards contained some offensive language. This has not happened before in the seventeen years this awards show has been on the air. We will take precautionary measures to see that it does not happen in future telecasts."[105] Of course, all of this was incredible PR for the world's most dangerous band, whose notoriety only grew as a result.

At Rumbo, Slash, Duff, and Steven continued to lay down basic tracks, working from GNR's long list of unreleased material. Steven was clearly struggling. Work would be aborted for days at a time while Slash and Duff waited on the drummer to appear. When Steven finally arrived, he would be so bombed he wasn't able to accomplish anything.

Slash downplayed any such issues in the press. "We're in the studio now and we're putting together a healthy chunk of songs. We've already done thirteen and we've still got another sixteen left to do," he reported, adding that the new record "goes to extremes. It's really heavy or really mellow. There's acoustics and horns and shit like that."[106] Despite the issues with Steven, the guitarist was happy to be working again, excited about GNR's forward momentum. "Me and Axl are on a roll right now. Last night we were listening to one of the new songs, trying to put lyrics to it. I went upstairs to get my hat, and he was singing. I got chills, thinking, man, this album is gonna be a killer. I'm really excited about it now. The distractions, the problems, the bullshit are truly behind us."[107]

But this initial burst of excitement quickly soured as the group listened to the recordings of the basic tracks. They had spent weeks working on and off at a cost of over $100,000 and the results were terrible. "We had recorded like eighteen tracks for the *Use Your Illusion* record with Steven and it just wasn't happening," Duff recalled.[108]

Slash was upset that Guns lost so much time and cash for tapes they weren't going to use. The guitarist nixed the remaining sessions at Rumbo. "Steven wasn't ready for it, so it turned out to be a waste of money. At this point I'm very aware of what our financial situation is. You have to be. You're forced to be. So, I cancelled the time in the studio. We had recorded all these songs, but a lot of situations went on with Steven not being altogether there in the studio."[109]

Frustrated and angry at Steven over the delays, Guns put out feelers to a few drummers who might be able to fill in. They considered finding someone to record the album while Steven tried to get in shape for the tour. If Steven couldn't get it together to go on the road, GNR would hire someone else to do that. Floating such possibilities was partly a scare tactic to get Steven to straighten out, but they were seriously considering a replacement. The Pretenders stickman Martin Chambers and Adam Maples from the Sea Hags both tried out, rehearsing *Appetite* standards such as "Jungle" and "Brownstone," but neither drummer meshed.

In late March, Steven pleaded his case and Guns agreed to give him one more chance, coercing the hopelessly drug-addled musician into signing a "probation" agreement stipulating that he work with a sober coach and remain free of hard drugs for the recording of the new album. This meant another delay while Steven went into rehab; GNR would not begin recording until May.

A whole new way of working

Axl used the downtime to write, adding tweaks and touches to the plethora of material that continued to pour out of him, including a newly penned series of measured, piano-driven numbers. "I was working on writing these ballads that have really rich tapestries and making sure each note is right," he explained. "It has to be the right note, and it has to be held the right way, and it has to have the right effect. I've got four of these motherfuckers now. I don't know how I wrote these, but I like 'em better than 'November Rain.' And I'm gonna *crush* that song. But now I've got four of 'em I gotta do, and they're all big songs. We play them and we get chills."[110]

Recording this material and sharing it with GNR's fans was at the forefront of Axl's mind. "This is our dream, to get these songs out there into the public. What's important is the recording of the songs."[111] To Axl, the second record was a do-or-die mission. "There's only one thing left, and that's this damn album. That's it. Guns N' Roses doesn't fully function to its utmost potential unless it's a kamikaze run. Like, fuck it, let's go down in flames with this motherfucker. That's how we are about this record, everybody's like, we're just gonna do this son of a bitch."[112]

"I *have* to make this album," the singer continued. "Our second album is the album I've been waiting on since before we got signed. We were planning out the second album before we started work on the first one."[113]

Appetite was born of collaboration, written and recorded by a bunch of guys living on top of each other and making music around the clock. For the follow-up, Axl explained, "We had to find a whole new way of working together. Everybody got successful and it changed things. Izzy's brought in eight songs at least. Slash has brought in an album; I've brought in an album. And Duff said it all in one song. None of this ever happened before."[114] The new material would be assembled more like the Beatles' *White Album*, a collection of distinct contributions from the individual musicians of a group.

As for Adler, "He was definitely out of the band," Axl said in early April. "We worked with Adam Maples, we worked with Martin Chambers. Steven plays the songs better than any of 'em, just bad-assed, and he's GNR. And so, if he doesn't blow it, we're going to try the album with him and the tour, and we've worked out a contract with him. It's finally back on. It's only been a few days so far and he's doing great. We're all just hoping it continues."[115]

While Steven was rehabbing and Axl was writing, Slash and Duff spent a day laying down bass and guitar tracks for Iggy Pop's *Brick by Brick* LP. (According to Pop, the pair showed up to an initial meeting toting "a gallon of vodka and a bowl of blow."[116]) Working with super-producer Don Was, the pair cranked out four tunes in a single live session, accompanied by drummer-for-hire Kenny Aronoff. Slash and Iggy co-wrote one number, "My Baby Wants to Rock 'n' Roll," right there in the studio.

Slash had known Iggy since he was a child. Slash's father was a British artist who designed record covers for Neil Young and Joni Mitchell. His mother was a black hippie designer who outfitted celebrities such as John Lennon, Diana Ross, and Janet Jackson. Famous actors, musicians, and industry moguls such as David Geffen popped by the family home regularly. After his folks split up, Slash's mom dated David Bowie. From the time they met, Axl was intimidated by Slash's cosmopolitan background, a stark contrast to his strict religious upbringing in rural Indiana.

Slash's session with Iggy Pop led to an invitation to play on Bob Dylan's forthcoming album, which was also being produced by Don Was. Slash's parents were huge Dylan fans and he jumped at the opportunity to record with the folk-rock legend. Slash arrived at the studio, where George Harrison was playing slide guitar, watched by actress Kim Bassinger. Dylan appeared next, aloof and indifferent. "He looked like an Eskimo," Slash recalled. "It was a summer day and he's wearing a heavy wool sweater with a hood over it and a baseball cap underneath the hood and big leather gloves on and appeared to be stoned out of his mind."[117]

Slash was asked to add guitar to a tune called "Wiggle Wiggle," an upbeat ditty with a jazzy feel. He recorded some chords on an acoustic guitar before turning to the solo. "Play it like Django Reinhardt," Dylan instructed, referring to a Belgian jazz pioneer from the early 20th century.[118] Slash understood what Dylan was asking for, but did not think the request worked for the song's structure. "The chords were a typical I-IV-V progression," Slash recalled. "With all due respect to Django, that would have been a great concept had it fit the song. The guy was impossible to work with. No matter how amiable I might be, Dylan was just impossible to relate to, to communicate with."[119] [120] [121]

Slash laid down a lead, ignoring Dylan's directive to imitate Django Reinhardt. "I did one of my best one-off guitar solos ever, one take – it was killer," he said. "Dylan was as indifferent as indifferent gets. That was the most miserable session."[122] [123]

In September, Dylan released "Wiggle Wiggle" as the opening track of his album *Under the Red Sky*. Slash was shocked to discover that Dylan removed the guitar solo, leaving only his acoustic strumming. "Bob said it sounded a little bit too much like Guns N' Roses, so he just took it off," Slash recalled.[124] "The space is still there in the song, so now when it gets to the guitar solo all you hear is me strumming these stupid chords. The whole thing was just a drag."[125] [126]

In early April, Slash and Duff attended a Cult concert at Universal Amphitheatre. Cult drummer Matt Sorum recalled the pair's rock-star arrival by limousine in the underbelly of the venue. "The door opened, and Duff climbed out of the car; he was so lanky it was more like he was being tipped out. Slash appeared next – in a cloud of smoke, dressed like classic Slash: with the hat and everything. Four super-hot, scantily clad girls climbed out next, and with one on each side of them, Slash and Duff walked straight past us with a bottle of liquor each, heading straight into an area that had been cordoned off for them backstage."[127]

Hanging out and watching the show from the soundboard, Slash and Duff were impressed by Matt's strong arm and steady groove. Matt was a strapping Orange County native who drummed for

Gladys Knight, and recorded an album with Tori Amos that was released on Atlantic Records. Matt was then recruited by The Cult to tour in support of 1989's *Sonic Temple,* which hit the top ten in the U.S. and the U.K. on the strength of the international hit "Fire Woman."

Nobody's child

On April 28, Axl and Erin took a three-hour limo ride from L.A. to Las Vegas, stopping for five minutes to get married at the Cupid Wedding Chapel. Becoming husband and wife seemingly did little to bring stability to their troubled relationship. Less than a month after eloping, Axl filed for divorce in a Los Angeles court, citing irreconcilable differences.[128] He then called off the divorce and the couple continued to try to work things out.

Around this time, Axl received a telephone call from George Harrison, who rang to solicit a new GNR track for *Nobody's Child: Romanian Angel Appeal,* a compilation whose proceeds would support Romanian orphans. The effort was spearheaded by Harrison's wife, who took up the cause after visiting Romania in the wake of communism's collapse. Due to the former Beatle's involvement, *Nobody's Child* was populated by rock royalty such as Elton John, Paul Simon, and Van Morrison. Looking to align Guns with figures such as these and flattered by Harrison's personal call, Axl immediately agreed to contribute "Civil War," the closest thing GNR had to a political number.

Built around a somber series of minor chords, "Civil War" showcased the more reflective side Guns had exposed on numbers such as "Patience." This was no hard-rocking thrasher, but something more mature, growing from acoustic ode to electric stomper over a seven-minute stretch. The number's quasi-political lyrics – with mentions of human rights, the Kennedy assassination, and something about the scars of history – were far from *Appetite's* tour de squalor, almost dipping a toe into U2 terrain. "A friend asked me to write a song about how crazy the world is," Axl recalled. "I just thought it was an interesting subject and Slash had this music and it exactly fit what I'd written."[129] Axl penned "Civil War" from a broad perspective, but his lyrics felt personal, too. The number's insistent rejection of political conflict seemed to push back against the racialized outcry over "One in a Million." Axl did not want to be dragged into anyone's war.

Thrilled to have the involvement of one of the top-selling acts in music, George Harrison immediately agreed to include "Civil War" on *Nobody's Child*, asking Axl to send over a tape right away. But there was one problem: Guns had not recorded "Civil War" yet and Steven was in no condition to go back into the studio. Axl was livid. Steven's drug problem was costing GNR once-in-a-career opportunities. Axl knew right then, Steven was gone.

Farm aid

GNR's only official live performance of 1990 took place at Farm Aid, held April 7 at the Hoosier Dome in Indianapolis. At the fourth and final Rolling Stones show in October, Slash had promised new material the next time Guns performed live and he kept his word. It would have been easy for GNR to play a couple of hits, but they opted for two unreleased tracks instead, a new original and an obscure cover.

A huge ovation rang through the Hoosier Dome as Axl strode out, dressed for the moment in frayed blue jeans, a wide snakeskin belt, a black leather jacket, and a straw-colored cowboy hat. An overly enthusiastic (and possibly overserved) Steven rushed on stage, attempting to leap onto the drum riser. Instead, he missed, and face planted onto the stage floor. Guns hadn't even begun and already it was a long night.

"I'd like to dedicate this to my Uncle Bob, who lives in Illinois on his farm," Axl told the audience. "This is something new we got." GNR offered a subdued version of "Civil War," its first-ever airing. Farm Aid was being broadcast live on network television and everyone in the band wondered if Steven would blow it. His drumming was fine, if unspectacular; "Civil War" never really took flight until the end when the group broke out into a rocking coda.

For the second number, Axl chose a cover of "Down on the Farm" by the English punk-rock quartet the U.K. Subs. "Wanting to be a rocker and growing up in the Midwest can get you a lot of critical abuse," the singer said by way of introduction. "So, for humor's sake, since we don't mind and you can take a joke, this is the only farm song we know."

It was the last tune Steven would play as a member of GNR, his final performance. Steven managed to avoid catastrophe at Farm Aid, but Guns were about to embark on an extended world trek, headlining their first ever tour. Axl did not want to wonder if his drummer was going to be too wasted to pull it off on any given night. Steven had to go.

But Axl wanted to get "Civil War" to George Harrison as soon as possible, so he begrudgingly agreed to use Steven for the recording, which began just days after the Farm Aid appearance. Rumbo was fully booked, so GNR recorded at a backup studio, the Record Plant, instead. "It wasn't in our normal studio," Slash recalled. "I didn't have a normal amp. I had to use a rented amp, and I wasn't particularly happy with the sound. We had to do it because we were doing it for a benefit album, and it was a rush thing. The song was great, but Steven couldn't play."[130]

Steven claimed the effects of a prescribed opioid blocker put him in a catatonic state when he cut the drum tracks for "Civil War." Everyone else just assumed he was plastered, like always. Regardless, Steven was unable to produce a single usable take during two days of recording. Duff recalled, "Bass and drums always got done quickly in the early days. I hardly ever had to do bass fixes because Steven and I were so solid as a rhythm section. But when we had tried to lay down the basic tracks for 'Civil War,' Mike Clink and I had to patch together the drum tracks from dozens of inadequate takes."[131]

Master plan

Among Axl's musical heroes was Elton John, whose piano-driven tunes were heavy without relying on Les Pauls cranked through Marshall stacks. "Elton John is it, especially the first seven albums,"

Axl enthused in an interview around this time. "Bernie Taupin to me is the best lyric writer that's ever lived on the face of the earth. And Elton John was just amazing in the studio and the recording of everything. Some of it is art. That's my classical music, because some of his stuff is classical. I listen to Elton John *all* the time."[132]

For years, Axl had been tinkering with his Elton John-inspired ballad "November Rain," and he was currently writing one grandly conceived, piano-driven number after the next. Axl had always wanted to add a keyboardist to GNR, particularly someone who could reproduce his piano parts live. He had the guy, too: Darren "Dizzy" Reed, a longtime associate Axl met when they were neighbors back in the club days. "He had a master vision, a master plan for the band before they got signed," Dizzy recalled. "He told me one night, 'We're gonna do the big record, and then an acoustic record or an EP, and then we are gonna do a double album. We're gonna add a keyboard player and it's gonna be you.' And he stuck to his word."[133]

Piano was central to Axl's aim of moving Guns away from metal on *Illusion* and aligning the group with classic rockers such as Elton John. Clocking in at over seven minutes, "Civil War" was longer and more ambitious than anything on *Appetite*. Axl insisted that Dizzy be added to the track, and he was so pleased with the results that he offered the keyboardist a permanent spot in GNR. No one could believe it. Slash was pissed. Including piano on a song was one thing, but it was preposterous to add a sixth member to a quintet whose history and musical chemistry were so intertwined.

Axl's move instantly created bad vibes within Guns, and Dizzy was mostly shunned by Slash and Duff. The instant Dizzy made a mistake during rehearsal, Slash was all over him, telling the keyboardist, "You screwed up there. Just don't play."[134] "Some of the guys really weren't keen on the idea of having me in the band," Dizzy recalled. "They made it a little difficult for me."[135] Slash conceded as much about a year after Dizzy came aboard, telling *Guitar World*, "I had to get used to the idea. At first, I thought, 'We don't need no stinking keyboards,' and I really gave Dizzy a hard time."[136]

Dizzy was an old buddy, but also a hired hand who got a lucky break, not someone who earned his position. Slash and Duff liked Dizzy well enough, but they did not respect him as an equal. That suited Dizzy just fine – the laid-back pianist knew his place and was happy to stay in the background. But the twenty-eight-year-old musician also knew this was his big break and he was determined to stick around.

One of the bros

GNR were not done making personnel changes. The same recording session that got Dizzy hired got Steven fired. Slash and Duff had spent months in rehearsal spaces and recording studios, trying to make it work with Steven to no avail. He was barely able to complete one number. It was time for the drummer to go. Axl agreed. Izzy went along with it begrudgingly.

Attorneys were notified and paperwork was signed. Steven was drug addled and hurt; everyone else was ready to move on and stopped returning his calls.

Finding a replacement did not prove easy. "I mean, we couldn't place an ad in the paper," Slash said.[137] Guns would've been besieged by every drummer on the planet. Besides, it wasn't just about securing a musician who could play the parts, it was about finding someone who got along socially. "We didn't want to hire some session guy," Slash said.[138] He and Duff put out more feelers and auditioned another series of drummers. None of them fit.

It was June and GNR had spent most of 1990 spinning their wheels. Frustrated and wanting to move forward, they started to look for a drummer who could simply record the album – they could always hire a touring drummer later. Getting someone short term would enable Guns to work with a player from an existing act who had the free time to record. Slash was interested in Steve Gorman, drummer for the Black Crowes. In late June, the guitarist hopped onstage with the Crowes in New York City for a cover of "It's A Sin," a slow blues number by Jimmy Reed. But Bowman was busy with his own group and not looking to make any moves.

Matt Sorum, who had just wrapped the Cult tour, was another stickman who came to mind. Slash phoned the drummer, telling him, "Our drummer is in rehab. It doesn't look like he'll be able to do this record. You think you could come play with us?" Matt instantly agreed.

GNR put Matt up in a Toluca Lake apartment building called the Oakwood, which was frequented by bands such as Nirvana and Aerosmith, who needed medium-term rentals when they were in town to record. Matt went to a rehearsal session at Mates, where Slash, Duff, and Izzy were on hand. Izzy played a cassette containing primitive acoustic demos of "Dust N' Bones" and "Bad Obsession." The quartet tried out those songs as well as "Locomotive (Complicity)," a tune Sorum found overly long. But the session went well, and Slash and Duff were especially enthusiastic about Matt's playing. Plus, he was easygoing and laid back. "Matt fit in within the first five minutes," Slash recalled. "No weird attitude. No rock star trips. None of that crap."[139] "That's as important as playing." Duff added." "We hung out and he was instantly one of the bros."[140]

Matt came back the next day, and then the next, and the next after that. Dizzy was at the Mates tryouts the entire time, but only observed and was not invited to join in. On day five, Axl finally made an appearance. He did not sing and did not stay long. "He walked slowly, in a wide arc, though the studio," Matt recalled. "As he passed the stage, he cocked his head a little and glanced at me with an intense look. Then he turned to Slash, nodded gently, and left the studio without saying a word."[141] Matt, it seemed, had Axl's approval.

GNR had agreed to contribute a song to the soundtrack for *Days of Thunder*, a forthcoming action film starring Tom Cruise. The deadline was fast approaching, and the group decided to give Matt a tryout in the studio. Guns didn't have time to work out new material, so they opted to record their popular cover of "Knockin' on Heaven's Door," which had long been earmarked for the second album.

They rehearsed the tune for an hour with Matt and then went to record, setting up shop at A&M Studios. The massive compound was originally developed by film director and star Charlie Chaplin and opened in 1917. Record industry impresarios Herb Alpert and Jerry Moss acquired the property in the mid-1960s and turned it into the headquarters of A&M Records. GNR's equipment was set up in the large Studio One, a sweeping space that could accommodate full orchestras. Five years earlier, "We Are the World" was recorded there.

Backup vocals were added by family R&B group The Waters, which featured Maxine and Julia Waters. The Waters sisters had a long career as backup singers for top acts such as Michael Jackson and Carole King. The two appeared on Don Henley's *The End of Innocence*, where they came to Axl's attention.

During the session, Matt easily nailed his drum parts, a stark contrast to the ordeal it took to get anything done with Steven. Guns immediately invited Matt to record the rest of the album and he agreed.

Slash, Duff, and Matt hit the rehearsal space in earnest, putting in four- or five-hour sessions every day for a month. Initially, Matt had been hesitant to get involved with GNR due to their reputation for volatility and drug abuse. "I had heard all the horror stories," the drummer recalled. "I thought I was going to be walking into an opium den, but it wasn't like that at all. It blew me away how professional everybody was. We worked our asses off, rehearsing or recording every day – five days a week – for a month. I think they knew that if they didn't do the album right then, it all might be over."[142]

"Matt saved the band," Duff said. "There was a real low point after we had to kick out Steve. Matt came in and kicked ass. And that put a foot up our ass. It was like, 'That's right! We're a fucking band, man!' We forgot we were a rock 'n' roll band that could kick ass. And it all came back."[143]

Matt was a seasoned pro who would have no problem learning the pile of songs GNR planned to record for *Illusion*. He was also an equal, already drumming in a world-famous act that had just issued a Platinum disc and spent eighteen months touring the world. There was no learning curve with Matt. He could step in and deliver from day one. A couple of weeks later, when Slash asked Matt to join GNR, the drummer used this leverage to come aboard as a member rather than a hired sideman. Guns were in no position to bargain. If anything, the group was thrilled. At last, their long-standing drummer problem appeared to be solved. The victory was sweet, but short-lived. As it turned out, much larger problems were just around the corner – and right next door.

Chapter 4

No More Patience

Slash, Duff, and Matt spent a month at Mates rehearsing the twenty-seven tracks they intended to record. Izzy dropped in from time to time, but Axl was rarely seen. Matt had a glut of material to absorb, and he approached it systematically. The drummer aimed to learn a new tune each day, writing out extensive charts of his parts as they went. Matt concluded some of this material would never make the final cut. "There were certain songs that I was like, 'This probably won't make the record, I don't know if this is great.'"[144]

Guns had attempted basic tracks for *Illusion* at Rumbo with Steven, and his signature hooks, fills, and turnarounds were already written for the pre-*Appetite* material as well as newer numbers such as "Don't Damn Me" and "Locomotive." Matt was easily able to incorporate Steven's parts, retaining some essence of his predecessor's style, if not his feel.

After a month of rehearsing, the group returned to the main room at A&M Studios where they spent the latter part of July and most of August cutting basic instrumental tracks for twenty-seven songs. For once, GNR set a deadline and stuck to it. "We had thirty days booked at A&M to do the basics, and we didn't want to go someplace else to continue," Duff said. "I like that pressure. To me it's good."[145]

The sessions were scheduled to begin each day at noon. A large coffee-bagel-and-booze spread was laid out for everyone's enjoyment, with the food and drink changed continually throughout the day. Axl loved to order in massive trays filled with sushi and caviar and insisted that champagne flow at all hours.

Matt's drums were set up in the sprawling main room, his kit surrounded by microphones, stands, cables, and sound baffling. Slash and Duff played alongside Matt, while Izzy holed up in a nearby vocal booth with a window that looked out at the others. In the booth, the guitarist installed a thick Persian carpet along with a chair and a lamp to give the space some vibe. Everyone's amplifiers were set up down the hall, where they could be recorded in isolation.

Taping the musicians as they played together enabled Mike Clink to better document the group's spirit and chemistry. "We know the way we are on stage, and the only way to capture that energy on the record is by making it somewhat live, doing the bass, the drums and the rhythm guitar at the same time," Axl explained. "That brings some energy into it. Because Guns N' Roses on stage can be out to lunch. How do you get that on a record?"[146]

Soft-spoken Mike Clink was a taskmaster, refusing to let Slash, Duff, and Izzy sit down or concentrate too deeply on their instruments. Instead, he instructed them to move around, interact with one another – to treat the recording session like an all-out performance. "It's always aggressive," Duff said. "Clink won't let you be otherwise. When I'm in the studio I'm ready for war. I use a lot of eye contact. When Matt hits a crash, I watch exactly when he hits the crash."[147] Hoping to recreate the *Appetite* magic, Duff was using the exact same bass and amp he wielded on GNR's debut.

Mike Clink hated using a click track, where the band plays along to an electronic beat, so the song is recorded in perfect time. "We played it just like it was live," Matt recalled. "They stood in front of me, and everyone jumped around."[148] The instruments were tuned down one note to D, which produced a deeper, heavier sound. Tuning down would also take some pressure off Axl, who could sing in a lower register and spare his vocal cords.

Guns began by recording the least complex material first, quickly hammering out numbers like "Perfect Crime" and "Back Off Bitch" in one or two takes. If the vibe wasn't there immediately, that was it.

They'd try the number again another day. "One run-through and then the red light was *on*," Slash recalled. "When it came to the basic tracks, all of those live takes had to be keepers."[149] There was a staunch refusal on the group's part to overwork the material. "Hey, what do you think about doing one more?" Matt asked Slash one day, following the second pass at a tune. The guitarist looked aghast. "You just want to suck the rock 'n' roll right out of it, don't you?"[150]

GNR probably could've knocked out the basic tracks in a week or two, but there was a deliberate refusal to rush the process. The band and Mike Clink were looking to capture a moment that was ephemeral and fleeting, a magic take. The group might attempt two or three straightforward rockers in a single session. They would then spend an entire day mapping out the arrangements for more complex material such as "Coma." "There were days when I could have done ten, but they didn't like to work that way," Matt said. "The attitude is how everyone feels, not just one person."[151]

From the vocal booth, Izzy strummed a series of Telecasters and Les Pauls in his usual style, minimal and sparse. "Izzy, even on the songs he wrote, put on a very bare-bones guitar part, just basic chords," Slash explained. "And sometimes, very rarely, a single-note melody." Izzy eschewed solos almost completely, playing just one on the entire *Illusion* set, at the outset of "Back Off Bitch."[152] Perhaps Izzy's most notable musical contribution was the sitar he added to the beginning of "Pretty Tied Up," replicating the sound on a rough demo he'd created earlier.

Izzy was irked by the intricacy of some of the *Illusion* material, particularly "November Rain," "Estranged," and "Coma," which featured numerous chord changes and tempo shifts. "Slash has this song, it's called 'Coma,' and it's fifteen minutes long," Izzy griped to a reporter. "I still don't know it, man. I have to use a special chord chart whenever we play it. There's like fifty chords at the end of it and I can't follow them."[153] Influenced by classics such as "Layla" and contemporary hits such as Faith No More's "Epic," several tracks concluded with elaborate musical codas that extended their length and complexity in ways that Izzy found insufferable. The entire group struggled to get "Breakdown" to work to their satisfaction.

Slash felt strained at times, too. The guitarist hated the phony environment of the basic track sessions, with his Marshall stack hidden off in a room somewhere. He disdained wearing sterile-sounding headphones, hopping around with Duff like they were onstage, hacking away at his axe. As he did on *Appetite*, Slash recorded basic tracks with the band, knowing he would erase all his guitar parts and re-do them afterward.

"It's very rare that I keep anything off the basic tracks," Slash explained shortly after *Illusion* was released. "I was just there for the general feel for the rest of the guys. I can't play for shit if it doesn't sound right. The only time I kept anything through headphones was on a punk EP we did that's going to come out eventually, which we mostly cut live in the studio."[154]

Slash was referring to five cover tunes he and the others cut in a single, live session during the month they spent at A&M. These included "Down on the Farm," the UK Subs number GNR had played at Farm Aid in April. Fear's "I Don't Care About You" was a group favorite that was immortalized in *The Decline of the Western Civilization*, a 1981 documentary that chronicled L.A.'s punk scene around that time. Also recorded were two of Duff's favorites, "Attitude" by the Misfits and The Damned's "New Rose." The session was capped by "Black Leather," a Runaways ditty that was written by members of the Sex Pistols. "We played all the songs in the studio live one day – just bashed it out, first take, real sloppy," Matt remembered.[155]

Guns had long wanted to release an EP of covers, and the success of *Lies* convinced them the idea was commercially viable. It had taken more than two years to get back into the studio and there was no telling when they would return, if ever. Recording covers during the *Illusion* sessions would give GNR more material they could later package and release.

When the group wasn't in the studio, they were generally across the street at a strip club called Crazy Girls. There were some days when Guns spent more time at Crazy Girls than they did at A&M,

snorting huge lines of coke and boozing it up with the dancers. Matt had always liked to party, but his intake went up immensely upon joining GNR. "He started to try to keep up with me and Slash on the drinking front," Duff recalled.[156]

Izzy was stone cold sober and increasingly tired of his bandmates' drunken antics. One night, Izzy sat waiting in the studio for hours while the group got hammered at the strip club. The frustrated guitarist was indignant by the time everyone stumbled back in the door, but Mike Clink knew an opportunity when he saw it. The producer quickly sat everyone on stools and asked them to perform an acoustic version of Izzy's "You Ain't the First." This drunken pirate take became the final cut.

Izzy wasn't just irritated by his bandmates' constant drinking and drugging; he was also frustrated by the glacial pace of recording, the amount of time it took for Guns to accomplish anything. "It progressed really slowly," the guitarist recalled. "Each song kept being taken to bits and analyzed again and again and remade, and before you knew it, weeks and months had gone by. When we finally finished a song, I'd forgotten how to play the others."[157]

Izzy's bandmates were put off by his apparent disinterest in the second album. He just didn't seem to care about it as much as everyone else did. Izzy was a gifted writer, but even getting him to work on his own material was difficult. "Izzy really wasn't that much involved anymore," Axl recalled after *Illusion* was finished. "He wrote songs, but those songs were on the record because I wanted them on the record, and because the band agreed to learn them and liked them, and we all worked on them. I really believed in Izzy. I was an Izzy fan for fifteen years and I wanted his songs to be a part of this project. But it was like pulling teeth to make that happen."[158]

Use your illusion

Axl had never been more famous – he was everywhere. Pick up the August 1990 issue of *Car Audio Electronics* and there he was on the cover, posing atop his custom convertible BMW 325i. In the article, Axl described tooling around Hollywood, listening to everything from

Frank Sinatra to Faith No More on a state-of-the-art stereo system that featured six amplifiers, 23 speakers, and a 100-disc CD player. "Every single day I listen to Steely Dan's *Decade* because it just pushes me to work harder," he said.[159] Axl's ear-splitting system was customized by Electronic Entertainment, which billed itself the "Car Stereo Store to the Stars" and whose client roster included MC Hammer and Michael Jackson.

After having dinner on Rodeo Drive one evening, the singer wandered into Hanson Gallery, a Beverly Hills art dealer. Axl was window shopping. He had never purchased artwork before – he had never had that kind money. The singer was drawn to a striking 48" x 36" red and yellow piece by Estonian American artist Mark Kostabi. The work was based on a small section taken from The School of Athens, a renowned painting by Italian artist Raphael from the early 1500s that currently hangs in the Vatican. Axl was struck by Kostabi's reinterpretation of a classic but also by its title, *Use Your Illusion*. The night before he had been wrestling with the lyrics for "Locomotive," which contained a line about illusions. It seemed meant to be. Axl purchased Kostabi's piece on the spot.

"It was the first painting that I've ever bought," the singer said, adding that "I wanted to use that picture because it was art that has a lot of controversy around it, because of Kostabi's methods. The background was taken from a very old painting. I don't know how I feel about how it was done, I just know I like it."[160] Axl compared this to GNR's scattershot approach to making music – they just wrote material they liked and that felt good, whatever it took to do so.

Axl adored Kostabi's artwork; he couldn't stop looking at it. A few weeks later, the artist received an offer. "Axl's manager called me and said Axl was writing songs about illusions and wanted to use the painting on his new album cover and also wanted to use my title," Kostabi recalled. "We negotiated a happy deal, and it made rock history."[161] The identical blue version that was used for the cover of *Illusion II* was created at Axl's behest by graphic designers at Geffen.

The singer couldn't wait to show the artwork to everyone in the group. He charged into A&M Studios one afternoon, having not been there in several days. "I love it all, it's all great," the singer said, excitedly, about the tracks that had been recorded so far. "Here's what we're gonna do. We're gonna make two records and release them simultaneously. We can have the same cover art for both records but distinguish between them by doing them in different colors. I found a perfect image."[162]

Everyone looked at their shoes. The plan had been for Guns to make a double album. Or record a bunch of tracks and choose the best ones for a single disc. Two separate releases made no sense – nothing like that had ever been done before.

Axl, drawing on the years he worked in retail at Tower Video, explained that double CDs were frequently kept behind the counter at record stores – their high value made them targets for theft. "We don't want our fans to have to go and ask for our record," Axl told the band. "We want them to be able to go to the bin, touch the record, and then buy it."

"This guy is a fucking genius," Matt Sorum thought to himself.

The title of Mark Kostabi's painting would eventually appear in the lyrics for "Don't Damn Me." Axl's patronage gave him a new career – the artist would go on to design album covers for the Ramones and jazz singer Jimmy Scott.

Axl's on-and-off relationship with Erin Everly was on again. One night the couple were hanging out on the balcony of the singer's twelfth-floor West Hollywood condo, located just north of the Sunset Strip, which Axl had purchased eighteen months earlier. They were joined by Skid Row vocalist Sebastian Bach, a 6'3" overgrown puppy of a twenty-two-year-old with a mane of blonde hair that he grew to his waist. Skid Row's self-titled debut was released in January 1989, blowing up later that year due to the success of the power ballad "I Remember You." Bass, as everyone called him, was a loveable loudmouth who was born to party, reveling in every aspect of his recently attained rock-stardom. The three were eating takeout, having some drinks, and blasting music. Bass was getting loud, as usual. A neighbor called the police to complain about the noise.

When the cops arrived, according to Axl, they were heavy handed, barging into the condo uninvited and threatening to take everyone to jail. Axl filed a complaint against the police, telling *People* magazine, "I want an investigation. I don't know if they're out to get me, but they hate my guts, and I don't know why. Maybe it's because if you're working the Sunset Strip and you saw long-haired guys with earrings who have no socially redeeming qualities going out with these girls you wished you had, it might tend to piss you off after a few years."[163]

Pat Boone, Debby Boone

Axl did not record any vocals during the basic track sessions at A&M, but he contributed piano on GNR's cover of "Live and Let Die," West Arkeen's "Yesterdays," as well as three numbers the singer wrote by himself: "November Rain," "Estranged," and "Breakdown." These lengthy conceptual pieces were among the most complex material on *Illusion* and Axl insisted they be treated as something more than tunes; the singer wanted to create works of art.

"It was in Axl's mindset to make this grandiose piece of music," recalled Matt, who was summoned to the studio late one night by the singer. Over caviar and chilled vodka shots, Axl laid out his vision to the drummer. *Illusion* would contain an epic, three-song suite consisting of "Don't Cry," "November Rain," and "Estranged." The three tracks would be linked lyrically, thematically, and musically, and together would tell a single story. Big-budget music videos would accompany each number, presenting the tale visually.

Over the studio monitors, Axl blasted Elton John's "Don't Let the Sun Go Down on Me" at top volume, swaying in time with the panoramic hit from 1974. In the tune, drummer Nigel Olsson repeats a simple, sweeping roll across his tom-tom drums. Axl's eyes lit up. "I want you to do *that*, something like that on 'November Rain,'" he told Matt. "I want you to mark every section with this signature musical fill that would be representative of not only that song, but I want you to use it again as a little snippet in 'Don't Cry' and I want you to do it again in 'Estranged.'"

Matt, new on the job and eager to do well, listened and nodded. "You want me to do the same drum fill?" he asked.

"Yes," Axl affirmed.

Matt went over to his drums and tried a few different rolls, eventually coming up with a simple tom-tom fill, something he jokingly called the Pat Boone, Debby Boone because that was the sound made by its A-B, AA-B pattern.

Axl loved it. "I want you to do it here, here, here and here," the singer enthused, pointing out exactly where the drum fill should go on "November Rain." Axl went into the isolation booth that housed his piano and sat down. He and Matt spent the next several hours painstakingly going through every note of "Don't Cry," "November Rain," and "Estranged." They also worked on "Breakdown," which had continually bedeviled the band during the basic tracking sessions. As they went through the songs, Axl instructed the drummer, "When I go to *this* chord, I want you to hit *that* cymbal."

"We had it all worked out," Matt recalled. "Axl wanted to make an epic record. We wanted to go forward. We wanted to move into a bigger arena, being epic, meaning we're gonna be an arena band, play stadiums."

When it came to the recording of *Illusion's* longest and most complicated numbers, Guns stuck to their self-imposed rulebook: No more than a few takes, played perfectly, all the way through. No overdubs, no corrections, no fixing it later in the mix. "The band doesn't believe in punching in anywhere, ever, so those eight-minute songs had to make it all the way to the end," Matt said. During one session, the drummer blew the very last fill on an otherwise perfect pass at "Coma." Matt asked if he could fix that one little part and was instantly rebuffed. "No way, sorry," Slash told him.[164] They would have to redo the entire thing. Some other day.

Still, after months of delays and frustration with Steven, the group was thrilled to be getting things done. Matt's positive, upbeat demeanor and tireless work ethic gave GNR the momentum they needed to lift the second album off the ground. "It was a miracle, he has saved the band's life," Axl marveled in an interview with MTV at the end of August, just after the basic track sessions wrapped. "He came in, he's in an up mood, he works real well with us. He takes suggestions well, he keeps everybody in line, keeps the timing great. I mean, he played twenty-nine songs in a month."[165]

Wall of guitars

Now that the basic tracks were in place, it was time for Slash to start over, erasing all his playing and beginning anew. Slash, Mike Clink, and engineer Jim Mitchell relocated to the Record Plant, where GNR booked two studios, one for Axl to begin working on vocal tracks and one for Slash to redo his guitars. Slash spent the next five weeks rerecording all his parts, overdubbing solos, and adding an array of stringed instruments. Slash refused to let anyone from the band attend the sessions. "I need to be in my own studio – away from where the basic tracks are done – in the control booth," he explained "That's really my element. I love it."[166]

Slash had an exacting process built around a daily routine that he followed six days a week. "When I get up in the morning, before I go in the studio, I pick the song I'm going to play; I get down to the studio and go, 'Okay, get me this guitar and this is how we're going to do it.'"[167] At the time, Slash estimated he had spent $400,000 on guitars, and he used about twenty of those on the *Illusion* sessions, mostly Les Pauls but also a Fender Stratocaster, a Music Man, and a Travis Bean for slide work.[168]

Once Slash had selected a guitar, he would have a series of amplifiers brought in to determine which one sounded best with that particular axe. Slash would sometimes try out and reject up to twenty amplifiers before selecting one that fit. "I won't play through something if it doesn't sound right," he said.[169] Slash eschewed all pedals and digital effects, save for a wah-wah and a voice box, fair game in his book because he manually controlled those devices.

Guns had completed twenty-seven tunes during the basic-track sessions that Slash wanted to redo. His goal was to finish one song per day although he frequently spent two days on the more complex material. The guitarist worked on one number at a time, re-recording his basic tracks and then adding additional guitars or instruments and a solo. He would not stop working on a tune until it was completely finished, frequently putting in ten-to-twelve-hour sessions. At night, Slash would take mixes home on cassette, listening back to the day's work and pondering what to do tomorrow.

Like a painter in his workshop, each day Slash immersed himself in a song. He frequently doubled or tripled his rhythm parts or recreated the same part an octave up, resulting in a beefier sound. Slash added slide to "Bad Obsession," "So Fine," and "The Garden" and played a Dobro on "You Ain't the First." He affixed a solemn Spanish guitar coda to the end of Izzy's "Double Talkin' Jive," and used a talk box to enhance "Dust N' Bones." He augmented Duff's bassline with a six-string bass on "Live and Let Die," and accompanied Izzy's acoustic with a back-porch banjo on "Breakdown."

Slash laughed off any notion that he was some sort of musical genius. To add the banjo part, he simply tuned the instrument like it was a guitar and played it with one of his picks. "I don't know shit about real banjo," he demurred.

Listening through headphones, on GNR recordings, Slash's guitars were panned to the right and Izzy's to the left, with guitar solos appearing in the center of the audio mix. This arrangement allowed for greater separation between the two players, producing a fuller sound. For *Illusion*, Slash created a wall of guitars on his side of the tracks and Izzy's sparse playing sounded thin by comparison. Slash compensated by adding more guitars to Izzy's side, all but taking over some numbers. "Izzy has only one guitar throughout the whole record. I did all the overdubs and harmonies, plus my regular rhythm track," he explained. "There are a couple of songs, especially ones I wrote, where I beefed up the tracks over on Izzy's side. Otherwise, it falls out of balance.[170]

This approach resulted in a very different overall guitar sound on *Illusion* compared with *Appetite*. Many of *Appetite's* signature lead lines and fills were played by Izzy rather than Slash, and it was the interplay of the two guitarists that helped give the album its thrust. Conversely, Slash dominated *Illusion*, and the musical interplay between the two axemen was virtually nonexistent.

In recording his guitar parts for *Illusion*, Slash's fountain of creativity resulted in hundreds of instrumental tracks collected on stacks of reel-to-reel tapes. For every instrumental flourish from Slash that made it to the final mix, there were probably three more that were not used.

As he did during the basic track sessions at A&M, Slash continued to prize inspiration over technical prowess. "It was always one or two takes, more or less," he said. "If the intonation was really off, Clink would tell me, and I'd go back and maybe punch in. When I leave something on a record, it's usually got to be something that kicks my ass, and at the same time, a really good performance. Then I'll leave it, even if it has a little mistake in it."[171]

Axl's lengthy piano pieces – "November Rain," "Estranged," and "Breakdown" – created some of the most challenging days in the studio for Slash. "The guitar and bass parts had to be thought out and done precisely," he said.[172] In some instances, Slash would spend an entire day working on a track and still not have it finished. At times, Mike Clink would gently nudge the irritated axeman out of the studio, telling him, "Look, you're pretty tired. Why don't you come in the morning and do it."[173]

Frustrations aside, Slash had a blast during the five-week session. "It was exciting," he enthused. "It was a challenge that I was really into. Adding it all up, as far as this band goes, with the amount of stuff I was involved in, besides just the actual getting to the studio and playing, I was working 25 hours a day on it."[174]

Always on the run

Slash's guitar prowess and instantly recognizable visage made him a popular choice for musicians looking to add a bit of devil-horns-flying metal to their projects. During the *Illusion* era, the guitarist would rise to become a professional hard-rock avatar of sorts, teaming up with a variety of musical artists. Slash's signature look – top hat, curly mane, leather jacket, Les Paul – made him a natural fit for collaboration with rockers such as Iggy Pop and Alice Cooper, but the guitarist's brand was so strong, he was also tapped by notables outside the metal world, including Lenny Kravitz and Michael Jackson,

Slash had run into Lenny Kravitz at the American Music Awards earlier that January, and the two realized they had attended high school together. Kravitz struck gold with his 1989 debut, *Let Love Rule,* a unique blend of rock, hippie soul, and funk that the multi-instrumentalist put together almost entirely on his own. The album became the toast of L.A.; Slash loved it. "We started talking and were excited to meet each other again, especially the fact we were both making music," Kravitz recalled. "We said we should work together sometime." [175] [176]

In late 1990, Kravitz was working on his sophomore effort in a Los Angeles recording studio and invited Slash to drop by and contribute a guitar solo to a tune called "Fields of Joy." To get a feel for the number, Slash tossed off a quick warm-up take, and Kravitz stopped recording. Slash was ready to play it again, but Kravitz shook his head. He enjoyed the rawness of first takes and insisted on keeping Slash's initial pass.[177] "It's the most out of tune first-take dry guitar solo – but he really digs it," the guitarist laughed.[178]

The two musicians continued to hang out that night, drinking vodka, smoking pot, reminiscing about high school, and jamming. Slash started noodling around on a slinky guitar riff he'd been kicking around for a few months, ultimately rejecting it as too funky for GNR. Kravitz immediately seized upon it. "Hey, what is that?"

Slash shrugged, "Oh, it's just this thing."

"That's psychotic," Kravitz declared.[179] "I'm going to make a song."[180]

A few months later, the two musicians reconvened in a New Jersey studio to record the track. "He had me get a gallon of vodka and a bag of ice and we went into the studio and bang, there it was," Kravitz recalled.[181] "The song just wrote itself. He came in with the riff, I got behind the drum kit and we worked out an arrangement and got it down real quick. I picked up a Les Paul and did the opposing part, which I call the funk part – the counterpart. The two guitars together just fit and weave perfectly together. I did the bass part, he played his solo, and that was it. I then took the track home, wrote the lyrics and melody, and went back in to finish the song. Did the vocals, did a horn chart for it, and there it was, man. It was just a beautiful combination."[182] [183]

"I had a great time hanging out in New Jersey," Slash said. "The guy is so down-to-earth. It's a pleasure to work with somebody like that, where there's no bullshit."[184]

Kravitz titled the composition "Always on the Run," issuing it as the lead single from his second record, *Mama Said,* in March 1991. The cut received considerable radio airplay and its accompanying black-and-white performance video became a mainstay on MTV.

Dangerous

Michael Jackson desperately wanted Slash to appear on his eighth solo album, *Dangerous.* Jackson famously featured an Eddie Van Halen guitar solo on 1982's "Beat It," and tapped Billy Idol axeman Steve Stevens for 1987's "Dirty Diana." Doggedly determined to top his previous efforts, for *Dangerous,* Jackson sought the highest-profile player in the hard-rock world, Slash. The guitarist was flattered. "I thought it would be cool, sort of an Eddie Van Halen spot where I could really shine," Slash said.[185] "I think Michael liked me because of the animated element of my persona. I think he saw me as a caricature."[186]

The eccentric Jackson spent $10 million making *Dangerous,* hiring dozens of producers and booking multiple L.A.-area recording studios for years at a time.[187] "The guy books the studio for two or three years and comes in once every six months," Slash said.[188] "The sessions were so unorganized. I like to keep a schedule and be punctual, but those dates just sat there for months and months until I kept thinking they didn't want to use me anymore. I got a call three months later to do it at such and such a date, but when that date came, it wouldn't happen."[189]

After months of rescheduling, the session finally took place at Ocean Way Studios in Sherman Oaks. Jackson was not there. That day, Slash worked on two numbers that were being considered for *Dangerous*: "D.S." and "Morphine." To record his parts, the producers would start the backing music and Slash would play his guitar riff one time. This sample would then be cut and pasted into the rest of the track. "That was probably the most business-like session I've ever done," the guitarist recalled.[190] "Everything is pieced together from samples; you use the same drum beat and chords then later add things to make it different in some places. That's way too automated for my taste. I come from the old school – you get in there and you play. Michael Jackson is great, but not the process. To this day I still don't know what's happening."[191] [192] [193]

The producers wanted Slash to record another song, but the session never came together. "Six months went by, and they called: 'Can you come down and finish?' I said, 'Yeah, when?' 'Well, we're trying to figure it out.' A few months later, I finally call them: 'Do you want me to finish this? Maybe Michael isn't hip to the stuff I put down.' And they said, 'No, you've gotta do it.' Ages went by and they called again. At this point I said, 'No, I'm doing our record and we're on the road. Too late.' I never met Michael through this whole thing."[194]

Feeling dizzy

After three months of consistent effort, *Illusion's* basic tracks were in the can and Slash's guitar work was complete, but GNR's second album was far from finished. There were still lyrics to write, vocals to record, and more instruments to add. Axl was insistent that Guns produce a masterpiece, with some songs so cinematic only a full orchestra could reproduce them. The singer began working closely with Mike Clink to augment the existing tracks with additional instruments, beginning with a two-week session with new keyboardist Dizzy Reed.

Axl was determined to pack *Illusion* with pianos, organs, and keyboards. The singer had already laid down piano on five of *Illusion's* basic tracks, including "November Rain," "Estranged," and "Yesterdays." On the latter number and "Don't Damn Me," Dizzy augmented the tracks with organ. Dizzy had spent months listening to the new material, suggesting places where he might insert piano or organ. "If I thought something needed piano and I tried it and they liked it, it was cool. So that's what I did. Piano, organ, and a little bit of clavinet. Just stuck to the basics."[195]

Dizzy's rollicking piano was a welcome addition to stomping, mid-tempo rockers such as "Dust N' Bones," "Bad Obsession," and "Pretty Tied Up." GNR's production team made strategic use of the additional instrument, panning it to the left alongside Izzy on "Bad Apples" to compensate for the mismatch between Izzy's lone guitar and Slash's wall of axes. At other times, Guns chose not to incorporate piano. The sweeping ballad "Don't Cry" could easily accommodate all variety of keyboards, but GNR opted to present the song in its original form. Likewise, adding a bit of barrelhouse piano to "You Ain't the First" seemed like a no-brainer, but Guns left it off.

Regardless, Dizzy's many keyboard contributions transformed GNR's sound. More than half the material on *Illusion* would feature piano, a radical contrast to *Appetite's* stripped-down approach. The overt addition of piano and keyboards on *Illusion* forever distanced Guns from their metal origins, enabling the band to explore different strains of the classic rock canon. Now GNR could do more than write material in the tradition of Black Sabbath and AC/DC; they could follow the paths paved by Elton John, Queen, the Stones, and others.

Illusion's choice of covers helped align Guns with two of rock's most consequential artists, Bob Dylan and the Beatles. Written by Paul McCartney and released by his post-Beatles outfit, Wings, "Live and Let Die" was the title track to a 1973 James Bond film. "I rented the movie, and I was watching it, and I just went, 'This song sounds like "Welcome to the Jungle 2."'" Axl recalled, just after *Illusion's* basic tracks had been recorded. "We ended up playing it a little bit in rehearsal. To me it's like Tom Waits meets Metallica or something. 'Cause the way I sing it, it's so rough and scratchy that I sound like Tom Waits."

"Knockin' on Heaven's Door" fit Guns hand in glove; the group so fully inhabited Dylan's tune, it almost sounded like a GNR original. "Live and Let Die" was a left-field choice and the group was unsure they'd be able to pull it off. Slash remembered, "It's one of those songs, like 'Heaven's Door,' that Axl and I have always loved. We were talking one night about a cover song and that came up, and we're like, 'Yeah! Let's do it!' So, I went to rehearsal with Izzy and

Matt and Duff, just to see whether we could sound good playing it, and it sounded really heavy."[196]

"It sounds like us," Axl affirmed of "Live and Let Die." "Everybody that hears it thinks that it sounds like the perfect song for us to do."[197] Axl's grandiose vision for McCartney's tune included piano, keyboard, a horn section, and even a full-blown orchestra. For the horn parts, Axl enlisted Matt McKagan and his fellow Suicide Hornsmen Robert Clark and Jon Trautwein. Matt McKagan's wife, Rachel West, came to the studio that day, too, and contributed piccolo.

Axl begged Mike Clink to hire an orchestra for "Live and Let Die" but the producer talked him out of the idea, insisting the cost and logistics were prohibitive. Instead, Clink assured Axl, they could reproduce an orchestra using synthesizers. Although the final version of "Live and Let Die" clocked in at under three minutes, Clink's over-the-top production made the number feel longer and more epic.

Interviewed around this time, Slash described the swelling vision for *Illusion*, and how he and Axl continued to make additions to the album's basic tracks. "There'll be a lot of different instruments. I've got guitars doing all different kinds of sounds and things. There are horns on 'Live and Let Die.' We didn't get into sampling, but right now, as we speak, Axl is in the studio with a rack of synthesizers, so we don't have to bring in an orchestra for a couple of songs. There might even be a bunch of kids singing on 'November Rain,' because it's that kind of song. It's very angelic. We'll do whatever it takes to make the songs as powerful as possible."[198]

Geffen was impatient for Guns to deliver their sophomore opus and were currently planning for an early spring release, aiming for April 1991. To the company's dismay, Axl continued to eat up studio time, tweaking the instrumental tracks, writing lyrics, and practicing his phrasing. He refused to rush the process. Axl had laid down a few scratch tracks here and there, but the singer still had not recorded one note of his vocals.

Then there was Rock in Rio, a large Brazilian music festival that had booked GNR for two headlining concerts in January 1991. The group had only played a few shows in the past two years and the new lineup with Matt and Dizzy had never appeared anywhere. Following the Rio shows, beginning in May, Guns were slated to release their second album and embark on their first-ever headlining tour, an international trek that would take them around the world over a two-year timespan. The band would play arenas and then coliseums, including gigs in Europe, South America, New Zealand, Australia, and Japan. Everything was contingent upon the new record being done.

Right next door to hell

Whatever progress Axl was making at the Record Plant was slowed in November after he got into a confrontation with his neighbor, Gabriella Kantor. The events would eventually inspire the lyrics to *Illusion's* opening rager, "Right Next Door to Hell." The thirty-seven-year-old Kantor lived next to Axl on the twelfth floor of Shoreham Towers, a condominium building located near the Tower Video store on Sunset where Axl once worked. Kantor alleged there was loud music emanating from Axl's condo at all hours, creating a 'round-the-clock disturbance. Axl claimed that Kantor was a crazed fan who continually harassed him, including blasting GNR from her own apartment and hosting "I live next door to Axl Rose" parties. "It's really weird, she cranks my music all the time," he told a reporter from the *L.A. Times*.[199] Axl was certain it was Kantor who had summoned police to his apartment in August with a noise complaint.

It was after 1:00 a.m. on October 30 when Axl and Kantor got into an argument in the hallway. According to Kantor, Axl was playing loud music, and she went next door to ask him to turn it down. When she knocked on Axl's door, "He was in one of those crazy moods and he attacked me."[200] Kantor claimed the singer snatched her keys and threw them off his balcony into a shared swimming pool below. According to Axl, Kantor showed up to his door drunk at 1:30 in the morning, carrying a wine bottle and threatening to cut him with it. Axl claimed he took the bottle away from Kantor, closed the door, and called the police.

"This lady lives in the condominium right next door to Axl Rose," West Hollywood police officer James Mortensen told the press later that night. According to Mortensen, Axl "confronted her in the hallway. She was carrying a partially full wine bottle. He grabbed that from her, poured some wine on the floor, and then hit her in the head with it. She was taken to Cedars-Sinai hospital. She is spending the night for observation there. And Axl Rose was arrested for assault with a deadly weapon."[201]

Axl was taken to the West Hollywood Sheriff's Station in handcuffs. He spent four hours in jail, making quite the scene in baggy shorts, an *Exile on Main Street* T-shirt, and red-and-white Converse high top tennis shoes branded with custom "Axl" lettering. He was released later that morning after posting $5,000 bail. Cameras surrounded the singer as he exited the jail, with members of the press snapping photos and shouting questions. Axl grinned and kept his game face on. "I live next door to a psycho," he told a reporter, making his way toward a waiting limousine.[202] The arrest made headlines around the world.

Axl had strutted confidently out of jail draped in a black leather jacket, but privately he worried about the felony charge. A few hours after his arrest, the singer spoke to MTV about the incident, denying he hit Kantor with a wine bottle, but conceding he was concerned about having to prove his innocence. "I don't know," he admitted. "I don't think I'm gonna have much of a problem. But then again, I'm not going to sit here and say that everything will be just fine, 'cause you never know in a court of law what can happen."[203]

Looking to avoid further confrontations with Kantor, Axl booked a room at a pricey boutique hotel, the Sunset Marquis. He felt trapped, locked out of his own apartment. And there were lyrics to write, vocals to record, an album to finish, and tour dates to prepare for. Axl used his condo partly as a place of business – it had a small office where he kept a desk, a fax machine, and important documents. He hated that work-from-home setup and yearned for an oasis, a place to get away from work and the stresses of the music industry.

Days later, Axl shelled out $800,000 for a 2000-square foot, two-bedroom house located in the tawny Beachwood Canyon section of the Hollywood Hills. The 1950s-era abode sat on 1.3 acres and featured a swimming pool and views of the L.A. skyline.[204] The place had been completely remodeled by the seller, but Axl and Erin called for a series of new renovations. A team of designers and decorators swooped in, redoing the floors and remodeling the kitchen. A pair of topiary elephants arrived via helicopter.

At Axl's behest, legendary rock photographer Neal Preston dropped by to take some pictures. Preston snapped shots of Axl and Erin embracing, their bodies intertwined on the black leather couch in their living room. On a whim, Axl invited Preston to the recording studio, where he captured a series of iconic black and white photographs of a pensive-looking Axl. "I had heard all the stories about his good days and his bad days," Preston recalled. "But this must have been a good day because he was great. He said he was going to the Record Plant, so I tagged along and got shots of Axl at his peak."[205]

Piece of me

Ten days after his arrest, Axl performed at the 4,000-capacity Hollywood Palladium for a concert celebrating *Rip* magazine's fourth anniversary. Axl had agreed to appear long before the Kantor situation and kept his word. That night, he played as part of Gaak, a supergroup that paired members of GNR with two acts that would become *Illusion* tourmates. To begin, Slash, Duff, Metallica drummer Lars Ulrich, and Skid Row singer Sebastian Bach pounded out headbanging takes on *Appetite's* "You're Crazy" and Metallica's "For Whom the Bell Tolls."

"Mr. Axl Rose!" Sebastian Bach howled after the second number concluded. Axl strode to the stage, shirtless and wearing a leather jacket over shorts. "Nice little surprise?" he asked the audience, smiling as the band launched into "Piece of Me," a hard charger from Skid Row's self-titled debut. Sebastian Bach sang "Piece" as a come-on, a sexualized tease from a hot rock star, but Axl interpreted it as a provocation, daring would-be adversaries to come at him. Midway through the tune, Axl had already tossed aside his leather jacket. It felt great to be onstage again, killing it in front of an adoring audience.

"Piece of Me" thundered to a close and Axl clapped Slash on the back. "We do this for a reason," he told the audience. "There's a lot of people that try to pit me and Bass against each other. This ego bullshit, fuck 'em."

Gaak launched into Nazareth's "Hair of the Dog," which Hollywood Rose used to play in nightclubs and Guns covered on the *Appetite* tour. Axl threw himself into it like a man possessed, a maniacal gleam in his eye. Axl turned the chorus into a declaration of war; in his mind, the singer was delivering every word straight to Gabby Kantor, his neighbor from hell. This was a *sonofabitch* she had messed with. As if to cement the point, Axl wore a wide belt whose buckle spelled out the words "Fuck You" in bold brass letters. Axl knew immediately "Hair of the Dog" would have to be added to GNR's covers EP. After two numbers with Gaak, the singer departed, replaced by Metallica's James Hetfield and Kirk Hammett.

Backstage at the Palladium was the usual cocaine-and-booze blur, but Axl was too tense to cut loose with the others that night. He felt anxious about his pending court date and pissed off about being forced out of his condo.

Axl and Erin never moved into the new house in Beachwood Canyon. Increasingly irritated by the situation with Kantor, his relationship with Erin, the unfinished album, and everything else, Axl snapped one afternoon while touring the renovations. "This house doesn't mean anything to me!" the singer roared. "This is not what I wanted. I didn't work forever to have this lonely house on the hill that I live in because I'm a rich rock star."[206] Axl shoved a grand piano estimated at $38,000 through a massive bay window that overlooked Los Angeles. It fell two stories, splintering on the asphalt driveway below. The singer was just warming up. He smashed all the living room and kitchen windows, then demolished a $30,000 granite fireplace that was affixed to a 30-foot glass wall. He finished by destroying a $12,000 statue. The total damage was estimated at

$100,000. Not to be outdone, Erin trashed the rest of the house the next day. "I had my own different reasons," she told a reporter.[207]

Meanwhile, Axl's arraignment for assault with a deadly weapon was scheduled for the end of November. On November 20, Axl won a restraining order against Gabby Kantor. His lawyers contended that Kantor was a Guns fan turned stalker, describing her as "a potentially dangerous rock 'n' roll groupie upset that she is not a part of Rose's social and or professional life."[208] Axl denied making any physical contact with Kantor, comparing her to Glenn Close's crazed antagonist from *Fatal Attraction*. "Gabby wants a big place in my life, and she can't take the rejection," the singer told *People* magazine. "Frankly, if I was going to hit her with a wine bottle, she wouldn't have gotten up. I would have become a criminal at that point, wondering what I was going to do next to not get busted over the quivering body in my hallway."[209] Axl even went so far as to take a lie detector test, publicly offering to cover the cost of Kantor's own test and compare scores.[210]

Kantor denied the allegation that she was a crazed fan, telling the reporter from *People*, "I'm not fanatical about anything." Kantor repeated her claim that Axl's loud music was the root of the problem, and that she now suffered from "post-concussive syndrome" due to his assault with the wine bottle.[211]

On November 28, the day before Axl's arraignment, the charges were dropped due to lack of evidence. Deputy District Attorney Elden Fox told the *Los Angeles Times*, "It just doesn't appear Rose struck her with a wine bottle."[212]

Axl was legally vindicated but the problems with Kantor had driven him from his condo, strained his relationship with Erin, and burned up more than a million dollars in attorney fees. And he still didn't have a place to live. Perhaps the only silver lining of the entire affair was that Kantor inspired *Illusion's* opening number. Axl told the reporter from *People* he was writing a song that "has a verse about life in L.A., and the chorus came when I was at home and couldn't figure one out. All of a sudden Gabby started beating on the walls and had her television cranked on ten to bother me, and I just wrote this chorus called 'Right Next Door to Hell.' It works really well."[213]

Axl's court victory was costly in other ways, too, further delaying the process of writing lyrics and recording the vocals for the more than thirty instrumental tracks GNR had in the can. The forward momentum of the past several months seemed to have slowed. Guns had promised to deliver their second album in the spring of 1991; two years' worth of headlining tour dates were lined up, starting in May. Geffen's impatience was growing by the day, and even Axl's bandmates were frustrated with the ongoing holdups.

A reporter from *Rolling Stone* asked Slash how Axl's personal troubles had impacted the making of *Illusion*, and the guitarist unloaded on him. "They're a pain in the ass and they keep things from getting done," Slash griped. He complained that GNR had spent more than $400,000 on *Illusion* so far with nothing to show for it. "There are moments when Axl's thing really gets in the way of what is productive, and we end up spending a lot of money. Axl has no idea, or has a very slight idea, of what the financial reality is. To me, $400,000 to make a record is ludicrous. So, I just sit there with my head between my knees, freaking out. Axl's craziness drives me crazier than it does Axl."[214]

Toward the end of 1990, Axl and Erin severed their relationship once and for all, an immensely painful experience that threw the singer from his bearings. In the divorce papers, which were published in the media, Axl claimed he "sincerely believed that Erin was my greatest inspiration. I was in a severe state of fear and depression that unless I married Erin at that time, she would leave me, and I would therefore lose the person whom I believed to be my greatest inspiration." Unfortunately, Axl wrote, their marriage had been characterized by "severe property damage, mutual acts of violence and humiliation and similar such activities."[215] Axl claimed Erin would disappear for "weeks on end without notice. She made it quite clear by her actions and statements that she had no intention of complying with her promise to raise a family and be involved in a well-adjusted marital situation."[216]

Axl felt abandoned. He had nowhere to live and his marriage to Erin was in the death throes. He had lyrics to finish, vocals to record, and an international tour on the horizon, beginning with two massive

stadium shows at Rock in Rio in January. It felt as if the entire world
was scrutinizing his every move at a time when he felt depressed, out
of shape, and exhausted.

Despondent and without a place to call home, Axl set up shop in
Studio A of the Record Plant, ordering assistants to bring in his king-
sized bed, exercise equipment, CD collection, Kiss and Elton John-
themed pinball machines, smoking jacket, and other belongings. The
singer was determined to record the vocals for *Illusion*, even if that
meant moving into the studio and living there until they were
finished. Rumors floated that Axl had gone mad, locking Mike Clink
and the band out of the studio, and re-recording all the tracks. But
those allegations were false. The singer had not recorded anything.
Despite GNR's monthslong effort to finish the second album, Axl
had still not recorded one note of his vocals.

Chapter 5

His World

Shannon Hoon was a vocalist and Lafayette, Indiana native who was five years younger than Axl. The two did not know each other growing up, but Axl had attended high school with Hoon's half-sister, Anna. After Axl made it with GNR, he would occasionally return to Lafayette to visit old friends. Hoon was already fronting a band by then and running in some of the same circles that Axl had. The two were introduced and Axl took an instant shine to Hoon, a talented Indiana kid from a troubled family who had dreams of rock stardom. The singer could relate. "Axl saw a little bit of himself in Shannon," said Hoon's friend Bill Armstrong.[217]

During one of Axl's trips to Lafayette, he and Shannon hung out, talked, and even sang a few drunken Bad Company karaoke tunes at a local bar. "Axl liked him," recalled Shannon's girlfriend Lisa. "Shannon was younger than Axl. They became friends."[218] This early encounter with Axl proved to be a catalyst for Shannon, who immediately began hatching plans to relocate to L.A. and join a band.

Shannon arrived by bus in the spring of 1990, around the time Guns were recording "Civil War." Axl was busy dealing with Steven Adler's issues, but he had his assistant secure Shannon an apartment, and hooked him up with an office job at one of Riki Rachtman's companies. Shannon, confident and outgoing, embraced the Hollywood lifestyle and immediately became a Cathouse regular.

Axl also invited Shannon to the studio to witness the making of *Illusion*. "Shannon was great," producer Mike Clink recalled. "He was this shy little kid from Indiana that used to sit in the back of the room, who was a friend of Axl's. And he would come night after night after night – sit there and listen. He was a sponge, taking it all in."[219] The precocious Shannon was no wallflower. He continually played demos for Mike Clink, seeking affirmation and a big break. Soon enough, Shannon was singing backup on *Illusion*, his airy falsetto blending with Axl's various vocal stylings.

In addition to letting Shannon sit in on and occasionally join GNR's studio sessions, Axl enjoyed playing kingmaker. The singer began taking his young protégée to exclusive nightclubs and private parties, introducing him to key players in the industry. "Axl was a big fan of Shannon's," recalled Bill Armstrong. "He really loved the way Shannon sung, and felt like, 'Here's a guy from my hometown, and I'm going to do anything to help this guy out.'"[220]

Shannon eventually fell in with some musicians and formed Blind Melon. Back in Indiana, he had written one undeniably great number, "Change;" the burgeoning group dashed off a few new originals and slapped together a five-song demo tape. Axl's endorsement of Shannon made the new act a hot commodity in Hollywood. Despite having just five tunes and zero gigging experience, every record label in town requested a meeting.

Dead by Christmas

In late 1990, Axl had been living at the Record Plant for weeks, brooding about his divorce and slowly working on the vocals for *Illusion*. "I couldn't leave the studio, but I couldn't go back to my condo because of my neighbor. That was a nightmare," the singer recalled. He resided in the studio full-time for about six weeks. "There was no heat in that room. It was a cold, lonely place, but it was the only place I could stay to keep myself in the work. It was cool-looking, but it was dark, cold and weird."[221]

Axl had several large pieces of exercise equipment brought into the $200-an-hour studio, including a Stairmaster, stationary bike, punching bag, and weights.[222] To combat his growing depression and sense of despair, Axl threw himself into a punishing workout routine that included more than 500 sit ups per day. Unlike his bandmates, Axl rarely did cocaine, but during his time at the Record Plant, he smoked pot incessantly. "I was in a lot of pain, and that was the only way I could keep myself together enough to work," Axl explained. "It was the only thing that could take my mind off my problems, so I could stay focused and record. Any other drugs just screwed me up. That was the only thing I could do to sedate me and keep me contained enough to not freak out on how depressed I was. I was doing it almost medicinally."[223] [224]

Industry insiders whispered that Axl had gone insane, claiming that he would stay awake for two- and three-day stretches and then crash for an equally long time. While much of this gossip was baseless, there was no doubt Axl entered a difficult period following his divorce, one that pushed him into a black hole of despair. "It got to the point that certain people could tell just by the way I was talking, the tone of my voice, that I wasn't right," Axl recalled.[225] The singer's macabre sense of humor probably did not help. That December, he made a point of blasting Hanoi Rocks' "Dead by Christmas" around the clock.

Shannon Hoon rallied around Axl, proving to be an ally during one of the singer's darkest hours. Shannon even moved into the Record Plant, so Axl would not feel so isolated. As Christmas approached, the Blind Melon vocalist planned to return home to Lafayette to spend the holiday with his family. He implored Axl to come with him, but the singer refused. Shannon did not want to leave Axl alone, so he made a series of frantic phone calls, trying to find someone who was willing to spend Christmas at the Record Plant with him.

Shannon eventually reached GNR booking agent Shelly Shaw, who agreed to watch over the singer. To lighten the mood, she brought along a few Christmas presents. "It was the holidays. Axl had been through a really quick divorce with Erin. He was sad and living at the studio – he was in a really bad way," Shaw recalled. "When I got there, he was sleeping a lot and going out to eat – there was no recording going on. He was just living there. And he had a lot to say. Axl loved to sit and friggin' filibuster."[226]

Axl told Shelly Shaw everything. His marriage was over, he was locked out of his condo, his new house was destroyed, *Illusion's* vocals were still not finished, hundreds of tour dates were booked, and Geffen was breathing down his neck. He was suffering from a deep depression. "I reached a point where I was basically dead and still breathing," he explained less than a year later. "I didn't have enough energy to leave my bedroom and crawl to the kitchen to get something to eat. I had to find out why I felt like I was dead. I was miserable and suicidal, and I realized I had to do this work or I would check out."[227]

Shelly Shaw was sympathetic, encouraging Axl to seek therapy as a way to deal with some of the overwhelming feelings he was having. Axl nodded and listened. With little to lose, he agreed to give it a try. The singer first wanted to finish recording his vocals and get through the Rock in Rio shows in January, but after that, he agreed to seek counseling.

The Axl treatment

Axl did not enjoy songwriting, but he loved recording, which appealed to his artistic nature and served as a platform for his creative pursuits. That winter, he threw himself into crafting and capturing the *Illusion* vocals. "Recording is my favorite thing because it's like painting a picture," he said. "You start out with a shadow, or an idea, and you come up with something and it's a shadow of that. You might like it better. It's still not exactly what you pictured in your head. But you go into the studio and add all these things and you come up with something you didn't even expect. You allow different shadings to creep in and then you go, 'Wow, I got a whole different effect on this that's even heavier than what I pictured.'"[228]

Axl's process for recording was the opposite of Slash's. The guitarist sought to capture the magic of a perfect first take and hated to play something more than one or two times. Axl was the kind of musician who liked to do three hundred takes of a vocal line and then spend a week debating which one to use. Slash liked to begin recording around noon and end in the early evening; Axl woke up at two or three in the afternoon, starting at sunset and working through the night. Slash would leave in a little mistake if the take was otherwise good. Axl could not live with anything less than one hundred percent perfection. Slash was a musical genius who erased all his original tracks and re-recorded everything in five weeks. It took Axl nine months to complete his vocals for *Illusion*.

Part of the delay was due to Axl's sporadic schedule, showing up to record once or twice a week, then staying there nonstop for weeks on end. "Or he might come at four in the afternoon and work 'til midnight the next day" Tom Zutaut recalled.[229] Axl would scrap recording sessions at the drop of a hat. One night, he snorted a single line of coke while partying with Matt and Metallica drummer Lars Ulrich. The next day the singer cancelled an entire week of sessions, claiming that the blow had compromised his voice.[230]

Another reason it took Axl so long to complete the vocals for *Illusion* was because he liked to stack multiple registers, pitches, and voices onto each song, sometimes dozens. "On this record, I just sang with myself," Axl explained. "It was in different keys, so there was some form of harmony. But it wasn't planned harmonies like on 'Sweet Child' or 'Nightrain' on the first record. I just wanted to sing with myself in a different octave."[231]

Furthermore, Axl had to be in the correct emotional state before anyone could even dream of pressing the record button. "I put myself wholly into whatever line I'm singing," he explained. "Whatever the line makes me think of, I go there. If it's a tear-jerker thing, maybe that situation was written, and I'm thinking about being in a park or something. Or I think about the emotions I had as a child that those lines relate to, and I go there while I'm singing it. That way I can get the best out of me because it's getting in touch with the base emotion, the base feeling and the base environment inside my head.[232]

Slash aimed to bang out a killer second album, a hard-charging single disc that proved Guns had not lost a step. Axl aspired to create nothing less than a sprawling masterpiece, a musical work of art that would stand the test of time for decades. He was inspired by Pink

Floyd's 1979 double album *The Wall,* a rock opera about a drug-addled singer who has a mental breakdown while on tour. *The Wall's* cinematic milieu was meticulously crafted by adding sound effects and dialogue from characters such as teachers, judges, groupies, and ER physicians. Similarly, Axl wanted material like "Coma" to resemble mini movies, and he and Mike Clink filled them with spoken passages and lifelike sounds, including a real defibrillator.

Even material that hewed close to the *Appetite* archetype got the Axl treatment. Izzy's "Pretty Tied Up" was built upon the same type of greasy, slip-sliding guitar riffage that drove *Appetite's* best rockers. The song's sleazy Hollywood setting and real-life description of a professional dominatrix fit perfectly with the cast of lowlifes who populated GNR's debut. Adding to this were Izzy's wry observations about life post-fame. Every bill someone hands him is suddenly higher now that he's got money. Everywhere he looks there is another rip-off artist, another shark, another million dollars in royalties some shady music-biz hustler forgot to mention. There was also the guitarist's almost shocking self-description of a hungry, street-level rock band that turned into a joke before imploding altogether. Through this sharp series of images, Izzy draws a sly comparison between the golden handcuffs of rock stardom and the sadomasochistic universe of the whip-cracking dominatrix. In the end, everyone is pretty tied up, bound by the pleasures and pains of wealth, celebrity, and dirty sex.

Unfortunately, Axl could not stop futzing with the track, adding keyboards, spoken-word non-sequiturs, sound effects and other gimmickry. Atop this already-busy foundation, the singer piled additional layers of vocals, doubling and tripling the pre-choruses and choruses with deep baritones and high falsettos. In the end, Axl's studio enhancements diminished the raw power of what might have otherwise been the standout number of the entire set.

Along these lines, the singer was determined to add Alice Cooper's speaking voice to West Arkeen's old tune "The Garden." Cooper's craggy timbre and spooky image were perfect for the number – Axl envisioned something akin to Vincent Price's horror-movie narration on the Michael Jackson song "Thriller." Guns and

Alice Cooper had recorded Cooper's "Under My Wheels" a few years back, gigged together many times, and remained friendly.

In the 1970s, Cooper was a coke-and-booze-swilling Mr. Hyde, but he had cleaned up his act years ago and his off-stage life now resembled that of a golf-loving grandfather. Cooper was lying in bed watching a movie at the Sunset Marquis late one night when Axl phoned. He invited Cooper to the Record Plant to duet on "The Garden." Cooper went over to and gave the track a listen. "I have a tee-off time tomorrow at seven," he told Axl. "We're doing this in an hour."

"I'm used to doing things in an hour," Cooper explained. "Axl likes to take his time, but if you can't get a vocal like that in an hour, there's something wrong."[233]

The two got to work on the spot. "When you're in the studio one-on-one with him, he's amazing – the guy can really sing," Cooper marveled. "You can't stay with him. I'm trying to do a duet with him, and he was two octaves ahead of me. I'm going, 'Okay, you do the real high parts and I'll stay down here.'"[234]

Like Slash, Cooper preferred to work quickly and was startled by Axl's drawn-out process. "As an artist, you gotta know when the painting is done," he said. "I did my bit maybe three times, but when Axl was doing his vocals, he treated it very intricately. Axl was a perfectionist – almost to the point where you want to say, 'At some point, Axl, it's gotta be good enough.'"

Axl's perfectionism and insistence on working only when he felt inspired led to growing tensions within the band. Slash in particular was frustrated with the endless delays and hassles in finishing the second album, which increasingly seemed to be due to Axl's personal troubles and emotional issues. Axl viewed Slash as unsympathetic, not only of his real-life problems but of the intense pressure faced by the singer to deliver a knockout second album and everything that went along with it, from starring in music videos to commanding center stage on a worldwide tour. Axl was the face of it all.

Izzy was the one member of the group who could still talk honestly to Axl. They had been friends for fifteen years and that history meant something to both men. Izzy pulled Axl aside and suggested they agree to some sort of timetable or schedule. Axl exploded, "There is no fucking schedule!"[235]

Axl's obsessive tendencies extended to the songwriting credits and royalties as well. For *Appetite*, the quintet split everything the same way, reflecting the democratic songwriting process of that album. Axl took a 25% share due to his greater contributions to the lyrics, Steven received 15%, and Slash, Izzy, and Duff each earned 20%. West Arkeen received credit for his co-authorship of "It's So Easy," and one-time Hollywood Rose guitarist Chris Weber collected royalties for contributing to "Anything Goes."

Illusion was complicated by having multiple outside writers and band members bringing in songs that were largely complete. Axl had not been on hand for some material GNR developed early on in Chicago, including "Garden of Eden," "Bad Apples," and "Get in the Ring," but the singer commandeered a large chunk of credit anyway. "Axl insisted upon splits that were like 22.75% or 32.2% per song for us core members," Slash wrote in his memoir. "It was mathematically worked out according to who wrote what. It was pored over and complicated things to a corporate degree."[236] Further incensing his bandmate, Axl demanded 100% of the songwriting credits for "November Rain" and "Estranged," despite Slash's significant musical contributions to both numbers. This became another point of contention, ratcheting up the growing tensions between the singer and guitarist.

My world

Appetite only featured a single keyboard – a synthesizer line on "Paradise City" – but Axl had always been interested in electronic music. "I might be using synthesizer," he told an interviewer a year earlier, when asked about GNR's second album. "I took electronic music in 11th grade at school. I don't know shit about digital synthesizers, but I can take a patch cord and shape my own wave forms. So now I wanna jump into today."[237]

Axl had always envisioned hiring a full orchestra to accompany Guns on "November Rain," but time constraints forced the singer to tackle the job himself, using a bank of synths. "I realized I only had one week, and no way I was gonna learn how to communicate with an orchestra. So, we brought in eight synthesizers. For eight hours I just sat there and played strings to 'November Rain' over and over and picked every single string sound to create my own 130-piece orchestra. We went through three thousand sounds. We had to sit there and go, 'Wait, is that one sound more real than that one?'"[238]

Axl's musical vision for GNR was expansive, and he was thrilled to add an array of instrumentation to the *Illusion* tracks. "Guns N' Roses just works with guitars, drums, vocals, bass. But working with the strings, and flugelhorns, and certain bells – and 'Is it the right bell?' It was almost like it was magical."[239]

Slash described Axl as being like a kid in a candy store as he sat behind his banks of synthesizers, meticulously working through each section of a track. Slash attributed some of Axl's obsession to his round-the-clock marijuana intake, but the guitarist gave credit where it was due. "Axl was into the grandiose production. He had so much integrity about it that he'd spend however long it took to ensure that the sonic drama was *perfect*. He spent hours dialing all of that shit in, getting the nuances just right. What he ended up with at the end of the day was brilliant. I've heard songs with real strings that sound less authentic."[240]

Slash and the rest of Axl's bandmates were staunch rockers for the most part, but the singer's tastes were more varied. He popped up backstage at a Pet Shop Boys concert that spring, professing his admiration for the British electronic duo. "Axl thought the show was gorgeous," Boys singer Neil Tennant told *Rolling Stone*. "He was extremely charming and knew our music quite well."[241] Conversely, Axl loved the hardcore gangsta rap produced by fellow L.A. denizens N.W.A – a ballcap featuring the group's logo would be nightly stagewear on early legs of the *Illusion* tour.

Axl described Faith No More as "the only band I'm jealous of."[242] The singer loved the way the group built their sound on a heavy rock foundation, effortlessly incorporating everything from rap to prog rock into the mix. That the group prominently featured a keyboardist was not lost on Axl.

He was also an early adopter of Nine Inch Nails' 1989 debut, *Pretty Hate Machine*, raving about Trent Reznor's bold artistry. Axl loved the juxtaposition of Reznor's deeply emotional vocals and lyrics set to the cold, relentless throb of electronica. That dichotomy perfectly encapsulated Axl's own feelings of rage and isolation.

All these influences came together on "My World," a track Axl wrote and recorded in three hours. He enlisted Johann Langlie, an electronic musician who had been brought in for sound effects work on "Coma."

"'My World' just kind of presented itself," Axl explained. "We had been working on 'Live and Let Die' all night and it was early morning. I'd been listening to a lot of industrial music and all of a sudden, I said, 'Hey, let's do something. Let's see what happens. Let's just make it short and sweet and see what we come up with.'"[243]

Langlie assembled the backing track, programming drums, keyboards, and effects into a Nine Inch Nails soundalike. It concluded with scenes from a bondage session, a woman moaning in ecstasy a la "Rocket Queen." On top of the din, Axl laid down a vocal that resembled a three-way tie between Faith No More, N.W.A, and Nine Inch Nails. Drawing on a variety of voices, Axl rapped, spoke, whispered, and screamed throughout the 85-second track. In the lyrics, the singer debated nurture versus nature, laughing at a woman, possibly a therapist, whose psychological troubles were rooted in biological disorders. (Implying that Axl had earned his scars the old-fashioned way.) Anyone who dared talk to Axl risked unleashing a closetful of skeletons and entering his world, a hazard zone filled with treacheries around each corner. "It's pretty much me and a computer engineer just putting things together, raw expression," Axl explained.[244]

"My World" was a lark, a one-off experiment Axl put together to see how it would turn out. He adored the results, telling a reporter, "I want to do a whole project like that by myself and with whoever else might want to be on it. It's something that I need to get out of my system, but it's not something I want to base my career and future on."[245]

"My World" was a head-scratcher to some of Axl's bandmates. Duff thought the track was slamming but Slash dismissed it as "new age music with synthesizers."[246] Izzy would later claim that the first time he heard the number was after *Illusion* had been released.

By mid-January, Axl's main vocals for all but four songs were finished. This still left backup vocals to be recorded, and Axl was as deeply involved in that aspect of the recording as he was his main tracks. The singer's endless studio time had cost GNR a fortune, but everyone breathed a sigh of relief that one of *Illusion's* most significant hurdles had been mostly cleared.

Being in the Beatles

"This is some way for me to show up to my first rehearsal in two years," Axl intoned with a grin, as he introduced "Patience." The audience at Maracana Stadium, 140,000 strong, roared in approval. Guns had played to large crowds at festivals on the *Appetite* tour, and there had been stadium shows, such as when they opened for the Stones. But never before had they witnessed such a large and rabid crowd there exclusively to see them, an audience that knew every word to *Appetite* and sang along at top volume.

To increase his visibility in the colossal venue, Axl arrived onstage in blazing white: white leggings, white T-shirt, and a custom white leather jacket emblazoned with GNR logos and ephemera – the same one he wore in the "Paradise City" music video. Ever on brand, Slash hit the rafters in a top hat and leather jacket, Sunburst Les Paul at the hip.

Rock in Rio was a $20 million dollar, nine-day music festival in Rio de Janeiro, Brazil, the sequel to a large gala first held there in 1985. The event ran from January 18-27 and featured international superstars such as Prince, George Michael, and INXS. Guns headlined on two nights, drawing the largest crowds of the festival. MTV dispatched a news production crew to cover the entire event.

GNR treated the whole thing as a vacation. They arrived days early and Izzy, Duff, Slash, and Matt brought their wives and girlfriends along. But when Guns landed at Galeao International

Airport, they were greeted by members of the press and a throng of three thousand fans that was so fired up, the band needed a military escort to get into town.[247] Fans screamed and threw themselves at the passenger vans taxiing the group and their entourage. Thousands more devotees gathered in front of the International Hotel where the tour party was staying. It almost resembled a rock concert, with fans blasting GNR music, waving banners, and shouting the names of their favorite members. If anyone in the group dared to peek outside their hotel room window, instant mayhem ensued. "It was like being in the Beatles," Matt recalled."[248]

The concerts were pure pandemonium. "I'm not sure that I've ever seen a more insane Guns N' Roses crowd – and that is saying something," Slash recalled, years later. "When we kicked into the bridge of 'Paradise City' people swan-dived from the upper tier of the stadium – seemingly to their death."[249]

For GNR, Rock in Rio marked a week filled with firsts. It was the band's first full concerts in more than a year, and Matt and Dizzy's first performances with the group. (Before Rio, the largest crowd Dizzy had played in front of was 400 people as an opening act.) At the shows, Guns debuted a number of *Illusion* tracks, including fiery passes at "Pretty Tied Up," "Double Talkin' Jive," and "You Could Be Mine." These were not tenuous takes on unfamiliar material; Guns approached the *Illusion* songs with conviction, easily integrating them with their classics. "Civil War" and "Knockin' on Heaven's Door" were greeted like old favorites, even though they were technically *Illusion* tracks.

"They're looking for this record to absolutely suck and go down the drain," Duff told a reporter while being interviewed in his hotel room in Rio. "I'm confident and fortunate to work and write songs with the guys in my band and be positive enough that I know that the album won't do that. Even if it's not successful sales-wise, which is not proof of anything."[250]

But Duff's faith in *Illusion* belied a growing sense of turmoil within the group. Guns had never been more victorious, yet something felt off. "We had somehow changed from a band into a traveling extravaganza in which we each just played a more or less independent role," Duff wrote in his memoir. "During that trip to Brazil, I sometimes felt completely alone and alienated even in my own band."[251]

The bassist sought relief in a bottle. His vodka intake had always been high but starting in Rio and for the remainder of the *Illusion* tour, Duff would consume a half gallon of vodka per day – the equivalent of 64 shots. "The shows in Rio were the beginning of the darkest days of my life."

In Rio, GNR were mobbed everywhere they went – the group members could not go shopping without security. As the most recognizable members of the band, Axl and Slash could not leave the hotel at all. "We couldn't leave our rooms, even go down to the pool," Slash recalled. "Because when we did, somehow people would launch themselves over the fifteen-foot wall and run up and basically attack us. They didn't want to hurt us, but they definitely wanted to break a piece of us off to keep for themselves. Any women seen in our company were taunted and basically marked for death by these fans."[252]

Izzy went out anyway, hitting the town in the early mornings to skateboard and surf. Izzy had transformed from the worst heroin junkie in Guns to a sober fitness enthusiast. He was still a chain smoker, but the guitarist's healthy-ish lifestyle was increasingly at odds with Slash, Duff, and Matt, who spent much of their time in Rio half-cocked.

To prepare for the shows, Matt had to learn all of Steven's drum parts on *Appetite* and *Lies*. MTV's Kurt Loder asked Izzy how things were working out with Matt and how his playing differed from Steven's. "As a drummer I would say, I don't know, it's good," Izzy replied, haltingly. "Different style, but they're both good drummers and Matt is working good. He's been busy learning a lot of songs, thirty or something like that."[253]

As the newest member of GNR, Matt was a curiosity in Rio, and he was happy to engage with the fans and chat with the press. "When I joined the band about eight months ago, everything was in turmoil," he told a reporter while touring the iconic Christ the Redeemer statue at Corcovado Mountain. "But the band has really come together, and we pumped out a lot of tunes for this new album, and everything is going really well."[254]

The Rio shows marked another first for Guns. Eight months after joining the group, Matt finally played with Axl for the first time. "It was my first rehearsal with Axl – in front of 140,000 people," the drummer laughed. "It was kind of wild because it was the first time I ever heard him sing with the band, with me playing."[255]

Steven Adler had favored standard five-piece drum kits. By contrast, Matt's massive setup was awash in extra drums, cymbals, and percussion doo dads. On both nights in Rio, Axl called for Matt to execute a drum solo after "Knockin' on Heaven's Door." Axl had not sung a full-length concert in ages and needed time during the set to catch his breath and let his voice rest.

"Axl wants you to do a drum solo tonight so he can take a break," Axl's bodyguard Earl Gabbidon informed Matt, the morning of the first Rio date.

"In which part of the show?" Matt asked.

"He'll let you know," Gabbidon replied. "There's no set list."

Affixed to the stage monitors at the Rio shows was GNR's "pick list," a handwritten inventory of tunes the band could summon at a moment's notice. During gigs, Guns loved nothing more than to launch one ballistic missile after the next, but the group learned the hard way the importance of varying the tempos. At the end of a fast-paced set in Donington, England in 1988, GNR were informed that two fans had been crushed to death. Now, when playing stadiums, the group was mindful to keep the audience's energy levels under control, turning up the heat for two rockers at most before cooling things back down with a ballad. This strategy helped keep the crowds from getting too out of control.

"I like that element of danger, that energy," Slash said during an interview just prior to the Rio gigs. "But then you have to stop the show for people to settle down, or else the casualty tent is filled with all these injuries. I have to change my music, so people don't get killed." Guns would be headlining a number of large stadium shows on the *Illusion* tour, Slash said, and they intended to include a fair amount of slower material "where everyone can chill out for a minute."[256] Those speedbumps included ballads such as "Patience," and "Sweet Child O' Mine," guitar and drum solos, and long instrumental intros, such as the dramatic version of the *Godfather* theme the band cooked up in rehearsal.

But even when Axl was singing a slow number, he worked the crowd tirelessly, sprinting from one side of the stage to the other, doing flying splits off speaker cabinets, and rocking out alongside the other members of the group. There were multiple outfit changes, including the debut of Lycra shorts with an American flag pattern during "Civil War." Axl liked the shorts so much, he ordered a set of tights in the same pattern. Both articles of clothing would become iconic stagewear on the *Illusion* tour.

Axl's shorts were practical, but they were also a deliberate poke at the tough-guy image of the rock frontman. "It isn't necessarily the most macho, male, rock 'n' roll thing to do – that's kinda why I did it," the singer said in a 1992 interview. "It began when I wanted to wear something different, and I wore a pair of red, white, and blue shorts when I was in Rio. I liked them. I could move around better because what I do is pretty athletic."[257]

GNR's second Rio concert was a celebratory affair, with the group relieved to have survived opening night. They premiered more *Illusion* tracks, including "Bad Apples," a rocker they would only play one more time before retiring it permanently.

Axl was relieved the shows went down so well, a positive harbinger of things to come. But he never forgot the severe impoverishment he witnessed in Rio, even if from a distance. "It ripped my heart out," he said. "The poverty down here is like nothing I've ever seen. When we were coming to the stadium to do soundcheck the first day, we went under the tunnel, and when I looked up and saw the houses, I thought of myself as a little kid here and having to try to make a life and starting that way."

Therapy and trauma

GNR returned to the States at the end of January and had about three months before the *Illusion* tour was scheduled to begin. The album had come a long way, but it was nowhere near complete. The Rio shows were exhilarating but exhausting. Axl did not feel physically or psychologically ready for a tour. But he knew the whole world would be watching and he was determined to be mentally and physically in shape.

Axl decided the only way he would be ready was by purging whatever demons were tormenting him. He began therapy in February 1991, not long after the Rock in Rio shows concluded, working with a woman named Suzzy London.

Suzzy London was an actress, singer, and dancer from Park Ridge Illinois, a suburb of Chicago. She attended the University of Iowa where she eventually earned an MFA in theater. Like many aspiring actresses, London moved to Los Angeles, where she tried to break into the business by taking any job she could. She worked in radio and did voiceover work. She sang at a resort, and even worked as a magician's assistant, climbing into coffins, and pretending to be sawed in half.

London also took to Southern California's woo-woo lifestyle and soon developed a side hustle in non-Western medicine and holistic healing. She earned PhDs in fields such as naturopathy, herbology, and phytotherapy, which drew from Native American and Sri Lankan traditions but did not certify one to practice medicine in the U.S. These paper-thin degrees were enough to allow London to call herself a "doctor" and use any available tool or technique to treat the mind, body, and spirit.

London's approach aligned well with Axl, who had long been an armchair student of alternative religions and systems of beliefs – Eastern ideologies, crystals, UFOS, reincarnation, you name it. Erin Everly claimed that after her dogs died, "Axl believed that he had the dogs' souls transferred [into new dogs]."[258] Maybe Axl had been a powerful person in a past life and that could explain his rise to megastardom. And so long as the checks were rolling in, London was happy to entertain Axl's wildest fantasies.

Once Axl began therapy with London, like so many things, he threw himself into the process completely. The sessions lasted five hours per day and Axl attended them Monday through Friday.[259]

Part of their work involved regression therapy, where Axl supposedly unearthed memories that dated to his conception. He would locate and re-experience these painful formidable events in an attempt to heal the torment they still caused him in the present day. "You go back and find the time that something happened and work through and finally find the base underneath," Axl explained. "And by letting it go, all of a sudden you don't have certain problems in your life."[260]

Through regression treatment, Axl pieced together a prenatal biography: His mother's pregnancy was unexpected and unwelcome; Axl's father treated his pregnant wife and unborn son poorly. Embryonic Axl was aware of these issues and blamed himself for causing so many problems. "That would tend to make you real fucking insecure about how the world felt about your ass," he explained, adding, "Everything is stored in your mind. And part of you is aware from very early on and is storing information and reacting."[261]

Axl claimed that upon birth, he was mistreated by his parents and grandmother. Some of the memories Axl unearthed during his therapy sessions were extraordinarily painful. "I was two years old and got fucked in the ass by my dad and it's caused a problem ever since," he told a reporter in 1992. "That's a fact. That's something that happened and that's some of the damage I've been working on."[262]

It is hard to think of a male rock musician of Rose's stature who had ever spoken with such candor about experiencing sexual abuse. In a 1992 *Rolling Stone* cover story, Axl offered details almost too grim to bear. "My father kidnapped me, because someone wasn't watching me. I remember a needle. I remember getting a shot. And I remember being sexually abused by this man and watching something horrible happen to my mother when she came to get me. I don't know all the details. But I've had the physical reactions of that happening to me. I've had problems in my legs and stuff from muscles being damaged then. And I buried it and was a man somehow, 'cause the only way to deal with it was bury the shit. I buried it then to survive – I never accepted it."[263]

From his earliest days, Axl felt white-hot rage, and had a hair trigger that fired at whim. Axl said in therapy he learned "my mental circuitry was all twisted in terms of how I would deal with stress because of what happened to me back in Indiana. Basically, I would overload with the stress of a situation by smashing whatever was around me."

Axl channeled a lifetime's worth of fury into GNR. The singer believed much of the anger, misogyny, and homophobia in his lyrics was rooted in traumatic childhood experiences, which established the foundation of his psyche. "I've had a lot of hatred for women. I've been rejected by my mother since I was a baby. My grandmother had a problem with men. Homophobic? My dad fucked me in the ass when I was two. I've got a problem about it. I wrote about my feelings in the songs."[264]

For Axl, the act of committing words to paper could be fraught with difficulty, requiring that he re-experience painful memories and summon negative emotions. Writing could be cathartic, but also psychologically wrenching. The singer had struggled for more than a year to finish the lyrics to Slash's "Coma." He would pass out every time he tried. "It's a defense mechanism sometimes. Your body shuts itself off," he explained. One day at the studio while working on the number, it happened again. When Axl came to, he grabbed a pen and wrote the entire ending to "Coma" in a single purging. "It was like, I don't even know what's coming out, man, but it's coming," Axl recalled. "It just poured out."[265]

Mixing

Geffen Records was increasingly anxious about GNR's delayed second album. The band had promised to deliver it in April 1991, giving the label time to prepare for an early June release. GNR's rabid reception at Rock in Rio only solidified everyone's confidence in the group's ability to sell records and draw crowds. GNR's management had already booked dates beginning in May for what would be one of the largest tours in rock history. But they had to have the album first and it was a long way from finished.

To expedite the process, Axl continued to tweak his vocals in Studio A of the Record Plant, while Slash and Duff worked in a separate studio down the hall, adding final touches to the tracks. The group also rented a third studio, and brought in Bob Clearmountain for mixing, where the level of each instrument and vocal is adjusted until everything sounds perfect. Clearmountain was one of the most sought after – and expensive – mixers in the music industry. His resume was dotted with career-defining chart-toppers such as Bruce Springsteen's *Born in the U.S.A.*, *Cuts Like a Knife* by Bryan Adams, and INXS's *Kick*.

Clearmountain was installed at Skip Saylor Recording, one of the only studios in L.A. large enough to accommodate the mountain of instrumental and vocal tracks Guns had amassed over the previous six months. For example, "November Rain" consisted of 24-tracks of basics – drums, bass, and Izzy's rhythm guitar. There were another 72 tracks of Slash's guitars, 24 tracks of Axl's vocals, and 48 tracks worth of pianos, keyboards, and even more vocals. All this was fed into Skip Saylor's massive console, which featured 84 channels to be mixed and adjusted.

Clearmountain preferred to work closely with musicians, and he badly needed the band's guidance on which tracks to use for the final mixes. But GNR were busy working at the Record Plant, and Clearmountain was largely left to his own devices to complete the job. The tensions between Axl and Slash had grown to a point where they were working separately and at different hours, communicating only as necessary by phone. Axl refused to come in and listen to Clearmountain's mixes when the other group members were there. If Axl liked a mix, Slash disliked it and vice-versa. It was "a very awkward way to work," Clearmountain recalled.[266]

Axl "seemed to have a lot on his mind at the time," Clearmountain added. "You wouldn't hear from him for a week, and then he'd show up. I'd ask if he listened to the last couple of mixes, and he'd say, 'Oh yeah, man, it's happening.' And that'd be about it. He basically wasn't paying attention."[267] Clearmountain claimed that Axl brought a lot of negative energy to the sessions. The singer was temperamental, quick to anger, and everyone walked on eggshells around him. "He would threaten to quit the band three times a week."[268]

Clearmountain ultimately mixed twenty-four *Illusion* tracks. Axl and Slash were at odds over just about everything at that time, but the two agreed on one thing – they hated the mixes. Guns served Clearmountain notice, and he was all too happy to move on. But losing him meant yet another delay for *Illusion*. The first tour dates were only weeks away and Geffen was increasingly frantic. Slash recalled, "They kept saying, 'When are we gonna see that record, guys?' Our attitude was, 'We don't know. When it's done, it's done.'"[269]

It was not until April that GNR were able to find a satisfactory replacement for Clearmountain, flying in Bill Price for a test mix of "Right Next Door to Hell." Price's credits included the Sex Pistols, the Clash, and Pete Townshend. Everyone enjoyed Price's mix as well as his wry humor and English temperament. He was hired and quickly got to work, with assistance from Mike Clink and Jim Mitchell.

Bob Clearmountain had not been able to get everyone in GNR into the studio, but Bill Price insisted that *Illusion* would be impossible to finish otherwise. "The only way to find out which tracks to use would be to get the entire band in the studio at the same time, which seemed like quite a normal thing to me. When I mentioned this to the band's management, they were totally horrified. The thought of Guns N' Roses all being in the same room at the same time was too much for them to bear. They warned me against it."[270]

Having already lost their first mixer and seeming to grasp all that was at stake, GNR acquiesced to Price's request to congregate. "They were very gentlemanly," Price recalled. "Axl walked in and said, 'Good afternoon, Slash. I know it's your guitar, and obviously you have the main say in it, but I do love that lick there. Do you think we could have it a bit louder?' Total gentlemen."[271]

"He brought a whole new life to the album," Slash said of Price. "He has a great overall idea of what separation's all about, as far as instruments go, especially because there were so many things going on in some songs. He was great to work with, and he has great ears, so it was a real relief, 'cause I thought the album was destroyed."272

Ten days later, *Illusion* was mixed. But Guns had burned through well over a million dollars so far, and they were still not prepared to hand in their new album. They had not even recorded everything that would end up on it.

Alan Niven is fired

Illusion was not ready, and neither was Axl. The singer was not psychologically prepared to go on the road. He'd been in therapy for several months and felt like he was just starting to make progress, just breaking through. *Illusion* was mixed, but there were still several more numbers to record and Axl in no way considered it finished. Yet the world tour in support of the record was beginning anyway. GNR's manager Alan Niven had booked North American and European dates months earlier, when there was optimism the group would deliver *Illusion* in the spring of 1991. Now Guns would be forced to finish the album while on tour.

Slash didn't care. He was dying to hit the road, the sooner the better. And what was more rock 'n' roll than playing unreleased material from an album you were still recording. But Axl had concerns. Touring without a new album meant fewer nights at the same venue, losing a valuable revenue stream. According to *Entertainment Weekly,* "By being on the road too early, the band is losing the promotional boost touring naturally provides, and very possibly alienating retailers and radio stations who've anxiously awaited the record."273 Furthermore, this was GNR's first-ever headlining jaunt. Axl felt like they should be playing the most prestigious venues in the country – Madison Square Garden, the Hollywood Bowl. Instead, Alan Niven had booked them into "sheds," soulless outdoor amphitheaters that catered to the beer, bratwurst, and shorts set. Poison's *Flesh and Blood* tour was playing many of the same venues that spring.

Axl had agreed to all of this, of course, but he believed part of the manager's job was to spot obstacles in the road ahead. Niven should have known that Axl wouldn't be ready, and he never should have booked the dates. And now, Axl couldn't get out of it. He had no choice but to go on tour.

The singer was furious, so angry that he fired Alan Niven and installed road manager Doug Goldstein in his place. This maneuver did not go down well with the rest of the group, who thought it was disloyal and wanted to be involved in major decisions. When they balked, Axl simply fired back, "All right, take *him* as a singer then, because if he stays, I leave."[274] "I felt really bad about it," Izzy said a few months after Niven's firing. "I felt I had to choose between him and the band. He was kinda like the sixth member of the group. He really helped put us where we are now. But Axl wants to do stuff his way, at his pace, in his time."[275]

In firing Niven, the point was made clear – it was Axl's world, everyone else was just living in it.

Chapter 6

In the Ring

GNR hit the stage of the Ritz looking like a band with something to prove. They opened with the 1-2-3 punch of "Pretty Tied Up," "Bad Obsession," and "Right Next Door to Hell," a trio of high-octane *Illusion* standouts. The songs were unfamiliar to most of the 1500 attendees, but the group presented the new material with confidence and energy.

"This is like my third rehearsal, since I never make it out to jam with these guys," Axl joked after the opening number, thanking the New Yorkers for their early and ardent support of Guns. The Ritz, of course, was the site of one of *Appetite's* most memorable concerts, shot in 1988 for MTV and broadcast ad nauseam. GNR would need to bring their A game in returning to the same venue three years later.

The Ritz appearance was the third in a trio of small warm-up gigs, before the Illusion tour's official launch with two sold-out dates at the 37,000-seat Alpine Valley Music Theatre in East Troy, Wisconsin. The first warm-up show was held May 9 at the Warfield Theater in San Francisco, which accommodated about 2300 spectators. The second took place two days later at the 2,700-seat Pantages Theater in Hollywood. Holding the invite-only warm-up shows in three major cities made strategic sense. GNR could get a few dress rehearsals under their belt before embarking on a massive world tour, but it also allowed them to fulfill the thousands of ticket requests they received in those cities from friends, family members, fellow musicians, music industry figures, journalists, and others.

"I swear I can't rehearse unless I got something like this happening," Axl said, gesturing to the audience at the Ritz, who cheered in appreciation. "I mean, you can work on a song, and you can work on recording it until hell freezes over, but if you're gonna play it again, you guys are the only thing that make it worthwhile."

The warm-up shows enabled Guns to take stock before embarking on their first worldwide trek as headliners. "The theater tour was killer," Slash said shortly after the Ritz stop. "It gave us a chance to get back and get toe-to-toe, and realize where the band really was, as opposed to going out there and jerking off for 40,000 people that are screaming just for the hell of it. We really have to actually play and perform."[276] Dizzy found the warm-up shows were more daunting than his debut at Rock in Rio. Unlike Rio, where the pianist was playing for total strangers, in L.A. and New York he was being scrutinized by half the music industry and everyone he knew.

Axl pointedly introduced Dizzy to audiences as an official member of GNR, but the pianist continued to lay back and play his part. If Slash didn't want piano on "Mr. Brownstone," Dizzy would tap on a nearby bongo drum – anything to have a reason to be there. "Lucky enough, Axl wrote a lot of the songs on the piano," Dizzy said. "He has a really good concept of keyboards and music. I just looked at it as another challenge. If I can pull this off, I can damn well do anything."[277]

Robert Hilburn of the *Los Angeles Times*, who frequently claimed that Axl was the heir to Jim Morrison, wrote a glowing review of GNR's L.A. appearance. Hilburn praised the *Illusion* material, asserting the group's forthcoming effort "mixed their aggressive and melancholy musical instincts in fresh ways."[278] Hilburn singled out the new tracks "Bad Obsession," "Don't Cry," and "Bad Apples," the latter of which received its second and final-ever airing at the Pantages. Hilburn pointed to the positive vibes and excitement that surrounded the band at the outset of the Illusion tour. On stage, they were "enthusiastic and relaxed, neither compelled to do something outrageous to reassert the group's long-standing 'bad boy' image nor wrap every song with overly dramatic emotion to give the show a false sense of occasion. For a group that has seen as much written about its image as its music, Guns N' Roses was refreshingly down to earth."

Axl had not wanted to embark on the tour at all, but he was getting into the groove. "I'm really happy with the way things are going," the singer told his friend Del James in an interview that week. "Professional rehearsals in front of people. It allows me to get into the mode I'm gonna have to be in when we start doing the big shows. Frisco was really cool; there was a different kind of hunger there for us. L.A. seemed to scrutinize us a bit more, and I welcomed that. I thought we went over real well in L.A., but I still look at it as rehearsals. I'm not really worried about what critics have to say about these gigs, but if they like these shows, in six months they'll be real happy."[279]

Axl's dream was to deliver a three-hour show, which would enable Guns to draw deeply from every period of their career. But a concert that long could not be spontaneous and off-the-cuff. The setlist would have to be curated for maximum impact. "Mick Jagger was working on getting that stage thing together for a really long time and I learned a lot from him," Axl told MTV just after the Ritz show. "We're hoping in six months we can actually have different set orders and have it planned out so it's a lot more dramatic."[280]

Jumping jack flash

Axl had been thinking about and planning GNR's first headlining tour for years. The singer's grand ambitions for *Illusion* as the ultimate album also applied to its accompanying tour, which he wanted to be the ultimate live musical statement. In planning *Illusion*'s stage show, Axl drew upon an extended history of rock entertainment, going to extreme lengths to deliver a superstar-caliber performance each and every night. Taking a page from Mick Jagger's playbook, Axl was a marvel of athleticism and energy, striding from one side of the stage to other, spinning in circles, crisscrossing ramps, and taking leaping scissor kicks from high atop the PA speakers.

When *Appetite* broke into the mainstream, Axl became known for his patented serpentine dance. For the Illusion trek, the singer added a series of dramatic poses that he would strike during key points in a performance. For example, as a number climaxed, Axl might splay his legs while bending his waist at a 45-degree angle, like Michael Jordan's Jumpman logo. A similar strategy was used by Michael Jackson, the most famous singer-performer of the era, whose dance poses were so distinct, he was recognizable in silhouette. "I try to make my own unorthodox moves," Axl explained.[281]

A long list of Axl's 1970s heroes were known for over-the-top stagewear, including David Bowie, Elton John, and Alice Cooper, followed in the 1980s by superstars such as Prince and Michael Jackson. Madonna was easily the biggest female singer-performer of the 1980s and was known for changing into a different costume for each number during concerts. In 1990, Madonna collaborated with legendary French designer Jean Paul Gaultier to create iconic costumes for her sold-out Blond Ambition tour.

Similarly, Axl took each song on the Illusion tour as an opportunity for a wardrobe change. At the warm-up shows, he never wore the same thing twice, at various points donning American flag tights, a black fishnet shirt, an N.W.A. ballcap, a purple leather jacket, a rhinestone encrusted belt, white bicycle shorts, an American flag coat, a cowboy hat, a Nine Inch Nails T-shirt, a UNLV Rebels starter jacket, a series of colorful headbands, and purple-tinted sunglasses.

On the side of the stage, Axl was aided by GNR's full-time wardrobe director, Joni Veage, who helped the singer change in and out of his various outfits between numbers. Guns met Veage in 1987 when they opened for Mötley Crüe on the *Girls, Girls, Girls* tour. Veage was the Crüe's wardrobe assistant and seamstress, skilled at altering Mötley's streetwear for the stage. "The stage clothes really weren't designed for athletic maneuvers, so they couldn't do the splits," she recalled. "I ended up having to modify the clothes for them. I would even have to make shoes that they could run around on stage in."[282]

At the Ritz, Axl began "Double Talkin' Jive" in rose-patterned tights, shirtless but wearing an oversized black parka made from what appeared to be wooly mammoth fur. "I wore this coat just to prove that you can buy *anything* in New York," the singer joked before throwing himself into the number. He frequently stripped off his jackets and shirts during songs and spent a good deal of the warm-up concerts shirtless.

Stair master

Axl had spent the past several months working out obsessively and it showed. At Farm Aid a year earlier, Axl hit the stage badly out of shape. Winded after GNR's brief two-track set, the singer collapsed onto a wardrobe trunk and spent fifteen minutes inhaling oxygen through a mask.[283] Axl vowed to get fit, spending hours per day on his StairMaster and stationary bike.

During performances, Izzy could slouch around in jeans and smoke cigarettes all night, Slash could fill his veins with Jack Daniel's, nicotine, and god knows what else, but the physical and mental expectations of Axl could not be greater. He had to lead a mass throng night after night for hours, often all but naked.

From the outset of the Illusion tour, Axl made physical fitness a priority, insisting that Guns travel with a personal trainer, a masseuse, and a small gym's worth of exercise equipment, which had to be set up and torn down at every tour stop. This included the ROM, a four-hundred-pound, $15,000 contraption that claimed to offer a full body workout in only four minutes. Axl's ROM gobbled up 55 square feet of floor space, and he parked it next to an almost equally large StairMaster machine.

"I work out on a StairMaster with my trainer," Axl explained. "We do a workout on the StairMaster that enables me to breathe and move better on stage. And what I'm doing on stage turns out to be something that helps build me up rather than tear me down by being so exhausting. At first when I was playing, it would just wear me out."[284]

Axl was eager to see the rest of the band members follow suit. "Now that we're starting a tour, everybody's gonna be starting to get in more shape while we're playing," he said shortly after the Ritz show. "We brought a trainer and everything. Everybody will get in better shape once we get some form of regimentation down."[285]

Slash wasn't hitting the StairMaster alongside Axl, but he worked with the masseuse to relieve the pain that sometimes caused his left hand to cramp. This was all part of the aging process. Like Axl, Slash had replaced his *Appetite*-era cowboy boots with high-top tennis shoes that allowed him to sprint around onstage. "Axl's always been very health-conscious; I'm the complete opposite," Slash explained shortly after the Ritz show.[286] "I'm no angel or anything. Before this started happening, I was sitting around drinking beer, watching cartoons at my girlfriend's house, and doing nothing all day until rehearsal. And I realized I'd better get off my ass and so I started exercising. But that's not my style. I mean, seriously, it's just not. So now I get my workout onstage. I'm back to normal just from the shows."[287]

Axl and Arnold

At the Ritz warm-up concert, following Matt's drum solo, Slash pointed to the number of camera operators on hand that night. "We're gonna do a tune off the new record," he told the audience. "There's a new *Terminator* coming out, it's *Terminator 2* and it's this big movie. This is the cut that they wanted for the end when the credits go on. We're gonna do a video for it but this isn't gonna be one of those movies where the band plays and then you see parts of the movie and then the band plays and it's all really corny. We're gonna try to make it really happening."

The opening beat kicked in and the group launched into a torrid take on "You Could Be Mine." The ballistic track was a leftover from the *Appetite* sessions and borrowed a lyric from a 1973 Elton John tune titled "I've Seen That Movie, Too." It was selected to help launch the most-anticipated movie of the summer, *Terminator 2: Judgment Day*, directed by James Cameron and starring Arnold Schwarzenegger. The video for "You Could Be Mine" would juxtapose live footage from the Ritz with clips from the film, including a serendipitous scene where Schwarzenegger as the Terminator conceals a gun inside a bouquet of roses. But true to Slash's word, a standalone plot was created specific to the music video, where the Schwarzenegger-Terminator attempts to assassinate GNR as they perform onstage. The music stops and the band exits the back door of the venue, only to come face to face with Schwarzenegger. The scene ends when Axl and Arnold square off. The Terminator concludes that attacking Axl would be a "waste of ammo" and concedes the battle.

"Arnold was great, really nice" Axl recalled shortly after the Ritz show. "He apparently is a Guns N' Roses fan. We let them listen to a lot of material and the song they picked was 'You Could Be Mine.' So, we shot a video for it, we filmed the show in the Ritz, and then I guess Arnold was flying back from Congress going, 'I want to be in the video.'"[288]

Schwarzenegger did not attend the Ritz concert – his footage was shot on a Hollywood soundstage and behind the Roxy nightclub in L.A. Everyone in the group except for Izzy showed up for the taping behind the Roxy, where the Terminator confronts GNR. Izzy skipped the shoot and did not appear in the music video's final scene.

Excited to meet one of his favorite bands, the gregarious Schwarzenegger brought everyone one of the bullet-hole-ridden leather jackets he had worn in *Terminator 2*. Slash, an avid movie buff, was over the moon. "The jacket I got was from my favorite scene. He gave them to us at random and I got my favorite one – he gets shot six million times and they all come through his back." Slash was so thrilled, he gave Arnold the top hat he was wearing in exchange.[289]

"You Could Be Mine" would be issued as a single in June, the third public airing of *Illusion* material, following the earlier releases of "Civil War" and "Knockin' on Heaven's Door." The finished video looked terrific, with Guns charging about energetically as they performed. At the Ritz show, during the taping of "You Could Be Mine," Axl took a flying leap on the side of the stage, landing badly on the cement floor and instantly breaking a bone in his foot. Axl finished the number with his left foot propped up on a floor monitor.

"You know that expression *break a leg*? I think I just did." he said to the audience after the song ended.

The singer had a chronic history of heel and ligament injuries dating back to junior high. "I got really excited, I was just jumping off everything," Axl explained of the Ritz concert.[290] The bone break occurred about halfway through the GNR's two-hour set. The group had put in a hard charging first hour but slowed down things considerably in the second half to accommodate Axl, who could barely walk. The singer played through the pain, beginning "Patience" seated on a speaker cabinet. "This is a ballad set now," Axl joked, but he could not contain himself for long and was moving around the stage again as Guns performed the next number, "Knockin' on Heaven's Door."

Afterward, Axl personally escorted Shannon Hoon to the stage. A few months earlier, Blind Melon had signed a major label deal with Capitol Records. Though the newly formed group had only written five tunes, Hoon's growing friendship with Axl turned Blind Melon into a hot commodity. "This is a song that was on our original demo tape," Axl told the audience. "This is my homeboy Shannon Hoon from Lafayette, who was covering that version on the demo tape in Indiana. And he did such a bitchin' job I said why don't you sing it on a record with me. He's in a band called Blind Melon and this is a song called 'Don't Cry.'" The two singers shared a single microphone, with Hoon taking the high harmony.

"Don't Cry" had been earmarked as *Illusion's* first single, the logic being that a ballad should follow the rocker "You Could Be Mine." "Ladies and gentlemen, Mr. Shannon Hoon, the twenty-seventh unofficial member of GNR," Axl joked as "Don't Cry" concluded. Slash conferred with Axl for a few moments. "Shannon, don't go too far," Axl said. "This is an Izzy Stradlin number. We recorded it for the album, but we never played this song together until a couple of days ago. This is something called 'You Ain't the First' Mr. Stradlin put together when our girlfriends were up our ass."

Guns tackled the swampy acoustic number with electric instruments, with Izzy aimlessly fingering the melody as Slash pawed at his Les Paul with a metal slide. In trying to cohere, the musicians rushed the tempo, speeding up the lolling back porch ditty to double time. Axl, Shannon, and Izzy shared a single microphone, harmonizing, with Hoon again taking the high notes.

Even Axl's microphone stand had to be unique. Freddie Mercury was known for using only the top half of his mic stand during concerts, giving the Queen vocalist greater mobility. Building on this idea, Axl had a half stand designed that looked like an upside-down crutch. The half stand could be used by itself or affixed to the bottom half of the mic stand, whose circular base resembled a car steering wheel.

The teleprompter

"This is a little baby of mine called 'Estranged,'" Axl said at the outset of GNR's Ritz encore. Rather than try to memorize all the new lyrics, Axl used a teleprompter that contained the words to every song. The video screens were held in floor monitor cabinets and placed strategically throughout the stage. When the band called for a number, one of Axl's assistants would pull up a primitive computer file and manually scroll through the lyrics as the musicians played. Singers have devised similar strategies from time immemorial, but Axl's was among the first public uses of a teleprompter at a rock show, and it generated negative press. In June, *New York* magazine ran a piece under the headline "Axl Rose Sings Tunes by Teleprompter." "Controversial rocker Axl Rose is running into trouble with his lyrics again, but this time, it's because he can't seem to remember them. At a concert last month, Rose got some snickers from the audience when he was seen reading lyrics off a teleprompter. 'It was hilarious,' said one person at the event. 'I've never seen anything like it.'"[291]

Axl explained that sometimes it was the old lyrics he would forget, losing himself in the moment. "On songs I'm supposed to know like the back of my hand, I start spacing out and thinking of other things. I prefer to do the new stuff. I love singing 'Yesterdays.' 'Right Next Door to Hell' is a blast. I'm just feeling my way through the songs right now."[292]

GNR closed the night with a barnstorming take on "Welcome to the Jungle," with the audience nearly breaking into a mosh pit when Guns tucked into the main riff. During the middle section, Axl hopped onto the shoulders of his hulking bodyguard, Earl Gabbidon, who walked the singer out to center stage to screech into the spotlight.

The Ritz show ended on a celebratory note, yet despite nine months of non-stop work, *Illusion* was still not finished. Slash and Duff had spent the week before the warm-up shows at mastering sessions, where the final mix is balanced so it sounds good on all types of music players and sound systems. But at the Pantages gig in L.A., the group introduced a new track, "14 Years," a piano-heavy Axl-Izzy co-write that had yet to be recorded. Following the May 16 Ritz show, GNR booked studio time in Wisconsin, where the Illusion tour was slated to begin on May 24.

Everybody knows

The first official concerts of the Illusion tour took place at Alpine Valley Music Theatre in East Troy, Wisconsin on May 24 and 25, 1991. At the time, the 37,000-capacity venue was the largest amphitheater in America. Guns walked onstage the first night to Leonard Cohen's "Everybody Knows," an opener they deployed frequently on the Illusion tour. The track featured heavily in the 1990 film, *Pump Up the Volume*, where Christian Slater played a brash, uninhibited pirate-radio DJ who used the number as his show's theme music.

The Illusion tour was a colossal operation, run by a crew of about 70 that included half a dozen sound technicians, eight lighting operators, six instrument technicians, four carpenters, a twelve-person catering staff, three site coordinators, a power technician, a six-man video production unit, and a production manager. A team of eleven semi-truck drivers hauled 150 tons of equipment that included a three-million-watt sound system, 134 speaker cabinets, 900 stage lights, 60 microphones, 50 guitars, and three giant video screens. The steel scaffolding that held the sage and lighting rig measured 72 feet wide, 64 feet deep, and 75 feet high. 250,000 watts of energy was required to power everything.[293] [294] [295]

The Illusion stage was designed to resemble an enormous, crashed B-52 bomber plane, with the drum riser at the nose and ramps that extended out on either side like wings. As was popular with metal bands of the day, the drum riser was situated high above the group, with stair steps leading up and down. A series of catwalks wound around the back, behind the drums, above the stacks of amplifiers. Similar to the Rolling Stones' Steel Wheels stage, the Illusion setup had a metallic look. The production was so large, GNR had to lease an airplane hangar at the Burbank airport in order to assemble the entire contraption and try it out. Slash and Duff hated how cheesy it looked.[296]

Due to Axl's broken foot, Guns did not deploy their complete stage and lighting setup at Alpine Valley, removing several ramps that extended out into the audience, hoping to reduce the chance of further injury. To increase his mobility on stage, Axl's foot had been tended to in Milwaukee by a team consisting of sports doctors and a tennis shoe manufacturer, who created a custom-fitted athletic splint that doubled as a cast. The singer would be somewhat hobbled, but he'd also be ambulant and able to perform. "The doctors seem to think it'll be fine," Axl told MTV's Kurt Loder, right after the first Alpine Valley concert. "We had all the top doctors from the Brewers and the Packers and New Balance Shoes all working on designing me something so I could run around. 'Cause without this boot, it's definitely limping. But we didn't want to call off the show."[297]

The opening round of the Illusion world tour – dubbed Get in the Ring – would last more than two months, with three dozen gigs lined up across North America through the end of July. The outing would culminate with four hometown shows at the legendary L.A. Forum. Ten days later, GNR would be playing stadiums in Europe. Wanting to ensure the tour was preserved for posterity, the band hired a two-man film crew to follow them everywhere, professionally recording every concert and videotaping the group hanging out backstage and at hotels. The intention was to have the footage compiled into a documentary, and the camera crew stayed on for the entirety of the Illusion tour.

Axl insisted he continue to pursue five-days-per-week regression therapy sessions with Suzzy London, and she was part of the Illusion touring party from the beginning. Despite his private reservations, the singer was relieved Guns were finally headlining after all these years. "It feels great," he told MTV. "We've been planning this ever since we started, aiming at it. On our second major album, we wanted a headlining tour and to do it right. And it feels great. We've got all the pieces in place and the morale is really high."[298]

In a separate interview that night, Slash concurred. The guitarist loved nothing more than life on the road. "I've been fucking going nuts. I've been a complete basket case. I've been through the mill since we got off the road last time. When we embarked on this thing, when we went to go do the theater tour, when we popped back to Los Angeles, I just stayed in a hotel. I didn't even go home."[299]

GNR invited Skid Row to be the first opening act on the Illusion tour, a pairing that made sense given Axl's friendship with Sebastian Bach. The timing was fortuitous – Skid Row's hard-rocking sophomore effort, *Slave to the Grind*, was scheduled to be released in mid-May, just as the Guns outing was getting underway. "The Skids, they're friends of ours and also the only band around that has an attitude that's genuine and brash," Slash said. "I couldn't see going out with Great White Lion Tigress or whatever."[300] Axl was equally enthusiastic, adding, "We wanted really high energy. Skid Row was doing great, and Sebastian and I get along great. The fact that we get along so well and that they're really into what they do – I mean, they get the crowd all worked up for when we come out there."[301]

With the always-down-to-party Sebastian Bach on hand, the Guns-Skid Row venture was one for the ages, but Alpine Valley was a mostly subdued affair. In the parking lot, tailgating fans from suburban Chicago and St. Paul, Minnesota hoisted beer and bratwurst as they professed love for GNR. It could be any concert anywhere or even a Sunday afternoon football game. Earlier that day, MTV shot footage of strait-laced Kurt Loder wandering around backstage, seeking out a party that was nowhere to be found. He roamed a sunny, tree-lined patio adorned with a few mostly empty tables shaded by red-and-white Budweiser-themed umbrellas. "Well, it *is* Wisconsin," Loder shrugged.[302] Those with a higher level of backstage pass were allowed into a private area that had been cordoned off by three large trailers parked in a U shape. In the center, were a series of round tables and folding chairs. A 32" TV was set up in one corner and potted palm trees were scattered about. One of the surrounding trailers housed Axl's dressing room, a second contained GNR's dressing room, and a third was dedicated to food and drinks for guests.

MTV did a piece about the array of pricey merchandise for sale: T-shirts, ballcaps, necklaces, tour programs, thong underwear, all branded with the red and blue *Use Your Illusion* artwork. But *Illusion* remained unfinished. To the immense chagrin of Geffen, Guns were now touring in support of an unreleased album. Prior to the Alpine Valley gigs, the band had used some days off to book time in a Wisconsin studio. There, they laid down tracks for "Don't Damn Me," Axl and Izzy's new tune "14 Years," and two old rockers from the club days, "Back Off Bitch" and "Ain't Going Down." "I'm actually gonna be recording some stuff here to finish it up," Axl told MTV. "Recording on the road."[303]

Geffen wanted *Illusion* in stores, but the singer refused to rush the process. He was determined to create a masterpiece, however much time it took. "We're competing with rock legends," Axl told a reporter from *Rolling Stone.* "We're trying to do the best we can to possibly be honored with a position like that. We want to define ourselves. *Appetite* was our cornerstone, a place to start. Now we're going to build something."[304]

Axl's plans did not end there. The singer was always thinking one step ahead. At Alpine Valley, he told MTV that an EP of punk covers would be released after the Illusion tour wrapped. The project was already in the can. "I want a lot of people to hear songs that they didn't hear," he explained. "There's selected cuts that you can't really find the original recordings that they're on, and B-sides and songs we think really rocked and way, way influenced us."[305]

Despite this display of confidence, Axl was nervous about the next two shows – back-to-back nights at Deer Creek Amphitheatre in Noblesville, Indiana. Everyone he grew up with would be there. "I'm going to play Indianapolis in a couple of days," the singer said. "There's a lot of people I'm not having come to my show. There's a lot of people I am. There's a lot of people I'm realizing are more important to me than the people I've worried about my whole life."[306] Axl knew Indiana was going to be a showdown, and the singer was looking for a fight.

Chapter 7

MGM Grand

Axl had a love-hate relationship with performing, and the singer was always especially tense on concert days, his thoughts consumed with that night's show. "Before the gig, I always don't wanna do that show and nine times out of ten I hate it," he told a reporter in 1990. "Most of the time I'm mad about something or something's going wrong. I don't enjoy most of it at all."[307]

Axl savored the spotlight as much as − or perhaps more than − the average rock frontman, but he was naturally inclined to introversion. During interviews, the singer was laid back to near comatose, speaking in a calm register like he was trying to pacify a growling dog. After spending time with Axl during the early Illusion dates, *Rolling Stone's* Kim Neely observed, "off the stage his manner is so languid that he gives the impression of carefully considering each movement before he makes it."[308]

Axl was a brilliant live performer and the same perfectionist tendencies that drove him to delay the release of *Illusion* until he deemed it flawless, made him want to deliver concerts that were transcendent, the stuff of legends. But introverted Axl could not just hop onstage and go from zero to ten in a flash. It took hours of mental and physical preparation for the singer to work himself into a state where he could deliver the type of performance that made him a star. "I am very shy and can be very insecure sometimes, but you have to find a way to communicate your feelings every night on stage," he confessed to the *L.A. Times* shortly after *Appetite's* lengthy touring cycle concluded.[309] Axl had just spent two years dazzling the world with his impassioned and awe-inspiring live performances. Even the singer's most ardent critics conceded he was among rock's most compelling entertainers. But it never, ever came easy. "You have to try to win the audience over," he told the *Times*. "It's very challenging, like an actor on the screen, in a way. The only difference is that I'm not playing a part. I'm playing myself, but I'm always looking for ways to go beyond the music itself to express what I'm feeling."

Overhanging Axl's anxieties about performing was the dark cloud of drama that simply seemed to follow the singer everywhere he went. Somehow, the turmoil always seemed to peak on concert days. "Something always happens before the show and I react like a motherfucker to it," Axl said. "I don't have this pot-smoking mentality of just letting things go by. I don't feel like Lenny Kravitz, like peace and love, man."[310] Some nights, just getting Axl onto the stage was the hardest part of the entire gig. "Axl was very shy, and he had stage fright," said Arlett Vereecke, who worked as a publicist for GNR from 1987 to 1992. "So, it took forever to get him on stage."[311]

For the Illusion tour, Guns retained a small army of professionals whose sole task was to help Axl prepare for showtime. On concert days, Axl would subject himself to one of Suzzy London's arduous, multi-hour regression therapy sessions, unearthing long buried demons and working through a torrid of negative emotions. Medical research has demonstrated the mind-body connection related to trauma. For example, soldiers return from war with PTSD that manifests itself in various physical ailments.[312] Axl believed some of his early ordeals were stored in his body the same way his painful childhood memories were buried in his brain.

After an extended therapy session, Axl sought physical relief through exercise and massage. He would put in a long workout and then get a massage from Sabrina Okamoto, who traveled with the Illusion tour as GNR's full-time masseuse. Exercise and massage relieved the singer's physical ailments and primed his body to perform that night. After that, he would take a long shower and get into his first stage outfit, selecting one of about six that had been laid out by an assistant. Axl then had his ankles taped, reducing the odds of rolling or twisting an appendage on stage.

Once he was dressed, Axl would perform a sixty-minute series of vocal warm up exercises, a routine he had done for years. This was necessary for the singer to prepare his voice to go full throttle for two-plus punishing hours. Until Axl's voice and throat were ready, he did not go on stage. Period.

At the outset of the Illusion tour, the singer also began working with Ron Anderson, a well-known celebrity vocal trainer. Axl brought Anderson on the road so the coach could witness his singing techniques firsthand and help him preserve his voice over the course of the tour. Anderson taught Axl a series of warm down exercises, an hour-long process Axl added to his post-concert routine. This was intended to preserve his vocal cords so he could do it all over again at the next gig. "I'm taking the steps so that I can ensure the people a good show and I'm up to my best," Axl said after the first Alpine Valley gig.[313]

Prisoners in Auschwitz

But Indiana was different. The hometown shows threw a monkey wrench into Axl's psyche he could not exercise away. The singer had originally envisioned the back-to-back Deer Creek concerts as a triumphant return home but setting foot inside Indiana brought feelings of dread. Axl had run off to California in 1980, leaving a lengthy arrest record and a string of bad memories behind. Now every cop, teacher, coach, boss, family member, and detractor who'd ever given teenage Axl the side eye was going to be at Deer Creek, hoping the singer would melt down on stage. Half of them had the nerve to request free tickets. Axl didn't want to sing for these assholes; he didn't want to sing at all.

Guns opened the first Indiana concert with a ferocious take on "Perfect Crime," chosen by Axl specifically for the song's warning to steer clear of his bad side. GNR's 9:45 p.m. arrival was greeted with rapturous-if-relieved applause by the 18,000 attendees. Skid Row's sixty-minute set had ended an hour-and-a-half earlier and the throng had grown increasingly restless. But Axl wasn't ready to sing just yet. He had something to say.

"This stage here in Indianapolis, Indiana, this time around, is the hardest stage I could ever walk on. It's not because of how hard it is to do what we do. It's because I grew up in this state for two-thirds of my life. And it seems to me that there are a lot of scared old people in this state. And for two-thirds of my life, they basically tried to keep my ass *down*."

Axl's local references received huge, knowing cheers from the spectators at Deer Creek. The singer continued. "I don't know anything about Iraq, I don't know that much about New York. I been in L.A. ten years and that don't mean shit. So, basically for me it's like I got a lot of cool fucking prisoners in Auschwitz."

The crowd went ballistic at this last line, and Axl's comparison of Indiana to a World War II concentration camp would make headlines the next day. But the singer was still not finished. "I know you didn't come here to hear me talk, but if I don't do this, I can't play," he said. Axl told a short story about a friend who supposedly got hassled by the local cops that afternoon for the way he was dressed. It brought back a million bad memories to Axl, made him not want to even bother to play that night.

"When I was getting all pissed off today, I had to remember something. What this stage and these people represent to me ain't the same thing as what you are. You're people that came to hear my band play. So, it's been a hurdle for me to get over my hatred of these people that tried to hold my ass down and tell me I was an idiot for twenty years of my life just 'cause they had their heads up their ass."

The group tore into the opening notes of "Out Ta Get Me" and GNR was off and running. Axl was fired up, which could result in a riveting performance, or it could go sideways. One thing was certain – when Axl was pissed about something there was no way he was going to clam up and let the music do the talking. The singer spent most of his return to Indiana griping about growing up in the state. "I know what it's like here," he told the audience over the opening strains of "Civil War." "Your parents, they try to tell you when you're in school to do it their way, and then when you're about seventeen or eighteen, you gotta figure out what to do about all the shit they didn't teach you to deal with. I know this doesn't really apply – I wrote this about shit in the Middle East and things. But I think the real civil war was on the home front." To introduce "Estranged," Axl told the crowd, "This is something I wrote about a woman, but now it looks like it's about this place. It's a place that makes me feel estranged."

In Noblesville, Axl introduced Izzy as a Lafayette native, resulting in a huge ovation. Izzy, who had been living in Indiana full-time for the past two years, was mortified by Axl's onstage behavior at the homecoming. In an interview two years later, the guitarist was still talking about that night. "When Guns N' Roses played Indianapolis, when Axl would start to go off on a tirade, I'd stand there and go, 'Oh, let's go. Next song, next song.' Kind of embarrassing. But there's no shutting him up. Once he gets going, that's it."[314]

Axl's 9:45 arrival at Deer Creek meant that for GNR to play a complete show, the band had to break Noblesville's 10:30 curfew for outdoor concerts held on weeknights. Violation would result in a $5,000 fine. Of course, Guns played anyway, refusing to quit until nearly 11:30. "I want to apologize for so much shit going wrong that you people had to wait on my ass to get here," Axl said toward the end of the night. "Being this is Indiana, it would be the only place that has a ten o'clock-something curfew. So, to return the favor of you waiting, as of eleven o'clock, which was about 45 minutes ago, we're paying an extra five thousand dollars just to stay here and play."

Axl's Indiana diatribes were panned by the local press, whose juicy reviews were reprinted in newspapers around the world. "Great Rock, Too Much Talk" read the headline in *The Indianapolis Star*,[315] while *The Indianapolis News* published a recap titled "All GNR Fans Needed Was a Little Patience."[316] These and other write-ups focused on Axl's between-song chatter, highlighting the most controversial bits of his onstage rants. Some quoted law enforcement officers, who blamed the show's problems squarely on the singer. For example, Hamilton County sheriff's sergeant Tom Gehlhausen told one reporter, "Axl Rose had problems getting to the event last night which delayed the concert."[317]

Axl had spent hundreds of hours in regression therapy, ruminating about the abuses he endured as a child and adolescent in Indiana. Axl's stepfather was a devout follower of the Pentecostal strain of Protestant Christianity, best known for evangelist preachers whose sermons include live snakes and speaking in tongues. Axl's household was so strict, he was forbidden from listening to rock music at all. As a teenager, he used to call friends, who would put the phone up to the radio, while Axl pretended to be chatting. Asked during an interview about his onstage comments at Deer Creek, Axl replied, "You get a lot of teaching in high school about going after your dreams and being true to yourself, but at the same time teachers and parents are trying to beat you down. It was so strict in our house that everything you did was wrong. There was so much censorship, you weren't allowed to make any choices. Sex was bad, music was bad. I eventually left, but so many kids stay. I wanted to tell them that they can break away, too."[318]

Izzy's relocation to Indiana had made Axl seriously consider doing the same. But those hours in therapy changed him. The connection he once felt to the region was gone, utterly extinguished. Axl tried to explain himself to a reporter from *Rolling Stone*. "I know the Midwest better than most places. A lot of scared people are living in their houses, and I don't ever want to be that way. You have to be really aware of stagnation. If you're shutting out the rest of the world without really knowing what it's about, it's like you're in a cocoon – a butterfly that never hatches."[319]

Axl was more restrained at the second Noblesville gig, at least between songs, where he curtailed the chatter somewhat. The singer chose the occasion to premiere "November Rain," sitting down at a piano to perform his beloved ballad for the first time in concert. The debut would forever change the experience of GNR performances – Axl seated at the piano singing a ballad would become a staple of the band's shows from that night on.

These adjustments were of no consolation to the local authorities, who charged Guns with two counts of curfew violation, levying a $10,000 fine against the group before they left town. Steve Nation, the Noblesville prosecutor who announced the charges, said the curfew violations were not significant crimes. "What makes this different is that Axl Rose said on stage that he knew about the curfew and thought it was stupid. And he said a few things about our county and about our state."[320]

Metalworks

As the tour continued, GNR kept performing without a setlist, with Axl usually calling for the songs spontaneously. The running order took on the same general structure, but the group continually mixed things up. "Thanks to our last manager we're out on tour a month early, so we might as well wing it," Axl told the crowd in Grove City, Pennsylvania. Just before going on each night, the group would huddle backstage and determine the first song they were going to play. They regularly opened with "Perfect Crime," and "Mr. Brownstone" was always the second number of the night. After that, it could be anything, in any order but Guns were clearly galvanized by the unreleased *Illusion* material. Axl called for "Double Talkin' Jive," "Bad Obsession," and "Estranged" at almost every show. "We feel like pussies if all we play is the old shit," he told the audience in Hershey, where GNR put in a killer performance of "Dust N' Bones," another *Illusion* cut they played at nearly every stop on the tour's first leg.

Other *Illusion* songs were played, but with less frequency, including "Right Next Door to Hell," "Pretty Tied Up," "Don't Cry," "Yesterdays," "You Ain't the First," "Dead Horse," "Locomotive," and "14 Years." In Dayton, the group performed "Used to Love Her" for the first time in two years after an audience member requested it. In Richfield, Ohio GNR opened with "Coma," the live debut of the Slash-Axl opus. "A lot of bands have a setlist and they say the same thing between songs every night," Duff told MTV. "That's akin to a 9 to 5 job to me. Rock 'n' roll is energy, and it's spontaneous, and it's violent. It keeps us on our toes, so there's a lot of energy every night."[321]

Guns were firing on all cylinders, with Axl putting in some of the most intense and athletic performances of his career. The group earned glowing reviews for the new material from *Illusion* and their eagerness to play so much of it. "Guns N' Roses Performance Simply Superb" raved the headline in the *Dayton Daily News*.[322] The group drew 30,000 fans to the Toledo Speedway in Ohio and delivered a concert described by the *Detroit Free Press* as "rock 'n' roll at its most enjoyable and its most liberating."[323] In Richfield, GNR were said to "assault the assembled mass with a 90-minute-plus onslaught of withering, hammer-and-tong rock that seemed to build with each offering."[324]

Countering this heavy praise, Guns were frequently reproached for going on late. Tickets generally listed a 7:00 p.m. start time. Skid Row would take the stage at 8:00. To help pass the time, the Skids had taken to playing long opening sets that frequently approached the one-hour mark. Then it might be another hour-and-a-half to two hours before GNR finally showed up. 21,000 attendees were on hand for the group's opening night in Toronto, where Guns started after 10 p.m. and blasted away until 12:30 in the morning.

On nights when GNR did not have a gig, they were scrambling to finish *Illusion*. Producer Mike Clink was traveling with the group, trying to squeeze in a quick recording session whenever possible.[325] Mixer Bill Price recalled, "The last half a dozen songs were recorded, overdubbed, vocal'ed and guitar'ed in random recording studios dotted about America when they had a day off between gigs. My mixing mode switched into flying around America with pocketfuls of DATs, playing them to the band backstage."[326]

After twin concerts in Toronto, GNR stayed in town an extra day for a session at Metalworks Recording Studios. Tom Zutaut from Geffen Records flew in for the session, too. Zutaut had signed Guns back in the club days and was instrumental in shaping *Appetite*, but his relationship with the group had grown increasingly strained.

Geffen was agitated over the repeated delays, by GNR's refusal to deliver *Illusion* once and for all. The record company's lack of patience infuriated Axl. It felt disrespectful to rush him after all he had done for the label. They should be grateful he cared so much about the album. Zutaut's presence added another element of pressure. Clearly, Geffen had dispatched the A&R executive to move things along. "I keep reading about delays in getting the record out," Axl said during an interview the night before the Metalworks session. "But as far as the band is concerned, there really have been no delays. The only rule we had was to make the best record we could, regardless of how long it took. But we had people at the record company come up with deadlines on when they wanted the record out and we'd go, 'Okay, we'll do our best' and we tried. But we were not going to give anybody the record until we felt it is done."[327]

At Metalworks, Guns laid down the final version of "Get in the Ring." The session began late and lasted all night, with the group finally wrapping up at 7:30 in the morning. Axl, according to someone at the session, was in one of "those moods" during the recording and bad vibes prevailed.[328] Whatever the case, it resulted in a venomous late addition to *Illusion*.

The music for "Get in the Ring" had been around since GNR's initial meetup in Chicago, but by this point Axl had sharpened the lyrics into a lascivious assault on the media, naming specific journalists and editors from *Spin*, *Kerrang*, *Hit Parader*, and *Circus*. The last three magazines catered to niche readerships and did not have widespread cultural relevance. Their pages were populated by Poison, Warrant, and Trixter – no one took them very seriously. So, Axl's all-out war on a major-label album seemed slightly beneath a star of his stature. Would legends like Mick Jagger or Elton John spend two seconds thinking about what some nerdy writer printed, let alone record a song about it? Moreover, these magazines, their staff, and their readers helped build Guns into a legend. Axl was on the cover of the May 1991 issue of *Hit Parader* at the same time he finalized the lyrics to "Ring." The singer's decision to bite the hand that fed – however justified he may have felt – came across as a dick move by a powerful, rich celebrity.

Mr. Invisible

Following the "Ring" session in Toronto, the Illusion tour advanced to New York and Pennsylvania. GNR and their entourage were traveling in style. The band chartered the MGM Grand, a 130-passenger 727 jet *Metropolitan Airport News* described as beyond opulent: "Individual swivel seats, velvet window curtains, plush carpeting, and lavatories adorned with smoked glass, Italian marble, and gold fixtures. Dinner was served on formally set tables with Royal Worcester china."[329] The entourage could fit in the front of the plane and there was a lounge in the middle with a fully stocked bar. Five flight attendants hovered around tending to every need. Axl, Slash, and Duff could relax in one of four private bedrooms, each with bed-convertible seats and large enough to hold two couches and a television. "They would use it even if they were going from New York to Boston," Skid Row drummer Rob Affuso marveled. "It's an hour trip. It would take them longer to get the thing off the ground."[330]

Of course, the MGM was just a way to get from city to city. Once the plane touched down in a new location, Guns and their entourage would decamp via limousine to a nearby luxury hotel, such as the Four Seasons or the Ritz Carlton, where two floors would be booked in the band's name. Axl would always have the presidential suite, with his bodyguard in the room next door and one of his two personal assistants on the other side. The rest of the group resided in luxury suites. No one, including Axl's fellow GNR bandmates, could reach the singer without first going through one of his personal assistants and his bodyguard. "We all agreed to him having this arrangement," Slash explained through gritted teeth. "He wants his own space and that's the way he chooses to deal with the incredible pressure that's on this band now. And if that's what it takes to get him in the right frame of mind, then that's okay by me. Whatever it takes to get him onto the stage every night is cool."[331]

Axl claimed touring in high style allowed GNR to better merge the personal and professional. "Most of us have figured out how to integrate our personal lives into what we do. We've wanted to live on the road and enjoy it, and everything is so nice, on such a big scale. I'd hate to go down the tubes and be back to a van going to the clubs. I don't take it for granted."[332]

Guns and their entourage flew the MGM, but Izzy went his own way. Izzy hated the jumbo jet. "I don't want any part of that airplane," he told Axl when the idea of renting the MGM was initially floated. "I'm not paying for it. I'm gonna buy a bus, and I'm gonna drive my bus with my girl and my dog."[333] That's exactly what Izzy did, purchasing a full-sized bus at the outset of the tour that he used to get from gig to gig. (The guitarist didn't actually drive it, though.) The bus pulled a trailer emblazoned with motocross stickers that carried Izzy's Harley Davidson motorcycle, and allowed the guitarist to bring along his girlfriend, Anneka, and Treader, a friendly German shepherd who wore a backstage laminate for a collar. "If you're driving, it keeps you in touch with the rest of the world," Izzy explained.[334]

The guitarist claimed even going by bus, he still got to the gigs faster than the perennially late GNR and their jet airplane. Izzy would do the soundcheck, play the show, and then take off immediately afterward, stopping at some anonymous roadside diner for a bite to eat.

There was a practical element to Izzy's strategy, too. The guitarist had been completely sober for more than 18 months, forgoing alcohol, pot, and everything else. "At first it was real hard," he admitted. "When I finally stopped and then started going out, just riding around on a bicycle, I thought 'Wow, this is really cool. How did I forget all this simple shit?'"[335]

Izzy had no intention of returning to his previous lifestyle, and there was virtually no chance the guitarist would be able to stay sober if he was riding on the Party Express with the coke and booze fiends in GNR. "I don't miss it," he told a reporter at a tour stop in Philly. "There is nothing like throwing up out a bus door going 65 miles an hour."[336]

Rolling Stone's Kim Neely traveled with Guns for the first two months of the *Illusion* tour and observed Izzy was "probably the only member who manages to lead a somewhat normal life."[337] While

Izzy's bandmates were sleeping off the previous night's excesses, the guitarist would wake up early and explore whatever city he was in, taking long walks with Treader, skateboarding, or riding a bicycle. In doing so, he frequently ducked GNR's security team, to the chagrin of management. The only time anyone from the group saw Izzy was onstage. At the Ritz warm-up concert, Axl introduced him as "Mr. Invisible of GNR."

Taking a shower

The pressure to deliver *Illusion* continued to escalate. The release date had been pushed back several times and the group had still not handed over the master tapes to Geffen. According to industry observers, by touring without *Illusion* in stores, GNR "may have weakened itself at the box office. The group has been doing good business – averaging almost 25,000 fans and a $605,000 gross per show. With extensive radio airplay from the new albums, the band might have been able to do more multiple-night engagements in various cities." [338]

Due to its proximity to the record business in New York City, Guns' June 17 stop at the Nassau Coliseum in Uniondale was besieged by Geffen personnel and other industry figures. Every one of them, it seemed, wanted something from Axl. Tom Zutaut was backstage with a stack of cassettes and a hundred questions about the latest mixes. An art director showed up with an elaborate set of boards that required the group's approval. Publicist Bryn Bridenthal was there, fresh from an all-night shoot with legendary photographer Herb Ritts. An image of the entire sextet by Ritts would end up on the cover of *Rolling Stone* but scheduling an important photography session so close to a New York concert infuriated Axl.

Photo shoots, like live performances, brought out the singer's worst anxieties. He dreaded them, sometimes stewing for days before a scheduled session with a high-profile photographer. "It was an insecurity thing," said publicist Arlett Vereecke. "He was concerned about his looks. When you're a frontman at that magnitude, it's easy to become insecure. People judge you on your hair, your pants, your shoes, your rings, your fingers. Your nails – are they short or long, too small? You're under a microscope."[339]

GNR's photo shoot with Herb Ritts went until 6 a.m. and by the time Axl got back to the hotel, showered, and got some sleep, the doors of the Coliseum were about to open. The athleticism and length of Axl's performances made it impossible for him to sing until he had completed his physical and vocal warm-ups.

Skid Row went on and played everything they knew, eventually departing the Coliseum stage at 8:30 p.m. after performing twice as long as their usual 45-minute set. It took Guns almost two-and-a-half hours to appear, a time during which the 17,600-strong capacity crowd grew increasingly restless, booing loudly and chanting "bullshit" as the wait continued. At 10:10 p.m. an announcement was made that GNR was "en route by helicopter and should be here shortly."[340] This may have simply been another delay tactic because Axl was nowhere in sight.

"Everybody's *freaking out* backstage, the whole arena is imploding, all the fans are screaming," Sebastian Bach recalled.[341] "I look down the hallway and there's this big commotion going on. It's a model holding hands with Axl. He's walking down the hall like nothing happened."

"Dude, where were you?" Bach asked.

"I was taking a shower," Axl replied nonchalantly[342]

It was nearly 11:00 p.m. when Guns finally took the stage, opening with a furious one-two punch of "Perfect Crime" and "Mr. Brownstone" Immediately afterward, Axl apologized for being late and the audience booed loudly, expressing their frustration. "I know it sucks, huh?" the singer said. "If you have any real complaints, you can do me a favor. You can write a little letter about how much that sucked and send it to Geffen Records and tell those people to get the fuck out of my ass."

GNR made it through "Bad Obsession" and "Dust N' Bones" before Axl was back at it, railing about the all-night photo shoot with Herb Ritts. "We got a *Rolling Stone* cover coming out in a month or two months. Do me a favor, don't buy it. If you really want it, steal it. 'Cause *Rolling Stone*, some of the people there are cool, but every time

I got a show in New York, they're up my ass. The only thing that matters to me when I'm on tour is the time I'm on stage. Nothing else counts or matters. You paid your money to see us play and I want to be in the best condition that we can to do that for you. I ain't up here to be working for Geffen Records or *Rolling Stone* magazine."

Axl stopped the concert several more times to denounce his record label and journalists that ranged from Jon Pareles of the *New York Times* to some poor scribe in Philly whose sole offense was not giving Skid Row their proper due.

The hours-long delay at Nassau and Axl's extended, colorful diatribes became the focus of the ensuing press coverage, overshadowing GNR's musical performance and setting the tone for the rest of the tour. On MTV, Kurt Loder suggested fans "bring a book to pass the time between sets," while the *New York Daily News* opened a review with the observation, "Punctuality has never been tops on Guns N' Roses' list of priorities."[343] An assessment from the *New York Times* focused on Axl's invectives, riveting because they were so clearly unscripted and antithetical to the formulaic stage patter of the average rock frontman. "The best parts of the show weren't musical. Rock shows are about drama, and Axl Rose, the band's charismatic lead singer, knows a thing or two about drama. The band was several hours late to its performance, and Mr. Rose was finding scapegoats in just about everybody except himself."[344] Axl's high-wire act gave an air of unpredictability and genuine danger to concerts, which made the group's hard-punching tunes feel that much more authentic.

No one was spared from the singer's onstage venom – the media, Geffen Records, other artists, the crew, security guards, and frequently the audience itself. At a June 19 stop in Landover, Maryland, a fan close to the front booed after Axl explained GNR would be playing a lot of new, unreleased material. He had already castigated the soundman for his mic feeding back. "Did I hear some boos? Then I guess you wasted your money, homeboy. You don't want to hear it, you might as well leave, sorry. 'I wanna hear *Appetite*, I don't wanna hear anything new.' Burned out, smoking pot, sitting on the couch and wasting your life away."

Three songs later, Axl was at it again, railing against Geffen and bands that supposedly cared more about being rock stars than making high quality music. "I was going to do something mellower," Axl said, but called for "Perfect Crime."

Guns followed this with "Civil War," but only made it midway through before Axl, seeing a security guard clashing with a fan, dove headfirst into the audience. The crowd went berserk, and a huge roar went up as the musicians continued to play. Izzy then stopped and walked to the front of the stage to get a better look at things. Axl appeared to be fighting with three security guards. Izzy shook his head in disgust and walked off, just as Slash and Duff rushed to the front.

Axl eventually made it back on stage, explaining to the audience, "A guy threw me his hat. I threw it back. A girl caught it. He went to get the hat and fell and got jumped by three security guards. I saw this guy get a cut eye and punched, and he didn't do shit except try to get his hat. So, it's stage dive time!" The audience loved this last line, cheering in approval. Axl asked for someone to check on the woman who was involved, to make sure she was okay. "We like to get crazy, but we don't want anyone to get hurt."

Little did Axl know his stage diving and fighting with security were about to cause the biggest disruption of the entire tour.

Chapter 8

Code 1000

On June 30, GNR appeared in Birmingham, Alabama, a night that was unremarkable until midway through the show when Axl suddenly walked off stage for no reason. The band covered for him, improvising a lengthy blues jam, followed by an even longer solo from Slash. Matt recalled, "Duff and I kept exchanging increasingly anxious glances, wondering, *What the hell's going on?*"[345] Axl eventually reappeared, but the unexpected incident left everyone in the group a bit rattled.

Two days later, the MGM Grand touched down in St. Louis, Missouri at 4 a.m.; Guns were scheduled to perform that night and spent the day sleeping at a nearby hotel. Izzy was already in town, having arrived by bus on his own schedule.

Located in Maryland Heights, Missouri, outside of St. Louis, the Riverport Amphitheatre was a brand-new venue that had opened weeks earlier. GNR was only the third performance to take place at Riverport, whose inaugural concert was a staid affair featuring Robert Cray and Steve Winwood.

Guns attracted rowdy audiences that liked their rock hard and their party substances even harder. In St. Louis, there was a heavy contingent of Saddle Tramps, a local motorcycle gang with a notorious reputation around town. Many were regulars at local concerts and were friendly with Riverport security. According to *Rolling Stone*, "The Saddle Tramps were making their presence known in the first row, allegedly intimidating other concertgoers."[346] This included Bill "Stump" Stephenson, who had come to the show with something he wanted to give to Axl, a printed card with the Saddle Tramps logo rendered in a manner similar to GNR's round pistols and flowers emblem, with the words "Welcome to St. Louis" written over it.

Stephenson was determined to personally hand the card to Axl, having done something similar at previous Guns appearances. GNR began with "Perfect Crime," their preferred opener during the Illusion tour's initial run. Axl wore his signature red kilt along with a baseball umpire's padded chest protector and a black leather military style cap. Stump Stephenson pressed close to the front, holding up the card for Axl. The singer, busy performing, did his best to ignore the annoying fan. "You have people yelling and screaming during the whole show," Axl recalled. "But this guy just wouldn't stop, and he was loud – almost as loud as my monitor. He's holding up a card, and I'm like 'Okay, yeah, that's great.' But he still won't stop yelling."[347]

After the fourth song, "Dust N' Bones," Axl paused to address the crowd. Stephenson again yelled at the singer and held up his card.

Irritated, Axl took it from him. "What am I supposed to do with this?" he asked, briefly scanning the card.

"Remember it," Stump hollered back from the throng.[348]

Axl turned and walked toward the drum riser, looking back at Stump and adding, "That was worth interrupting me for? No, it wasn't, dude." Axl tossed the card onto the drum riser, took a quick gulp of water, and walked back to the front of the stage.

The singer explained to the audience how Guns liked to vary the setlist running order from night to night. "There might be a delay between different songs because we just have this big list and we pick which song we're gonna play next as we go, to see how it feels best with you. That way, we don't get bored and you don't go, 'I saw that show in Toledo.' Fuck *that* shit. We'll be playing a lot of new stuff, seeing as how you people have waited for a really long time for the album to come out."

The "You Could Be Mine" single had been released a week earlier and proved to be another in a string of home runs for GNR. Its *Terminator 2*-themed video with Arnold Schwarzenegger paired the band with the summer's hottest blockbuster, slated to hit theaters on the coming fourth of July weekend. "You Could Be Mine" debuted at number sixty-four on the Billboard Hot 100 singles chart, no small feat at a time when the top ten was populated by acts such as Paula Adbul, Color Me Badd, and Jesus Jones. The hard-rocking single would eventually crack the top 30. The video, GNR's first in more than two years, played continually on MTV.

"We got a new song out that people like you put on number one on requests on MTV and radio stations across the country," Axl told the crowd in St. Louis, which roared in approval. "We're real surprised. We never thought it would happen with that song. We just kind of threw it out there so that the rockers would have something to listen to while we were working on our ballad shit. But you guys stuck a firecracker up its ass, and it just took off."

Guns charged through an energetic take on their new hit single after which Slash enthused, "Fuck yeah, St. Louis, this is happening." Matt recalled, "Twenty thousand people were in the audience, and at first, the atmosphere both on and offstage felt great."[349]

"Give me a little Rod Stewart," Axl said, calling for the brief instrumental passage from Stewart's "I Was Only Joking" GNR were playing as a segue to "Patience." Immediately following that singalong anthem, Axl was at it again. The singer's rants were now a regular feature of the show, with Axl stopping every few tunes to deliver another invective. The audiences seemed to anticipate these tirades, cheering even when Axl was railing against the audience itself.

"How can you ask me these questions when you're a Guns N' Roses fan and you've listened to our albums, and you've listened to us talk?" Axl asked hypothetically after "Patience" concluded. "I know there'll be things in the press that someone else wrote and they'll be twisted and upside down. What is it? I must have some huge reputation for lying my ass off all the time. Basically, if you're talking to Axl, argue with him and don't believe him because he's just known for lying in his music and in his personal life. He just lies all the time, I guess."

Axl went on for a while longer, eventually turning around and grabbing a cup of water, taking a quick swing before tossing the cup aside.

"Maybe I just make shit up all the time," the singer continued.

"Alright, Axe," Izzy said sharply, urging Axl to end his harangue.

He seemed to get the message. "Maybe I am so full of shit, that I am nothing but a double-talking jive motherfucker." Matt launched into a beat and the show was up and running again. Afterward, Axl sat down at the piano to play "November Rain." "This is something that you already may own since it sold three to five million bootlegs," the singer griped, adding. "Impatient motherfuckers." The song got a huge ovation. Despite touring without a new album, Guns were playing four well-known numbers that would eventually be released on *Illusion*: "Civil War," "You Could Be Mine," "Knockin' on Heaven's Door," and "November Rain." There was also a familiar Paul McCartney cover, "Live and Let Die."

Following "November Rain," Axl told a long story about taking a Greyhound bus from Lafayette to St. Louis when he was seventeen. Upon arrival, he hitched a ride with an air conditioning repairman. "I was exhausted and beat and I'd never been out of my town on my own in my life. We went to some hotel and crashed out, and I woke up and this guy was trying to fuck me. You can be male, female, you can be a fucking dog, I don't care what you are, man, that shit ain't right. No, but I guess I'm just homophobic, that's my problem. Anyway, I pinned this guy against the wall between the door of the hotel with my straight razor – and it took everything I had not to slice his jugular vein. So that was my first experience of knowing where I was. Do you know where you are? All I know is when I was here and I was seventeen, I was in the middle of the *jungle* baby."

Near the 75-minute mark, Axl called for Matt's solo, which enabled the singer to take an extended break while the drummer pounded away at the skins. This was followed by a long solo from Slash, which segued into the instrumental *Godfather* theme. Axl then returned for "Rocket Queen," having changed into white bicycle shorts, a black feather boa jacket, and a military style cap.

From his position near the front, Stump Stephenson started snapping photos, infuriating Axl, who demanded that security confiscate his camera. "Hey, take that, take that! Now, get that guy and take that."

"I had taken pictures throughout the show," Stephenson recalled. "After I took the picture, he just started hollering and pointing down at the crowd. I moved a little to the left, a little to the right, and he was following me with his hand and finger."

Axl's demands that security confiscate Stephenson's camera went unanswered, so the singer decided to resolve the matter himself. "I'll take it goddamn it," he bellowed, diving headfirst into the crowd, leaping directly for Stephenson.

"He hit me blind-sided and we went over the chairs," Stephenson recalled.[350]

Axl did not deny it. "I got a hold of the guy and wouldn't let go of him," the singer said in an interview shortly after the incident.[351]

From the stage, the other members of GNR scanned the crowd, trying to locate their singer in the fracas. "As far as I could see, they were both going at it with clenched fists, and black feathers from Axl's jacket were swirling through the air," Matt recalled. "My jaw dropped as I tried to keep up the beat."[352] But Slash was not particularly concerned. "We've been jumping into crowds our whole career – that's how we do things," the guitarist shrugged.[353]

Riverport security rushed in and tried to pull Axl off of Stump Stephenson. Axl punched one of the guards in the face, later claiming several members of the security team had hit him first.[354] Axl was hoisted back onto the stage. He had lost a contact lens in the melee and was struggling to see. He was furious over the lack of assistance from the Riverport security, who had enabled Stump's behavior and then refused to stop it. *I'm out of here. I'm paying these guys' salary, I don't need to be treated like that*, the singer thought to himself.[355]

"Thanks to the lame-ass security, I'm going home," Axl shouted to the audience, throwing his microphone to the floor. It crashed with an explosive crackle some purportedly mistook for gunfire. The singer turned and stormed from the stage.

"He just smashed the microphone, so we're outta here," Slash told the crowd, following Axl offstage. The rest of the band joined them shortly after.

As soon as Guns walked off, the audience began booing, and within seconds chants of "bullshit" thundered across the amphitheater. Some launched bottles and cans toward the front, which smashed into other concertgoers and members of the Riverport security team, mostly teenagers earning $7 per hour. According to one reporter who was on the scene, "Security forces ringed the stage, as roadies frantically attempted to remove the group's equipment. When some of the debris fell short, a few of the GNR staffers began taunting the audience. One of them repeatedly grabbed his crotch and made jerking-off motions toward the crowd, further inciting their anger."[356]

An announcer came on the PA system, stating the band would return and play two more songs if the audience promised to settle down. This did nothing to appease the crowd, which was growing increasingly restless and emboldened.

Without warning, the venue's house lights were turned on, signaling the end of the show. Debris rained down on the stage: bottles, cans, seat cushions, and even seats flew toward the front. Hundreds of fans rushed forward, collapsing the barricades that separated the audience from the stage production and equipment. Police and firefighters poured in through the backstage corridors.

"Suddenly all hell broke loose," Slash recalled. "There were people being pulled in backstage and blood was all over the place. I was sitting in the dressing room, quietly drinking from a bottle of Jack Daniel's, when it was suggested we should get out of the building. To do what? Get caught in traffic? Where were we gonna go?"[357] Slash had a hard time understanding why the audience was so enraged. "I don't know who the crowd were mad at – us, the police or the security."[358]

Things were turning to complete chaos out front, where thousands of fans were tearing the place apart, destroying anything in sight, be it a seating pad or a Marshall stack. The mob was ripping entire sections of seats from their bolts in the concrete floor. SWAT teams with shields arrived, pummeling concertgoers with batons. Police used fire hoses and pepper spray on the crowd, enraging the audience and further inflaming the situation.[359]

Guns offered to go back on and appease the mob. "It was getting crazy, and we decided we were going to go back out and try to play, because we didn't want people to get hurt," Axl said.[360]

But it was too late. Fans breached the Riverport stage, destroying or making off with everything in sight. The rioters climbed into the scaffolding, tore down lights, and hung from the two-story high video screens until they ripped in half. GNR's roadies managed to salvage their vintage guitars, but nearly all the rest of the equipment was either smashed or stolen. Audience members rolled giant speaker cabinets right off the stage and walked off with the mixing boards. Back on the lawn, attendees demolished chain-link fences, ripped shrubs from their roots, rolled up sections of sod, and set fires. Rioters tore down all the signs in the parking lot, making it difficult for people to find their cars as they tried to leave.

"I've never seen anything like it in my life," Axl told the *Los Angeles Times* a day after the event. "The only thing that would be uglier or heavier are things that have happened in soccer games, where the seats collapsed."[361]

"Some of our guys got stitches," Slash recalled. "Backstage, there were people on stretchers, bleeding, cops coming through. It was real intense."[362]

According to the *Riverfront Times*, "On-site security was overmatched by the crowd, and for the first time in St. Louis County history, a Code 1000 was called, summoning all available police officers to the Riverport. An estimated 400 officers from thirty police departments descended on the venue."[363]

John Reese, GNR's tour manager, insisted they leave the Riverport immediately. "It's not safe," he told them. "We've gotta get you guys out of the venue."[364] Izzy had already departed in his tour bus, but the rest of the group huddled in a van together, ducking down to avoid being noticed as they fled the parking lot. When Guns arrived at their hotel, they could already see the riot all over the news. Moreover, local authorities were searching for Axl. The band members grabbed their luggage and immediately returned to the van. Reese ordered the driver to transport them across the state line, into Illinois, where the St. Louis police had no jurisdiction.

It took approximately 400 officers more than ninety minutes to gain control of the venue.[365] The *Riverfront Times*, St. Louis' local alternative weekly newspaper, wrote, "It was nothing short of a miracle that no one was killed. This was the worst riot St. Louis concertgoers have ever seen."[366] There were 75 reported injuries, including thirteen law enforcement officers, one of whom suffered a broken kneecap.[367] Authorities made sixteen arrests for charges such as assaulting a police officer, resisting arrest, and destruction of property.[368] In addition to GNR's lost equipment and staging, the Riverport Amphitheatre suffered an estimated $2 million in damages.[369]

Axl was desperate to explain his side of the story. Within hours, he was on the air at KSHE-FM, St. Louis' biggest rock radio station. "I regret what happened last night," he said.[370] "I didn't have a choice," the singer told *Rolling Stone*, "I couldn't even see, and was injured, and did not feel safe on the stage. I was concerned that people didn't get more of a show. But some fans don't take responsibility that they should take. There's a lot of people not taking responsibility for the damage they did at that place."[371]

Axl would make his feelings clear later, donning a T-shirt onstage bearing the slogan "St. Louis Sucks," and including a small tribute in the *Illusion* CD booklet: "Fuck you, St. Louis!"

Aftermath

The St. Louis riot made headlines the world over, with the media blaming Axl for the crowd's destructive behavior. The press coverage typically included quotes from law enforcement officers, who also pointed the finger directly at the singer. For example, John Wachter, a Maryland Heights police sergeant, told the Associated Press, "This is the first incident we've seen in which a bandleader attacked someone in the crowd, and that is what precipitated the riot. I know groups don't like to have their pictures taken, but they should have exercised a little more judgment."[372] The negative stories frequently mentioned the long waits at GNR concerts and Axl's onstage rants, cementing the singer's reputation for tardiness and bile.

Guns were forced to cancel upcoming appearances in Chicago and Kansas City, scrambling to replace virtually all their equipment and get the tour back on track for two sold out gigs in Dallas. This meant repurchasing or renting everything from amplifiers and guitars to the entire lighting rig, sound boards, monitors, two pianos, and more.

The riot was not only expensive and a logistical headache, there were also legal implications, including potential criminal charges and a slew of lawsuits already being prepared on both sides. Promoters also became increasingly wary of working with Guns. Following the riot in St. Louis, county administrators in Salt Lake City demanded organizers review the safety procedures for GNR's upcoming appearance at the Salt Palace, threatening to cancel the concert if necessary.[373] Beefed up security, additional fencing and barriers, and thorough searches upon entry became standard features of Guns concerts. These measures cut deeply into profit margins. "Let's just say that there will be more security at this show than at one by James Taylor," a California promoter said dryly.[374]

Perhaps more importantly, the riot was a stunning blow to GNR's psyche. Like the deaths that occurred at Donington in 1988, the St. Louis melee served as a massive check to Guns, forcing the group to question the very instincts that had made them so successful. "A crowd never freaked us out until St. Louis, when the place exploded," Slash said shortly after the incident. "I don't think the band realized how much power we can have over that many people."[375] The guitarist expressed relief St. Louis was not a repeat of Donington, that no one had lost their life. But he vowed the incident would never be forgotten. "This will stay with us for all time. At the back of our minds there will always be a fear of St. Louis being repeated."[376] GNR would not play St. Louis again for twenty-six years.

Dallas

"For the last few days, I'm watching CNN and I'm reading this shit in the papers about how I incited a riot," Axl told the audience in Dallas at GNR's July 8 concert at the Starplex Amphitheatre. The venue's management had brought in additional security for the night as a precaution, including police with riot gear. Forty-one off-duty officers joined a team of private guards to maintain order.[377]

Axl wore a white T-shirt that read "Public Enemy" in bold black letters, along with the New York rap outfit's crosshairs logo. He continued. "I realized that no matter what we did tonight and how good or how bad we played, there'll be one person in the press here that for some reason didn't dig it and he'll write some lies." Axl continued on for a bit before adding, "It's hard to figure out why we get up on stage to do this. Because sometimes it's fun and other times it takes all the physical energy we got to get up here and do what we do for a living."

Axl paused a beat before stating flatly, "They helped kill Jim Morrison with a *lot* less pressure."

It had taken the singer forever to steel himself enough to step on stage and confront an audience again. The group went on around 10:15, two-and-a-half hours after Skid Row finished. "Almost every night we heard the crowds get antsy and then ugly," Duff recalled. "After about an hour of waiting, kids would start to chant. Then they would start to throw beer bottles and rocks and whatever else they could find. From backstage, it was difficult to know whether people had started or would soon start to scale the security fences or rigging and break into full-on riot mode."[378]

By the time GNR stepped on stage in Dallas, the frustrated audience was incensed, booing and throwing things. Like Axl's on-stage tirades, however, Guns arriving late was becoming a convention of their concerts, a part of the experience. As a review of the Dallas appearance in *Entertainment Weekly* put it, "By Guns N' Roses' standard, it had not been an unusual show. The band arrived onstage two hours late, and Rose had something to tell his expectant and impatient audience."[379]

This type of press coverage may have encouraged Axl to keep concertgoers waiting. It was now part of his image – the rock star who doesn't care whom he keeps waiting and for how long. But Axl's late arrivals were becoming a source of growing tension within the group. No one felt like they could say anything to the hypersensitive singer. Doing so might trigger him to show up even later. As Izzy would recall shortly after the Dallas gig "It can get pretty tense at times, particularly when you're supposed to be on-stage and you're sitting there, literally counting the seconds, thinking 'Man, we've just had a riot in St. Louis. Now we're in Texas. What the fuck is going to happen *here?*'"

The sound was glitchy in Dallas, too. GNR's hastily purchased replacement equipment was not identical to the top-shelf gear they had hand-selected to take on the road months earlier. To get back on tour, Guns had to make do with whatever monitor boards and amplifier heads they could get their hands on. "I apologize that the sound quality isn't up to par," Axl snarled onstage in Dallas. "If you have a real problem with that you can go talk to fucking St. Louis." The singer wasn't done with the Missouri city by a long shot, concluding the show memorably with, "Thank you, Dallas, fuck you, St. Louis, and God bless America."

Backstage after the first Dallas stop, there was a palpable sense of relief. The tour had threatened to career off the rails after St. Louis, but GNR had somehow managed to keep the train on the tracks. "Tonight was a real turning point for this band," Duff said after the gig. "The crowd were really pissed off at having to wait a while for us to appear onstage. But we went on and turned them totally around. They were throwing shit at us for the first three or four songs, and I got really aggressive out there. I went right up to the front of the stage as if to say to them 'Come on, I dare you to come up here!' But we pulled it off and it was important for us, because this was the first date we've done since the riot in St. Louis."[380]

Slash agreed, sitting next to Duff shirtless and sweaty, a towel wrapped around his head. "There was a certain tension before we went onstage tonight. After all, the riot will always be at the back of our minds, and we were playing with new equipment. Still, it went really well."

"Actually, despite what people outside might believe, things have been going like clockwork on this tour," Duff added with a laugh. "The only thing is that for us the clock is always kinda lop-sided."[381]

Duff and Slash enabled each other's partying, hanging out before and after the shows and indulging their day-to-day vices and ingesting whatever else happened to come their way via fan or friend. "We're still not angels by any means," Duff told the *L.A. Times*. "We still do that sex, drugs and rock 'n' roll thing. But it's not our lifestyle anymore. We know how to choose what and where and when. We're not going to let it destroy the band or kill us."[382]

Setting Axl's life force free

Duff and Slash snorted and drank away the shock of St. Louis, and Izzy dealt with it by disappearing further into the ether. This left Axl alone, dead sober, and feeling vulnerable. He had been crucified by the media over "One in a Million," and the St. Louis riot gave his detractors another round of ammunition. The singer coped by waging war with everyone in his universe: the press, Geffen Records, audiences, members of the crew, management, his bandmates, and even himself. The intensive routines Axl underwent to prepare for concerts were *just* enough to keep the demons at bay and get him onstage one more night. But the group was fraying at the seams, the pressures were mounting from all sides, and *Illusion* had not even been released. Desperate, the singer sought anything he could to alleviate his inner turmoil and keep the tour from falling apart. Money was no object. As Matt put it, "Our management was willing to do whatever it took to keep us on our feet."[383]

Backstage at the second Dallas appearance, Axl was introduced to Stephen Thaxton, a twenty-five-year-old diehard Guns fan who had just completed his coursework in chiropractic. Thaxton had been hired by the promoter in Dallas to give free adjustments to everyone backstage – the group, their wives and girlfriends, the crew, Axl's personal assistant, and so forth. Everyone was raving about the results.

Following GNR's second Dallas concert, deep into the early morning hours, Thaxton was summoned to Axl's dressing room. The singer was certain if he could achieve perfect physical and mental health, he could deliver the flawless performances he aimed for.

"Thank you very much for treating my crew, my band," the singer told the somewhat-awestruck Thaxton. "I hope you can do something for me."

"Be honored," Thaxton told the singer in a thick Virginia drawl. "What's going on with you?"

"Well, my back's been hurting," Axl said.

Thaxton gave Axl a thorough spinal adjustment.

Afterward, Axl sat up and twisted his torso. "Wow, you really know your shit."

Thaxton later adjusted Axl's therapist Suzzy London, joking to her that his treatment had "set Axl's life force free." That was more than enough for London, who phoned two days later and asked Thaxton to join GNR for their next gig in Salt Lake City. He never left the tour, remaining on the road with Guns for the next two years, flying on the MGM Grand and staying in five-star hotels.

"Axl's physical performance was very, very important to him on the *Use Your Illusion* tours," recalled Thaxton, who later worked as a chiropractor and trainer for Bon Jovi. "Axl was clean. And it was important for him to be clean – and probably why he and I bonded so quickly. I mean, within a couple days, I felt like I was his brother and we got super tight as a result of that. My non-drug stance and what I represented fit very well with what he was trying to do with his life at the time. The other guys had different ideas."[384]

"I work out on a StairMaster with my chiropractor-trainer," Axl explained. "We do a workout on the StairMaster that enables me to breathe and move better on stage. And what I'm doing on stage turns out to be something that helps build me up rather than tear me down by being so exhausting. At first when I was playing, it would just wear me out."[385]

Axl was a serious guy, but he was known to occasionally poke fun at his tempestuous image, as he did around this time by pairing with MTV to give away his West Hollywood condo in an "Evict Axl" contest. Axl appeared in promo commercials, sporting a blue blazer, sunglasses, and a cowboy hat as he offered a tour of the apartment where he'd had so many highly publicized fights with his next-door neighbor. "This beautiful Sunset Strip property has everything a rock 'n' roller could ever want," the singer said with a sly grin, impersonating a sunny real-estate agent. "A bar, a barbeque, and a pool within throwing distance. The bed's never been slept in. I'm not saying it hasn't been *used*, it just hasn't been slept in. This wall's only been smashed once – some guy's head, but it's been repaired. It's like new now." As Axl showed off the condo, a voiceover intoned, "Evict Axl Rose. Take possession of his condo, his furniture, his stereo, and his aura. And after you move in, Axl will throw you a housewarming party." At the end of the promo, Axl boarded a tour bus, looking directly at the camera and stating, "You can have the pad, I'm keeping my aura."

At the time, Axl's condo had an estimated value of about $425,000. MTV received more than 400,000 entries. The winner was Erika Alden, a twenty-one-year-old college senior from Ohio.[386] "I was so excited," Alden said of the phone call she received from MTV. "I thought it was a one in a million chance."[387]

A lousy show

County administrators in Salt Lake City demanded additional security measures be taken during GNR's concert at the Salt Palace on July 13. Earlier that year, three spectators had been crushed to death at the same venue during an AC/DC performance when the audience rushed the stage. That tragedy, combined with alarming headlines about the riot in St. Louis, led to concerns about what might occur at the Guns appearance. Organizers capped attendance at 12,500, and more than 200 security officers were on hand, including nearly twice the usual number of ushers.[388] They "patrolled the aisles of the arena doing everything from extinguishing cigarettes to making sure fans who tried to edge closer to the stage returned to their assigned seats."389 A review in the *Salt Lake Tribune* described the atmosphere as sterile and Axl's performance as "tame. He screamed only a few expletives in his between-song chatter and was mild in comparison to Sebastian Bach."390

It was a lousy show, and Guns departed without playing their usual closer, "Paradise City." "There were people sitting there like they were bored off of their asses," Axl recalled. "Finally, we left. Why should we play the encore? We just wanted to get out of there. My attitude was, 'Man, I only have a few bands that really get me off at a show. What do you want? What do you have to do tonight that's better than this?' Maybe they wanted to go home and listen to something else."391

Four days later, from the stage of the Tacoma Dome outside Seattle, Axl denounced the audience in Salt Lake City, describing the gig as "the most boring concert I ever played." Axl had heard crackling sounds earlier he assumed were firecrackers. "I know you want to get rowdy; I want you to get rowdy but be good to each other down here," he admonished the crowd. "The reason it sucked in Utah is those people didn't care that much about each other and they ended up running over each other's ass until they killed three of themselves. Now, their concerts are ran by the military police and if you go to smoke a cigarette and be rowdy, you get thrown out. So for us, the show *sucked*. Be good to each other down here so you can have this whenever a band comes to town."

When Axl wasn't chastising Salt Lake City, he was deriding St. Louis. After "Dust N' Bones," the singer donned a plastic pig's snout, which he claimed with a gift from the Seattle police, a middle finger to the cops in St. Louis. But GNR were tight and put on an energetic show, striving to leave the tribulations of Missouri in the past.

The appearance was a return home for Duff, who had played in dozens of underground Seattle outfits before moving to Los Angeles and joining Guns. "This is a dream come true," the bassist enthused to *The Seattle Times*. "I saw Bowie at the Tacoma Dome; I saw Rod Stewart there."392

Seattle was going well until about the 95-minute mark, when someone launched a bottle rocket near the end of "Rocket Queen." The firework ricocheted off the ceiling and exploded near the stage, narrowly missing Izzy on the way down.

Axl was livid. "Hey, that's a good way to stop the show," he said after "Rocket Queen" ended. "If you saw whoever did that, we'll give you ten minutes to turn them in. We'll be back."

Axl strode off stage and the audience immediately began booing. "We are one of the few bands that will stop our show two or three times if the crowd is getting too outrageous," Axl told the *L.A. Times* shortly after the St. Louis incident. "We like people to have the greatest, wildest time they can, but if people are getting hurt, we'll stop the show."[393]

Contractually, Guns were required to perform for 90 minutes and could end the Seattle appearance if they chose. But the memory of St. Louis was still potent, and no one wanted to see a repeat, especially mere days later. Within seconds of departing, Axl returned to the stage, telling the crowd two fireworks had been launched at the group that night. "We played our 90 minutes. I ain't up here for us to get hurt, or anybody in this crowd to get hurt, by some *stupid drunk pussy* who thinks he's cool 'cause he's drunk and he's high."

Axl was seething. Describing what happened somehow made the events feel even more dangerous and further enraged the singer.

"It's up to you," he told the audience. "Get him outta here. If you get him and he's outta here, we'll come back. Otherwise, peace." With that, Axl threw the microphone to the floor and stormed off stage.

Organizers of the Seattle concert had brought in extra security that night in case something like this happened. There were shouts and rumblings from the arena floor as confusion reigned.

Within less than a minute, Axl was back onstage. "You may have your different opinions of the way I handle things. The authorities may have their opinions." The singer recounted a story about how Motörhead frontman Lemmy Kilmister told him not to tolerate audiences throwing things because it could lead to other bands getting hurt. "We ain't up here to play games, it's our job. I ain't trying to fuck you up. Anyway, hopefully, you beat the fuck out of that asshole. Let's hear some Bob Dylan." Slash began plucking at his Les Paul and order was restored. *The Seattle Times* praised the night as "spectacular, one of the best concerts here in years."[394]

"The St. Louis gig taught us a lot," Slash said during a late-night, brandy-fueled interview after the Seattle show. "That made us realize you have to play it a certain way. You can't just split – because the people are not gonna understand. But M80s and whatever that bomb was that went off tonight – that's so dangerous. Why would you wanna do that? I guess people like to see the band react."[395]

Segregation and separation

GNR concluded the first leg of the *Illusion* tour with eight California concerts, beginning with back-to-back appearances at the Shoreline Amphitheatre outside San Francisco. By this point, the band was sequestered into different camps that had less and less interaction. The only time they were together was on stage, but even then, there was isolation – each member had a private room underneath the stage where they could hang out by themselves during breaks. "Most of the time now I stay in my hotel room and see the people I'm close to," Slash told a reporter a couple of weeks earlier. "I hang out and listen to my stereo, dealing with my own personal stuff. Then I go to the gig and do the best I can. It's a weird lifestyle."[396]

British journalist Nick Kent was backstage at the first Shoreline stop and was struck by the distance between the group members. "They prefer to segregate themselves in separate environments," Kent observed.[397] Axl was locked away in a private trailer, furiously exercising. In another trailer, Slash nursed a wicked hangover as he tucked into a fresh bottle of booze. Next door to him, Duff woozily discussed the solo album he was working on. Duff began recording while he was waiting around for Axl and Slash to complete their guitar and vocal tracks for *Illusion*, playing all the instruments himself. The bassist already had a deal with Geffen. Finally, there was Izzy, holed up in his own trailer and wishing he was anywhere else.

Izzy had divorced himself almost entirely from the rest of the band, traveling in his own bus and staying in separate hotels. He'd arrive thirty minutes before Guns were scheduled to perform, waiting around for Axl to get his head together enough to actually go onstage.

Everything revolved around Axl. Nick Kent described an organization ruled by the singer's iron fist. "Axl Rose runs the group. Consequently, everything has to be done pretty much his way."[398] Axl made the decision to fire Alan Niven. *Illusion* was delayed due to Axl's perfectionism and determination to release four records worth of material. On tour, everything from the pre-show music to the opening act was hand-selected by Axl.

But the singer's authoritarian style was rubbing his bandmates the wrong way. Izzy claimed to have no idea when *Illusion* would be released, his exasperation palpable. "It's gotten to the point where I don't even ask when it's coming out 'cause every time I ask it's a different date. Three months ago, they were mixing. Other than that, I'm just not up on it at all. They're still mixing is all I know."

Previewing some of the *Illusion* material for Nick Kent backstage, Izzy was dismissive. He didn't even recognize some of the tunes. "These albums are just so far from me now. The life of these songs for me is in playing 'em every night live. Otherwise, they're just product that's going to be marketed."[399]

Asked about the future of the group, Izzy chose his words carefully. "Guns N' Roses will take its natural course. Even though it could all end tomorrow night, I think we'll take a long break and then come back and do it again. That's what it feels like could happen. But then again, two years ago, I never really thought this tour could happen. Frankly, I didn't think any of us would have this much of a future."[400]

Even though all members of GNR were present and accounted for backstage, Axl kept the San Francisco fans waiting more than 90 minutes after Skid Row wrapped up. Wary of a St. Louis repeat, alcohol sales were cut off and the audience grew increasingly restless and irate. Legendary Bay Area promoter Bill Graham even had to come out and plead for calm.[401]

Axl put in his usual dynamic performance that night, but waged an onstage battle with Tom Mayhew, a crew member who picked up a microphone stand the singer had thrown to the ground. According to the journalist Nick Kent, Axl kicked Mayhew. Hard.

"I said don't pick that mic stand back up, motherfucker!" Axl raged at Mayhew, who stood there frozen. "Fuck, Tom, you're too efficient tonight." The Shoreline crowd roared in approval.

"Hey, check it out," Axl told them sardonically. "I'm having one of those irrational temper tantrums you keep reading about in the press."

Later in the show, when Axl came across another offending mic stand, the singer flung it like a javelin at the unfortunate Mayhew, who swerved at the last second and narrowly avoided injury.

"You know, I work on my stupid irrational temper," Axl told the audience. "But when I lose it, you fuckers get off on it. I guess being a psycho basket case helps my career."

Kent was unimpressed, describing a lackluster concert from a band that seemed too hungover to deliver the goods. "Certain members appear to be too physically worn down from partying to perform a two-and-a-half-hour rock gig. Slash looks dissipated and sounds disappointing. The pallid McKagan has to spend several numbers lying flat-out, his eyes closed, smoking a cigarette."

Backstage after the show was always a party, when the hardest drinkers and cocaine users – Slash, Duff, and Matt – would really cut loose. They were frequently joined by Sebastian Bach and members of Skid Row, industry figures and musician friends who were in the same town, and scores of attractive women. "There are wall-to-wall blondes," observed a journalist who was backstage in Seattle. "I'm waiting in a room with twenty-one of them for a while, all hand-picked by the Guns crew from the Tacoma crowd – all of them panting, preening and eager to fuck a Gunner."[402]

Backstage at the Shoreline, it was more of the same. Slash and Duff could barely walk, while Dizzy and Matt trawled for groupies. "Every night's a fuckin' party, man. Chicks, beer, you name it," Matt enthused. "Take any chick you want, man. It's just like being in a candy store."[403]

Izzy sat off to the side, shaking his head. He usually didn't stick around to watch this sort of thing anymore. GNR's backstage shenanigans were utterly foreign to him now. "These guys, they still drink, they still party. Probably way too much for their own good. These guys like to trash themselves. Tomorrow they're going to wake up and feel like shit. They really haven't changed much."[404]

"Izzy just doesn't dig it at all anymore," Matt explained. "He don't dig the drinking, even. Me, I like to party. I'm your typical drummer, I guess. Sometimes I go overboard."

There was no booze or women for Axl tonight; the singer was strictly business. The first leg of the *Illusion* tour was ending, and the albums still were not released. "This is crazy, isn't it?" Axl told journalist Lonn Friend immediately after stepping offstage at the Shoreline. "Three months on the road with no record! It's nuts. I sat in my hotel room all day today, looking at a pile of faxes and papers, a million things that needed my attention. And something just came over me. I took my Halliburton briefcase and smashed every light fixture in the room with it. Sometimes I don't know what's real anymore, and what isn't."

Here we go again

Tensions within GNR had reached a boiling point as they careened toward Los Angeles. On the way to their July 25 appearance in nearby Costa Mesa, Axl got into an altercation with television traffic reporter Bob Tur while boarding a helicopter at the Santa Monica airport. According to the *L.A. Times*, "Rose suggested Tur tried to interview him. Tur, who reports for both KCOP television and KNX-AM, said it was just a coincidence he was at the airport and had no intention of interviewing Rose, who he said berated him with expletives."[405]

To close out GNR's first Costa Mesa appearance, Axl stormed offstage as they were about to encore with "Estranged." Guns had played the opening notes, but Axl's monitors were not working so he stopped the musicians and asked them to start over. The singer stood there impatiently. "You can start over any time," he told his bandmates, sharply.[406] They did but Axl's monitors continued to give him issues. Seconds later he threw his mic to the ground and stomped away, done. The rest of the group looked at each other sheepishly.

Oh no, here we go again, Izzy thought to himself. He set down his guitar and walked offstage, followed shortly afterward by Matt and Dizzy. Slash and Duff improvised a blues jam, hoping Axl might change his mind and return. But after three minutes of flailing they gave up, too. "We've run out of songs," Slash told the audience with a shrug. Eventually, there was an announcement the concert would end one tune early due to technical issues.

A review in the *L.A. Times* praised GNR's raw authenticity during live performances. "You can tell from tension on stage, and the frequently surprised expressions on the band members' faces as the drama unfolds each night, that Axl's following his emotions on stage, not a script."[407]

The opening leg of the Illusion tour was capped by four consecutive appearances at the L.A. Forum – GNR's first time headlining an arena in their hometown. The shows were packed with celebrities that included Arnold Schwarzenegger, Cher, Johnny Depp, Billy Idol, Keanu Reeves, N.W.A, and more. Guns went on late and were fined for playing after midnight at every one of the four appearances.[408]

Before the second concert, Axl's limousine was stopped for making an illegal left turn as it was arriving at the sold-out Forum. Axl was already more than an hour late and felt being pulled over for trying to get to his own gig was ridiculous. He angrily stuck his head out of the sunroof and yelled at the motorcycle cop, who promptly issued Axl's driver a summons. "Before a show, Axl is volatile. It's a sensitive time," Geffen publicist Bryn Bridenthal said, adding, "Someone had told the limo driver to turn left."[409]

By the time Axl finally made it to the Forum, he was seething with rage, and refused to perform unless the ticket was dropped. The panicked promoters got a friendly police officer to "investigate" the summons so the concert could go on. Accused of engaging in celebrity justice, police captain James Seymour defended the action.

"We don't need 19,000 people at the Forum rioting over a traffic ticket," he told the *Times*. Axl thanked the police from the stage that night for "enabling us to have a show," but a week later, the ticket was reinstated, and the limo driver was fined $60.[410]

Moments before the final gig at the Forum, Slash found Matt backstage and informed him, "Axl wants us to play every song we know tonight."[411] The singer was determined to break Bruce Springsteen's record for longest concert ever held at the Forum. But there was also reason to celebrate. More than two years after Guns convened in Chicago to begin the writing sessions for *Illusion*, the project was finally complete – mixed, mastered, and ready to go. In only weeks, the two albums would be on record store shelves.

At their final Forum date, GNR played thirty-one songs in a show that lasted more than three-and-a-half hours. This included all of *Appetite* save for two tracks, and nineteen *Illusion* cuts, including "Dead Horse" and "Locomotive," which had only been performed a handful of times. Shannon Hoon joined in to help sing another rarity, "You Ain't the First," played for only the sixth time.

Everyone felt relieved Guns had survived the first leg of the Illusion tour. There were moments of serious doubt they would make it across the finish line. For once, the night felt not like a struggle, but a celebration.

"Los Angeles can be one of the hardest places on the earth sometimes, but L.A. offers you something that a lot of places don't," Axl told the audience from the stage. The singer was feeling reflective, thinking about all he had achieved since first making his way to Southern California more than a decade ago. "If you're different or you've got different ideas or something, you can come out here and you can find some people similar. L.A. offers you *opportunity*."

A rave review in the *L.A. Times* compared the epic concert to marathon shows by U2 and Bruce Springsteen, calling it "a blistering and absorbing display of rock 'n' roll passion."[412] But there were storm clouds forming on the horizon. In late July, ex-drummer Steven Adler filed a lawsuit against the members of Guns, claiming they "continually strove to live up to their wild reputation. In doing so, the other members of the band introduced Adler to hard drugs and provided them to him."[413] Adler was suing to annul the probation agreement he had signed the year before and break up GNR's assets. Axl was offended by Adler's lawsuit. "Maybe we should just have somebody on heroin in our band so fucked up that we wouldn't be doing this show for you," the singer said sardonically at the second Forum show. As it turned out, Steven was the least of GNR's personnel problems at the moment – one of the most important members of the group was on the verge of quitting.

Chapter 9

Where's Izzy?

Axl selected the Sid Vicious cover of "My Way" as the walk-on music for the first European date of the Illusion tour. The Euro leg began on July 13 with back-to-back shows in Helsinki, Finland. Once again, Skid Row were on hand as openers. While touring Europe in support of *Appetite*, Guns had mostly stuck to the U.K. and Germany. The Illusion tour would take the band to more than a dozen European nations they had never played before.

The North American dates that just wrapped had been a three-month treadmill and Axl felt exhausted. The singer demanded the European setlists be shorter, so the group chopped about five songs, bringing the concerts closer to two hours instead of two-and-a-half. Axl also insisted the European shows begin with two tracks from *Appetite*, rather than "Perfect Crime," GNR's preferred opener on the North American leg. As a capper to the concert, Guns started playing an end-of-show cartoon, a violent clip of a butcher chopping off his thumb, arm, and head before drowning in a pool of his own blood.

At the first Helsinki appearance, everyone was jet lagged from the flight from America, and half the band was hungover from a visit to a Black Crowes show at a club the day before. Something was off that night. About 45 minutes into the set, Axl sat down in the middle of "Civil War," his mind whirling. He continued to sing the words, almost feeling as if he were watching himself perform from the outside. "I just couldn't understand why I was doing what I was doing," he later recalled "I was kind of looking at my lips while I was singing and looking at the microphone and looking at the roadies, and everything just shut off."[414] Afterward Axl briefly introduced "Double Talkin' Jive" in a flat monotone, rather than using it as a platform for a diatribe, like he usually did.

Following "Patience," Axl called for "Welcome to the Jungle." The singer usually prefaced "Jungle" by talking about whatever city GNR were playing, inevitably asking the audience, "Do you know where you are?" while Slash teased the song's opening notes. In Helsinki, Axl simply nodded for Slash to begin, muttering, "Take it away." Confused, Slash played a few notes of "Jungle" and then paused, tantalizing the crowd with the instantly recognizable chords. The guitarist started again and then stopped. Axl was getting impatient for Slash to begin. After a few more moments of on-and-off riffing, Axl screamed, *"Do you know where the fuck you are?"* staring at Slash and prompting him to begin. But the guitarist continued to paw at his Les Paul, refusing to start the number. Axl glared at him incredulously and then suddenly threw his microphone to the floor and stormed off stage. Slash almost immediately began the riff and the band launched into "Jungle" but it was too late. Axl was gone.

GNR ground away at an instrumental take on "Jungle" for nearly five minutes, with Slash peeling off solo after solo. But Axl did not return. The group finally stopped and huddled at center stage, trying to figure out what to do next. They decided to play "14 Years," which featured Izzy on lead vocals. Guns proceeded to execute an Axl-free version of the song, with Duff struggling to cover for Axl's distinct backup vocals. This was followed by a long drum solo from Matt and an even longer guitar workout from Slash. Finally, after nearly 25 minutes, Axl returned to the stage and the band picked right back up where they left off, launching into "Jungle" like nothing happened. In the end, the show clocked in at just under two hours, with Axl on stage for the requisite 90 minutes.

Axl hated it when this type of thing happened at concerts. The singer insisted every *Illusion* appearance be videotaped, and he would fastidiously review the recordings each night after the show. His commitment to being mentally and physically prepared to deliver a knockout performance never wavered, but the singer found it difficult to maintain his arduous routine when things were going wrong in his personal life – which was most of the time. "The pressure of having to do the show when whatever else is going on in my life is hard to get past," Axl explained. "If a heavy emotional issue surfaces and you've got a show in four hours, you have to figure out how to get that sorted out really quick before you get onstage, so that you're not in the middle of 'Jungle' and have a breakdown. That doesn't make for a very good show."

For Axl, getting into the right headspace before a performance was as critical as his physical and vocal warmups. A few days later in Sweden, the singer was three hours late to GNR's gig at the Stockholm Globe Arena because he stopped to watch fireworks at a street festival. To Axl, the delay was worth it because the fireworks got him in the right frame of mind to give his all in concert.

Izzy was incredulous. The singer's perpetual lateness had resulted in hundreds of thousands of dollars in curfew-violation penalties the group had to pay collectively. Izzy thought Axl should have to cover those fines since he was the one who was never on time. But it really wasn't about the money. "It was bumming me out to be waiting there because someone else is late," Izzy said. "It's just not fair to the audience, to the other band members. And the crew – when you go on three hours late, that's three hours less sleep they get."[415]

Axl was in high spirits on stage in Stockholm that night, calling for a world-beat improv in the middle of "Knockin' on Heaven's Door." "Rastaman, give me some reggae," he yelled back to Matt, who began drumming in double time. Dizzy leaned into the organ keys while the singer did his patented circle dance, spinning and twirling about the stage. On one of the ramps, Slash was laid out flat on his back, still strumming along gamely. "That's what happens when you smoke too much pot," Axl joked of GNR's impromptu reggae foray.

But the singer's jocular air was broken moments later during-the-call and response portion of "Knockin'" when he chastised some members of the crowd for their lack of energy, for not giving back all he had given. "On this one maybe you people who've been falling asleep the whole show can sing along, too," he intoned, pointing his finger at a section of seats. "If you were bored you should have saved your money and gone and seen the fireworks tonight."

Audiences like this were emotionally draining to Axl, but months of punishing, marathon concerts were beginning to catch up with him in other ways, too. The singer was having difficulty with his voice. Following a show in Copenhagen, Axl flew to Paris to see a throat specialist who recommended he rest his vocal cords as much as possible. Heeding this advice, Axl canceled a sold-out show in Oslo, Norway at the last minute, disappointing fans, who were already inside the venue, and his bandmates, who assumed Axl was just being petulant as usual. According to Duff, the cancelled Oslo show was the final straw for Izzy.

"I could see right then and there that Izzy wasn't going to last," the bassist recalled. "The cadence of his walk was different now. I saw it as clearly as the lurch of a bicycle with a misshapen wheel. His face was drawn, his eyes blank, his body language exhausted."[416] Izzy threatened to leave the tour, but after thinking it over, the guitarist agreed to finish out the last two European dates, one in Germany and a final stop at Wembley Stadium in London.

Nine inch nails

GNR's show in Mannheim, Germany was held at Maimarktgelände, a massive outdoor stadium with a capacity north of 75,000. The doors opened at 1:30 p.m. with the concert scheduled to begin at 4:30. Nine Inch Nails performed as the third act on the bill, hand-selected by Axl, who continued to praise the group to anyone within earshot. By all accounts, Trent Reznor and company's synth-based industrial goth was not well received by the German fans, who were impatient for Guns to take the stage. The crowd was slightly more tolerant of Skid Row's brain-bashing metal, but everyone was there to see GNR – the sooner, the better.

Guns were only five songs into their set in Mannheim when Axl was struck by an object thrown from the audience. The singer was standing to the far-left side of the stage, high up on a platform, out of sight from the rest of the group. Axl felt insane with rage. Night after night, he went on and had objects thrown at him by his supposed fans. "Thanks a lot," the singer said sarcastically and strode offstage, tossing his microphone up in the air behind him as he went.

The band was in the middle of playing "Live and Let Die" and the number quickly ground to a halt. Everyone looked at one another, puzzled. No one had seen what happened, so they assumed the singer was just doing his rock-star prima donna trip again. "Axl walked off for what reason I have no idea," Slash recalled. "He wasn't getting heckled as far as I could see, no one hit him with a bottle or anything, but he wasn't having it."[417]

"We're gonna take a quick break for a second and change guitars," Slash told the spectators with a straight face. "We'll talk to you in a second." No one was buying it. When Guns walked off stage, the entire stadium began booing. By this point, the group's reputation for shortchanging audiences was known the world over. Everyone in the crowd knew Axl might stop a show after twenty minutes, never to return.

"When Axl left the stage in Germany, another riot looked inevitable," Duff recalled.[418] The band tried to confront their singer, but they could not find him. The outdoor venue's stage was located a mile from the dressing rooms and production area, and the only way to get there was by van. When Axl walked off stage he hopped into a van and ordered it to take him to the dressing rooms. But the driver could not budge. The promoters had locked the gates surrounding the stage, prohibiting Axl from driving off. The increasingly restless concertgoers continued to boo, chant, and throw things, as police in riot gear prepared for the worst. With little choice, Axl finally exited the van, returned to the stage, and finished the concert, averting tragedy by a hair.

Out the door

The minute the show in Germany was over, Izzy was out the door. Guns had a week off before they had to be in London to play

Wembley, so the entire band – minus Izzy – flew to Ibiza, where they were booked into a boutique hotel for several days.

By all accounts, GNR's final gig with Izzy as a member was a good one. Axl showed up exactly on time and the group gave their all before a sold-out throng of 72,000. "We played spectacularly well, as fierce and inspired and together as ever before," Duff recalled. "It could have been mistaken for one of our club shows."[419] By the time Guns hit Wembley, road-tested tunes like "Bad Obsession" were coming into their own, with Matt and Duff locking into a tight groove as Dizzy peppered the top with piano notes.

Despite the strength of the *Illusion* material, the audience saved their biggest applause for the *Appetite* classics. And whether it was at the Ritz or in Rio, no song got a bigger reception than "Welcome to the Jungle." Guns frequently saved "Jungle" for the encore, sometimes even closing with it. At Wembley, the number appeared early in the setlist to hype up the crowd as much as possible.

MTV was videotaping a track at Wembley, to be broadcast six days later as part of the 1991 Video Music Awards. With GNR out of the U.S. on tour, MTV was willing to do almost anything for the VMAs to include a live clip from the world's hottest rock band. If a pre-taped concert recording was the best they could do, they'd take it.

"You Could Be Mine" was nominated in two VMA categories: best hard-rock/metal video and best song from a film. (GNR would lose to Aerosmith and Chris Isaak, respectively.) MTV requested Guns tape a live rendition of the *Terminator 2* hit, but Axl wanted to feature something newer, selecting "Live and Let Die" – the perfect tune to broadcast from the Beatles' homeland.

"This is something we recorded for Mr. Paul McCartney. It's something we'll be filming for the MTV music awards, with all you fuckers in it. It's something on *Use Your Illusion I*, a little different than you'll hear it tonight. This is called 'Live and Let Die.'"

GNR submitted an abbreviated version of the tune. During the performance, Axl sported his now trademark tartan kilt and red flannel, which he wore over a T-shirt bearing a "no martyr" slogan. There were few overt signs of tension between Axl and Izzy, other than Axl again recusing himself for the bulk of "Dust N' Bones." The singer sprinted onstage at the very end of the song, sharing a single microphone with Izzy and Slash to close out the number.

Axl was on his best behavior at Wembley. Other than a short diatribe against the press to introduce "Double Talkin' Jive, the singer mostly kept the proceedings moving forward. He wrung every ounce of drama from "Civil War," sporting an American flag overcoat and a white cowboy hat.

To close out the night, Axl thanked several members of the crew by name. "This is the end of our first two legs of this Get in the Ring tour. We'd like to thank you for coming and making our last night the biggest night of this tour. And if we're real lucky, maybe you'll like the album and you'll have us back next year." Guns finished with their preferred closer, "Paradise City," an *Appetite* classic that never failed to bring the house down. The Illusion trek's rocky European leg ended on a triumphant note at Wembley, but Izzy's growing disenchantment left the group rattled as GNR made their way home to L.A.

Give in to me

Slash loved touring so much, he stayed in hotels when he wasn't on the road. In early August, shortly after Guns returned from Europe, the guitarist was in his room at the Hyatt Regency on Sunset when the phone rang. "Slash?" a timid voice asked. It was Michael Jackson, calling to tell the guitarist he had a tune for his forthcoming effort, *Dangerous,* he would not include unless Slash played on it. Jackson overnighted Slash a demo of a slow-burning ballad called "Give in To Me." According to Slash, the tape had no vocals and "no guitars other than some slow picking. I called him and sang over the phone what I wanted to do."[420] Jackson immediately agreed. "He's going to delay the project until I can get into the studio," Slash said. "The song is perfect for me. I'm practicing it right now; I'm going to wail."[421]

The "Give in To Me" session took place at the Record Plant. When Slash arrived, Jackson was there and the two finally met in person. Brooke Shields was there, too. "I really want to thank you so much for being on my album," Jackson told the guitarist. "I can't wait to hear what you come up with."[422] Jackson and Brooke Shields left, and Slash taped his parts for "Give in To Me."

A few days later, Slash returned to the Record Plant and laid down guitar on Jackson's track "Black or White." His parts were not included on *Dangerous*, although a snippet of his unused playing was incorporated into the introduction of the "Black or White" video, where child actor Macaulay Culkin irritates his parents by playing loud music in his bedroom.[423]

Father figure

Josh Richman was an actor and trust fund kid who had grown up in the Hollywood entertainment business, doing everything from radio voiceovers to bit parts in movies such as *River's Edge* and *Heathers* and TV shows such as *21 Jump Street*. Richman, whose father co-founded the Seattle Supersonics, grew up around the other children of Hollywood's well-to-do set, including Erin Everly. Now twenty-six, Richman owned a place in the Hollywood Hills, close to Axl, and was a man about town. A would-be eccentric, Richman wandered around wearing socks with no shoes and toting an eight-ball topped cane.

Richman's wealth, local connections, and access to drugs made him a Sunset Strip insider whose constellation included players such as Taime Downe, Rikki Rachtman, and Slash. Through these concentric social circles, Richman eventually befriended Axl. Axl was a huge *River's Edge* fan, and was somewhat awestruck by Richman, who knew half of Hollywood and seemed to understand everything about the filmmaking process.

Axl had been unhappy with the music video for "Patience," which he believed had been put together in a haphazard manner and then streamed endlessly on MTV. The video for "You Could Be Mine" was buoyed by Arnold Schwarzenegger's star power but was unremarkable otherwise. "I want to make big-time videos," Axl told

Richman, showing him George Michael's "Father Figure." "*That's what I want to do.*"[424]

A series of brainstorming sessions ensued. The pair used "Without You," a short story written by Axl's friend Del James, as the foundation for a longer narrative that would take place over three music videos. "Without You" was inspired by Axl and Erin Everly's troubled relationship. "It was frightening to be around them," James recalled. "There was so much insanity that was brought upon by their love and their insecurities that had inspired me to write this short story."[425] James' narrative chronicles the tragic tale of Mayne, a troubled rock star, and his tumultuous encounters with a woman named Elizabeth. As with "Sweet Child O' Mine," Mayne writes a song about Elizabeth that tops the charts and yields international fame, but also brings out the singer's obsessive tendencies. "He'd called her a dozen times over the course of two days, leaving message after message on her answering machine," James wrote. "Even though she never responded, he'd left her ten all-access passes at Will Call. She never showed."[426] Seeking reconciliation, Mayne eventually barges into Elizabeth's apartment, only to find she has committed suicide. In James' short story, the hit single Mayne writes about Elizabeth is called "Without You." After James completed the story, Axl was inspired to write the song "Without You," whose title the singer later changed to "Estranged."

"We started talking about the story, we started writing it and storyboarding it," Richman recalled of his collaboration with Axl.[427] They drew liberally from James' "Without You" but also from Axl's own life, including his experiences with regression therapy. They added new scenes, including a wedding and a funeral. They mapped out a complete narrative, to take place over a trio of videos. *Illusion's* lead single "Don't Cry" would be the first, followed by "November Rain," and then "Estranged." Each of the videos would be linked, collectively recounting the larger tale.

Axl insisted *Illusion's* videos be on par with megabudget, high-concept fare from superstars such as Michael Jackson and Madonna. He had initially tapped Sean Penn to direct "Don't Cry," but by the time Guns were ready to begin, Penn was busy shooting *The Indian*

Runner. Instead, Axl hired Andy Morahan, the director of George Michael's "Father Figure." Morahan, mild-mannered and British, had also helmed iconic videos for some of the biggest names in the business, including Van Halen, Elton John, and Billy Joel.

The "Don't Cry" shoot took place over several days in Los Angeles in September 1991, not long after GNR put in their last gig with Izzy at Wembley. In the video, Axl portrays Mayne through a series of past and present-life selves. He appears as a literal demon, naked and done up in garish green body makeup. He staggers drunk through a snowstorm wearing an 18th-century military uniform, toting a revolver and a bottle of booze. He struggles to keep from drowning amidst a rollicking ocean storm. He shakes while undergoing regression therapy in the office of a psychologist, played by Axl's real-life therapist Suzzy London. He lies in a hospital bed where he is confronted by two alternate versions of himself. Near the end of the video, a tombstone is engraved with the words "W. Axl Rose 1962-1990," there because "I was a walking dead man," according to Axl.[428]

In the video, Mayne's relationship with Elizabeth, portrayed by Axl's new girlfriend supermodel Stephanie Seymour, is depicted as troubled. They sit for a picnic lunch in a graveyard. Elizabeth becomes jealous when she sees Mayne chatting with a woman as he plays piano in a restaurant, so she throws the competitor to the floor and strikes her repeatedly across the face. The couple has a physical altercation in Mayne's condo that involves a gun. "With our video, you don't necessarily know what's going on, but in real life that happened with Erin and myself," Axl said. "I was going to shoot myself. We fought over the gun, and I finally let her win. I was kind of mentally crippled after that."[429]

Axl had always drawn upon his past and present relationships to write song lyrics, but there was something surreal about reenacting those experiences with Stephanie on a film set. "It's weird to be involved in a relationship where the person I'm involved with is actually playing parts that are written about the two of us, about fictional characters, about things in my past relationships. It's a very touchy thing to do."[430]

Even more difficult was the drowning scene, which Axl described as one of the hardest things he'd ever done. The sequence was shot in a huge indoor swimming pool at a Hollywood studio lot. There were bubble machines that could reproduce a violent sea. The cameras would roll, and Axl's flotation device would be pulled away. He would struggle and pretend to go under. When Axl couldn't handle any more, he would flash a peace sign and four scuba divers would rush in to pull him to the side of the pool. "After three takes I was done," the singer said. "I couldn't do it again because I was so exhausted. But it was a real mind trip because that's how my life had felt for I don't know how many years, especially in my last relationship. I've always felt like I was drowning, trying to save us both, being pulled down."[431]

After the scene was taped, Axl went back to his trailer and broke down. "That was just a metaphoric scene of how I really felt. It was really disturbing and hard to do, but by doing it, it helped me heal and get over certain things."[432]

"Don't Cry's" most iconic sequence takes place when Slash drives a vintage Ford Mustang through a series of canyons while being screamed at and slapped by a beguiling hellcat in the passenger seat. Fed up, the guitarist steers the car off a cliff, and it explodes in a burst of flame and fire. The camera pans up and we see Slash survived, casting off a solo on his Les Paul, shirtless on a mountaintop.

In another memorable scene, GNR perform "Don't Cry" live atop the Transamerica skyscraper in downtown Los Angeles at night. Izzy is missing, his absence noted by a sign asking, "Where's Izzy." Shannon Hoon was on hand, duetting with Axl, and the resulting footage was cinematic. Director Andy Morahan recalled, "We had two police helicopters flying with their big spotlight beams, and that felt like we were shooting the biggest movie at that time."[433]

As always, there were grand ambitions behind these endeavors – and driven by them. "If it works, it's the first step towards bigger types of projects," Axl said on the set of "Don't Cry." "Not necessarily just for videos; if we want to film something feature-length, this is our first try at it."[434]

By all accounts, the production was challenging, with Axl's perfectionism and insistence on greatness keeping tensions high. The singer peppered the video with Easter eggs and tiny details. At one point, he can be seen wearing a St. Louis Cardinals baseball cap. There are also shout outs to Jane's Addiction, Nirvana, and the Red Hot Chili Peppers, a nod to the explosion of interest in the burgeoning alternative rock genre. "He's difficult," Richman said of Axl. "If he didn't like the way the picture was hung on the wall, it would have to be moved. He was such a stickler for detail. Everybody walked on eggshells."[435] Axl's mood swings added to the air of unpredictability, according to Morahan. "It just depended on what was going on in his life on that particular day – sometimes he was in the mood for it, sometimes he wasn't."[436]

During the shoot, the production team spent a good deal of time trying to keep the peace between the band members, all of whom required various degrees of placation and ego stroking. Duff was upset the video did not feature him in a standalone scene, the way it did Axl and Slash. So, Morahan quickly cooked up a vignette where a woman confronts Duff in a hotel lobby and smashes a bottle dramatically on the floor. Only a few seconds of the footage made the video's final cut, but it was enough to appease Duff on the set. "I was wrangling not only the creative forces – Axl and Slash – while also having to go and have meetings with the other members of the band to tell them what was going on," Morahan recalled. "It was a constant state of juggling everything."

The finished video came across more conceptual than narrative-driven, but the images were striking, heightening the drama of GNR's earliest ballad. "It was essentially meant to be a trailer for this trilogy and then the ultimate movie that Axl wanted to make," Richman said. "People were sniffing around; Scorsese was sniffing around."[437]

Sedona

Guns issued "Don't Cry" as a single in early September, a couple of weeks before *Illusion's* release. The CD single featured an alternative version Axl cooked up in a fit of inspiration one night in the studio. The alt version contained a different melody and lyrics, laid over the same instrumental as the original. Axl insisted both versions appear on *Illusion*. The "Don't Cry" single also included the original 1985 demo, taped at GNR's first-ever recording at Mystic Studios in Los Angeles.

The "Don't Cry" demo featured Steven Adler on drums, giving listeners a sense of how the *Illusion* track might have sounded had he remained in the band. The demo's production is wanting, the tempo is slower, and there is a brief spoken-word passage in the mid-section, a sweet, youthful nod to Hanoi Rocks' "Don't You Ever Leave Me." But Slash's solo is nearly identical to its *Illusion* counterpart, and Axl brings the number to a climax almost entirely with the power of his siren wail. Even in primordial form, "Don't Cry" was clearly a smash. It is no surprise Guns revisited the track during two subsequent demo sessions in 1986.

Like the cover of *Illusion*, the artwork for the "Don't Cry" single was acquired by Axl on a whim. Earlier that spring, the singer and Stephanie Seymour were visiting Sedona, Arizona, where they happened into Gallery One, a downtown art retailer. Axl was awestruck by *Ascension*, a 60-by-40-inch abstract painting by Santa Fe artist Kirk Hughey. "I dreamt this last night," the singer told Seymour, before purchasing the acrylic painting on the spot.[438]

"His business manager immediately sought me out to buy the painting and get the reproduction rights so that they could use it on the album," Hughey told a reporter, adding that "Don't Cry" was his favorite track on *Illusion*. "It took a lot of negotiating between myself and Rose's business managers and lawyers. I feel that we made a pretty good deal. We took the high road, and they negotiated down a little bit. I'm very happy with it."

Axl was in Sedona to see Sharon Maynard, a purported psychic energy healer who was recommended by his therapist Suzzy London. Axl sought out London, Maynard, and other holistic and spiritual therapists because he wanted to know himself, to make sense of his life. As a child, Axl was raised under horrific conditions, surviving only through an unyielding faith that one day he would be a rich and world-famous rock star. That Axl was seemingly able to manifest this destiny through sheer force of will, instilled in him an almost supernatural belief in mind power and other unseen forces. It was Axl's lived experience that one could become a powerful shaper of their own destiny through intensely channeled thought. How should he make sense of this? What did it mean? And how might he harness that power going forward?

London suggested they try past life regression, where a patient is hypnotized and supposedly remembers traumas they experienced in previous incarnations, some dating back hundreds or thousands of years. "Patients may speak in the voice or the language of that long-dead being, whether it be a Roman ruler or a Southern plantation slave. Past-life adherents tend to believe that one lives one's life with different incarnations of the same group of people."[439] This widely discredited practice has been compared to fortune telling and palm reading, predicated largely on the power of suggestion. Through these past-life regression therapy sessions, Axl became convinced he had been married to both Erin Everly and Stephanie Seymour in multiple past lives.

Sharon Maynard and her husband Elliott ran a Sedona nonprofit out of their home called Arcos Cielos Corporation that offered consultations to high-end clients.[440] Sharon claimed to be an expert in psychic energy, providing insight through aura readings and cleansing her clients of negative energy from current and past lives. Maynard claimed she could even read someone's energy from a photograph. At Suzzy London's suggestion, Axl traveled to Sedona that spring so Maynard could read his and Stephanie's auras and cleanse them of any impurities. Axl would continue to hire Sharon Maynard for her supposed psychic energy expertise throughout the Illusion tour. Skid Row drummer Rob Affuso claimed Maynard sometimes advised Axl as to the best time to go onstage. "Axl would be like, 'I can't go on until 11:17 and thirty seconds because that's when my healer told me the stars are aligned right.'"[441] Axl thanked Sharon and Elliott Maynard in *Illusion's* liner notes.

Paying dividends

On September 17, 1991, *Use Your Illusion I* and *II* were finally released, with more than 1,000 record stores around the U.S. opening at midnight to sell them. At Tower Records on the Sunset Strip – across the street from the Tower Video outlet where Axl once worked – more than 400 fans waited in line to be among the first to snap up the twin discs. Geffen reported selling an average of 500 copies of *Illusion* at each store that held midnight sales, accounting for more than half a million CDs and yielding more than $5 million.[442]

After years of waiting and reportedly spending more than $1.5 million to produce *Illusion*, the record company's investment was finally paying dividends.[443] Geffen took out a four-page ad in *Billboard* that week to celebrate. "This is the most exciting thing that's ever happened in the music business," president Eddie Rosenblatt gushed to the *L.A. Times*.[444]

In the U.S., each *Illusion* release retailed for $15.98 on CD and double LP and $10.98 on cassette. "I like this more than having a $29.98 album," said Lew Garrett, vice-president of purchasing for Camelot Music, a 300-store chain. "It's a real innovative move. Nothing like this has been tried."[445]

In retail outlets, *Illusion I* and *II* were stickered with a warning label: "This album contains language some listeners may find objectionable. They can f?I* off and buy something from the new age section." As a result of the curse word on the sticker, Walmart and Kmart refused to carry GNR's new release. Despite the prohibition, *Illusion I* sold 685,000 copies and *II* sold 770,000 in their first week.[446] (By comparison, Metallica's "black" album had been released weeks earlier and sold about 600,000 units.) The records would enter the Billboard chart at numbers one and two, the first time in history any act ever achieved that feat.[447] Within a year, each release would sell more than four million copies in the U.S.[448]

Illusion's two standalone albums filled an entire 76-minute CD apiece, totaling thirty tracks that yielded about two-and-a-half hours of music. The cover art was identical save for the color schemes, with *Illusion 1* in red and yellow and *Illusion II* in blue and purple.

Legacy

How do you follow up the best-selling and most critically acclaimed debut album of all time? If you are Guns N' Roses, you overwhelm the listeners with new material. Axl never viewed *Illusion* as anything other than a singular musical statement, an epic composition that didn't let up for two-and-a-half hours. "I've never looked at it as two separate albums," he said. "That was Geffen Records' marketing plan. I've always looked at it as an entire package. For me it fits together perfectly for the thirty songs in a row."[449]

The sprawling, thirty-track opus had something for everyone, from face-peeling rockers to orchestral ballads to left-field experiments. Those looking for hard rock found plenty to enjoy in tunes like "Right Next Door to Hell," "Garden of Eden," "Perfect Crime," "Don't Damn Me," and "You Could Be Mine." Mid-tempo groovefests such as "Bad Obsession" "Dust N' Bones," "Bad Apples" and "Pretty Tied Up" provided swagger and swing in equal measure. The lighter-lofting balladry on "November Rain" and "Don't Cry" both looked back and added to the legacy of the band that spawned *Appetite*. "You Ain't the First" gave a nod to the ribald acoustics of the *Lies* sessions. Guns looked ahead on complex numbers such as "Estranged" and "Coma" which contained tempo shifts and took place across multiple musical movements. "My World" sounded like nothing the group had ever produced.

GNR included plenty of throwback material on *Illusion*. Pedestrian rock tunes like "Back Off Bitch" were clearly drawn from the band's club days. But Axl came into his own as an artist on *Illusion*, contributing to 22 out of the 28 original numbers. The singer's newest material – "Estranged," "Breakdown," "Locomotive" – and his extravagant vision for epic tunes such as "November Rain" forever freed Guns from their Sunset Strip roots.

The addition of Axl and Dizzy's piano, keyboard, and organ on more than half the tracks made *Illusion* sound utterly different from *Appetite*. Nothing changed GNR's sound more than this element, generally for the better. This enabled Guns to expand their musical horizons and helped achieve Axl's goal of positioning the group alongside their classic-rock heroes of the 1970s. The emergence of Izzy and Duff as lead singers enabled the band to paint with a broader palette, too.

Matt Sorum also brought something new to the table on *Illusion*, burdened with the unenviable task of replacing Steven Adler. Sorum has been heavily criticized over the years for his supposed leaden feel and lack of musical chemistry — reproofs that have sometimes come from members of GNR. But those critiques have not stood the test of time. Simply, Sorum puts in a powerhouse, two-and-a-half hour performance brimming with creative playing and iconic moments. His propulsive energy drives rockers such as "Double Talkin' Jive," "Locomotive (Complicity)," and "Garden of Eden." He locks into swinging grooves on "Bad Obsession" and "Pretty Tied Up." Matt's musical instincts elevate "Live and Let Die," where he adds signature flourishes and fills that easily topped Wings' original. And his collaboration with Axl on the trilogy of "Don't Cry," "November Rain," and "Estranged" resulted in a symphonic flavor that made the songs sound larger than life. That Sorum had less than sixty days to learn all the material, write iconic drum parts for each number, and then record everything in single takes makes his contributions to *Illusion* even more significant.

Less present was Izzy Stradlin, who wrote some of *Illusion's* standout tracks, but did not distinguish himself as a guitarist the way had on *Appetite*. "Izzy basically left while we were recording the *Illusion* records," Slash said in 1994. "He's not on half of those records. He hardly even played on his own songs."[450] Slash was happy to pick up the slack, of course, sometimes dominating both sides of the tracks with a legion of six-string instrumentation. "Where the hell is my guitar? It's gone!" Izzy said to himself after hearing the final mixes.[451] But Slash's intentions were pure. The amount of care he and Axl put into Izzy's material — the lilting Spanish guitar coda on "Double Talkin' Jive," the multilayered backing vocals on "Dust N' Bones" — proved how important they considered his compositions to be.

If *Illusion* had a drawback, it was that Axl and Slash overdelivered, filling every millimeter of space with sound. Axl and

Slash's divergent instincts paid off beautifully on *Appetite*, a built-in system of checks and balances that was musically complex without feeling busy. On *Illusion*, Slash added a full orchestra's worth of six-stringed devices, sometimes layering dozens of instruments onto the tracks. Not to be outdone, Axl doubled and tripled his lead vocals until they were as thick and impenetrable as pavement. As if this wasn't enough, the singer threw in a choir's worth of howls, wails, moans, whistles, cries, laughs, asides, and affirmations, all in different pitches and timbres. Unlike *Appetite*, there was no one willing to restrain Axl this time around. Let him go crazy and we'll fix it later, the thinking seemed to be. With no room to breathe, the songs suffocated.

This came from a place of ambition and heart, of wanting *Illusion* to be the greatest album ever produced. It also stemmed from Axl's perfectionist tendencies. "Everything on that record is exactly the way we wanted it," the singer declared a year after *Illusion* dropped. "I can find a couple of points where a note wasn't quite in time, and a couple of things like that, the vocal speech at the end of 'Breakdown.' The mix on the speakers we did the mastering on was loud enough, but on other sets of speakers it's not. It depends on what stereo you're hearing it on."[452]

Of course, this was not the first time a musical artist has swung for the fences by issuing an ambitious double LP, and minor quibbles aside, Guns absolutely knocked it out of the park. Had the band broken up after *Appetite*, they would still be considered legendary, but *Use Your Illusion* forever cemented their legacy and earned them a place alongside the most important acts in rock history.

Critical responses

When GNR released *Illusion* that September, the group was at the apex of their fame, appearing on the cover of nearly every major rock and metal magazine, including *Rolling Stone, Musician, Rip, Kerrang, Hit Parader, Circus, Raw, Melody Maker, Faces,* and *Vox.* The September 1991 edition of *Spin* included a lengthy article on the band that was featured in bold letters on the magazine's cover.

In addition to the raft of feature stories, most of these outlets also published reviews of *Illusion*. Wanting to avoid leaks, Guns were hypervigilant about keeping the unreleased material under wraps. Reviewers seeking advance copies were told the only way to hear *Illusion* was to sit and listen to it at the offices of Geffen Records, under the supervision of a staffer. "Security was so tight," complained Janiss Garza of *Entertainment Weekly*. "I was searched and my purse temporarily confiscated. Only then, with no chance that I might tape the CD or walk off with it, was I allowed to hear *Illusion*. What's the world coming to when reviewing a record feels like being in jail?"[453]

Despite the harsh treatment, Garza liked what she heard, grading the project an A in her review: "The band's often-neglected search for light is honest and open, and so is its fatal attraction to darkness; on both *Illusion* albums the quintet teeter-totters between the two extremes." *Kerrang* also gave *Illusion* five out of five stars, proclaiming the set to be a "flawed masterpiece" and "the albums of the decade."[454]

Rolling Stone rated both efforts four out of five stars, describing *Illusion I* as "physically assaultive, verbally incendiary and at times downright screwy." The reviewer praised "Don't Damn Me" as the disc's high point, but criticized "Don't Cry" for being "too sweet and pleading" and described "Dead Horse" as a "desultory acoustic complaint."[455] The *Los Angeles Times* assigned 3.5 and 4 stars out of a possible five to *I* and *II*, respectively, with the reviewer noting the set "shows added ambition and authority as GNR moves in new and accomplished directions."[456]

Reviewers applauded the band's desire to expand their sound and explore new musical terrain. They enjoyed Axl's piano ballads and cheered Slash's guitar wizardry. Guns were regularly compared to hardcore rappers such as N.W.A, who also foregrounded anger in their art. "There are more ballads but less bliss on *Illusion*," wrote the *LA Weekly* in a lengthy dissection of the release. "They are the angriest two records to ever sit at the top of the charts."[457]

Many reviews were critical of GNR's cover of "Live and Let Die." For example, in an otherwise glowing assessment, *Vox* opined, "Axl's singing borders on self-parody" on the number.[458] Others criticized the growing sense of victimhood on songs like "Don't Damn Me." *Time* magazine accused Guns of having an "inexhaustible capacity for self-pity. Having been coddled from birth by their record company and by MTV and having been given a free ride by the rock press, the Gunners nevertheless cannot get off the whinemobile, as they moan about the demanding life of a rock star. According to *Forbes*, the Gunners will earn $25 million in 1990-91. These guys don't know how to take yes for an answer."[459]

Reviews published by the outlets Axl called out by name in "Get in the Ring" either highlighted or completely ignored the track in their write-ups. Asked about the tune, *Spin* publisher Bob Guccione Jr. told the *Los Angeles Times*, "If Axl wants a fight, he's got it. I'm willing to get in the ring with him, anyplace, anytime. Either Axl should back up his threat or he should stop singing the song."[460]

Izzy shuffles off

Rumors Izzy was quitting GNR were rampant at the time of *Illusion's* release. The October 5 edition of *Billboard* magazine included two front-page features on Guns, one about *Illusion's* first-week sales and chart performance and another titled "Izzy or Isn't He Leaving GNR?" The latter story pointed out the guitarist's no shows in the videos for "You Could Be Mine" and "Don't Cry," his traveling separately from the group on the road, and his apparent reluctance to take on a long, international megatour. The story claimed the next leg of the Illusion trek was scheduled to begin in mid-October but had been pushed back due to "Stradlin's tenuous status as a touring member of the band."[461]

Izzy didn't stick around for the release of *Illusion*; he was back in Indiana, driving a motocross through the backwoods and thinking about what to do next. He was ambivalent about GNR, uncertain if he should walk away or continue to weather the storm. "My interest in Guns N' Roses was starting to wane," Izzy admitted.[462] "It didn't feel like it used to. Something wasn't happening that used to happen for me."[463]

In early November, the guitarist returned to L.A., where GNR were scheduled to rehearse for the group's upcoming North American tour. It proved to be a showdown of sorts, and a series of long discussions between Axl, Slash, and Izzy took place.

Izzy's ongoing reluctance about Guns was immensely frustrating to everyone in the group. "There were certain things we weren't getting from Izzy, that we really wanted," Axl explained. "We thought that everybody should give energy in a certain way to Guns N' Roses, and we weren't getting that." They couldn't believe Izzy blew off video shoots but still expected to be paid the same as everyone else. "You're not giving an equal share," Axl told him.[464] Axl and Slash urged Izzy to do more, to get involved, to start showing up and acting like he gave a shit.

"He wouldn't do anything," Axl complained to *Rolling Stone* a few months after the L.A. showdown. "Slash and I are having to do too much work to keep the attention and the energy up in the crowd. I'm onstage going, 'This is really hard, and I'm into it and I'm doing it, but that guy just gets to stand there.' When the guy's getting up at 6:30 in the morning and riding bicycles and motorcycles and he's donating all this energy to something else, and it's taking one hundred percent of our energy to do what we're doing on the stage, we were getting ripped off."[465]

Izzy was offended. He wasn't the one who was always late to shows, who continually walked offstage, who caused riots, and marred the group's reputation with the public. He wasn't the one who generated hundreds of thousands of dollars in fines and penalties. Nor did he spend every waking hour in a drink-and-drug stupor. GNR's founding guitarist didn't feel like he owed anyone in the group anything. Izzy skipped the next rehearsal.

Axl called Izzy and the two longtime friends had one final talk. The singer informed the guitarist his standing as a full partner of the band was being adjusted downward. The argument was the other full partners – Axl, Slash, and Duff – were conducting the lion's share of the group's business, everything from doing interviews with the press to working the crowd during live performances. Given Izzy was not putting in an equal share of the work, he should not be entitled to an equal share of the pay. Axl encouraged Izzy to continue writing for Guns, earning royalties and maintaining his connection to the band.

The guitarist shook his head and smiled. So that's how it was going to be, after fifteen years of friendship. Izzy felt like the decision was being made for him. "Axl made it real clear to me that he was going to be running things, so to speak, and there were some conditions put up that I was going to have to go by. He was trying to make it good for me as well, I guess, but at the same time I realized that was it, I was done."[466]

The next day, Izzy officially resigned, retaining GNR's former manager Alan Niven to negotiate his exit. Izzy's businesslike withdrawal irked everyone in the group, who considered the guitarist to be a friend. "When he left, he didn't even resign to us," Slash recalled a couple of weeks later, still stinging from Izzy's departure. "He called the office and sent out a memo to everybody. There was a certain amount of hurt in that."[467]

Axl was blamed for Izzy's quitting Guns, but it was the last thing the singer wanted. "If people think I don't respect Izzy or acknowledge his talent, they're sadly mistaken," the singer said. "He was my friend. I haven't always been right. Sometimes I've been massively wrong, and Izzy's been the one to help steer me back to the things that were right."[468]

Just as Izzy and GNR were parting ways, the group issued a music video for "Live and Let Die." Directed by Axl's actor buddy Josh Richman, the video blended images and film clips of the band members as children with live footage taken from the first two legs of the Illusion trek. The video captures the raw energy, athleticism, and high fashion of the tour, making ample use of the MTV broadcast of "Live and Let Die" from Wembley. The piece was also bittersweet because it chronicled Izzy on his final outing with the group he helped found with his old friend from Indiana. At one point, a milk carton flies across the screen featuring a picture of Izzy with the word *Missing* over it.

But Izzy wasn't missing, he was gone. And with their guitarist and key songwriter out of the band, Guns were down to three original members just as the biggest release of their career was hitting the shelves. Arena gigs were only weeks away and once again GNR had to scramble to find someone to step in. Steven Adler's departure slowed the group down as they looked for a new drummer to record *Illusion*. This time, they had just weeks to find a suitable replacement for their iconic and beloved rhythm guitarist. Failing to find a substitute for Izzy meant total disaster, the collapse of the entire Illusion tour.

Chapter 10

Thriller

"Do you know where the fuck you are? You're in the Garden, baby, and you're gonna dieeeeeeee!" It was sometime past one o'clock in the morning and GNR were more than two hours into their first-ever headlining performance at Madison Square Garden. This was night one of three sold-out shows and Guns were giving it their all.

As usual, the band went on late, beginning at nearly 11 p.m. and refusing to let up until 1:30 in the morning. Per custom, they were fined for doing so, more than $24,000 in union overtime fees, according to Axl, who told the crowd they were worth every penny. It was business as usual in other ways, too. Axl stopped the show to offer a long-winded diatribe about *Circus* and *Spin*, two magazines that had earned his ire.

But much had changed since GNR stepped off the stage in London three months earlier. Izzy was no longer there to sing lead, so "Dust N' Bones" and "14 Years" were excised from the setlist and Duff was recruited to give Axl's voice a break. At the Garden, the bassist slammed through an amped-up cover of the Misfits' "Attitude," a track that eventually wound up on GNR's cover album. Later in the show, Duff sang lead on his *Illusion* contribution, "So Fine."

There were a few other surprises, too. In the middle of "Rocket Queen," Axl threw in a couple of verses from "It Tastes Good, Don't

It?" a tune he once described onstage as "Guns N' Roses version of a rap song." GNR had only played the ribald hip-hop number a few times in concert, and Axl airing it at the Garden was an indicator that his mood was upbeat.

For everyone involved, selling out the Garden was a moment, perhaps *the* sign they had made it. No other venue in the world carried the same weight. "I arrived in this band that was the modern version of Led Zeppelin," Matt Sorum told me. "I remember riding in a limo up the back way through Madison Square Garden and going, 'Man, this is exactly like *Song Remains the Same*.' I was in the limo, driving up the ramp, getting on the private 747 jet – living everything I'd dreamed."[469]

The second North American leg of the Illusion trek was even larger than the first, taking GNR across the country as they headlined large arenas and titanic stadiums. Axl had put together a new wardrobe for this part of the tour, retiring many of the iconic pieces from the earlier rounds. At Madison Square Garden, the singer took the stage in a rose-colored tuxedo jacket over matching red bicycle shorts and black combat boots.

For "Civil War," three oversized flags were unfurled from the rafters: Confederate, Russian, and USA. Axl wanted to make a point about how nations battle one another but also themselves. He began the number in a black leather jacket with the word "rebel" on the back above a Confederate flag. The so-called "rebel flag" was a pop-culture staple in the 1970s and 1980s, cropping up in TV shows like *The Dukes of Hazzard* and on Billy Idol's guitar circa *Rebel Yell*. In an ostensible plea for national unity, midway through "Civil War," Axl changed into the Stars-and-Stripes jacket he'd made famous during the early Illusion concerts.

Slash wore a Superman T-shirt at the Garden, appropriate considering his musical powers and unbound energy. The boots-planted headbanger of the *Appetite* era had been replaced by a ramp-dashing dervish who enjoyed taking five-foot leaps off the risers.

GNR opened with "Nightrain" and "Mr. Brownstone," getting two *Appetite* staples out of the way before launching into "Live and Let Die," whose music video had just been released to MTV. The video featured highlights from the opening legs of the Illusion trek, but it was a different band onstage at the Garden. There, for the first time, Axl was backed by the group he'd always imagined.

Big guns

Ever since Axl spent time around the Rolling Stones on the Steel Wheels tour, his vision for the Illusion trek included a large ensemble that could faithfully recreate the studio tracks. Axl wanted another keyboard, backup singers, horns, strings, percussion, everything. Part of this was motivated by the singer's artistic ambition and perfectionism, but it was also driven by his insecurities about performing. An ensemble that size could help Axl entertain stadium crowds and absorb some of the attention. Like the small army of specialists who helped the singer prepare for a concert, he wanted a team of pros on stage to help him deliver the best possible show.

A rocker through and through, Slash had no interest in adding to GNR's roster, but he wanted to appease Axl and maintain some semblance of control over the music. So, after Guns returned from the dates in Europe, the guitarist took it upon himself to hire some new touring members. "When this first started coming up, it was around the time that Izzy split," Slash recalled. "At the same time, I was trying to audition musicians to make 'November Rain,' 'Heaven's Door,' and stuff to sound a little bit more like it did on the record. Axl really wanted to get into that, so I got the job of going out and finding something to simulate it. I didn't want anything corny."[470]

Slash's first recruit was Teddy Andreadis, who played harmonica and keyboards for BB Chung King and the Buddaheads, a long-haired, hard-rocking blues act similar to the Black Crowes. Axl wanted someone who could handle Michael Monroe's harmonica part on "Bad Obsession," and Andreadis came recommended. Upon meeting, Axl dubbed him "Zigzag" due to his resemblance to the Jesus lookalike on packs of Zig-Zag rolling papers.

Using Andreadis onstage as a second keyboardist would enable Guns to recreate *Illusion* tracks such as "Yesterdays," which featured both piano and organ. After touring with Dizzy for the past several months, Slash had come around to using keys in GNR, at least in concert. "Keyboards can be difficult to deal with, to balance them with guitars without sacrificing at least one instrument's dynamics," he said. "But keyboards are great, especially live. They give us many more expressive options."[471] In response to Slash's approbation, Dizzy began to insert himself more deliberately into GNR's material during shows.

Axl insisted Slash hire a horn section for the next leg of the Illusion trek. Ever since their club days, Guns had incorporated horns into tunes such as "Move to the City," and their latest single "Live and Let Die" was rooted in them. Slash decided if GNR were going to be forced to add a horn section, it was going to be an all-*female* horn section. The guitarist asked Teddy Andreadis if he knew anyone.

Andreadis was an L.A. industry musician who had a side gig as a keyboardist in a television studio orchestra. One of his bandmates was a saxophonist named Lisa Maxwell. "Hey, I'm looking for some chick horn players. So, I recommended you to Slash," Teddy told her. A week later, Maxwell sat in with Slash at a Hollywood nightclub and was immediately hired. "Can you put a horn section together?" the guitarist asked her. Maxwell enlisted two friends, trumpet player Anne King and CeCe Worrall, who could handle sax, flute, and clarinet. The trio was dubbed the 976 horns and outfitted in bondagewear and lingerie, a fair indicator of how they were initially thought of by Slash and the guys.

"Fishnet body stocking and leather chaps," Lisa Maxwell recalled. "They had a costume designer make these outfits for us. It was like, 'Could we pick out our own outfits?' We kept going back and forth with the band. I don't know if it was the manager or Axl or Slash or whatever, but they were trying to make them look like a slutty bondage-y kind of thing."[472]

Slash spent two weeks rehearsing Andreadis and the horn section at SIR studio on Sunset Boulevard, working out arrangements for "Bad Obsession," "Live and let Die," "November Rain," "Paradise City," and more. At Madison Square Garden, "Move to the City" was buoyed by extended jam, with Teddy grooving away on organ as the horn players traded lines, transforming GNR's old, slight tune into a showstopper.

Just go with it

If Guns had a limitation as a live unit, it was backing vocals. Axl aside, there were no great singers in the group. Izzy and Duff could pull off a passable lead vocal, with plenty of assistance from Axl, but neither were worth a damn as backing vocalists. Backup singing featured heavily on *Illusion* tracks such as "November Rain," "Knockin' on Heaven's Door," and "Live and Let Die," and Axl was adamant GNR faithfully reproduce them in concert.

There was also a practical element to adding backup singers – Axl's vocal cords could not sustain the collateral damage of rigorous touring. Guns had a reputation for playing long sets, which were hard on Axl's voice. Despite hours of vocal warmups and cool downs, his guttural shrieks and wailing cries did serious damage. And the singer held nothing back. Axl exacerbated this by smoking cigarettes. He needed help.

Roberta Freeman was a rising backup vocalist who had already performed with A-listers such as Pink Floyd, Lou Reed, and Nile Rodgers. She had just completed the Heartbreak Station tour with Cinderella and was recommended to Slash by drummer Fred Coury. Slash and Coury were friends – the stickman had subbed for an injured Steven Adler for a few shows on the *Appetite* trek. Slash had the *Illusion* CDs sent over to Freeman and called her the next day, speaking as if she already had the job.

"Did you listen to the album? Just do the arrangements, all the vocal arrangements," Slash instructed."[473]

Freeman was taken aback by Slash's lackadaisical approach. She had listened to *Illusion* and didn't hear a lot of backup vocals, especially female singers. She hoped for some direction, maybe some suggestions from Axl.

"Just do what you think would sound good," Slash told her. "And, oh yeah, we need another singer, too. Can you get another singer?"

Freeman recruited Tracey Amos, whom she had worked with previously. They mapped out vocal arrangements and choreography for several numbers, and she and Tracey joined Slash and the others for rehearsals at SIR.

Slash loved to rehearse, but Axl hated it. Per custom, the singer skipped practices, which made Freeman anxious, worried he would not like the arrangements and she and Tracey would have to start over on a tight schedule. But Axl was nowhere to be seen. "He was kept separate from the other band guys," Freeman recalled. "It was hard to get in to talk to him. He didn't really come to the rehearsals. So here I am, this new hire in charge of creating parts and choreography and I don't have feedback."

Slash was easygoing, mainly because he hated the entire idea of adding backup singers. "Axl is the one who wants this," he told Freeman. "Whatever you think is right, just go with it."[474]

Freeman asked Doug Goldstein if she could speak to Axl, even briefly, but she was rebuffed. "I was told that I could not talk to him," she said. "I didn't know how guarded that whole camp was. They didn't like people to go in and talk to him. It was not like any other gig. It was another level."[475] In the end, Freeman did not meet Axl until after she played her first concert with Guns.[476]

Black or white

On November 14, Michael Jackson released a music video for "Black or White," the first single from his forthcoming album, *Dangerous*. At the time, a new video from Jackson was a cultural event. "Black or White" premiered simultaneously in 69 countries; half a billion viewers tuned in to watch, the largest audience ever for a music video.[477] The piece was directed by acclaimed filmmaker John Landis and was among the first to incorporate a new technology known as morphing, where a series of faces appear to melt from one to the next as they mimed Jackson's song.

Slash had worked on "Black or White" during the *Dangerous* sessions, but his parts were scrapped. A tiny snippet of his unused playing was incorporated into the introduction of the "Black or White" video.[478] In promoting the video, however, Jackson's publicists implied Slash had played on the track, too. Slash was pissed. "That's not me," he said. "That doesn't sound anything like me. So, I was a little pissed off, after all the work we'd done in getting together, when I realized Michael was promoting it as such."[479]

Slash's association with "Back or White" was forever cemented the day after the video premiere when he and Jackson performed it together for MTV's 10th Anniversary Special, which was taped before a live crowd at the Santa Monica Airport. Jackson's set was done up to resemble an inner-city ghetto, including metal trash cans and a dilapidated, graffiti-covered car propped up on cinder blocks. The two music icons ran around the stage, posing and performing together. At one point Slash soloed, kicking over one of the trash cans with his leather boot as he played. Later, he blasted out a second solo while Jackson threw down with a series of his thrilling trademark dance moves. To conclude, Slash blazed away at his Les Paul for a bit and then hurled the instrument through the car's windshield, which shattered in an explosion of smoke and fire.

The MTV anniversary special aired on ABC television on November 27. "I've gotten to know Michael since we first met in the studio and the guy's just a bonafide amazing talent," Slash said of Jackson.[480] "He works really hard, which is something I can appreciate because I don't like to fool around and waste time. He's real personable – and we got the stuff done. It was actually probably easier than anything we do in Guns."[481]

During the taping, Slash also caught a glimpse of Jackson's world when he wasn't on stage. "When he wasn't working, or in production or whatever, it was then you could see that he was sort of at the mercy of his own success," Slash recalled. "All the people he had around him, the tugging, and the yes people, you could tell that he knew ninety percent of them were full of shit. I felt sorry for him in that sense."[482] Slash and Jackson would work together again during the Illusion era, but for now, the guitarist had to return to his own band.

The whole catalog

With Izzy out of the group, GNR had only weeks to find a replacement. They decided to hire a guitarist for the tour, rather than seek a permanent member. Axl was a huge Jane's Addiction fan and badly wanted Dave Navarro for the job. Guns reached out and invited him to a rehearsal, but Navarro was deeply addicted to heroin at the time and never showed up. Guitarist Marc Ford was also invited to go on the road with GNR but turned down the gig because he had just accepted an offer to join the Black Crowes. Ford snubbed Guns in the press, telling the *L.A. Times* playing with the Crowes would be "a lot more fun – it's more my kind of music. I didn't think twice. I'm far more into the Black Crowes' music than the Guns N' Roses thing."[483]

GNR had less than two weeks until their opening night in Massachusetts and were desperate to find a replacement for Izzy. Axl reached out to an old friend from Indiana, Mike Staggs, and Duff called a long-lost buddy, Richard DuGuay. Neither worked out. Slash and Duff held meetings with a number of candidates, just seeing if anyone would fit, but the vibe did not seem right.

Gilby Clarke was a twenty-nine-year-old Cleveland native who had known Guns back in the club days. Gilby's bands, Candy and Kill For Thrills, had played gigs alongside some of Matt's groups, and the guitarist had been acquaintances and jammed with Izzy. After ten fruitless years of trying to make it, Gilby was scraping by as a soundman at a Hollywood nightclub. Rumors were flying around town that GNR were desperately seeking a guitarist. Gilby knew Josh Richman through the local music scene and got him on the phone to ask about the gig.

"We don't know if Izzy's gone for good or what's happening," Richman told him. "But they are looking for a guitar player. You know what? I'm going to give Slash your number."[484]

Slash called Gilby later that night and invited him to audition at Third Encore Studios in North Hollywood. "Hey, man. Will you come down and play? Just learn three songs and come down tomorrow."

Gilby arrived the next day, having learned "Knockin' on Heaven's Door" and "Civil War." Similar to the experience they had with Matt, Gilby fit in instantly and effortlessly. Slash asked him to learn three more numbers and return the next day. Gilby did so and that was it.

Axl did not attend the audition, but he was adamant Gilby was not a suitable guitarist. "I wasn't into it," the singer said. "He was cool, but I didn't want to work with him."[485] Axl did not want a carbon copy of Izzy, he wanted a far-out gunslinger like Dave Navarro who would push GNR in bold new musical directions. But Guns were out of time; Gilby would have to do. "We pretty much had to go with this person, or we were fucked," Axl said, pissed.[486]

A few days after his audition, Gilby's phone rang. It was Slash. "You got the gig. We leave next week. Learn the whole catalog."

Gilby was incredulous. "What? The whole catalog? Don't you have a set of twenty or twenty-five songs?"

"There's no setlist. Axl just calls 'em out, so you gotta know the whole catalog."[487]

Gilby quit his soundman gig and got to work learning the fifty or so tunes he'd be playing in GNR. "I don't know how I did it," the guitarist recalled. "I didn't have songbooks, and nobody even knew what Izzy played. They gave me the records. I'd learn five songs a day. I'd rehearse with them during the day. At night, I would learn five new songs."[488]

Exactly one week after he was hired, Gilby debuted with Guns in front of 14,000 fans at the Centrum in Worcester, Massachusetts. It was his first time playing with Axl. A few days later, they began a three-night stand at Madison Square Garden. "We brought somebody with us who felt a little more like touring and moving around for you people," Axl said, introducing the guitarist to the audience at MSG. Gilby's life would never be the same.

Heels n' horns

The live version of GNR was now twelve members strong and filled the band's multi-tiered stage. The three-piece 976 Horns were set up on a catwalk directly behind Matt's drum riser, high above center stage. Backup singers Roberta and Tracey flanked them to the left and right, and Teddy Andreadis's keyboards were placed on a platform to Matt's left, directly facing Dizzy.

Gilby did his best to fill Izzy's old spot, literally and figuratively. On the opening legs of the Illusion trek, Izzy would introduce "Patience" with a short rhythm guitar piece. The day before his first Guns appearance, Gilby was told to have something ready. Not wanting to encroach on Slash's status as GNR's resident six-string hero, Gilby chose to strum the opening chords to the Rolling Stones' "Wild Horses" while Slash improvised lead notes over the top. Like Dizzy, Gilby intuited the best way to fit in with Guns was to avoid standing out. Besides, Gilby looked and dressed so much like his predecessor many concertgoers never knew the difference. "Yeah, Izzy! All right, Izzy" they shouted from the front rows.[489]

The jumbo-sized GNR was too unwieldy for all-out rockers so the Garden setlist invariably leaned toward mid-paced and slower material. Backup vocalists Roberta and Tracey were prominently featured on "Patience," elevating a song that had always been dragged down live by Duff and Izzy's tuneless yowling. The singers also added their voices to "So Fine" and "Don't Cry," which featured a guest appearance from Shannon Hoon at Madison Square Garden. "Estranged" was given new vocal arrangements as was "Yesterdays," which Guns played at the second Garden show.

"Live and Let Die" featured the entire twelve-piece unit, with CeCe Worrall switching from saxophone to flute. Teddy Andreadis, costumed as a Sunset Strip biker-pirate, sang backup and bashed away at a tambourine, while Roberta and Tracey hit the high, sweet notes. "November Rain" sounded majestic accompanied by the synth strings, piano, organ, bass pedals, and backing vocals. These were not reinterpretations but more fully realized versions of their studio counterparts. As "November Rain" concluded, Andreadis worked the synthesizer, climaxing with the horns at full blare and the backup singers holding their own against Axl's piercing wail. The crescendo was massive, soaring like a Broadway show tune. At last, Axl had musical and vocal support in accordance with his talent and stature as a singer. "Slash put this new band together, did all of the groundwork," he enthused in an interview the following year. "He did such an amazing job that I just can't believe it really happened. I'm glad to be a part of it. It's a pretty huge thing."[490]

At the end of the night, everyone in the twelve-piece ensemble came together at the front of the stage and took a collective bow, arm in arm. Axl tossed roses into the front rows, smiling and wearing a robe. The singer did not want any more riots. After all the problems that occurred on the first legs of the Illusion tour, he was thrilled to add some female energy to the concerts and give them a friendlier vibe.

A review of the retooled GNR in *The New York Times* was disparaging, describing the audience as "oddly restrained. Beyond the front rows, many people simply stood and watched as Mr. Rose raced around the stage, shimmying his shoulders, or twirling his microphone stand and changing his costume every song or two." Writing in a tone similar to a myriad of assessments to come, the *Times* dismissed the female musicians for the way they looked. "The band has added two backup singers and three horn players, all women dressed in black lingerie. It's a horn section valued primarily for its G-strings."[491]

The *Times* review infuriated Axl, who, of course, made it the focus of a long tirade at the final Garden stop. "Anybody here ever happen to take the time out of their busy schedule to read *The New York Times?*" he asked. "We got some horn players, Lisa, Anne, and CeCe. They aren't using tapes. They're playing their horns; they're wearing the outfits they want to wear. But no, we're a sexist organization forcing these girls to wear G-strings. And that's the only reason the horn section is any good, because of the G-strings, but the quality of their playing doesn't exist."

Axl was thinking Steel Wheels when he ordered Slash to some backup singers, but he got Girls, Girls, Girls instead. The 976 Horns were nearly identical to the three-piece all-female horn section on Mötley Crüe's 1987 excursion. The critics excoriated GNR's new roster of female musicians. The venerable *Rolling Stone* described the women as "silly, a female brass section and backup singers decked out in heavy-metal harlot lingerie."[492] *The Boston Globe* dismissed the 976 Horns as "three women in skimpy halter tops."[493] *The Hartford Courant* sneered at the "bikini-clad horn section as well as new backup singers (hired primarily for sex appeal)," and asked readers to imagine the tryouts: "Yeah, you're pretty good on sax, but can you play in a bra?"[494]

"Heels and horns, our hair was down to our ass. I loved it, I loved dressing up," Lisa Maxwell recalled. "A couple of the other women were more resistant like, 'I don't wanna dress like that.' I was like, 'Sure, I'll dress like a slut.' It was all a costume and dress-up for me. And they're like, 'It objectifies us.' And I'm like, 'So what?' Now, I probably wouldn't wear that, but it was still fun. It was a blast."[495]

Axl seemed to be enjoying his new band. On night three at MSG, Guns opened with "Perfect Crime" for the first time since who knew when and aired *Illusion* rarities "Pretty Tied Up," "Breakdown," and "Locomotive." As always, they closed with "Paradise City." "We came in at the end of 'Paradise City' and that was really fun because it was always the last tune," Lisa Maxwell said. "And it was such a party and there's so much energy on the stage. It was like New Year's Eve every night. That's kind of the vibe – a pop-the-champagne-bottle kind of feeling, all positive. Everybody's feeling good. Everybody's dancing. Everybody's happy.[496]

Everybody but Slash, who resented having to do so much heavy lifting at the behest of Axl, who insisted on getting his way. "He'd dumped all of the band responsibility personally on me, from finding Matt and Gilby to hiring the support musicians," Slash complained.

Cake dive

On December 19, during a brief Christmas break from touring, Guns stopped in Los Angeles where they spent three days filming scenes for the "November Rain" music video. The video, which would take nearly two months to complete, would serve as the second part of the trilogy Axl and Josh Richman had mapped out before shooting "Don't Cry." Andy Morahan was brought back to direct, but Richman had been banished from GNR's inner circle. Richman has offered few details about his expulsion but hinted the directive came from Suzzy London or Sharon Maynard. "Prior to production on 'November Rain,' there was a very non-linear, ethereal falling out that encompassed things about past lives and such. It was weird," he explained. "Axl went off into the ether into Axl World."[497] Ultimately, the finished nine-minute music video cost more than $1.5 million to produce, roughly $3.5 million today.

All that money was on the screen – "November Rain" looked stunning. The video's plot continued the tale of Mayne and Elizabeth, based on Del James' short story "Without You." Morahan's nonlinear narrative used flashbacks, premonitions, and images inspired by Axl's regression therapy. In the video, Mayne takes some pills on his nightstand and falls asleep, tossing and turning on the bed as if having a nightmare. There are scenes from a wedding. Elizabeth, played by Stephanie Seymour, walks down the aisle in a mullet dress by designer Carmela Sutera. At the altar, she joins Mayne, played by Axl, who is wearing a royal blue suit with a white ruffled "pirate" shirt. We cut to the Rainbow, the notorious Sunset Strip rock club, where the band members and their wives and girlfriends hang out and enjoy some drinks. Back at the wedding ceremony, the bride and groom exchange vows and rings and then kiss. Slash wanders out of the church, exiting the front doors and stepping into a vast, open plain. His suit is now black leather, and he grips a low-slung Les Paul. The guitarist peels off a solo, captured by a dramatic series of diving aerial shots. Mayne and Elizabeth exit the church as the guests throw rice. They smile and step into a white convertible, but Elizabeth's pensive look belies inner turmoil. Slash plays a second epic solo. We move to an outdoor reception, where Mayne and Elizabeth cut slices of cake, as guests that include Rikki Rachtman look on. There are toasts followed by dancing. A small ensemble is led by an accordion-playing Teddy Andreadis. Suddenly, it begins to rain, and the guests rush for cover. In the ensuing mayhem, bottles of wine spill and one guest dives face-first into the multi-tiered wedding cake. At the seven-minute mark, the music changes and we cut to a funeral in a church, where Elizabeth lies in a casket, half her face covered by a mirror. Mayne looks stricken. As the song climaxes, we cut to a gravesite where Elizabeth is laid to rest. It starts to rain, and the attendees seek shelter. As the number ends, we return to Mayne's bedroom, where he awakens from the nightmare. We flash back to Elizabeth tossing the bouquet at her reception, then to the gravesite, where Mayne kneels in the pouring rain. The final shot shows Elizabeth's bouquet atop her grave.

The music video's narrative scenes were augmented by footage of GNR performing live at the Orpheum Theatre, a 2000-seat Beaux Arts movie palace originally built in 1926. The twelve-piece version of Guns appears on stage, backed by a full orchestra. Axl sat at a grand piano, wearing an ornate red military jacket and matching bandana. To film the music video, GNR invited fans to attend and every seat in the L.A. venue was filled. Rather than miming along to the studio track, Axl insisted the group and orchestra play "November Rain" live. At last, Axl was performing his beloved song as he'd always intended. "It was a way for me to be around an orchestra and see what that was like, to hear an orchestra actually play something I had written on keyboards and see how well it worked," he said.[498]

Axl was nocturnal and during the filming, he would arrive sometime after dusk to get started. Guns were "pulling apart at the seams," at this point, according to Andy Morahan. "They would only really want to work at night. So even if you had a call sheet that said 'daytime,' there's a good chance they wouldn't turn up till after sunset."[499]

The second night of the video shoot took place at Saint Brendan Catholic Church, where Morahan captured the wedding ceremony. "Axl and I wanted this *Godfather*-type of ostentatious wedding," Morahan recalled.[500] Axl insisted the wedding look and feel totally authentic. There were few extras – the guests were mostly real friends and acquaintances. The singer hired an ordained priest to conduct a real ceremony and exchanged personally written vows with Stephanie.

The funeral was filmed at the same location as the wedding, immediately afterward, using all same the same characters. The sequence took so long to shoot Stephanie Seymour fell asleep in the coffin. Axl reportedly struggled with some of "November Rain's" emotionally charged scenes. "It freaks me out to be acting these parts out with Stephanie, when some of the situations are based off things that happened in another relationship," he said on the set.[501]

Afterward, the production moved to the Rainbow Bar and Grill on Sunset Boulevard to shoot the scene of the band relaxing and hanging out. That taping lasted late into the night and involved plenty of real drinks from the actual bar. The minute the Rainbow footage was in the can, the production bolted twenty-five miles north to Sierra Madre to tape the reception sequence at Villa del Sol d'Oro, a luxurious Tuscan-style estate built in the 1920s. Working at a furious pace, the crew readied the cameras, lighting equipment, and rain machines. "I always liked a cinematic look," Andy Morahan explained. "I'm also a huge fan of locations. So, I'd rather do a wedding reception outside on location with three or four rain machines than try and emulate that in a studio."[502] The sun had just risen when the cameras began rolling.

One of the most memorable moments at the reception was the wedding cake dive, which was a last-second decision on the day of filming. Someone came up with the idea and one of the extras volunteered to face plant into the cake. There was only one cake on set so there was only a single take. "Without a proper stunt coordinator, we should probably never have ever done it, but it literally was our last shot so we thought 'What harm can it do?'" Morahan said.[503] "It is supposed to be a tongue-in-cheek bad dream, where everything just goes to shit. For me, that scene was like pissing on the wedding reception in *The Godfather*. It's an upside-down nightmare version of that wedding."[504]

Morahan did not like how the cake dive turned out and omitted it from the first edit of the video, prompting an immediate outcry from Axl. "It looked a little bit too jokey to me," the director recalled.

He showed a cut to Axl, who recoiled. "Where's the cake? I love the cake." Morahan put it back in.

Axl's erratic behavior meant Morahan had to improvise during the production. The final shot took place at the cemetery where Elizabeth's body would be laid to rest. The crew had assembled all the equipment, and the actors and extras were in place, but Axl never showed up. After hours of waiting and losing daylight fast, Morahan taped the scene without him. "Axl eventually came once it got dark, which is why you see him by the grave in his cape and it's nighttime," Morahan explained. "He's not in the scene with the priest and the extras. It was constantly trying to keep the whole show on the road. And of course, when things like that happen, the costs escalate."[505]

GNR were due back on the road, so the remaining scenes were shot piecemeal at later dates. As with "Don't Cry," Slash's solo became one of the most iconic moments in the finished work. Morahan spent weeks searching for a little church out in the middle of nowhere but could not find a location he deemed suitably remote. Eventually, the director was able to rent a chapel on wheels from the Cerro Pelon Movie Ranch in Galisteo, New Mexico, where the movie *Young Guns* was filmed. The tiny white church and accompanying fence had been used in the 1985 western *Silverado*. The sweeping, diving images of Slash were shot with a Louma Crane, a Steadicam, and a helicopter. "The helicopter was dive-bombing toward me at full speed, almost knocking me off my feet," Slash recalled. "The hard part was doing it take after take after take from all different angles. The propeller blades were so close."[506] The expensive, elaborate shoot only yielded about thirty seconds of footage, but they looked like nothing else on MTV.

At one point, there had been talk of turning Del James' short story "Without You" into a feature film, but for now the focus was on the trilogy of music videos. "There's a condensed version of the story in the visual," James explained. "'Don't Cry' segues into 'November Rain,' and hopefully, if there's time, 'Estranged' – the third part of it, and it'll all kind of make sense and will tell this pretty heavy tale."[507] Morahan confessed he never fully understood Axl's vision for the series. "It was never really fleshed out," he said. "It was to do with Axl falling in love with a girl, and he was going through personal regressive therapy, whatever that was. Things that had happened in his past and all that kind of stuff, I couldn't really begin to explain what it all meant."[508]

The video's illusory nature was partly intentional. Mayne and Elizabeth struggled over a gun in "Don't Cry," but we never learn how she died in "November Rain." "Music videos need to be a bit obtuse, have a bit of complexity to them, so that as you watch it a third, fourth, fifth, sixth time, you're getting something new," cinematographer Daniel Pearl noted.[509]

"November Rain" was released as a single in February 1992 and rose to number three, the second highest-charting song in GNR's catalog. The video debuted on MTV's "Headbangers Ball" and immediately went into heavy rotation. The hype surrounding "November Rain," as well as its narrative form, length, and excessive cost, made it comparable to Michael Jackson's "Thriller" – a music video that was also a cultural event.

But the audacity of Axl's creative ambition cut both ways in 1992, when grunge and alternative rock were on the rise. Low-budget works such as Nirvana's "Smells Like Teen Spirit" practically mocked the excesses of cinematic endeavors like "November Rain."

Outshined

GNR closed out 1991 by playing Miami's 40,000 capacity Joe Robbie Stadium on New Year's Eve. It marked the first time Guns had ever headlined a stadium. Opening on the second North American leg of the Illusion tour was Soundgarden, a 180-degree contrast to GNR's earlier choice of Skid Row. Axl was a long-time fan of the Seattle quartet, praising vocalist Chris Cornell to *Rolling Stone* in 1989, well before they were known outside the Seattle region. "The singer just buries me. The guy sings so great."[510] Soundgarden had recently released their third effort, *Badmotorfinger*, which broke the group nationally on the strength of the singles "Jesus Christ Pose," "Outshined," and "Rusty Cage." Soundgarden was one of several relative unknowns who released albums that fall and scored surprise hits, Nirvana being the most notable.

Guns and Nirvana were labelmates at Geffen and Axl had been given an advance copy of the grunge trio's second record, *Nevermind*. He was an early and ardent fan, sporting a Nirvana T-shirt in the "Don't Cry" music video well before the group's breakthrough. *Nevermind's* inaugural single "Smells Like Teen Spirit" was an unexpected phenomenon, lighting up the airwaves in the fall of 1991 and heralding a sea change that would sweep through rock music. The same week GNR headlined Madison Square Garden, *Nevermind* passed the twin *Illusion* albums on the charts.

Metal titans such as Mötley Crüe, Def Leppard, Bon Jovi, Van Halen, and Guns ruled the second half of the 1980s. During that time, underground rockers such as Jane's Addiction, the Red Hot Chili Peppers, Soundgarden, the Pixies, and Faith No More were experimenting with new sounds and styles that pushed the boundaries of guitar-driven music. It wasn't just the songs that were alternative, the entire culture was different. These new groups had images and ideologies that rejected metal's machismo and party-hearty vibe. "We came from different worlds," Jane's Addiction guitarist Dave Navarro explained when asked about GNR. "They were from the Sunset Strip rocker world. We were from the alternative world. We were both coming up at the same time and there were times when they wanted to do shows with us, but we wanted to keep it on a more alternative level."[511] Jane's Addiction and their underground peers inspired a new generation of artists that would change the face of music in the 1990s.

Nirvana, Pearl Jam, the Red Hot Chili Peppers, and Soundgarden issued albums in the fall of 1991, at the same time Guns dropped the twin *Illusion* records. GNR's new release was stuffed with leftovers such as "Back Off Bitch" and "Bad Obsession" that dated back half a decade, to a different era of rock. Lighter-lofting power ballads such "Don't Cry" and "November Rain" were pure 1980s, while GNR's alt-rock competitors were creating the music of the future.

If Guns had any prayer of remaining contemporary, they needed to affix themselves to the new generation. Inviting Soundgarden on tour that winter was a no-brainer. The Seattle quartet seized the opportunity, turning in potent hourlong sets of lumbering sludge metal that stirred up plenty of noise using a lineup a third of the size of GNR's. Along the way, they converted audiences and earned glowing reviews in the press. "Soundgarden played with the attitude of a headliner," raved the *St. Petersburg Times*. "Most concertgoers were unfamiliar with the songs, but the music's bracing power had a strong visceral effect. The wiry Chris Cornell was bare-chested for much of the set. He wore baggy shorts and military boots. His long, wavy hair draped over his face. As he strutted around the stage, flinging his locks and wailing, he seemed a cross between Jim Morrison and Robert Plant."[512] *Badmotorfinger* would earn a Gold record by the end of Soundgarden's stint with Guns, denoting sales of half a million.

But there was also pushback to the pairing, accusations the underground Soundgarden was selling out by taking the slot with the arena friendly GNR. A profile from the road in *Kerrang* depicted an ambivalent Soundgarden, resorting to playing their "butt rock" tunes in front of GNR's crowds. By all accounts, Soundgarden were well treated in their role as openers, there at Axl's behest. Still, some members of the group struggled with life on the perimeters of the Guns carnival. In the busy backstage corridors of the Target Center in Minneapolis, bassist Ben Shepherd was asked what he was getting from the Illusion trek. "I'm testing myself, testing my threshold of anger and temper and my personal theories," he replied.[513] But drummer Matt Cameron countered, "I'm certainly not gonna forget about it. The experience is great; it's a coveted opening slot which was given to us, and we're not gonna throw that in anybody's faces."

For the rest of his career, Chris Cornell told anyone who would listen Guns treated his band better than anyone they had ever played with. But the singer was struck by the distance that had grown between Axl and the rest of his group. "You were not allowed to be in a hallway or anywhere where Axl might see you when he was walking between the dressing room and the stage," Cornell recalled.[514] The singer found Slash and Duff to be down-to-earth and easygoing – musicians who just wanted to get out there and play. "Then there was this Wizard of Oz character behind the curtain that seemed to complicate what was the most ideal situation they could ever have been in: They were the most successful and famous rock band on the planet. Every single show, hundreds of thousands of fans just wanted to hear songs. For some reason there seemed to be this obstacle in just going out and participating in that."[515]

The power differential in GNR was increasingly tilted toward Axl. Around this time, a journalist from *Musician* magazine observed Guns now consisted of "three original members and three hired sidemen. You're one man away from a Steely Dan situation." Steely Dan was a group controlled entirely by two members, Donald Fagen and Walter Becker. Everyone else was anonymous and expendable.

"Slash and I are *avid* Steely Dan fans," Axl fired back with a grin.[516]

That spring, Guns included a letter in their regular fan club mailing, Conspiracy Incorporated, announcing Izzy's departure and other changes taking place within the group. They insisted Izzy and the band "split on good terms," but conceded "losin' him is kind of a shock for us too. But we're confident that things will work out better for everyone this way." They reported Gilby would be taking over rhythm guitar duties, at least for the time being. "It sometimes takes a while for the chemistry of band members to develop and meld. So, we'll see how Gilby will fit in but right now, he's doing a killer job." They also notified the membership, "for this tour, we are bringing along an extra keyboard player, three lady horn players and two backup singers. So, when you see us in concert, it will sound as close as possible to how the albums sound, maybe even better."

The cheery tone used to describe the decidedly mixed news was an indicator of the current mood within GNR – everyone was white-knuckling their way through a period of immense turmoil and change. As it turned out, the band was about to face some of their biggest challenges yet – particularly Axl.

Chapter 11

A Rough Night in Dayton

You know it's going to be a rough night in Dayton when you have to open with an apology. "The main power amp on the monitor system on the stage has been blown out so we're trying to fix it," Slash told the audience just before midnight. Soundgarden had left the stage 90 minutes ago.

"Bullshit!" a concertgoer hollered from the crowd, which roundly booed the guitarist's announcement.

"There's nothing we can do about it," Slash continued. "They're working on it as fast as they can. We're all here, we're just sitting around like you guys are. They said it won't be too long before they figure it out and we'll be out. So, just hang out. I'm sorry – I didn't build the equipment; I just play through it."

Thirty more minutes would pass before Guns finally took the stage at 12:25 a.m., possibly their latest arrival yet and one that again garnered national headlines. "It became part of the GNR persona," Alice Cooper said. "The audience actually embraced it. It built the mystique."[517] A mass of more than 11,000 restless spectators were packed into the Nutter Center at Wright State University for the January 13 show, which had an 8:00 p.m. start time. Soundgarden went on at 9:30 and played for sixty minutes, leaving a gap of nearly two hours before Guns finally arrived.

It had been another one of those nights where just getting Axl onto the stage took every ounce of soothsaying, salesmanship, manipulation, and manpower the GNR organization could muster. Axl's stepfather was from Dayton and the singer had spent time there as a child. The bad memories came flooding back the second the MGM touched down at the airport and had not let up since.

Those tasked with getting Axl onstage that night included his manager, bodyguard, two assistants, therapist, chiropractor, masseuse, and his sister, Amy. Also along for the tour was Sharon Maynard, Axl's psychic healer from Sedona, who would purportedly cleanse the venue of negative energy before a show. "She didn't really speak much to anyone," backup singer Tracey Amos recalled. "I saw her and was in her presence, but she was in her zone, and she was there for a purpose."[518] Axl's bandmates disdained the diminutive, soft-spoken, elderly Asian woman, barely concealing their contempt and giving Maynard the derisive nickname Yoda.

But for Axl, it was all part of the process, "what it takes to face that big audience. I wouldn't call it stage fright. It's something else, and you have to psyche yourself up for that."[519] But the personnel and the process separated Axl from his bandmates, who spent countless hours, sitting backstage, waiting for the star to finally show up. "With all the doctors, specialists, therapists, fans, and everyone in his organization trying to help him, he just sank further into his cocoon, alienating himself even more," Del James wrote of Mayne in "Without You," his thinly disguised "fictional" portrait of Axl.[520]

Most of the musicians brought three or four suitcases on the road, Axl travelled with ten. This included a large trunk that toted twenty different types of specialized bath salts that could not be purchased in stores.[521] These large, unmarked plastic bags of white powder had created no shortage of issues at border crossings and police checks, but the drug-free Axl was never detained for long.

Axl's entourage also carried bags full of syringes, but they were used for the B12 vitamin shots that were administered to everyone in the group before shows. "I'm on very specific, high-tuned vitamins," the singer explained in an interview around this time. "My body needs these vitamins. I'm also involved in extensive emotional work to reach certain heights with myself that doing hard drugs would interfere with. I'm doing several detoxing programs to release trapped toxins that are there because of trauma. Doing coke would definitely get in the way of what I'm trying to accomplish."[522]

Even with all of this, Axl almost didn't make it to the gig in Dayton that night. "The Midwest – you all know how that's just one of my favorite places," the singer told the crowd sardonically. "No offense, but if you believe that – I mean, my stepdad is from here in Dayton and I used to come here when I was a kid. This is not a pleasant place for me to be. But I gotta realize that it doesn't have anything to do with you who came to see the show."

There were cheers of approval but after four and half hours of waiting, most of the audience members didn't want to hear it.

"Who cares?" a concertgoer yelled from the arena floor.

"Shut up and play a song!" shouted another.[523]

They were rewarded with Matt's 2 a.m. drum solo. But GNR played plenty of tunes, too, not letting up until a little after 3:00 in the morning.

Twenty hours and thirty minutes later, Guns were back onstage in Dayton to do it all over again.[524] The evening began on a sour note when, three numbers into the set, Axl's microphone stand snapped in two, cutting his hand to the bone. Duff took over to sing "Attitude" while the singer was tended to by medical staff backstage.

The laceration was serious and there was no doubt Axl would need stitches. The doctor warned him to not play the piano that night, lest he permanently injure the nerves in his hand. Axl agreed to go to the hospital, but he was committed to finishing the concert, which he could see and hear from a backstage monitor. "Let's get it taken care of, so I can finish the show" he said.[525]

Following "Attitude," Slash ambled up to the mic. By the time Axl finally showed up for gigs, Slash would be completely wasted, having spent the evening drinking and doing whatever else. Miraculously, it had no impact on his playing. Night after night, no matter how much he'd imbibed, Slash blasted out note-perfect renditions of his solos with ease. Tonight, he stalled for time, addressing a crowd that had been kept waiting for hours. Someone called out for Axl.

"It's called a clothing change. Just be patient," Slash replied.

Watching from the monitor backstage, Axl jolted upright, seething with rage. "*Costume change?*" he roared, holding his bandaged hand aloft.

From the stage, Slash continued to stall for time. "I want to introduce the newest member of the actual band. Somebody that came in during a period where we almost didn't make this tour because of a little band member mishap that we had. But Gilby Clarke helped us out so we're gonna play a little Rolling Stones for you."

Slash had sensed Axl's injury was more serious than initially thought. "Hey Gilby, let's make this a long one," he said. Gilby and Slash strummed the Stones number for a few minutes, after which Slash told the audience, "We had a physical mishap on stage, so we're gonna do a song called 'So Fine,' while Axl gets bandaged up. So, hold on. We'll be all right. He just cut himself to the bone, but we'll take care of it."

The group launched into "So Fine," with the backup singers doing their best to cover for the wounded Axl. The number concluded and GNR's lead vocalist had still not returned to the stage. They had already played both of Duff's numbers and Gilby's Stones piece, so it was time to get creative.

"Axl's getting taped up," Slash told the attendees. "He cut his hand all the way to the bone, so he's still back there. So, let's do a blues jam for a bit. Let's get the keyboards out and we'll do it in A. This shit happens but what the fuck."

Slash and the band were just about to start the blues jam when suddenly a roar rose up from the audience. Axl was back.

The singer strode on stage and rushed straight for Slash.

"Costume change?" he demanded in the mic for all to hear. If Slash was going to talk shit about him to the crowd, that same crowd was going to hear this, too.

A roadie jumped in and tried to separate the two, but Axl pushed him away, yelling, "Get the fuck back."

The singer got directly in Slash's face. "Costume change? Yeah, I was watching on TV, punk motherfucker."

"I said costume change," Slash stammered. "I said he cut his hand."

"Yeah, yeah, okay, you're fucking stoned," Axl said, dismissively. "I'll kick your ass right now!"

"No, no," Slash pleaded. "I didn't say that!"

Axl walked away. "Isn't this fun? Are you getting your money's worth?" he asked the onlookers.

Somehow, Guns managed to launch into "Welcome to the Jungle," a surefire way to get any audience back on their side. And even burning with animosity toward one another, Axl and Slash were able to deliver their signature tune like they always had.

"This is a little song that gets a little contradictory with the term brotherly love," Axl said afterward, introducing "Live and Let Die." Axl's bandmates seemed happy to be playing music again, not trying to cover for their singer's hand injury or fighting one another onstage. But Axl wouldn't let up. As soon as the number ended, he was at it again, this time railing against GNR's crew, who allegedly had been gossiping about Axl wanting to fire the group's manager, Doug Goldstein.

"A lot of shit gets said about this band, things that never happened. People like to start stories cause they ain't got nothing better to do in their own goddamn lives," Axl said, to confused applause. "I'm sorry, this is the only time I get to be around the crew," he explained to the concertgoers. "I'm mainly talking to our crew, with their little stories. They can take a walk *now*."

Axl was spinning out of control, the words coming out before he could even think about what he was saying. "We don't have tape decks rolling under the stage, we don't got other people playing the parts underneath the stage. This ain't no Mötley Crüe show." More applause.

"We got reviews that we should call the albums 'Our Hitler' and we're David Duke's house band. Fuck David Duke!" Axl roared to more clapping. Duke was a controversial white supremacist and one-time leader of the Ku Klux Klan. "If you think supporting something like David Duke's what we wrote a song like 'One in a Million' about, then you're a real disillusioned motherfucker and you oughta just leave."

Axl was not quite finished, saving a parting shot for his bandmate. "Oh, and Slash, the shit is on tape – I saw it on TV. Anyway, this is called 'Double Talkin' Jive' motherfucker." Matt instantly launched into the number, not wanting to give Axl the chance to continue his diatribe. Thankfully, the remainder of the night was less eventful as Guns worked their way through another seven tunes as well as the usual guitar and drum solos and instrumental interludes. Despite the onstage skirmish and Axl's hand injury, GNR managed to play for more than two hours.

But Axl could not possibly play piano that night, and "November Rain" had to be eliminated. "I apologize," the singer told the crowd toward the end. "We're gonna do a few more songs and cut this a little short so maybe I can play piano next time I see you people."

After the concert, everyone insisted Axl watch the videotape of Slash's onstage comments. Axl reviewed the tape and realized he had made a mistake. "We had a run-in in Dayton because I thought he took a potshot at me," Axl recalled. "I came back onstage and was a dick to him and told him I'd kick his ass in front of 20,000 people. That was fucked up. I was wrong, and I apologized the second I realized I was mistaken."[526]

To his credit, Slash was understanding of Axl's tempestuous outbursts from the stage, at least publicly. "With me it's pretty simple. It's 'Get the fuck up there and plug in that guitar and go,'" Slash told a reporter shortly after the Dayton debacle. "With him it isn't that simple. There's a lot going on apart from the three hours that we spend up there and it's *that* shit that affects him. A lot of it comes from just unbridled sincerity. Everything about him as a performer and a singer comes from his personality, so the shit that makes him crazy or the shit that he finds hard to deal with is, at the same time, what makes his talent."[527]

Due to Axl's injury, GNR had to reschedule their next two gigs, just outside of Detroit, and resume the tour a week later. If his bandmates were frustrated, they kept it to themselves. Axl knew he had the upper hand at all times, that he held all the cards. In an interview with *Musician* magazine around this time, a reporter observed, "It seems like you have the other guys in the band over a barrel sometimes. Everyone knows you're capable of saying, 'The hell with it, I won't go on' or won't record or won't show up. Doesn't that force the band to say, 'We better do it Axl's way or it ain't going to happen at all?'"

Axl's response was blunt. "Yeah." The singer left it at that – nothing further needed to be said.[528]

Pressed

Axl's dictatorial tendencies were not limited to his group. The singer had always been hypercontrolling of GNR's press. Early in the *Illusion* touring cycle, Guns stated they would only grant interviews to publications that signed a contract agreeing to submit their finished articles to the band for pre-approval. Most media outlets balked, and Guns embarrassedly withdrew the stipulation after *Spin* published a copy of the agreement GNR's management faxed over. But it demonstrated the lengths Axl and company would go to in order to control their image.

Axl hated having his picture taken and was frequently a wreck on the eve of a major photo shoot.[529] Longtime Guns associate Robert John had served as the band's official photographer since the early club days, and he was still the go-to source for official GNR photos. John's iconic shots of the group appeared on everything from magazine covers to the *Illusion* CD booklets. Similarly, Axl gave a series of exclusive interviews to "Without You" author Del James that were published in national publications such as *Rolling Stone* and *Rip*. The April 1989 cover of *Rip* featured a solo shot of Axl taken by John and a feature story inside written by James.

For all the venom Axl directed at the press, the singer knew he needed major media outlets to help cement GNR's status as a legendary band. Axl frequently relied upon friendly media outlets to make public announcements, reach his audience, or do damage control. During the Illusion tour, he granted *Rolling Stone* reporter Kim Neely unprecedented access, allowing her to travel alongside the band for three months. Neely envisioned herself seated next to Slash, scribbling notes as he snorted cocaine off a groupie's hindquarters, but mostly found herself ostracized by an organization wary of the press by default. "Sitting on the band's chartered plane from New York to Los Angeles, I felt as if my section of the aircraft had been quarantined," Neely recalled. "At the hotels, I spent most of my time in my room, wondering what I was missing."[530]

Neely's article about her experiences on the Illusion tour appeared in the September 5, 1991, issue of *Rolling Stone*. Axl had waited to see how the story turned out and, sufficiently satisfied, contacted Neely with the exclusive of a lifetime. "Axl called and informed me that he wanted to talk on the record about being sexually abused as a child," the reporter recalled. Both parties knew the story would be a bombshell. That was okay with Axl. He wanted to be understood, he wanted people to know where the anger came from. The two eventually sat for a long interview in late January 1992, the night before a GNR concert in Las Vegas. "Rose can be a disarming – and formidable – conversationalist if you catch him at the right time," Neely wrote. "When he is relaxed, he seems to delight in the challenge an interview presents, and it is all but impossible to rattle him."[531]

During their conversation, Neely told Axl bluntly the public viewed him to be a rich, spoiled brat. "That's true," Axl responded immediately, disarming the reporter with his candor. "Yeah, I'm real spoiled. I've spoiled myself. I'll get better at dealing with that, though. I mean, it's still new."[532]

Le Dome

From the outset of their careers, the members of GNR discussed their appreciation for Metallica during interviews. "We listen to Metallica all the time," Axl told a reporter in 1987, not long after the release of *Appetite for Destruction*. "Metallica is amazing – the sincerity. A lot of their stuff is more dark, getting out their anger, and we do that in our way, too. I was telling Slash last night that there's a really good chance that if we get along, there could be some form of weird fusion, and I got this feeling there might be like Gunica or Metalliarose."[533] "I really like Metallica," Slash told a reporter the following year. "They're the best band doing anything in rock 'n' roll in the past ten years. They're just the greatest."[534]

Metallica drummer Lars Ulrich recalled meeting Slash on the set of a Mötley Crüe video shoot in the fall of 1987. "The minute that I met him, it was like, this guy's totally real – I felt like I'd known him all my life. Over the course of making *And Justice for All*, we became real good friends, super tight – and just saw them a lot and hung out and got up to a lot of no good: women, drugs, you can pretty much imagine. I mean, we weren't doing a lot of charity works for the homeless together."[535]

A Guns-Metallica tour was an idea that members of both organizations had kicked around for ages, two of the top-selling and most-credible acts in metal unite for a marathon blowout. The idea took place "over numerous late-night gatherings all over the country," Ulrich recalled. "I had these conversations with Axl and Slash, and it was always, 'One day we've got to go out and do gigs together.'"[536] The drummer continued, "It got to the point where we talked about it so much that it was just like: Fuck, we gotta actually see if we could make this happen."[537]

Both bands issued landmark new releases in fall 1991, and with grunge and alternative rock on the ascent, the time seemed right to forge an alliance. It would be the biggest tour of the year and dominate the headlines.

GNR had just wrapped up their latest North American leg and had a couple of weeks at home in L.A. before they were due in Japan for a three-night stand at the Tokyo Dome. Metallica were on the road in support of their behemoth "black" album and were in town to play back-to-back dates at the Great Western Forum.

A meeting was held at Le Dome, a swanky West Hollywood restaurant that catered to powerbrokers from the music and film industries. In attendance were Axl, Slash, and Doug Goldstein, along with Metallica's James Hetfield and Lars Ulrich and their managers. They discussed logistics and hashed out terms. The popularity of the two bands meant the tour would play nothing but large, outdoor stadiums that held upwards of 80,000 spectators. Both groups would play complete, headline-length sets, but questions arose about curfew laws, which varied from city to city. Due to GNR's reputation for going on late, Metallica offered to play first, ensuring the concerts began on time.

Two hours later, everyone shook on the deal. Guns and Metallica were finally going to tour together. "I remember late-night conversations years ago with Axl about someday doing stadium shows," Lars told the *L.A. Times*. "So, it was great after the meeting, me and Axl were standing outside the restaurant, talking about how surprised people were going to be once the event was announced and how everyone would be saying, 'I can't believe it, it'll never happen.'"[538]

Guns and Metallica were eager to solidify the bill with a hot opening act that would bring credibility to the tour and align it with alternative rock and grunge. For Axl, there was no question Nirvana should be the band.

Axl had championed Nirvana ever since hearing an advance copy of the trio's second album *Nevermind*. Like many listeners, the singer connected deeply with Kurt Cobain's music, particularly "Smells Like Teen Spirit," which seemed to reach listeners like nothing else at the time. "The world has gotten really bored, really fed up and really pent up with frustration, and that comes through in Nirvana," Axl said shortly after the meeting with Metallica. "A lot of people were aware of that feeling and he happened to find the song that touched it and was able to let that feeling out in people. I'll do anything I can to support it. That's why we want them to play with us."[539]

Axl was obsessed with "Teen Spirit," which caused him to reflect on his own position as a singer tasked with entertaining fans. "To write a song like 'Smells Like Teen Spirit,' making fun of your songwriting and then have it used as an anthem has got to be a complete mindfuck," Axl said, adding, "The man definitely has a mountain to rise above."[540]

Cobain was already being hailed in the press as both the voice of Gen-X and the second coming of John Lennon. Axl believed "Teen

Spirit's" themes of apathy and dissatisfaction were universal. "Have you ever been let down by family, friends, something you wanted, or maybe just life in general?" the singer asked on stage, outside of Phoenix, just before the meeting with Metallica at Le Dome. "You know the mood I'm talking about. It's kind of like this band, Nirvana, why this teenage spirit, why this song's such a success. People relate to being let down. They say, 'Why are you always late?' I don't know, maybe I'm always in a bad mood about something. And this is my life, this is my love, and sometimes it doesn't mean anything to me, 'cause I'm just too bummed out."

At Le Dome, when Axl floated the idea of letting Nirvana open the Guns-Metallica trek, everyone immediately agreed. It was perfect. "I don't think the Skids are gonna be on it," Slash told a reporter shortly after the meeting. "We're talking about doing it with Nirvana, but we need to see where those guys are at. Metallica, Nirvana, and us sounds good to me. I went and saw Nirvana last night and they're pretty good friends of mine, so hopefully that'll help, even though we're very different bands."[541]

Too different as it turned out. Nirvana couldn't stand GNR and wanted nothing to do with them. Guns represented everything Nirvana opposed – a massive, successful, multimillion-dollar, commercial hard-rock outfit. Kurt Cobain and other members of Nirvana had repeatedly slagged GNR in the press and scoffed at the idea of touring together. The answer to the offer was a firm no.

But Axl refused to be swayed. The singer was desperate to pair up with Nirvana, leaving multiple voicemails for Kurt Cobain and using the press to pass him messages. "It's back and forth," he informed *Musician* magazine a few weeks after the dinner at Le Dome. "They're having a lot of problems with who they are and who they want to be and trying to hold onto it at the same time, at least Kurt is. I'd like to be as supportive as I can, but I don't know how much he will allow support."[542]

Eventually it became clear Nirvana was never going on the road with Guns under any circumstances. "They don't want to go out, and the vibe, from my point of view, is just because they don't wanna deal with 'mainstream,'" Slash said. "I love their record, but I can't stand the attitude. Because we spent our entire career as a band doing what we wanted to do in the way that we wanted to do it, going totally against the mainstream and getting to where we are now. We're in the mainstream only because the mainstream has become part of us. It's adapted to what we do."[543]

Slash might point to the members' various endorsement deals as an example of the mainstream bending to accommodate GNR. The most reputable musical instrument and equipment manufacturers in the world were lined up to do business with Guns. Slash had a deal with Gibson guitars, appearing in the company's "Only a Gibson is Good Enough" ad campaign in 1992. He was also a pitchman for Guild acoustic guitars and Ernie Ball strings. Duff endorsed Gallien-Krueger amplifiers and RotoSound strings, and Gilby shilled for ESP guitars. Slash, Duff, and Gilby were spokesmen for Seymour Duncan pickups. Meanwhile, Matt had monetized every element of his kit, cutting deals with Yamaha drums, Zildjan cymbals, DW pedals, and Easton sticks.

Axl was not immune to endorsement deals, either. The singer appeared in Shure microphone's 1992 print ads, which featured a dramatic photo of Axl gripping a mic in his fist and belting with all his might. Cheesy ad copy completed the cartoonish image: "What you hear is very real – the searing live sound of Guns N' Roses and Shure Beta microphones help create it. So take a cue from Axl. Visit your Shure dealer today."

Print ads featuring GNR members littered the pages of the rock and metal press. This was standard practice throughout the 1980s, when rockers such as Eddie Van Halen struck lucrative deals with the likes of Kramer guitars. But what was a sign of success then was a marker of selling out now. In 1992, being the face of a corporation was increasingly viewed as phony by the anti-establishment grunge acts. Pearl Jam vocalist Eddie Vedder was reportedly furious at drummer Dave Abbruzzese for taking endorsement deals, hastening the stickman's departure. GNR's notion of success – sold-out stadiums, multimillion dollar videos, horn sections and backup singers, endorsement deals – was anathema to Kurt Cobain.

Addicted to love

Guns travelled to Japan in late February to play three sold-out gigs at the Tokyo Dome. The final stop on February 22 was taped for Japanese television and later released on home video. To film the shows, GNR brought in Paul Becher, who had directed music videos and live performances for AC/DC, Prince, and others. The resulting two-hour-and-forty-five-minute concert film showcased GNR's expanded twelve-piece lineup. With a few months of gigs under their belt, Big Guns were firing on all cylinders.

In his interview with *Rolling Stone* a few weeks earlier, Axl had brushed off accusations the group had lost their edge, the raw vibe that had once made them so potent in concert. "I don't think it's losing any of its energy. There's a lot more energy now," the singer said, adding, "There are people who like a girl that had the same haircut she had ten years ago, too. I understand that, but we're evolving."

GNR's new recruits continued to learn the ropes live. The horns and backup singers were not featured on every song, and because there were no setlists, when they were not on stage they would huddle in the wings, watching for their cues on a monitor and waiting to go on if needed. Much to his chagrin, the backup singers and 976 Horns would hole up in Matt Sorum's private man cave, located directly behind his drum riser.

"They were in my dressing room," Matt told me, exasperated. "Behind my drum riser, I used to have my own room and I had a bar in there and I used to have little groupie chicks running around naked. Then these fucking girl horn players and background singers came on the tour, and they used to have to sit in my room – sitting down there doing their makeup."[544]

Reviewers continued to denigrate the women for their clothing, which remained a point of contention internally. Some of the horn players wanted to adopt the iconic style of Robert Palmer's "Addicted to Love" video, which featured a string of lookalike models in heavy makeup, stiletto heels, and black Chanel dresses. They brought the idea to the band's management but were rebuffed. "No, we like the slutty look," the women were told.[545]

Accompanying Axl in Tokyo was Sharon Maynard, who insisted the singer's team collect data on Japan's atomic energy facilities and the Tokyo Dome's power system. According to a former employee, "It was something about the magnetic forces that exist in the universe and where those things are in comparison to where Axl would be spending his time. If it was any exotic, wonderful place around the world, the advisers generally had to be flown in at some point. They had to accompany Axl to Japan to make sure that the bad-energy waves didn't capture him there, but if it was Kansas City, everything was really fine."[546]

There was widespread concern Axl was being taken advantage of by his alternative healers and therapists. "Look at how Yoda, Sharon Maynard, conned him," ex-manager Alan Niven said. "$75,000 for an 'exorcism.'"[547] According to Niven, Axl regularly attended upscale psychic retreats in Sedona that ran $10,000 a head. Maynard claimed to have expertise in reading the energy of spaces and places but failed to predict the riot in St. Louis. Sometimes her advice seemed nonsensical. According to Al Coury, a staff member at Geffen, "One time we had a meeting with Axl, and he left to go to the dentist. His psychics told him he had to change the fillings in his teeth because his current ones were giving him bad vibes."[548]

But Axl believed the work he was doing with his alternative healers was helping. "I've found a lot more peace in the last year than I've ever known, and I feel a bit more creative than ever," he said, attributing this to his sessions with Suzzy London and Sharon Maynard. "I've done a lot of emotional therapy and getting in touch with my real self, rather than the self that I've created to deal with life. Even though I was fighting to be myself, I wasn't really in touch with who I was."[549]

Axl claimed it didn't matter to him if his uncovered memories, past life experiences, or chats with dead relatives were "real" or not. The point was they helped him and that was real enough. "You could go to a medium and talk to someone in your family who had died and when you come out, you'll feel much different," Axl explained a few weeks after the Tokyo concerts. "Someone will say, 'Was it real?' and you'll say, 'I don't know, but I know I feel a lot easier with the situation.'"[550]

Savannah

GNR took the month of March off, which was Slash's worst nightmare. The guitarist hated downtime. He refused to stay at his house, holing up in hotels and chatting happily with any journalist who cared to interview him. "I might go and do a session," he said. "I like just to work all the time. Dead time just kills me. I don't know what to do with a day off – sitting around getting drunk all day. It's too lethargic."

On April 1, Guns returned to the road for back-to-back shows in Mexico City. The following day, Axl's explosive *Rolling Stone* cover story hit the shelves. On April 3, the group returned to the States, where a very on-brand Slash was seen openly having sex with porn star Savannah at the Scrap Bar in New York City. Owner Stephen Trimboli told *People* magazine the duo got it on "right there at the bar, in full view of everyone" before making their way to a limousine parked outside.[551]

To Slash, the incident was another example of the loss of privacy he experienced upon becoming famous. GNR's profile was higher than ever, and things had only become worse in this regard. "I didn't have any privacy in the last couple of months. All of a sudden, I can't just walk up and down the street or go into this pub or go into this club. That's changed and that's the biggest hardship. The three hours we play on stage makes it worthwhile, so you try not to bitch about it too much. But it has its moments where it gets to be like, 'I can't believe people are writing this.'"[552]

Three days later, Guns headlined at Myriad Arena in Oklahoma City. Chicago quartet Smashing Pumpkins were tapped to open. The Pumpkins were still relatively unknown outside of alternative-rock circles, building a fanbase on the strength of their 1991 studio debut, *Gish*. The group was soundly booed in Oklahoma City, and singer-guitarist Billy Corgan pushed back hard, dedicating a number to

Satan and telling the crowd, "The only reason you're so mad at me is you're all living on stolen land." Drummer Jimmy Chamberlain was pegged with a quarter. Four years later, the Pumpkins would return to the Myriad as headliners.[553]

In Oklahoma City, GNR went on after midnight, opening with three songs from *Appetite*. Oddly, they forgot to play "Welcome to the Jungle," one of the only times that ever happened. Axl was in a feisty mood, telling the crowd, "They don't want you to see some little loudmouth like me, who crawled out of some shithole and worked his way up onto this stage. There's something deep inside you that knows what it is you're supposed to do with your life. And no matter what anybody tells you, if you keep looking and you keep digging, you're gonna find it. And you can be the person you're meant to be on this planet. And don't let anybody ever get in your way, including me."

The singer was still smarting over the loss of Izzy. "There may be a lot of you who are pissed off that Izzy's not here with us," he told the audience. "Well, we're kinda pissed off that Izzy's not here with us. But if Izzy was with us, we probably wouldn't be here in Oklahoma right now." During the encore, Axl called for Izzy's rarely played "Pretty Tied Up." It was the last time GNR performed the number on the Illusion tour. Thirty-one years would pass before Guns played it again.

An extraordinary update

Axl's *Rolling Stone* cover story had been out for nearly a week and the singer's revelations of child abuse made worldwide headlines. The offices of *Rolling Stone* were flooded with emotion-filled missives from readers. "The response to that interview was overwhelming," Kim Neely, the story's author, recalled. "Letters poured in from survivors of sexual abuse. Some wrote they felt less alone, others that the piece had given them the courage to tell parents and counselors about abuse they'd kept secret for years. For the first time, I felt that a story with my byline had transcended the boundaries of reporting and actually touched lives."[554]

Axl had tried to reach out to his family in advance, warning them about what was to come, but he was rebuffed. "I haven't talked with my parents in over a year-and-a-half," he confessed to a reporter a few weeks earlier. "I sent them some letters just recently to let them know this was happening, but when I started to uncover things, they let me know, very adamantly, to drop the issue.[555]

On April 9, GNR headlined at the Rosemont Horizon outside Chicago, the first of two make-up dates that had been cancelled right after the riot in St. Louis. The Smashing Pumpkins were on board again as openers, receiving a better reception from the local crowd.

Axl only made it through two songs before he started talking about the *Rolling Stone* article. "Shut the fuck up," he warned the audience, mocking the teenage headbangers in attendance. "'Yo, Axl! Cool! Metal, dude! Rock 'n' roll! Party! Do cocaine! Yeah!' I ain't here for that."

A friend of the family had called to admonish Axl that his relatives had "'taken a great offense at what I said in this magazine. Look what he's done to his mother. His mother can't even go out of the house now.' It was amazing my mother could have gone out of the house before, knowing the shit she knew."

The singer was spinning out now, barely able to contain himself. "I tried being nice, I tried being cool about it. I tried being friends and offering forgiveness and love. All I got was, 'You know how much we love you, but let's keep the screws on and keep you down like we always have.'"

Axl was bringing a therapy session to the stage, and the Rosemont was hanging on every word. "Why is he talking about this?" the singer asked rhetorically. "Because it might not have happened to you, but it might have happened to the two or three people that are standing around you, who've got some fucked up family life that's gonna come back to haunt them when they hit twenty-five. And then you gotta try to climb your way out of what you thought was your life, but it looks more in your head like a car wreck that no one told you about."

A review in the *Chicago Tribune* called Axl's confession "an extraordinary update of this latest chapter in his now public struggle.

He can't seem to fake his way through a performance."[556] The *Tribune* acknowledged the growing criticisms of Axl, that the singer had "become a joke in certain quarters because of his erratic behavior, but once on stage, Rose goes about his business with a ferocity that few performers have ever matched"[557]

Axl told the audience he was done with being the cool rock frontman everyone wanted him to be. "It ain't about doing cocaine, it ain't about how much vodka can I drink and how much I can drink someone else under the table." The singer stared at Slash and Duff, who looked away. "It ain't about what a macho-man-rock 'n' roller I can be. That shit don't work no more. That's great for a little kid, rock 'n' roll bullshit, but it don't work no more in the real world. I can't come up here and go, 'Yeah, I'm bad, I'm rock 'n' roll, we're doing this rock 'n' roll thing' if my life is falling apart. I can't fake it no more."

Few rock frontmen had ever let it hang out so openly on stage, at least not those who were sober. But for Axl, there was a point to all of this, a message. "If a scrawny little junior high 90-pound weakling can finally get up here and take this shit on, so can any one of you that have the same problems in your life," he said to the crowd, which roared to the rafters.

There were nights when the show itself was a healer and tonight was one of them. Axl started to feel better as the evening wore on, losing himself in the music and the moment, the sheer physicality of his performance shaking loose some demons. "There's something about being able to be up there moving around during it that's actually a present, a gift or something," Axl said of "Estranged." "Being able to dance and rejoice in a song that came from situations and emotions that were killing me."[558] Axl called for a piano and spent more than three-minutes thrilling the concertgoers with his dexterous keyboard work before turning in a sublime "November Rain." The singer didn't want to get off stage that night, refusing to leave for nearly three hours.

Axl was supposed to return the following evening for more of the same, but the singer cancelled the second date at the Rosemont and two booked in Detroit after that. This time, Axl's problem wasn't performance anxiety or stage fright. This time, the singer cancelled because there was a warrant out for his arrest.

Chapter 12

On the Run

"Axl Rose, the bad boy of rock and roll, stirs up trouble wherever he goes in keeping with his image," *Entertainment Tonight* co-host Mary Hart said to open the national TV show's segment on GNR. "Most of his antics are part of the act, but now he's a real-life fugitive from justice being hunted by the law."

St. Louis County prosecutor Robert McCulloch charged Axl with four misdemeanor counts of battery for fighting with fans and security at the Riverport Amphitheater the previous summer. Axl was also cited for property damage of less than $1,000 due to some items he smashed in a dressing room.[559] McCulloch had attempted to have Axl detained after GNR's show in Oklahoma City, but the singer managed to evade arrest.[560] Frustrated, McCulloch increased Axl's bond by ten times, raising it to $100,000. Axl was facing up to four-and-a-half years in jail and $4,500 in fines.[561] "We've given him eight months to turn himself in at his convenience, and he's ignored us," McCulloch complained to the press.[562]

Seeing that GNR was playing near Chicago, McCulloch contacted the Cook County sheriff's department and asked them to enforce a bench warrant for Axl – to arrest the singer and extradite him to St. Louis.[563] [564] On their way over to the Rosemont, the sheriff's office contacted the concert's promoter to inform him Axl would be taken into custody that night. With 18,000 fans slated to arrive at the sold-out venue, the police did not want a disturbance or riot, so they gave Axl the option of surrendering after the show.[565]

At 7:30 p.m., fifteen minutes before the Rosemont doors were scheduled to open, GNR cancelled, turning away thousands of fans waiting outside.[566] The group also announced the cancellation of two upcoming gigs just outside of Detroit, dates that had already been rescheduled in the wake of the St. Louis riot. A spokesperson for the sheriff's department told the press Axl was considered a wanted man. "If he is determined to be in Cook County, he is a fugitive at this point. These warrants will be outstanding."[567]

But Axl was already on his way out of town on the MGM Grand. "Rather than go to jail, Rose left the sheriff's jurisdiction," Bryn Bridenthal of Geffen Records told reporters, estimating GNR lost $1.5 million in ticket sales due to the cancellations.[568] "He wasn't anxious to spend any time in jail without reason. To suddenly extradite him over a misdemeanor charge, there's no cause."[569]

"I consider the charges serious," prosecutor McCulloch countered to *Entertainment Tonight*. "Obviously, he considers the charges serious. He's gone to such drastic steps to avoid answering the charges." McCulloch claimed it was not unusual to extradite someone for misdemeanors and asserted Axl was being treated like anyone else.[570] The prosecutor vowed to have the singer arrested and brought to justice wherever GNR played next. "He is easy to find," McCulloch said. "Wherever he goes, we'll be waiting for him. If he wants to cancel his whole schedule, fine. If he leaves the country, we'll notify Customs to get him when he comes back."[571]

Axl's run from the law generated national press. "Concert Is Canceled After Band's Singer Flees to Avoid Arrest," read a headline in *The New York Times*.[572] "Rock Star Evades Long Arm of Law" cried the *St. Louis Post-Dispatch*.[573] The *Chicago Sun-Times* ran a story titled "Axl Rose a Fugitive After Show Cancelled."[574]

A tribute to Freddie

Ten days after fleeing the authorities in Illinois, Axl was onstage in front of 72,000 rabid fans at Wembley Stadium. The singer had not exactly been keeping a low profile since evading the cops back in the States. A few days after the aborted Rosemont gig, he attended parties hosted by U2 while they were in Los Angeles touring in support of their 1991 opus *Achtung Baby*.

At Wembley, Axl was the star attraction at the Freddie Mercury Tribute Concert for AIDS Awareness. The Queen vocalist had passed away from AIDS-related complications at the age of 45 the previous November. Tickets for the show sold out before the lineup was even announced, illustrating how beloved Mercury was to his British followers. The Mercury tribute featured an A-list of British rock royalty, including David Bowie, Robert Plant, Roger Daltrey, Elton John, and George Michael. The four-hour event was being broadcast in 76 countries around the world. As usual, Axl skipped the rehearsal sessions that took place a day before the show.

For the first two hours of the concert, Metallica, Def Leppard, and GNR performed two- or three-song mini sets of originals. Guns played "Knockin' on Heaven's Door" and "Paradise City." "Shove it!" Axl called to a spectator hoisting a sign that read *Piss off, Axl.*

The second half of the event featured the surviving members of Queen playing the group's classics, fronted by a series of vocalists and guitar players. Queen axeman Brian May served as genial bandleader, smiling and nodding as he urged the musicians to greater heights. Slash joined Def Leppard singer Joe Elliott to perform "Tie Your Mother Down." Matt, Gilby, and Duff watched the proceedings from the royal box, alongside Prince Charles and Diana, Princess of Wales.

Toward the climax of the show, Elton John and Queen submitted a transcendent take on the opening of "Bohemian Rhapsody." The number's operatic midsection was handled by the members of Queen, as videotaped in the 1970s. As the musicians broke into the tune's final "rock" section, Axl came charging out onto the stage in a black leather kilt and a football jersey, tackling Mercury's vocal with all his might. Wembley exploded. Axl returned a song later and brought the house down with a stadium-shaking take on "We Will Rock You." There was a lot of star power at Wembley that night, but even among this heady crowd, Axl remained peerless.

Few rock stars of any caliber can step into a stadium packed with 72,000 spectators and tear the roof off the place with nothing other than a drumbeat and their own charisma and vocal prowess. But Axl was that good and, once again, he delivered mightily, doing Mercury more than proud in the process. Simply, he crushed it.

The grand finale brought the stars big and small back to the stage for a rousing sing-along of "We Are the Champions." Even Broadway diva Liza Minnelli was swaying to the music. Per usual, Duff had been drinking all day and was almost too wasted to join in. "Backstage, I let it go too far," the bassist wrote in his memoir. "I was too drunk to talk, too drunk to walk. Elton John literally carried me to the side of the stage, propped me upright, and helped maneuver me out onto the stage where almost 100,000 fans awaited the showstopper. About fifty performers lined up in a chorus line with Liza Minnelli singing lead. I remained upright through the song – no doubt using the sets of shoulders on either side of me – then I had to be carried back to my dressing room, unaware of what was happening around me."[575]

You better run

GNR had a few weeks off before the next round of dates began. Slash was a diehard road dog who always got antsy between tour legs. "Being on the road for me is heaven," the guitarist explained. "I am into it; it doesn't tire me out or anything like that. When I come home off a tour, I don't know exactly what to do with myself. You're forced into home life, this mundane kind of existence, which I'm just not into. The pace is too slow."[576]

To keep himself occupied during the downtime, Slash recorded a couple of tracks with Motörhead. "You Better Run" was a bluesy stomper but "I Ain't No Nice Guy" was far from a prototypical Motörhead tune – it was a reflective, acoustic-driven ballad. "It's a classic song," Slash told a reporter. "It gave me chills. It's sort of rare to go into somebody else's session and get chills from their song. So, I think it's gonna be on their new record."[577] Motörhead convinced Ozzy Osbourne to team up on the number, and "Nice Guy" became a superstar effort and a single. Both tracks were issued on Motörhead's 1992 album *March ör Die.*

Axl was dismissive of Slash's collaborations, believing the guitarist was too willing to work with others, particularly pop singers such as Michael Jackson. In Axl's mind, it cheapened Slash's personal brand and reflected poorly on GNR. The singer felt increasingly irritated by Slash's musical activities outside Guns. But the guitarist believed it enhanced his brand and his playing. Besides, it gave him something to do when he wasn't on tour, a healthy alternative to jabbing himself with heroin needles. "It keeps me active, it keeps my chops up," Slash said of his guest appearance with Motörhead. "When you play with other people in their environment, it makes you a better player. As far as Guns N' Roses goes, there's no real similarity; we do what we do. When I do something on the side, it's their thing. So, it's just me going and trying to adapt to their situation."[578]

To that end, Slash also used the downtime between tour legs to link up with the legendary singer-songwriter Carole King. The guitarist hopped onstage with King at the New Orleans Jazz and Heritage Festival on May 3, sticking around to play on three tunes. "It's summertime, we're in New Orleans," Slash said, setting the scene for a reporter. "I was up there with no shoes, no shirt, leather pants, sunglasses. It was fun. I didn't rehearse anything – just went up and winged it. I've known her since I was a kid; it's like she's part of my family."[579] The pair were joined by soulful vocalist Aaron Neville, practically royalty in New Orleans, working through the classic sixties tune "Loco-Motion," which was written by King. They also performed "Hold Out for Love," which Slash would later add a solo to for King's 1993 album *Colour of Your Dreams.*

Nine days later, the guitarist joined Metallica drummer Lars Ulrich for a press conference to announce the Guns-Metallica co-headlining trek, which would hit two dozen North American cities that summer. The two acts had held a dinner meeting before the Freddie Mercury tribute concert to finalize the logistics of their outing together.[580] Slash noted GNR and Metallica did not have much in common musically but shared an uncompromising approach. "Attitude-wise, there is a lot of similarity," he said. "It's one of the reasons we wanted to do it together – we've gotten really far away from conforming to the industry. Both bands will open a lot of doors for other bands and open up the attitude of some of these very stiff white-collar executive types at the record companies and let them know this commercial attitude they've got isn't necessarily the way to go. So, we have that similarity, plus we're just good friends."[581]

While Slash and Lars were chatting with the press, Axl was conferring with his legal team. The singer had promised to surrender to the authorities in St. Louis on May 11 but canceled at the last minute.[582] Through attorneys, the singer offered to pay a fine and even perform in concert for charity, but the prosecutors declined. "Axl's not going to get off with a slap on the wrist and a fine," Dan Diemer, assistant county prosecutor, told reporters. We consider a fine for Axl Rose a slap on the wrist because he has millions. We're thinking in terms of probation."[583]

When a reporter asked Slash about Axl's "fugitive" status, the guitarist just shrugged. "We made an ass out of St. Louis and this prosecutor is pissed off," he said. "So, he's trying his hardest to make things difficult for us. But I don't think he's gonna win in the long run. He's sort of pathetic, actually."[584]

Slane Castle

On the second European leg of the Illusion expedition, GNR ventured to several countries they had never played before, including Czechoslovakia, Hungary, Switzerland, Spain, Portugal, and Italy. They debuted on May 16 at Slane Castle in Ireland, about thirty miles north of Dublin. Slane was an 18th-century castle located next to a sweeping natural amphitheater that could accommodate 50,000 spectators. Guns had flown in two days earlier, setting up shop at the luxurious Berkeley Court Hotel.

The early arrival enabled Duff to connect with more than a hundred distant relatives who lived in the region, including his maternal grandfather. It was the bassist's first visit to Ireland, and the day before the concert, he was taken on an extended pub crawl followed by a family reunion and barbecue at a nearby home.

At one point, a great-aunt pulled Duff aside, grabbed the bassist by the cheeks with both hands, and insisted, "You drink too much." Duff took a look around the gathering, filled with heavy Irish drinkers who appeared to be half sloshed. *I drink too much compared to these folks?* he thought to himself. *Really?*[585]

The Slane Castle show was scheduled to begin in mid-afternoon, one of the few times GNR agreed to play during the day on the Illusion jaunt. Even with a long lead-up, Axl still didn't make it to the gig on time. Following sets by openers My Little Funhouse and Faith No More and a stretch of nearly two hours, the restless crowd began forming human pyramids, mooning each other, and throwing full cups of beer at the stage.

"I was concerned that there might almost be a riot," castle owner and concert promoter Lord Henry Mountcharles told *The Irish Times*.[586] He rounded up Slash backstage and insisted Guns go on immediately. "Axl Rose wasn't even on site. He was still in his hotel suite in Dublin," Mountcharles recalled, incredulous. A helicopter was dispatched to Dublin, and Axl was persuaded to board. Mountcharles described the Illusion tour as a "typhoon of chaos" but conceded GNR ultimately delivered a five-star performance. "Credit where credit is due. When they went on stage, they really turned it on – but there was a lot of stuff going on in the background."

Slash shrugged off any backstage tension as part of GNR's modus operandi. "The band has always been tense, because this isn't a day job," the guitarist said just after the Slane gig. "Most bands in the business nowadays do the show in their sleep. We go up there, every night is different, and we care about every single show. If something happens during one particular show, yeah, it's tense. Because it's not premeditated. We don't have a setlist. So, it's always hard and it's always tense."[587]

Guns had been off for a month, so they had to shake off a bit of rust before locking back into the groove at Slane. Axl, sporting a newly grown beard that matched his red hair, told the crowd GNR had an affinity for Ireland due to "having a McKagan in the band

and being half-Irish myself – but you can't tell, right?" The singer delivered another stellar performance, throwing himself into the end of "Don't Cry," with abandon.

Dublin kings U2 were on the road, but they had sent over a welcome gift – a barrel of Guinness and a crate of forty-year-old Irish whiskey. Axl would return the favor on stage at Slane, singing a few lines of U2's recent single "One" as an intro to "Sweet Child O' Mine." Later that year, Axl would describe the U2 tune as "one of the greatest songs ever written."[588] At Slane, Axl premiered "It's Alright," a lilting solo piano take on a Black Sabbath tune that would frequently serve as an introduction to "November Rain" for the rest of the tour.

From Ireland, GNR ventured to Prague, another city in a country they had never played before. As with the first round of European dates, the group nixed several numbers from the set, reducing the concert lengths to about two hours instead of their usual two-and-a-half or three. Duff would later claim he was so wasted during the second European expedition, he could not even remember performing in Czechoslovakia. A couple of days after the gig, he woke up in a Budapest hotel room and saw a passport stamp for the Czech Republic. "We played a stadium show in one of the most beautiful cities in East Europe not long after the fall of the Berlin wall, and the only way I knew I'd even been in the country was because of the stamp."[589]

"This is a song that Freddie Mercury asked us to play for you," Axl told the audience in Budapest at GNR's May 22 gig. "He'd be here to sing it for himself for you, but he had some other plans that he had to take care of tonight. We tried to learn this in the dressing room, and we didn't do a very good job of it. So maybe you won't mind helping us out." Axl then sang "Tavaszi Szél Vizet Áraszt," a Hungarian folk tune Queen had played in Budapest in 1986. As soon as the concertgoers recognized it, they went crazy, clapping and singing along at the top of their lungs.

U2's multimedia Zoo TV tour was playing Europe at the same time as GNR, and the two bands saved a few dollars by sharing the MGM Grand.[590] In Vienna, Austria, the Illusion and Zoo TV excursions were booked in the same outdoor stadium on consecutive nights. At U2's gig on May 24, Axl joined the Irish quartet onstage for a cover of "Knockin' on Heaven's Door," a tune Bono and company had also been covering for years.

Invading Paris

Ever since Axl performed with the Rolling Stones in Atlantic City, the singer yearned to have his own pay-per-view special. Like the Stones, he envisioned celebrity musical guests and a concert that would be simulcast live around the world. Axl decided Paris would be the perfect location. GNR's June 6 appearance at Hippodrome de Vincennes would be broadcast on FM radio as well as internationally on pay-per-view under the heading *Guns N' Roses Invade Paris*. "This promises to be the biggest rock pay-per-view event in history," enthused John Soher, president of Polygram Diversified Entertainment, which was producing and distributing the show. "I fully expect this Guns N' Roses telecast to exceed the numbers achieved by the Rolling Stones and the Who. The mystique and curiosity surrounding Guns N' Roses concerts on their most recent tour adds a certain element of danger to a live telecast."[591]

The pay-per-view event was another outrageously expensive proposition. Axl tapped Lenny Kravitz, Jeff Beck, and Aerosmith to guest star, flying everyone first class to Paris, putting them up at the five-star Hôtel de Crillon, and laying out the royal treatment every step of the way.

A rehearsal was held the day before the show, giving GNR and the musicians a chance to walk through the songs together. "Always on the Run" was the perfect choice for Lenny Kravitz, whose collaboration with Slash had been a hit. The Paris concert would mark the pair's first live rendition. "I've been waiting a long time to get to actually play live with them," Kravitz said after the practice session. "They called me a week or so ago and said, 'Come to Paris and play.' And today in rehearsal, it went really well. It's always fun to play with other people and do something different from what you normally do. Especially when you're on tour and you're doing the same thing every night."[592]

"Always on the Run," a sparse, stripped-down rocker, was given the big-band treatment by GNR, with eleven musicians backing Kravitz and his six string. "We're just a big jam now, everybody's playing," Kravitz enthused. "We've got two keyboard players, three of us on guitar, bass, drums, horns, background singers. It's kind of a big jam on the tune."

Legendary British axeman Jeff Beck was invited to perform "Locomotive (Complicity)," one of the longer and more complex *Illusion* tracks. Beck had heard of GNR, but he had never listened to their music, agreeing to take the gig on the advice of his manager. The night before rehearsals, he ran into Matt, Duff, and Gilby at the hotel bar. The trio invited Beck upstairs and offered to teach him "Locomotive." Drinks went around, and before long, Duff was guiding Beck through the chord changes. "Fifteen years ago, ten years ago, a year ago, if I would have seen myself showing Jeff Beck a song on the guitar, people would have thought I was nuts," Duff said.[593]

As Beck worked on "Locomotive's" chord changes, Duff began soloing over the top. Gilby laughed, recalling the memory. "Jeff Beck, Duff, and I are in the room and Duff's soloing. Perfect. 'Duff! Let him do it!'"

The next day at rehearsal, Beck and the group took a stab at "Locomotive." The gum-snapping guitar wizard traded blistering solo lines back and forth with Slash, while Beck superfans Steven Tyler and Joe Perry watched from the wings, enthralled, smiling and bobbing their heads in time with the music.

Everyone agreed the Paris summit could only conclude with all the musicians playing "Train Kept a Rollin'," a cover tune Beck performed with the Yardbirds in the 1960s and Aerosmith popularized in the 1970s. "It was the best idea if we were gonna play at the end," Beck told a reporter from MTV the day of rehearsals. "Everybody thought it was Aerosmith's song. I stole it back. But it's a good number for everybody. As long as I can hear what I'm doing."

Beck's hearing was of genuine concern. After decades of playing loud rock music, his ears were shot, plagued by tinnitus that manifested itself as constant hissing. "They don't know how to get rid of it," Beck explained to MTV. "The hearing mechanism that we have is the same as the Iron Age."[594]

Guns had always been devout Aerosmith fans. They closed *Live ?!*@ Like a Suicide* with a raucous cover of 1973's "Mama Kin." Likewise, the Boston quintet big-brothered GNR in 1987 as openers on a tour that saw Guns rise to prominence. At the end of the months-long trek, Aerosmith gifted the entire band with metal Halliburton suitcases – something to last them on the many excursions ahead. "It's great to see them doing what they're doing," Aerosmith guitarist Joe Perry told MTV in Paris. "We haven't really played together that much, but we can play a song like 'Mama Kin,' and it seems to mesh pretty well."[595]

"We toured with Aerosmith," Duff added, "so we're already like family with them."

Not so for Axl, who skipped the practice session like he always did. The singer told everyone he wanted to preserve his voice for the concert, but Slash was incredulous. They needed to prepare, to work out the material so they'd be ready for prime time. The guitarist thought Axl's failure to show up and rehearse with guests the singer had personally invited was rude and unprofessional.

Unfortunately, the rehearsal turned out to be Beck's sole appearance with GNR in Paris. Beck's ears gave out during the practice that day. "I was going through misery with the tinnitus, I was thinking I was gonna die, and I couldn't deal with it," the guitarist said. "We'd rehearsed in the dressing room and went out to do a sound check. Matt hit one bass drum, and it was like forty million watts going through me, and I had to walk away."[596]

Beck pulled out of the concert on the day of the show. Everyone felt terrible. "He was rehearsing with us all day yesterday, and he was having a real problem sleeping last night with this huge ringing in his ear," Matt told MTV. "So, he called and he said that he talked to his doctor, and they thought that it'd be a better idea if he didn't play, 'cause it could cause damage. So, he thought it'd be better if he sat out of this one. But it was great to meet him and play with him in the rehearsal."[597] Beck did his best to make it up to Guns the following week in London, where he laid down some licks on two tracks that would appear on Duff's still-in-process solo album.

This I love

The Paris concert showcased the twelve-piece version of GNR performing at an outdoor venue in the daytime. The daylight hours were necessary to accommodate the largest possible pay-per-view audience. On either side of the stage hung 50-foot rectangular banners with the dual images of the *Illusion* cover art, red on the left, blue on the right. Faith No More and Soundgarden were on hand as openers.

Guns began with a barnstorming pass at "It's So Easy," with Axl and Slash dashing from one end of the stage to the next. Axl came on wearing a T-shirt from the Bollock Brothers, an obscure British electronic duo, before removing his shirt and changing into a bright red blazer and matching bicycle shorts a few songs later. Throughout the show, Duff and Slash performed standing on top of the monitors and Teleprompter boxes so they could be seen better by the audience.

GNR were about twenty minutes into the set and had just wrapped "Bad Obsession" when Axl announced, "We're gonna play something, so I don't know," and abruptly left the stage. Everyone looked puzzled as the band members scrambled to figure out what was going on. The audience, sensing something was wrong, began to chant "Guns and Roses" over and over. Slash admonished them. "Fuckin' hold on. We're trying to get something together here. It's cool, don't worry about it, just relax." Although he was not slated to appear until later in the set, Lenny Kravitz was sent to the stage.[598] "This is a little tune that Lenny Kravitz and I penned together," Slash said, introducing "Always on the Run." Despite the shambolic entrance, Kravitz and Guns nailed it, locking into a hard groove and rocking out. Axl remained backstage the entire time.

Kravitz departed and Axl emerged in a blue and red sport coat, irritated. He introduced the next number by calling out Warren Beatty, a fifty-five-year-old Hollywood actor with a longstanding reputation as a lothario. Over the years, Beatty had been linked to a string of actresses and supermodels, including Diane Keaton, Jane Fonda, Cher, Madonna, and Elle MacPherson.[599] After three decades of serial bachelorhood, Beatty finally settled down in early 1992, marrying actress Annette Bening. But he'd once dated Stephanie Seymour, a fact that continued to eat away at Axl.

"I'd like to dedicate this next song to a man who lives his life playing premeditated games," the singer began. "A man who is so empty that's all he can do is play fucking games. A man who is a parasite. A man who lives his life on sucking off other people's life force and their energy. An old man who likes to live vicariously through young people and suck up all their life, 'cause he has none of his own. I'd like to dedicate this song to a cheap punk named Warren Beatty. A man who has a family and a baby, but he's gotta spend his time fucking around with other people 'cause he doesn't know what to do with his own life. A man who uses you, uses the media, and uses everybody just to fulfill his parasitic needs. Well, listen home fuck, if you think Madonna kicked your ass I'm betting my money on Annette, you stupid fucking asshole. This is a song called 'Double Talkin' Jive' motherfucker!" A review in the *L.A. Times* declared that Axl's bizarre rant "seemed like it was beamed in from Venus."[600]

Throughout GNR's set, Axl showcased a series of outfits, including a T-shirt that proclaimed, "Nobody knows I'm a lesbian" during "Patience." For "November Rain," his grand piano rose from beneath the stage on a hydraulic lift. As the instrument emerged, Axl hopped on its lid and rocked it back and forth as if riding a surfboard. The singer donned the ornate red military jacket he wore in the "November Rain" music video, sat down at the piano, and proceeded to play Black Sabbath's "It's Alright," his fingers sweeping across the keys. "This is a song about unrequited love," the singer said, introducing "November Rain."

During his time in Paris, Axl completed a new composition called "This I Love," whose lyrics he retooled to express his devotion to

Stephanie Seymour. It was a piano ballad in the vein of "November Rain" Guns had worked on during the *Illusion* sessions. More than sixteen years would pass before "This I Love" would see the light of day, appearing on *Illusion's* 2008 follow-up, *Chinese Democracy*.

Axl was in a convivial mood later that night when he introduced Steven Tyler and Joe Perry. The Aerosmith leaders joined GNR for ripping takes on "Mama Kin" and "Train Kept a Rollin'." The forty-four-year-old Tyler remained one of hard rock's preeminent frontmen, but his stage spins and twirling mic stand were no match for Axl, who delivered as usual.

Axl's pairing with Aerosmith was yet another means by which the singer intentionally aligned GNR with the legends of classic rock. As Matt Sorum later told me, "Axl wanted to heighten; he wanted to cross Guns over into a super group. And he was very smart about the way he did it. He used to bring artists onstage with us – Elton John, Brian May, Lenny Kravitz, Steven Tyler and Joe Perry. And his whole thing was you are who you hang out with. To a certain degree, the band achieved super group status because of the strategic things that Axl always thought up."[601]

Back in Indiana, Izzy shelled out $24.95 to watch the pay-per-view event on television. "It was bizarre, like an out-of-body experience," GNR's former guitarist said. "I didn't really recognize them all together. They had horn players and harmonicas and girl singers. Of course, I was Gilby for the night. It was weird. I was happy to see that they carried on without me. That's all I would hope."[602]

Everything, all the time

The size and scale of GNR's summer romp across Europe, which played eighteen colossal outdoor venues in six weeks, meant the group usually had two or three days off between shows. It took that long for the crew to disassemble the enormous stage and other equipment, transport it to the next location, and set up everything again. Following the Paris pay-per-view event, Guns had an entire week off before resuming in the U.K.

Part of the delay was due to the postponement of GNR's June 9 gig in Manchester, which was rescheduled to the 14th because Axl pushed himself too hard at the pay-per-view event in Paris. According to one report, "Doctors told lead singer Axl Rose, who is suffering from physical exhaustion, to rest for thirty-six hours." The Manchester gig was cancelled just hours before the gates opened, leaving thousands of fans fuming outside the venue. A spokesman for Guns promised the group would make up the missed date. "The band is dead set on playing Manchester and are really disappointed about what has happened today. A grueling tour like this one really takes it out of the band and there was just no way Axl could go on today."[603]

On days off, the group members were not content to lounge in their luxury hotel suites. Instead, Doug Goldstein kept them busy with an array of pricey distractions – chartering luxury yachts, taking snorkeling expeditions, renting out entire go-kart tracks and bowling alleys, going on shopping sprees at exclusive boutiques, closing down restaurants and hosting gargantuan feasts for the group, their entourage, select crew members, and industry contacts. "There was a spare-no-expense attitude on this tour, which was new for us," Slash recalled.[604] "It was all senseless spending. Doug approved one crazy idea after another to fill our free time at our expense." "Everything had scaled up," Duff added. "We often flew from our hotels to the venues in helicopters, plural – even massive double-prop Chinook helicopters. Everything had become outsized."[605]

The excesses could be found everywhere. In concert, Guns kept adding introductions to the songs or extending those already in place. Teddy Andreadis' brief harmonica intro to "Bad Obsession" turned into an extended full-band blues vamp. In addition to GNR's covers of Bob Dylan and Paul McCartney, which were played at every show, a veritable classic rock radio playlist was incorporated into Guns originals or used as intros: The Rolling Stones' "Wild Horses," Queen's "Sail Away Sweet Sister," Eagles' "Hotel California," Alice Cooper's "Only Women Bleed," Pink Floyd's "Mother." In Paris, Axl's use of Black Sabbath's "It's Alright" as a prelude to "November Rain" took a full five minutes.

The drum and guitar solos got longer, too, sometimes stretching out ten minutes or more. "I play a lot of different things," Slash explained. "I play the beginning of 'Young Frankenstein,' the violin piece. I play 'The Godfather,' I play Hendrix stuff sometimes. I play 'Red House.' I play 'Voodoo Child' before 'Civil War' all the time. I play the 'Scarface' theme sometimes."[606] As a result, GNR featured fewer originals in each set.

Adding to the onstage surfeit were even more wardrobe switches from Axl, sometimes in the middle of numbers. "Civil War" now featured four costume changes and "Paradise City" had two.

Between songs and intros, or when one of the musicians was taking a solo, Matt, Duff, and Slash would sneak off to their dressing rooms under the stage to snort huge rails of coke. The overindulgence that characterized every aspect of GNR's touring machine was becoming glaringly obvious. In Paris, a writer from *NME* described Duff as "punch-drunk, swollen and decaying."[607]

Axl smoked cigarettes and enjoyed a flute of champagne from time to time, but otherwise, he never joined his bandmates in their pursuit of the perfect high. The physical and mental routines the singer undertook in order to stay in shape and prepare for shows filled the bulk of his time. Instead of cocaine and groupies, the singer's dressing room was home to an oxygen tank, a humidifier, echinacea supplements, homeopathic potions, and an assortment of herbal teas to keep his voice primed during shows.[608] [609]

On days when he wasn't performing, Axl's fame was so vast merely stepping outside required extraordinary planning and personnel. While Axl's bandmates spent days off shopping in high-end boutiques or deep-sea fishing in the Mediterranean, the singer was frequently stuck in his hotel room. "I could do without touring in a lot of ways," he confessed. "I'm not a big fan of it. I like the transportation, I like flying in a private plane, I like riding in limos. I like the grandiose nature of those things and the material comfort. But other than that, I don't have a lot of time to really enjoy myself. I can enjoy that I've got a nice room and a police escort, but I don't have much time to take in a movie or just sit and relax."[610]

Faith based

Axl assumed his deeply confessional *Rolling Stone* cover story would be the ultimate rock star conquest, a massive middle finger to his family printed for all the world to see on the front of rock's bible. But the singer's victory proved to be short-lived. Just two weeks after his *Rolling Stone* cover story, Nirvana appeared on the front of the same magazine. In the photo, Kurt Cobain wore an olive-green thrift-store sweater over a T-shirt bearing the handwritten slogan "Corporate Magazines Still Suck." The iconic image perfectly captured the irony of grunge's anti-establishment stance amidst its assimilation into the mainstream. *Rolling Stone's* Nirvana issue included a companion piece about the sudden prominence of grunge and alternative rock music, hailing Seattle as "the new Liverpool" in reference to the Beatles' birthplace. The 1980s Sunset Strip scene that spawned Guns was officially dead.

Faith No More was a San Francisco alternative-metal quintet who broke through with 1990's "Epic," a pioneering rock-rap single taken from their sophomore album that went top ten. The band spent the next three years touring and working on their third effort, *Angel Dust*, which was scheduled to be released in June 1992, while they were on the road as GNR's opening act. Axl was a longtime fan and vocal advocate of the Faith No More. He loved the quintet's prominent integration of keyboards and their ability to incorporate multiple genres into a distinct sound. It was his idea to invite them to open for Guns that summer.

Like so many of their alt-rock contemporaries, Faith No More were spotlight avoidant, rejecting the trappings of rock stardom even as they pursued fortune and fame. Unlike many of their peers, FNM were genuinely weird, with an uncompromising art-rock streak that ran through everything they did. Rather than cashing in on the success of "Epic," the group rejected rock-rap on *Angel Dust* in favor of complex, head-scratching experiments with titles like "Crack Hitler" and "Jizzlobber." FNM were every record executive's worst nightmare, which was exactly what their dedicated fans loved about them.

Unsurprisingly, the quintet struggled throughout the European tour with Guns. They preferred to play tiny clubs packed with sweaty superfans, rather than gigantic stadiums where they were at the bottom of the bill. The group hated the downtime between gigs and were appalled by the excesses of GNR's day-to-day operations. Unwilling to play nice and placate their corporate overlords, Faith complained loudly about Guns to every journalist who interviewed them that summer. Their willingness – eagerness, even – to dish the dirt, generated plenty of attention from reporters, who were always on the hunt for backstage gossip.

"We may not like GNR," vocalist Mike Patton told one publication. "We may not like playing in open air stadiums in broad daylight, where we sound like shit and look like shit on a much too large stage that wasn't built for us, and we may not like the fact that people are paying too much money for a ticket. That's all true. But the fact is, it's a very good opportunity to reach a large audience that otherwise wouldn't have come to see us."[611]

"We're not made for this kind of stadium show," bassist Billy Gould added. "It may be good from a business point of view, but if we had our way, we wouldn't be doing this. The sound is shit, the place is too big, the crowd is a mile away. It just lends itself to more of a cabaret act, the kind of band who want to indulge in all that theatrical bullshit, with costume changes every other song."[612]

Gould's disparaging remark about costume changes was clearly aimed at Axl, the most frequent target of Faith's press attacks. "Touring with Axl has been like touring with Michael Jackson," Gould griped. "Although I think I've seen Michael Jackson more times on this tour than I have Axl."[613]

"Didn't Axl speak to you yesterday?" drummer Mike Bordin asked cheekily.

"No, it was Patton," Gould replied. "He said, Huhrrrmmmnn as he flashed past with his minders."[614]

"I'm confused about who's who in Guns N' Roses," keyboardist Roddy Bottum chimed in. "There's Dizzy and Iggy and Lizzy and Tizzy and Gilby and Giddy. Shit man, onstage now there's a horn section, two chick back-up singers, two keyboard players, an airline pilot, a basketball coach, a couple of car mechanics."[615]

Perhaps more than anything else, Mike Patton detested Axl's teleprompter, telling a reporter he wanted to "take a shit right on top of those TV screens, in front of tens of thousands of people. To me, there's no real reason why we're doing this tour."[616]

Faith's inclination to bite the hand that fed them that summer was partly due to the lag time between the interviews they granted and the publication of the ensuing articles. By the time GNR got wind of Faith's disparaging remarks, the tour would be over. "When is this interview going to be printed?" Billy Gould asked a reporter from the British music magazine *Select*. "I have to watch what I say but hey, fuck that, just print this: I hate the whole circus thing, we all hate it. We're just gritting our teeth and getting through it the best we can. Every band in the world might think they want to open for Guns N' Roses, but lemme tell you, it's been a real ugly personal experience, having to deal with all the shit that surrounds this circus. I've always hated that aspect of rock music and I've never wanted to be part of it, so to find myself being associated with a tour this big kinda sucks."[617]

A completely different thing

On June 13, GNR returned to Wembley Stadium where Queen guitarist Brian May joined the group to revive their covers of "Tie Your Mother Down" and "We Will Rock You," both of which had been performed at the Freddie Mercury tribute concert at the same venue in April. This was followed by stadium shows in the U.K., Germany, Switzerland, and the Netherlands.

On June 25, Slash, Gilby, and Teddy Andreadis were flown on a private jet to Munich, Germany to shoot a music video for Michael Jackson's "Give in To Me," which Jackson planned to release as a single. "When it came time to do the video, Mike put the whole thing in my hands," Slash recalled.[618] At Slash's behest, Andy Morahan was brought in to direct. The video shoot took place in a small club with Jackson performing the tune alongside a band. Also on hand were former Living Colour bassist Muzz Skillings and ex-Chic drummer Tony Thompson. Besides Slash, none of these musicians had anything to do with the recording of the song. Fans of Jackson and GNR were invited to the shoot, appearing as audience members in the finished video. "We're in this tiny space and it's very rock and roll," Slash said. "It's a completely different thing for Michael."[619]

Immediately after the shoot, Slash, Gilby, and Teddy flew straight to Italy for another stadium show with GNR. While in Italy, Axl took a rare shopping excursion to purchase wares from Armani and Versace. Fashion mogul Gianni Versace was heavily involved in the world of music, designing outfits for notables such as Madonna and Elton John, who was also headlining stadiums in Europe that summer. Elton John superfan Axl and the forty-five-year-old Versace attended one of John's concerts together and became fast friends. "Versace is a huge Guns N' Roses head," Axl enthused around this time. "He loves Guns N' Roses. His fashion shows, the majority of music is Guns N' Roses. He's just really, really into Guns N' Roses. He wants me to do a fashion show. He wants to make me clothes to wear."[620] During GNR's tour stop in Italy, Axl and Stephanie Seymour dined out with Gianni Versace's sister, Donatella, and supermodel Naomi Campbell.

Guns closed out the summer excursion of Europe with shows in Spain and Portugal. The band only had two weeks before their co-headlining trek with Metallica was scheduled to begin in the States. Duff used the downtime to party with his girlfriend Linda, whom he married on July 11. Duff would later describe Linda as "a Penthouse Pet and an enthusiastic co-conspirator in drug use. I don't remember the wedding. I think we got married on a boat at Lake Arrowhead, which was still party central – all about cocaine and debauchery. We were drinking with a bunch of friends; I woke up a few days later and we were married. I guess boat captains can marry people. That I could do all my coke – even crack – in front of her was pretty much the basis of our bond."[621]

Gilby used the two-week hiatus to lay down rhythm guitar for the impending covers album. Former axeman Izzy Stradlin played on several numbers the band cut during the *Illusion* sessions, and Axl insisted his parts be erased and re-recorded. There were also some covers GNR had completed without Izzy. Working one-on-one with Mike Clink, Gilby was given just one day to learn the material and record his guitar over the existing tracks.[622] "It was strange, because it wasn't like we went in to make an album," Gilby recalled. "They had seven songs already recorded, then I went in and re-did all Izzy's guitars or put on guitars where he didn't play on 'em."[623]

During GNR's summer expedition through Europe, Doug Goldstein fielded numerous calls from anxious promoters in North America, who were worried about Axl's legal case in St. Louis.[624] There was growing concern Axl would not be free to co-headline with Metallica. GNR's final European show took place on July 2, exactly one year after the St. Louis melee took place. "One year to the day, our anniversary riot day," Axl told the audience that night, dedicating "Double Talkin' Jive" to his nemesis, St. Louis prosecutor Robert McCulloch.

But McCulloch was done talking. The prosecutor filed Axl's name with U.S. Customs, ordering federal agents to arrest the singer the second he set foot in the country.[625] And that is exactly what happened when Axl touched down in New York City on July 12, a mere five days before the tour with Metallica was set to begin.

Chapter 13

The Dream Team

Axl stepped off the Air France Concorde jet at John F. Kennedy airport in New York and was arrested by federal agents as he passed through customs. It was a bit after noon on July 12, 1992, and the singer had been accompanied on the flight from Paris by Doug Goldstein, Stephanie Seymour, her son Dylan, and Beta Lebeis, the child's nanny, who would play a key role in Axl's life in the ensuing decades. The singer was held at the Port Authority office for about three hours and then handed over to the New York City police, who took him to Queens for booking. Axl was charged with four counts of misdemeanor assault and one count of damage to property. Conviction of all charges could mean serving up to four years in jail.[626]

Axl's legal team immediately dismissed the notion that the singer's arrest was some sort of surprise. "He's been on the customs' computer for months," said Arthur Margulis, Axl's attorney in St. Louis. "We knew he ran the risk of being arrested any time he entered the country."[627] Doug Goldstein added, "He was going to be arrested. That's why I was there. I called him in Paris and said, 'Do you want to sneak back into the country? We've done it before or do you want to put this behind you?' and he said, 'Let's get it over with.'"[628]

Axl's lawyers claimed they had worked out a deal with St. Louis County prosecutor Robert McCulloch for the singer to turn himself in. "Axl Rose Planning to Surrender Here" read the headline of a July 10 piece published in the *St. Louis Post-Dispatch*. "Rocker Axl Rose will surrender early next week on the warrant that was issued for the off-stage ruckus last summer at the Riverport Amphitheatre. The matter will then rest with St. Louis County Associate Court Judge Ellis Gregory."

The singer was caught off guard when he was taken into custody at the New York airport. "I'm doing great, the prosecutor reneged on a promise he made," a handcuffed Axl told MTV's Kurt Loder as he was being escorted to the Queens booking office. "I'm going there on the fifteenth and he said this wouldn't happen and he lied."[629]

Now Axl was being threatened with extradition to St. Louis. "There was no need for all of this," Bryn Bridenthal informed the press. "The prosecutor was told Axl would come to St. Louis to turn himself in to face the warrant this week."[630] She added, "We're being told the authorities will try to extradite him to St. Louis and, of course, Axl will fight that every step of the way. It would be much nicer to go voluntarily, without handcuffs."[631]

"He's been saying that he'd turn himself in, but he hasn't," Robert McCulloch countered to reporters. "We decided to not take any more chances; we decided not to take him at his word anymore. He's had a year to show up on his own."[632]

In New York, Axl spent a total of about eleven hours in jail before being released on $100,000 bail. "I basically spent my time writing autographs for cops and talking with them about rock 'n' roll," the singer told Kurt Loder immediately after he booked out, riding in the back of a stretch limousine. "All these totally cool cops, they were telling me about when they went to Woodstock and everything. It was great. New York cops are the best."

Axl added the only reason he had not turned himself in already was because the prosecutor refused to sign off on an agreement that would have resolved the matter. "We've just been waiting for the case to get somewhat solidified in writing before I go [to St. Louis]. I don't want to go there and get set up. 'You come here and it's going to be like this,' and it's a whole different story. And you end up sitting in St. Louis for a long time."[633]

Axl claimed to have no problem being on probation for the next two years. "I'm not really worried about any of that because I really don't spend my time breaking the law," he told Kurt Loder. "It just depends on if you play someplace where somebody doesn't like rock 'n' roll or Guns N' Roses. They could say I did something. You never know what will happen."[634]

GNR was slated to begin their excursion with Metallica five days later at RFK Stadium in Washington, D.C. Axl said he had no plans to cancel any of the shows. He also envisioned touring internationally after the outing with Metallica ended. "Hopefully in December we will be doing South America and then we'd like to try to do some really strange places – we're working on China. I'd like to play Israel; I'd like to play Moscow."[635]

The singer spent the night in New York City while his legal team negotiated the logistics of his surrender in St. Louis. "I don't know how they're getting here, or when," Arthur Margulis, Axl's St. Louis attorney, told reporters. "I feel confident that he's going to appear and he's frankly looking forward to it because he wants to get this matter resolved."[636] Margulis met with assistant prosecutor Dan Diemer on Monday, July 13 and attempted to work out a plea deal, but the two were unable to come to terms.[637] The prosecution sought a guilty plea, but Axl's legal team warned him pleading guilty would make it difficult to beat the seventeen civil suits that had been filed against him by concertgoers and security guards, who claimed they were injured in St. Louis. Axl was also being sued by his insurance company and the owners of the Riverport Amphitheatre.[638]

To avoid extradition, Axl and his legal team traveled to Clayton, Missouri, outside of St. Louis, for a court appearance on Tuesday July 14. A crowd of approximately fifty fans, journalists, and radio DJs gathered outside the courthouse that morning, hoping to catch a glimpse of Axl, but the singer entered through a basement door and avoided the throng. Decked out in a salmon-hued Versace suit with a string tie, the singer was accompanied by four attorneys, Doug Goldstein, and two bodyguards. Before appearing, Axl was fingerprinted and photographed by police. He also posted $100,000 bond.[639]

Axl spent less than ten minutes in court. The arrest warrant incorrectly listed his name as William Bailey. "Is your name William Bailey?" Associate Circuit Judge Ellis Gregory asked the singer. "No," Axl replied, stating he had legally changed his name to W. Axl Rose.[640] He pleaded not guilty to the misdemeanor charges, and a trial was scheduled to begin on October 13. Axl gave Doug Goldstein a hug and then exited through the back door of the courthouse, heading straight for the airport and flying back to New York City. For now, it was over.

"Axl's fine, I talked to him yesterday," Slash told MTV that afternoon. The co-headlining tour with Metallica was scheduled to launch later that week, and the guitarist agreed to head up GNR's media commitments while Axl and his team of lawyers wrangled with the singer's legal issues. "He's dealing with the logistics of this guy in St. Louis. I don't want to say anything that's going to put the band in a weird position – I think the guy's an asshole. So, he's dealing with him, and he's got a good attitude about it."[641]

A historic package

The Guns-Metallica outing was scheduled to run from mid-July until the beginning of October, stopping in twenty-seven U.S. and Canadian cities over a span of about three months. By combining their drawing power, the two mega groups would perform in massive stadiums rather than the large arenas they could fill individually in the States. An estimated 825,000 fans would attend the shows, which were priced at $27.50.[642] Both acts would play a complete set – more than two hours apiece – and Faith No More would open. Adding in the time it took the crews to change over the staging and equipment, the entire event would run more than seven hours. Neither band wanted to play during the daytime, so everything would likely end sometime after midnight – and with the notoriously late GNR, who knew how long it might last.

"I think this tour will have a huge effect," Gregg Perloff, president of Bill Graham Presents, a large concert production company, told the *L.A. Times*. "You have two major headliners playing together in a historic package. Other acts who normally tour alone are going to look at what is happening here and think it makes sense for them, too. This tour is a return to the spirit of the '60s and '70s, when you had lots of bands playing together, a time when you could see the Who and the Grateful Dead together."[643]

But this was not the 1960s and the headbanging headliners did not draw flocks of peaceful hippies. Stadium managers and city officials were nervous about hosting a late-night, hard-rock event of this scale.[644] There were security concerns, curfew restrictions, and challenges in routing a production this size across North America during the summer, when stadiums were already booked with sporting events. Chicago, Atlanta, Philadelphia, and Cleveland passed altogether. "Venue management and city politics have actually been the biggest obstacle to getting into the stadiums," Alex Kochan, GNR's booking agent, told the *Detroit Free Press*. The itinerary was made up of "just about every place that would have us."[645] "We wanted it to go to the thirty biggest cities in the country so all the fans could get a chance to see this once-in-the-lifetime thing," Lars Ulrich said. "But the stadiums there, they just weren't interested. They said, 'Oh, Guns N' Roses and Metallica will come and mess up the stadium.' We tried, believe me. We tormented our managers, and our booking agents: 'Find us a racetrack, find us a field, find us a yard, we'll play in a sewer.' I mean, Philadelphia is the fourth biggest market in the country; it's a joke this tour isn't going there."[646]

Beyond the logistical challenges were king-sized egos on both sides. GNR and Metallica were superstars who were used to having things done their way. According to Metallica frontman James Hetfield, "There were a lot of meetings trying to figure out what cities we were going to play, how many shows in a row, whose voice could hold out, who was going on last, who was playing the longest, guest lists – a bunch of political crap."[647]

Axl had a reputation for being hyper controlling, but Metallica was also known to micromanage every aspect of their live appearances. The San Francisco quartet insisted on bringing their own equipment, refusing to share lighting rigs or any other stage gear with Guns.[648] Thus, each headliner had their own complete production, requiring more than thirty trucks and a crew of 175 to haul around a stage that was 300 feet wide and 60 feet tall.[649] Metallica demanded use of their "snake pit," an exclusive fan section located at the front of the stage, which had to be dismantled as soon as they were done performing. Lars Ulrich's drum set required an elaborate hydraulic contraption to move around the stage. Metallica's show also featured elaborate pyrotechnics displays, which they insisted on bringing. A sound system would crank out 250,000 watts of power while giant video screens on either side and behind the stage would capture the groups in action.

Although both acts were headliners, everyone agreed to let Guns close each night. GNR's notoriously late starts could spell disaster for all involved. "We don't want to end up going on at three o'clock in the morning," Metallica guitarist Kirk Hammett told *The Boston Globe*. "You never know when those guys are gonna go out on stage."[650]

Despite these elaborate behind-the-scenes negotiations, Duff insisted "both bands are good friends. We hang out in Hollywood together. Literally, at bars we talked about why we should tour together. And it finally came together. It was really the bands that made all the decisions, and it got legislated through the management. It's not a corporate tour."[651]

"They said it would never happen," read advertisements, but the dates were booked, and the outing was set to begin. To drum up excitement, Slash and Metallica drummer Lars Ulrich made a series of joint media appearances in the days following Axl's arrest, popping up together on Rockline, a nationally syndicated radio program, and MTV's metal show, Headbanger's Ball. "The reason that we're getting together and doing this is because it's getting away from the norm and getting away from the hype and all the hysteria that goes on," Slash told the Rockline listeners. "It's got that anti-establishment rock 'n' roll thing. It's not, like, a Bon Jovi show."[652]

Lars Ulrich echoed Slash's upbeat tone. "We both incorporate a lot of different things," he said on Rockline. "These guys have been out playing stadiums for a while in Europe and they got their whole trip. And we've got our whole thing. So, both our bands are gonna have the normal surroundings that we're used to playing in. And we'll each play for forever, so pack your lunch and don't make any plans for the rest of the week, 'cause we don't know how long we're gonna keep you there."[653]

Slash and Lars swore egos would not get in the way because the two acts were longtime associates with a great deal of respect for one another. "It's really simple when you actually sit down and talk about it amongst friends," Slash said. "When you let management deal with it, all of a sudden it becomes corporate.'"[654] Lars added, "It was 'Look, let's check our egos at the door.' We all had to make sacrifices to make this happen. But we have a lot of mutual respect for each other. The real reason this is happening is a genuine desire between the main guys of both bands to make this happen. That makes it stronger than what the lawyers or booking agents or managers would throw our way. You can sit around and speculate until you're green in the face, but this is a once-in-a-lifetime situation."[655]

Slash conceded there were differences between the two groups in concert. Guns thrived on chaos and uncertainty, going on whenever they felt like it and playing without a setlist. Metallica was a finely tuned machine that relied on discipline and military-like precision. "There's an unpredictability about GNR, as opposed to the rigidity of Metallica's whole trip," Slash said.[656] "Both bands have different ways of approaching things in terms of how we run our band on a day-to-day basis," Lars Ulrich conceded.[657] "We try and mix it up as much as we can. But any band that plays as many live gigs as we do comes to a point where they realize what their optimum setlist is, and what flows better, and what makes them the most confident."[658]

Regardless, the drummer insisted, the groups had more in common than they had differences. "The real Guns N' Roses fans and the real Metallica fans are a lot closer than people think," Ulrich said. "I'm talking about our foundation audiences – the first two or three million people who buy the Black Album or who buy *Use Your Illusion*, those fans share a lot of attitudes that we share in terms of doing things your own way, not catering to what the music business tries to force bands to do."[659]

But Metallica bassist Jason Newsted was somewhat more mercenary in explaining why his group was pairing with GNR that summer. "When it comes right down to it, if we worked for the same amount of time on our own, we wouldn't play to as many people and we wouldn't earn as much money," he said. "We have a chance to make a few more million dollars over a six-week period, then we're *going* to do it."[660] The *L.A. Times* disagreed with Newsted's math, explaining how the increased production costs meant both acts were "doing the stadium shows for about the same money each receives for a successful show in a much smaller arena."[661]

Yoda

As the Guns-Metallica tour was about to commence, rumors circulated that Sharon Maynard, Axl's psychic advisor, had ordered him not to play cities that began with the letter M. Key markets such as Milwaukee, Miami, and Memphis were not on the itinerary. Allegedly, Maynard was "concerned about energy fields around Minneapolis and other areas of the country that had a strong magnetic field concentration."[662] According to the *Star Tribune*, a concert scheduled in Minneapolis on August 5 was canceled at the behest of Maynard.[663]

The chatter regarding cities that started with the letter M was widespread enough that several members of the press asked about it during interviews. Slash and Duff both vehemently denied the rumors. When asked about it on Rockline, Lars Ulrich responded, "Somebody somewhere got hold of some very long-winded story that was floating around. There was a story going around about cities that began with M that we were omitting, but obviously we're playing Minneapolis, we're playing Montreal. So, this whole thing that we didn't wanna go to Milwaukee because it begins with 'M,' that's just a crock of shit."[664] But Metallica frontman James Hetfield indicated there was truth to the rumor. "They have a lot of people out with them, and who knows who tells who what to do?" he said to the *Star Tribune*, when asked about Guns taking orders from Axl's psychic advisor. "I couldn't confirm it, but I think it did have something to do with his psychic or his psychic's assistant."[665]

St. Anger

Following his arrest at customs and court appearance, Axl's wrath about St. Louis reached new heights. GNR's legal team cautioned the singer and the rest of the band to keep quiet, but Axl was infuriated and had no intention of holding back. "I've been advised not to say anything derogatory about St. Louis," he said, two songs into GNR's set at the tour's opening night on July 17 at RFK Stadium in Washington D.C. "Well, St. Louis can suck my dick. You saw the news – an 'unexpected arrest.' It wasn't unexpected. I knew the motherfucker lied and was gonna have me arrested. And the only way we would be here tonight to do this tour was to let that asshole have his fucking way and shove it *back* down his motherfucking throat! Now the son of the bitch wants to work it out. Too late, home fuck! Because I'm fighting for what I believe in and what I feel is the truth. And I'm fighting for the people whose lives were threatened in that riot, because that place doesn't know how to have a rock concert. I mean, the last show they had was Jimmy fuckin' Buffett – give me a break! So now, it will come down in October to one of two things: either his career or my career. And *fuck* him!"

Guns launched into "Live and Let Die," which was punctuated by explosive cannon blasts. During "Welcome to the Jungle," a pair of giant inflatable monsters that resembled the flying creature on the original cover of *Appetite for Destruction* floated above the stage on either side. "If anything, it just got bigger," Slash told MTV about GNR's production on the co-headlining tour. "The stage is a little bit different and it's more dynamic. There's some pyro stuff, some explosions that go off, and we've been having a good time with it."[666]

But the St. Louis situation continued to weigh on Axl. "I got this thing on my mind," he told the audience in D.C. later. "It's trivial – no big deal, but I just can't get it off my mind."

For the first time since anyone could remember, Guns were getting to the stage on time. But that did not mean they showed up at a reasonable hour. Faith No More began at 6:30 p.m. and played for 45 minutes. Metallica went on at 8 p.m. sharp, putting in sets that lasted about two hours and fifteen minutes. Because both bands brought their full production, there was a 90 to 120-minute gap between Metallica's exit and GNR's entrance.

The long waits tended to produce restless, rowdy behavior from spectators, who occupied themselves by tossing beach balls, doing the wave, and throwing everything in sight – cups, plates, bottles, food, toilet paper rolls, clothing, inflated condoms, you name it.

GNR often began around midnight, with the performance wrapping sometime after 2:00 in the morning. "This tour seems poorly organized," griped a reviewer in assessing the opening night. "In festival situations such as this, it is customary for bands to share the same lighting and staging. But Metallica and Guns N' Roses are touring with separate stages, which forces long setup times, prompts audience restlessness and invites debauchery."[667] GNR manager Doug Goldstein defended the arrangement a few weeks later in the *L.A. Times*. "We could have cut a lot of corners – and saved a lot of money – if each band did shorter sets and used the same staging, but the whole idea was to make this tour unique."[668]

But standing in a stadium in the summer heat for eight hours was a grind for even the most devoted audiences. By the time Guns finally got onstage, the sunbaked and beer-drenched crowds were on their last legs – if they had not already given up and gone home. "You can tell that they're heat fatigued, and you can sense it's been a long day," Slash conceded a few dates into the trek. "Especially when it's 105 degrees. You can't expect 60,000 people to stand there for 12 hours. It might be difficult for them to deal with the entire thing, because it's a long day."[669]

Facing stadiums half-filled with exhausted fans brought out the worst in Axl, who relied on the crowd's energy to perform at his peak. As one reviewer noted, "By the time the set ended at 2:10 a.m. – long past many of the teenage fans' bedtimes – Mr. Rose was the most energetic person in the stadium."[670] Almost two hours into one especially dead show, Axl announced, "We're gonna take a little break while these people sitting down decide if they're too tired and want to go home." A few songs later, the frustrated singer asked the audience, "Is it past your bedtime or something?"

Metallica's willingness to perform before Guns was starting to look less like a selfless gesture and more like a strategy to reach audiences that were still fresh and energetic. GNR's twelve-piece band and Axl's numerous costume changes starkly contrasted Metallica's jeans, T-shirts, and bare-bones metal. The press praised Metallica to the heavens, making GNR appear lesser by comparison. The headlines were often brutal: "Guns Fail to Come up Smelling Like Roses" wrote the *Asbury Park Press,* while the *Observer-Reporter* opined, "Guns N' Roses Fires Mostly Blanks on Tour."[671] [672] "Guns N' Roses Misfires," read the headline of a review in *The Record,* whose critic wrote, "The energy Metallica generated could have lit the bright lights of Manhattan for a month. Guns N' Roses couldn't have powered a 9-volt battery."[673] Even longtime advocates such as *Rolling Stone* appeared to be siding with the San Francisco quartet: "If GNR had been in top form all night, they couldn't have topped Metallica's galvanizing set. The night belonged to Metallica. On song after anthemic song, Metallica achieved a pristine brutality that was riveting."[674]

Despite the initial love fest about friendship and cooperation, rivalry became the dominant vibe as Metallica strove to blow their tourmates off the stage each night. "There was always an air of competition the minute Lars stepped into a room," Matt said. "During our entire tour with Metallica, it was like he was competing with us."[675] According to Lars Ulrich, Metallica's desire to one-up their fellow headliners was friendly rather than contentious, propelling both bands to greater heights. "You need something to inspire you or force you into giving a little more of yourself," he said. "Knowing Guns is going to be on the same stage each night is something that pushes you to another level of playing – and I'm sure the same is true for them."[676]

Metallica's thirst to outdo GNR in concert galvanized them to beef up the amount of pyrotechnics used in their show. "They kept adding more and more fireworks to their set," Matt said. "At first, they were only using them in three songs, but before long they'd added them to every single track."[677] Before the trek started, the bands had agreed on the amounts of fireworks in advance – it was written into the contract. According to Matt, Metallica did not honor the agreement.

In response, Guns upped their own pyro spectacle, concluding their sets with a firework display that lasted a full five minutes and featured dozens of bangs, sparkles, airbursts, flashes, waterfalls, and fountains, followed by another hundred explosions. When the group lined up at the front of the stage each night to take a collective bow, Axl arrived sporting a red silk robe and boxing gloves, a fair indicator of his take on things. Each night before the show, the singer would autograph the boxing gloves backstage, tossing them into the audience as he made his final exit.

Afterparties

The competition that grew between the Guns and Metallica camps was not limited to the stage. Looking to one-up Metallica, Axl decided GNR would host extravagant backstage parties on every stop of the tour, an idea he nicked from the Rolling Stones. As always, Axl set out to outdo everything that had come before. The singer put his siblings, Amy and Stuart Bailey, in charge, giving them a $100,000 per party budget and insisting on an over-the-top experience: hors d' oeuvres, an open bar, pinball machines, video games, a pool table, a twelve-person hot tub, and strippers galore. "I want ice sculptures, I want champagne fountains, I want a casino, and I want to give people money to play craps and poker," Axl ordered.

The singer wanted each backstage party to have a unique theme. "We're gonna do a casino, we're gonna have dealers. And when we go to Indianapolis, I want Formula One cars. I want a Greek theme when we get to Pittsburgh. I want them to bring in a pig. Down in Orlando, I want a hippie party, with a sixties vibe."[678] The 1960s shindig featured daisies scattered about, lava lamps on every table, and slogans painted on the walls: "Acid is Groovy," "Kill the Pigs!" A 1970s rave-up included Twister mats and go-go dancers. There was a beach jamboree, a Mexican fiesta, a disco night, a Caribbean soirée, a Western hoedown, a Hawaiian Luau, a voodoo carnival, and a party based on horror films. In Pittsburgh, there was a Roman orgy theme, replete with extras dressed in togas. "They brought in a pig on a stick, a big skewer with a full hog that had been roasted," Dizzy recalled.[679] "We almost carry a circus with us for after shows," Gilby said. "We make our own parties – it's great! If you work your ass off all these years to get to this point, you have to take advantage of it. And that's what we're doing."[680]

The themed afterparties embarrassed Slash to no end. He refused to attend any of Axl's lavish affairs. "The whole idea of it was just too self-indulgent, too self-centered, and too showy for me to think about participating in good faith," the guitarist wrote in his autobiography.[681] Asked about the events by a reporter, Metallica frontman James Hetfield scoffed. "They blow big money on parties after the show. I think they could use that money somewhere else."[682]

The bad guy

Concerts in Indiana always heightened Axl's anxieties, triggering memories of the singer's worst childhood and teenage traumas. Approximately 39,000 fans attended GNR's July 22 appearance at the Hoosier Dome and Axl loathed every one of them.[683] The singer took the stage just after midnight sporting a Mike Tyson T-shirt, chiding the Indiana jury that convicted the boxer and sentenced him to prison. "Indi-fucking-ana – conservative, backwards-ass motherfuckers," he griped. "A bunch of quiet, mild-mannered people that just let the world go by around them. You helped put Dan Quayle in the president's office. But *I'm* a bad guy."

Audience members were screaming "Fuck you!" at the top of their lungs in response to Axl's insults, but the singer was just getting started. "At the same time this place tries to teach you morals and values and the truths and the things that make a country strong and a person strong, they try to break you down every step of the way here. You got a life. You got any life out there that you want to live and you can find in your heart. But you don't have any time to waste to try to get that life. Otherwise, you'll be thirty-five sitting in your trailer park, thinking about some girl you lost when you were twenty-five, wondering where did I go wrong?"

On the co-headlining tour, promoters routinely forbid alcohol sales at the stadiums. This reduced the potential for fighting and other problems inside the venues, but often led to parking lots filled with rowdy tailgaters, pregaming for the concert. In Indiana, police made 214 arrests in and around the Hoosier Dome for crimes such as public intoxication, disorderly conduct, weapons, and drug-related violations.[684] Axl drew cheers from the boozed-up crowd when he asked them, "What'd you do this week? Get off work and pick up a cold twelve or something? Think about fucking the guy or the girl down the street or at work? Watch some TV? Do you really think you got time for that?"

"There ain't nothing else to do!" an audience member cried in response, infuriating the singer. "If there ain't nothing to do, why don't you get the fuck out and find yourself something to do," he raged. "Or turn this place into something other than a corn-producing, pharmaceutical-making beer factory. Fucking cornfield Japanese-owned car company that has a choice of deciding if you can live or die by hiring you to give you money to eat. You're the only people who can make a difference in this place. You *got* to know that. Your parents didn't do it, their parents before them didn't do it. They're still sitting on their ass. You got to make a difference." Guns were only five songs into their set. Slash sighed. It was going to be another long night.

Blind Melon vocalist and fellow Indiana native Shannon Hoon joined the band onstage to share vocals on "Don't Cry." But the appearance of Axl's protegee during the encore didn't improve the singer's mood any. When GNR departed at 2:30 in the morning, everyone looked dejected.

The next day's headlines were unsparing: "Axl's Unrestrained Ego Bigger Than Hoosier Dome" decried the *Journal and Courier*.[685] "Rose's Music Hath More Charm Than He" asserted *The Indianapolis News*.[686] "Guns More Mouth Than Music" read the headline in *The Indianapolis Star*, which sharply criticized Axl's anti-Indiana screeds.[687] In response, Axl wrote the reviewer a letter, condemning his "basic

Indiana attempt at journalism."[688] "Indiana needs to wake up. If that takes a little taunting and two-and-a-half hours of music + a fireworks show + a cartoon to wake up maybe 5% of a 48,000-plus crowd, then so be it. I can also suffer your redneck, blind, narrow minded refuse about ranting – you nor anyone will <u>ever</u> dictate my actions, attitudes, comments, orientation, and musical performances on stage. I came here to enrage, and I succeeded. You're just gonna sit on your wannabe ass and watch me, born a Hoosier, grow larger than you could ever imagine or ever be able to stop. That's not to say I didn't appreciate your anger, hostility and general ignorance. It shows me my so called 'RANTS' are a much needed, missing piece in our puzzle of society."[689]

If local concertgoers were turned off by Axl's tirades at the Hoosier Dome, they didn't show it. GNR remained in town, and the next evening, Axl hopped into one of the three limos parked on standby outside the group's hotel and headed over to Arni's, a local Italian joint. Almost immediately, he was surrounded by fans. Axl's pizza run made the local papers. One devotee picked up the singer's still smoldering cigarette butt from the sidewalk as a souvenir. "I'm going to put it in my room, frame it," he gushed.[690]

Vegemetarian

Guns and Metallica didn't hang out backstage or interact much that summer, preferring to stay ensconced in their separate bubbles. "I don't even go to the gig until right before we go on," Slash told the *L.A. Times*. "I haven't seen Metallica since we started touring because I don't want to be intimidated or influenced, even subconsciously."[691] Duff had his own reasons to keep his distance. "We are buddies with Metallica, but I've seen them only once this tour. I don't like coming down to the shows early because there's too many drug dealers around. It's too tempting. So many people will push drugs on you."[692]

James Hetfield could barely contain his contempt for Axl. The Metallica frontman couldn't stand what he saw as the singer's prima donna, rock star bullshit, his massive entourage, "ego ramps," multiple costume changes, and use of a teleprompter. "I tried to communicate with Axl," Hetfield told the *Star Tribune.* "He's got a lot of yes men, which doesn't help him mentally, but speaking with him is really difficult. I don't really like hearing shit secondhand from people: 'Oh, his psychic said this.' I hate the whole gossip thing. Guns have so many people on tour, it's amazing. Who knows what those people do?"[693]

When asked to name something he *did* like about GNR, Hetfield praised their musical capabilities. "I like the fact they're really loose and they just play any song at any time. The fact that they have other instruments up there – piano, harmonica, horn section – is really cool. They've got no limits on what they're doing musically. Oh, I like Axl's shorts; they're really cute."[694]

Hoping to generate some camaraderie, the night before the July 29 stop at Giants Stadium, Axl treated 160 members of the touring party to a feast at the Old Homestead restaurant in New York City. Steak, prime rib, and lobster were accompanied by bottles of Dom Perignon champagne and Chateau Margaux, a French red wine. During the event, Axl gave a speech thanking the crew for their hard work. "You're the greatest – the best support crew I ever worked with," he said sincerely.

As the dinner continued into the night, a waiter named Randy mentioned he would be late for a class he was taking. Axl personally penned a note to the teacher: "Dear Mr. Sacco, I'm so sorry Randy was absent from school as he was working hard to feed starving heathens. Please excuse him, and with any luck it will happen again. Sincerely, W. Axl Rose."[695]

Backstage at Giants Stadium, Slash insisted Axl had made significant changes that had improved their musical partnership. The singer was less mercurial and more mature. "We had always been friends, but there is really a bond there now," Slash said. "We'd have fights because of something I was supposed to have said about him in the press or something he was supposed to have said about me. All these problems have pushed us closer together, so that we communicate better and avoid the misunderstandings. He can lean on me, and I can lean on him. He has opened up more. He's not like a firecracker anymore, who just explodes."[696]

Metallica drummer Lars Ulrich agreed Axl's persona was far different than the man himself. "I find it amusing that the minute you start saying Guns N' Roses, everybody conjures up all these pictures that are the result of images and rumors," Ulrich said backstage at Giants Stadium. "I know a lot of people said the tour will never happen or Axl'll never show up, but I never had any worries. I know Axl and when he really wants to do something, he can do it. Both bands have enough mutual respect for each other not to drag each other down."[697]

But James Hetfield was not convinced. Backstage at Giant's Stadium, he mercilessly poked fun at Axl's list of pre-show requests while a documentary crew filmed. "Horrible truths. Guns and Metallica piddly wants and wills and needs for certain folks on the road. Axl Pose dressing-room requirements – absolutely no substitutions. One cup of *cubed* ham. It's gotta be cubed up right, so it can get down his little neck. One rib-eye steak dinner. I didn't even know the guy ate meat – he looks like a 'vegemetarian.' One *gourmet* cheese tray. Pepperoni pizza – fresh. I think that's just for throwing around. Cans of assorted Pringles chips. You know, the greasy shit that he uses to put his hair back. Sue Bee honey that makes him *sing like this*. A bottle of Dom Perignon – that's where the money's at, right there. Just fuckin' crap, a bunch of hooey." Hetfield threw the list on the floor and stomped on it.[698]

GNR would not find out about Hetfield's making fun of Axl until Metallica released a documentary that featured the scene in November 1992. Asked about it by *Rolling Stone* magazine, Hetfield dismissed his comments as "Metallica humor. It didn't really matter what the hell was on it. Just the fact that Axl had his own rider was funny. It's hard to grasp. When we saw he had his own dressing room, I just didn't understand that."[699]

That night at Giant's Stadium, Axl was hit several times by objects thrown from the audience, eventually leaving the stage after being nailed in the groin by a cigarette lighter. Guns were already two hours and fifteen minutes into their show, so Axl's early exit went largely unnoticed. But the singer strained his vocal cords, and a physician advised him to take a week off. Concerts that were supposed to take place in Boston, Minneapolis, and Columbia, South Carolina were postponed, with rescheduled dates to be announced at a later time. The GNR-Metallica trek resumed on August 8 in Montreal, a gig that turned out to be the venture's most notorious stop.

Montreal

Metallica were frustrated by Axl's postponement, viewing it as another example of the singer's supposed diva-like behavior. Metallica's management informed Guns they intended to continue with or without them.[700] Although Axl did not feel as if his voice was fully healed, GNR agreed to resume the tour at the Olympic Stadium in Montreal. More than 57,000 fans attended. "It was the first show back after Axl had some problems with his throat," Lars Ulrich recalled. "So, we're back again in Montreal, everybody was very excited, and for the first hour and ten minutes, it was great. It was looking to be one of the best ones."[701]

Midway through Metallica's set, disaster struck. Looking to outdo Guns, Metallica had continued to add more and more pyrotechnics to their production. According to Matt Sorum, the band's stage "was starting to look more and more like a minefield."[702] During the introduction of "Fade to Black" there was a miscommunication regarding where some new pyro devices were placed. James Hetfield ended up moving to a location on the stage directly above where a twenty-foot flame tower would launch. When it ignited, the frontman was engulfed in fire and severely burned. Metallica immediately ended their set and Hetfield was rushed to Montreal General Hospital. "There was an incident with the pyrotechnics," Lars Ulrich explained to the crowd, flanked by Kirk Hammett and Jason Newsted. "Unfortunately, James is on the way to the hospital right now, and we're very sorry but we can't continue the concert for you tonight. But we promise you one thing, we will come back and finish our concert and play again for you as soon as we can."

Guns were not on site when Hetfield was scorched – everyone was still at the hotel. The promoters asked GNR to go onstage immediately, an impossible request given it took roughly ninety minutes to tear down and set up the two bands' equipment. Furthermore, even on the best nights, Axl needed about four hours to prepare for a show. The singer was roughly halfway through his routine – and still dealing with serious voice issues. But everyone agreed to rush over to the stadium and get onstage as soon as possible. "Okay, guys, let's go up there and do this as quick as we can," Axl told the group.[703]

The delay between Metallica and Guns took about two hours – a fairly common changeover time on the co-headlining tour but one that always generated restlessness and hostility from audiences. "I sat backstage monitoring the sounds drifting in from the arena, drink in hand, and could feel the crowd's mood change," Duff remembered. "The rumble of tens of thousands of people beginning to get angry is a deep, low sound that penetrates walls and vibrates the fundamentals of buildings, where dressing rooms are located. It's a horrible sound. After letting the crowd reach its boiling point, we finally went out and started playing."[704]

"When we got up there it was just really dead," Matt Sorum recalled. "The people were sitting down."[705] By all accounts, GNR's monitor system was plagued by technical issues – the band could not hear themselves at all. "The PA fed back the entire time, the monitors fed back the entire time," Slash said. "The crowd was non-existent. It was driving me crazy."[706]

Five numbers into the set, Axl told the audience, "This is the theme song to a movie we've been filming since we started this tour." Guns then played "Perfect Crime" for the final time on the Illusion trek. As of this publication, they have never played it in concert again.

Axl, already suffering from vocal cord issues, strained to be heard over the din, pushing his fragile throat to the limits. "I was having to sing over fifty kilowatts of sound or something," the singer remembered. "I didn't do major damage to my vocal cords, but I did enough that if I sang anymore under those conditions, I wouldn't be singing. In order to hear myself, to see if I'm on key and tell how loud or how hard I need to push to sing a song properly, I have to try to sing over the PA, which was impossible."[707]

Axl was frustrated and angry to be put in this position once again. *I'm gonna hurt myself*, he thought. "Two more songs; if we can't get it fixed, I gotta go," he told Slash.

"We just came back from a seven-week tour of Europe. This has pretty much killed us for the last year and a half," Axl said to the crowd. "I don't want to fall apart by the end of this tour, so in case anybody is interested, this will be our last show for a long time. This is called 'Double Talking Jive' motherfucker." Axl slammed his microphone to the floor and stormed off stage as the musicians launched into the tune. Moments later, the singer returned clutching a new microphone and finished the number.

GNR then played "Civil War," the sound cutting in and out. Axl had had enough, telling Gilby, "Dude, I can't hear." Duff replied, "I can't hear either." The band was less than an hour into their set. As Slash plucked the outro on his Les Paul, Axl decided to cancel.[708] "Thank you. Your money will be refunded," he told the audience. "We're outta here."

The concertgoers were infuriated. They lit GNR T-shirts on fire, threw bottles, overturned concession stands, and damaged the stadium's seating.[709] They smashed the windows at a store that sold Expos baseball merchandise and then looted it. As they exited the venue, they threw rocks and bottles at the police, injuring eight officers. Outside the stadium, they set fires in garbage cans, flipped a police car over, and damaged twenty-six more, slashing tires, smashing mirrors and windows.[710] "Everyone was yelling: 'Kill them. We've got to destroy everything,'" a female ticketholder recalled. "We didn't know if we were going to die." Approximately 10,000 attendees took part in the riot, which was eventually contained by 300 police officers wielding riot clubs and tear gas. Twelve arrests were made.[711]

"This time the riot didn't start near the stage," Duff said. "We didn't even see it. In fact, our crew did their normal teardown of the set, oblivious to the riot already raging out of view. Only when our buses pulled out of the parking enclosure did we see the full extent of the situation – cop cars turned over, vehicles on fire, lots of broken windows."[712]

James Hetfield, who suffered second-degree burns to his face, arms, and hands, heard about the situation from the emergency ward. "I was at the hospital. They drugged me up. So, I had one of the guys who works for us go and get my boom-box. I was tuning through the stations, and all of a sudden, I heard, 'James Hetfield got burned, and there's a riot going on.' I went, 'What the hell?'"[713]

The Montreal riot made headlines around the world, with blame for the incident falling squarely on Axl. "Everybody agrees singer Axl Rose is to blame for what happened," the *Montreal Gazette* wrote a few days later.[714] The story the press told was Axl walked off stage because he had a sore throat. Metallica pointed fingers at Axl, too, furious over what they viewed as more prima donna behavior from the rock star singer. "We went into the dressing room, and they're acting like nothing happened," an incredulous Kirk Hammett recalled to VH-1. Jason Newsted added, "Axl's down there with the cigarette holder in one hand and the champagne glass in the other, and he says, 'My voice is giving me trouble.' If your voice is gonna give you trouble, you shouldn't probably be drinking and smoking."[715] In an interview with *Rolling Stone* a few months after the incident, James Hetfield said, "I was so disappointed in him. He could have won so many people over by continuing the show. And he went the exact opposite way and made things ten times worse and jeopardized people's lives. There was a lot of unnecessary violence because of his attitude. He could have turned it into a great evening."[716]

Even Axl's bandmates blamed him for what took place in Montreal. "We could have saved the day by going right on and playing a long set," Duff wrote in his memoir. "It would have been a great gesture to the fans and to the guys in Metallica. It would have been the professional thing to do, the right thing to do. But no."[717] Publicly Slash was supportive of Axl, but privately he was embarrassed by the singer's behavior. "I'd lost face with everyone in Metallica," he recalled. "We didn't keep our promise to them, the fans, or to ourselves to put on the best show possible, come what may. When it had mattered the most, it felt like we'd given even less. I felt like an ass. I couldn't look James, Lars, or anyone in their band in the eye for the rest of the tour."[718]

In the wake of the Montreal incident, Axl was defensive and unapologetic. "People want what they want," the singer told MTV a few weeks after the riot took place. "If there's a problem on stage and you have to stop the show, they don't really care. They're still upset. There were technical difficulties in Montreal, and we had to leave, and the crowd was really upset about that and they didn't take the time to think about what went on for us. I don't feel responsible for that."[719]

GNR were sued by the promoters and hit with a lifetime ban from performing at the Olympic Stadium.[720] "Every time we have one of these happy-go-lucky riots, we are the ones punished," Slash told *Guitar World* later that year. "It's really disappointing because we'll probably never get to play there again. You never set out to cause something like that. But people think we set out to provoke it."[721]

Due to James Hetfield's injuries, six dates had to be postponed and an August 10 concert in Vancouver was cancelled. From the time the tour began in July, only nine of the first nineteen shows took place as scheduled. "Sometimes it seems like Guns has had to deal with every possible obstacle throughout our career," Slash told the press, sounding shellshocked. "Things that would stop any other band in its tracks. Those things are just tests, and every day there is a new one. It gets frustrating because you always wonder, 'Is there ever going to be a break? Is there ever going to be a cruise period?' Nothing phases me now."[722]

Chapter 14

Body Count

James Hetfield took a couple of weeks to recover from the burns he received in Montreal, pausing the Guns-Metallica tour for the second time. GNR used the unexpected downtime to shoot a music video for the old West Arkeen song "Yesterdays." Andy Morahan, who helmed "Don't Cry" and "November Rain," was brought on board to direct. Unlike those elaborate big-budget videos, "Yesterdays" was a relatively straightforward affair, taped in a single-late night session. GNR's instruments were set up in an airplane hangar as they performed the song, with Axl miming into a vintage microphone. Teddy Andreadis handled an organ alongside the six members of Guns.

Shot in black and white and augmented by vintage photos of the band, "Yesterdays" was a throwback to the classic video for "Sweet Child O' Mine." "It was a relaxed, simple black-and-white warehouse performance," Morahan recalled. "It was supposed to be the opposite of the big stage with all the bells and whistles – a bit more organic, edgy, and rough. So, it just felt more naturalistic."[723]

During the shoot for "Yesterdays," in a fit of late-night inspiration, Morahan suggested they create a second video for one of his favorite *Illusion* tracks, "Garden of Eden." Morahan had a concept in mind – shoot the frenetic song in a single take, using only one camera with a fisheye lens. The production team would flash lights to give the footage an odd, stop-motion look. GNR's instruments were already on site, so setting up the shot would only take a few minutes.

"We're here, we should just do it," Morahan told Slash, who was skeptical Axl would agree to make a second video that night.

"You can ask Axl, but I bet he doesn't want to do it," Slash told the director.

"Axl was tired, he was a bit cranky," Morahan recalled, but the director pleaded his case. "Just give me *one* take and if you don't like it, fine."[724] Reluctantly, Axl agreed. It was nearly six in the morning when Guns ran through the number. "It was at the tail end of the day, and we just shook our heads like madmen for about two minutes," Slash recalled. "It was a hell of a lot of fun."[725]

Morahan showed the clip to Axl, and he loved it. "This is amazing!" he enthused and immediately agreed to try a few more takes. "Once they saw what it was, they all got it," Morahan said. "We did five or six takes. It's kind of a manic track, so they performed it like that. I never cut. The worst thing you can do when you're doing a one-take shot is to stop it. Because their energy is so high."[726]

In the take that was ultimately used, GNR blasts through the frenzied, three-minute number, with Axl mugging for the camera as Dizzy and Teddy dance and flail in the background. Guns were famous for their expensive, high concept videos, but here they produced a single-take gem that was, in many ways, just as iconic. There were no plans to issue "Garden of Eden" as a single, but the simple, energetic piece remains one of Morahan's favorites. "It was a relief to do something that was back to their roots, that didn't have the pressure of all the big money and half the band not turning up on time. It was just one of those great moments. 'November Rain' has won all these things and it's an iconic video, but in a weird personal way, 'Garden of Eden' is my favorite video with them."[727]

Gilby was interviewed two days after the videos were shot, telling a Canadian publication, "We just got in from shooting a video. We did two actually – one for 'Yesterdays' and one for 'Garden of Eden.' Whether they both come out or not, we don't know. These are cool – they're back to the basics, just the rock 'n' roll band stuff."[728]

Slash was thrilled GNR had created a pair of music videos that stripped away the largesse of "Don't Cry" and "November Rain." "We don't want to be so-called video entrepreneur types, trying to make huge videos that sell a lot of records, and stupendous and technical and stuff. It's just really to get the expression of the band across."[729]

No more faith

While GNR were on hiatus, a number of the interviews Faith No More had given in Europe began to be published. The stories were filled with disparaging remarks about Guns, especially Axl. An interview with bassist Billy Gould published in *New Musical Express*, a major U.K. music outlet, quoted him as opining that, "GNR and their management are like a small government. Axl's the president, and his manager's a personal advisor. A couple of the other more visible band members are vice-presidents. Then there's the little guys who come underneath, to make sure only the right information is leaked out. They're dependent on the band for their living, so they will police themselves. Keep your mouth shut, enjoy the ride and everything will be cool. Open your mouth and jeopardize your own position."[730]

Vocalist Mike Patton declared to *Melody Maker*, another prominent U.K. music publication, that Axl was losing his hair. "He really is! They were playing one night and Duff walks up to Axl and pats him on the head like a loving comrade-type thing and Axl Rose immediately brings the show to a halt – this is in front of 80,000 people – and he screams, 'Don't you ever touch my head again, motherfucker!' Duff just walked away, wounded. We found out later that it was 'cause he's going bald and he's worried that if you touch his hair, it will fall out."[731] While in London, Patton told a reporter from *Details* magazine, "These are the most boring shows I've been to. The crowd is so safe. Backstage is so boring. I wouldn't go to the show. It's a spectator sport."[732] Patton further claimed a crew member was fired for accidentally bumping into Axl.

FNM's gleeful slagging did not end in Europe. In an article previewing the Guns-Metallica tour's upcoming stop in New Mexico, bassist Billy Gould told the *El Paso Times* Faith No More had nicknamed Axl "The Little Prince," and that the singer had cancelled dates in Munich and Madrid due to his psychic's "M" prohibition and scrapped six U.S. gigs because a fan hit him with a hotdog.[733] The music journalists, looking to make names for themselves and sell magazines, printed every word. They didn't care if FNM's outlandish tales of rock's most notorious singer were true or not – it made great copy.

Faith No More's smearing of Axl and company was so widespread reporters started asking GNR about it during interviews. "They're not too crazy about our band," Gilby admitted five days before the tour was set to resume. "The reason we got Faith No More on the bill was it was our way of bringing a broad spectrum of music together that we still had something in common with – people who have our record have Metallica and Faith No More records. If they're not crazy about the band that's up to them, but we're not going to kick them off the bill just because they don't like the band. I can't slag someone for having their own opinion. It certainly doesn't affect us."[734]

Gilby was being diplomatic. In reality, Axl was angry and hurt. He was a huge FNM fan and had personally invited them to tour with Guns in Europe and to open on their excursion with Metallica. He couldn't believe they would repay his generosity by insulting him in such a public way. Axl and Slash called a meeting with Faith No More and made it clear they needed to quit bad mouthing GNR if they wanted to remain on the tour. "If you don't like it here, just fucking leave," Slash told the group. "It can't be like this. Either let's do this thing and make it great, or forget it, go home."[735]

FNM agreed to bite their tongues for the remainder of the dates. "Call me back in ten days," Billy Gould told a reporter just before their final show in September. "I'll tell you anything you want to know. That's when we get off this tour. All I'll say is, everything you've heard is true."

Faith No More would later come to realize they had been played by the press, duped into dishing dirt to reporters who happily used them to sell magazines and make a name for themselves.

The next shot of insulin

When GNR's venture with Metallica resumed on August 25 in Arizona, Metal Church axeman John Marshall had taken over rhythm duties for James Hetfield. The Metallica frontman appeared onstage with a heavily bandaged arm and spent the remainder of the tour singing but unable to so much as hold a guitar.

The Arizona show took place at the Phoenix International Raceway, which had never hosted a concert before. The date had originally been booked at Arizona State University's Sun Devil Stadium, but wary promoters pulled out at the last minute, necessitating an eleventh-hour venue change. A flood struck the area just days before, and a swollen river that annexed the Raceway forced the closure of several roads. The resulting six-mile traffic jam caused a three-hour delay. Several concertgoers had to be rescued after they got stuck attempting to cross the flooded river. A nineteen-year-old attendee was swept away by the current and died.[736] The incident marked yet another tragedy in a tour beset by difficulties.

The headlines over the latest riot in Montreal cemented Axl's reputation for volatility. At this point, some concertgoers deliberately provoked the singer, hoping to cause an explosion, meltdown, or maybe even a riot. At GNR's August 27 appearance in New Mexico, Axl threatened to leave the stage after fans continually threw things at him. "It's like people who go to watch the Indy 500," Doug Goldstein told the press. "They don't go to watch the race; they go to see the crash."[737]

Axl conceded it was difficult to manage audiences that cheered for him, but also hoped he would lose it and do something stupid or crazy. "It can be tough to deal with," he said in an interview earlier that summer. "It's very disguised. It's not like, 'Aw, you suck!' They're screaming and happy, but they want to see blood. I've done shows where to the naked eye it looked really positive, but onstage, being sensitive to it, these people were out for every last drop they could get. It's hard to stay positive when there's that kind of anger in the crowd. It's hard to stay focused when you're getting beat up by the energy. To rise above that and still satiate the crowd is a tough job."[738]

Audiences that lacked energy were challenging, too. GNR's late-night closing sets meant performing for concertgoers who had been on hand for several hours and heard more than three hours of music from two bands. In New Orleans, Axl became frustrated by the lackluster reaction from the attendees in the first few rows. "How much did you people pay for your tickets?" he asked them. "I'll pay you back right now 'cause this just ain't gonna work. We might as well just sit up here and take a nap. No offense, I know. It's a hard day, and you're tired, and we go on really late. I understand. It's just kind of hard to work up here with people taking a fucking nap. If we put you to sleep, I'm really sorry."

In response, GNR's setlists began to feature more songs from *Appetite*. The *Illusion* cuts were pared down, save for hits such as "Civil War" and "November Rain," and the *Appetite*-era favorite, "Knockin' on Heaven's Door." Slash explained, "We are aware the audience is pretty tired by the end of the night, but we've fought through that. Even though the crowd is tired, we've felt that the response has been warm and appreciative."[739]

In many respects Guns had never been more popular. The *Illusion* albums were approaching sales of eight million in the U.S. alone. "November Rain" had been slowly moving up the Billboard Hot 100 chart that summer, peaking at number three on August 29 – GNR's second highest-charting single ever. But the band members were increasingly weary after more than a year on the road. Things were "so explosive, it could have blown up any day and the whole thing could have been over," Stephen Thaxton, the tour chiropractor, recalled.[740] The group seemed fragile, perpetually on the verge of falling apart. "We don't really know either," Gilby admitted when asked about GNR's future. "We certainly make plans for the future, but this is a very volatile rock 'n' roll band and whatever happens is going to happen."[741]

To manage the challenges of nonstop touring and keep the anxieties at bay, Guns continued to prop themselves up with drugs and alcohol. A journalist from *Life* magazine was on hand in New Orleans and observed Duff was "a gentle, silly and delightful man, even when he is drunk, which nowadays seems most of the morning and most of the afternoon and a good part of every evening. Duff is having a hard time with life on the road."[742] The bassist concurred his day-to-day existence had become a blur. "A lot of nights I wake up and I'm like, where am I? What city?" he told the *Life* reporter. "You run to the window and look out and try to figure it out. You actually forget who you are. I am completely blank. I end up a lot of times just sitting on my bed, and I'll find tears start coming out of my eyes and my heart is just aching. 'Please let there be another show soon.' Can you get the next shot of insulin?"[743]

Alternative

When the idea of a Guns-Metallica excursion was initially floated, everyone desperately wanted Nirvana on the bill. Since releasing their second album, *Nevermind*, on September 24, 1991, just a week after GNR's *Illusion* albums dropped, the Seattle trio had shot to the top of the rock world. Axl was a major fan who sported a Nirvana ballcap onstage and in the behind-the-scenes interviews for the "Don't Cry" music video. He felt Kurt Cobain was a kindred spirit who, like him, had transformed his childhood trauma into music filled with rage, yet belied a sensitivity. Guns had offered Nirvana opening slots on several occasions but had been soundly rejected by Cobain and company. "I think there is a part of him that has the strength and desire to do it," Axl told *Musician* magazine that spring. I just don't know if he's able to get in touch with it."[744]

Everyone was flabbergasted at Nirvana's unwillingness to play third on the bill at the GNR-Metallica venture. "It was kind of annoying when they refused to go along because Nirvana is another band with attitudes similar to Guns N' Roses and Metallica," Lars Ulrich told a reporter at the outset of the co-headlining trek. "They kept saying they didn't know if they wanted to play stadiums or even go on tour. I couldn't understand it. We were saying, 'Here's the biggest tour of the summer. Come on out and you'll play to 50,000 people four times a week. Do you want to stick to playing clubs?'"[745]

Throughout the Illusion trek, Axl had recruited credible alternative-rock opening acts such as Soundgarden and Faith No More, but still Nirvana refused to associate themselves with Guns. Axl had become increasingly fed up with the entire alternative-rock nation, which threatened to usurp GNR's supremacy. "We've had our share of problems with so-called alternative bands," the singer told 48,000 spectators at Orlando's Citrus Bowl on September 2. "What is this word? I mean, I didn't find myself using it. *Alternative.* Like someone who leads an alternative lifestyle. All I know is that when Guns N' Roses started, ain't no fucking radio stations wanted to play our shit, either. Ain't no radio stations wanted to play Metallica. So, I think we have the world's biggest alternative crowd here tonight."

The audience roared in approval. Axl continued, building up a head of steam. "The problem starts when you start thinking that you're different from everybody else on the planet. You may be a little different in what you're doing and how you're going about doing it, but I got a good feeling that you're probably a human being, right?"

Kurt Cobain and his wife, Courtney Love, generated international controversy over a September 1992 *Vanity Fair* article, which portrayed them as heroin-abusing junkies on a downward spiral. "They are expecting a baby this month, and even the most tolerant industry insiders fear for the health of the child," *Vanity Fair* wrote, insinuating Love was shooting heroin while pregnant.[746] Axl, disdainful of heavy drugs and triggered by tales of child abuse, was apoplectic.

"Right now, 'alternative,' the only thing that means to me is someone like Kurt Cobain, who basically is a junkie with a junkie wife. And if the baby is born deformed, I think they both ought to go to prison. And he's too good and too cool to bring his rock 'n' roll to you. Because the majority of you, he doesn't like or want to play to – or even have you like his music. It seems to be a general feeling among a lot of alternative bands, that they don't want the majority of people even liking them. They like it on the outside."

Axl's venom was partly spurred by several disparaging remarks Cobain and Love made about him in the *Vanity Fair* writeup, which pointed out Nirvana had turned down the GNR-Metallica outing and refused an offer to perform at Axl's thirty-sixth birthday party. Axl's onstage rant about Cobain in Orlando was covered by several national publications, helping to further the animosity between the Guns and Nirvana camps.[747]

Axl's petulance was a permanent part of GNR's show, but his onstage tirades began to generate increasingly negative press coverage. A review of the Orlando appearance in *The Tampa Tribune* described the singer as a "bratty millionaire."[748] The group also garnered scornful headlines in Florida for inviting a dozen female fans onstage, who promptly removed their shirts while dancing to "You Could Be Mine."[749] "It was a total surprise," Joanne Grant, a Citrus Bowl executive, told a reporter. "We've had many phone calls, and we are directing them to management. For me to send officers up on the stage would have caused a riot. It was a decision to just let it happen and it will be over in a few minutes. I'm certainly not happy about it."[750] Tour publicist Wendy Laister shrugged off the incident. "Any kids who come to a Guns N' Roses show are certainly going to have seen a breast before," she said, "Those offended were in the minority."[751] Slash seemed unbothered, too. "We're not angels by any means," the guitarist said. "We're still the eternal teenager band."[752]

Following the Orlando appearance, GNR traveled to Texas where they performed in Houston and Dallas. After their September 4 concert at Houston's Astrodome, Axl sat for a 4 a.m. interview with MTV's Tabitha Soren. She asked about the number of cancelled or postponed summer dates and the riot in Montreal. "Everybody had wanted this tour so bad and worked so hard to be able to do it," Axl said. "We thought it would just be perfect, that it would be so cool. Well, it kind of turned out to be the hardest thing we've ever done."[753]

Axl noted he was getting to the stage on time more often, despite the amount of preparation it still required. "I had to change my whole life in order to be able to keep doing this," he explained. "You do a show and then you'd be shot for three weeks, but no, you've got a show tomorrow. So, it'd take all these hours of preparation."[754]

Axl compared his job fronting Guns to being a competitive sportsman, trying to avoid injuries and ingesting sixty vitamins per day so he could execute at the highest level. "Every show we play is kind of like the Super Bowl," he said.[755] Like professional athletes, the physicality of Axl's performance required a team of trainers and medical staff. "It's like I have a pit crew and I'm a car. We do muscle testing and kinesiology. We do chiropractic work and acupuncture. We do cranial adjusting. On a daily basis, I'm putting my life back together and I'm using everything I can."[756]

Axl explained these various forms of physical therapy were central to his mental-health routine. Similar to his psychotherapy sessions, the goal was to uncover and heal hurts from the past, including his childhood. "When certain traumas happen to you, your brain releases chemicals that get trapped in the muscles where the trauma occurred," he said. "I've been working on releasing this stuff, but as soon as we release one thing and that damage is gone, some new muscle hurts. That's not a new injury, it's a very old injury that, in order to survive, I've buried. When I get a massage, it's not a relaxing thing; it's like a football player getting worked on. I've had work done on me – muscle therapy, kinesiology, acupuncture – almost every day that we've been on the road."[757]

Axl's time-consuming daily routines, however, meant the singer kept mostly to himself, friendly but distant, continually surrounded by a small circle of handlers and helpers. The singer stayed at different hotels from the rest of the group and maintained a separate backstage area. At this point, the only time Axl had any interaction with his bandmates was when they were onstage. "Nobody really has contact with him other than his close friends, his assistant, his chiropractor," Lisa Maxwell, GNR's sax player, told *The Boston Globe*. "But he's always been totally great with us – he jokes around when we pass him in the hall."[758]

Video vanguards

On September 9, Guns returned to L.A. to appear on MTV's Video Music Awards, held at UCLA's Pauley Pavilion. The broadcast featured live performances by rock legends such as Eric Clapton, Elton John, and Bryan Adams alongside up-and-comers the Black Crowes. The VMAs also included incendiary live numbers from a trio of newly crowned alternative-rock kings: Nirvana, Pearl Jam, and the Red Hot Chili Peppers, each of whom had issued a multiplatinum smash in the previous year.

L.A. alt-funksters the Chili Peppers were the most celebrated act of the night, nominated in nine categories for the songs "Give It Away" and "Under the Bridge." L.A. hard-rock heroes Van Halen were nominated in seven categories, taking home the prize for Video of the Year for their positive-thinking anthem, "Right Now." GNR were up for two awards for "November Rain," which won for Best Cinematography. For their contributions to the medium over the years, Guns were being honored with the Michael Jackson Video Vanguard Award.

The Pauley Pavillion did not have enough backstage space to accommodate all the artists and their entourages, so a series of tents and trailers was set up outside the venue. MTV newsman Kurt Loder and supermodel Cindy Crawford hosted a preshow from the makeshift backstage, yapping about the nominees and interviewing anyone willing to talk. Metallica's Lars Ulrich, who along with Kirk Hammett would serve as a presenter that night, stopped by to explain why his band was not performing. "James is not great, but he's getting better and better every day. He's up in San Francisco right now for this three-day break in the Guns N' Roses-Metallica tour, seeing a specialist. The fact that he's out there singing every day and the fact that he's sweating into the sores, it's not a pretty sight. I'll spare you the grizzly visuals. Can you say blood blisters?"

MTV's Tabitha Soren was also on hand, interviewing rockers such as Black Crowes frontman Chris Robinson. Axl and Stephanie Seymour could be spotted in the background but declined to stop and chat. Soren did, however, show clips from the recent interview she conducted with Axl in Houston, as well as brief snippets of discussions with Slash and Gilby.

The growing feud between GNR and Nirvana came to a head backstage when Axl and Stephanie Seymour passed by Kurt Cobain and Courtney Love, who were tending to their newborn daughter. "Hey, look, it's Asshole Rose!" Love yelled in front of dozens of onlookers. "What are you doing, Asshole?"[759] Axl tried to ignore them, but Love continued to provoke the singer. "Do you want to be godfather to our daughter?"[760]

Axl was stunned. He worshipped Cobain's music and had been a longtime Nirvana supporter. The singer was baffled Cobain and his wife hated him so much – they had never met, shook hands, or had even a five-minute conversation. "Are you a model?" Seymour asked Love sarcastically. "Yeah, are you a brain surgeon?" Love fired back. Axl had enough. "You better get a handle on your woman," he told Cobain. The Nirvana frontman looked over at Love and told her robotically, "Woman, you better listen to me," drawing laughter from their entourage.[761] Axl and Stephanie stormed off.

"We were just joking around," Cobain told MTV. "He turned around and started pointing his finger at us, really aggressive and mean, threatening to beat me up and stuff. I couldn't help but laugh because I haven't been in that kind of a situation since I was in sixth grade."[762] Cobain milked the encounter with Axl for everything it was worth, with the tale getting more outlandish each time he retold it. "Axl had, like, twenty bodyguards with him and I had a little helpless child in my arms," Cobain said onstage at a Nirvana concert shortly after the incident took place.

The bad vibes between the two camps continued to simmer throughout the night. At one point, an inebriated Duff – flanked by a couple of bodyguards – challenged Nirvana bassist Krist Novoselic to a fistfight. According to MTV executive Amy Finnerty, "After the show I went back to Nirvana's trailer. As I got there, I saw Duff McKagan and a couple of the guys from the Guns N' Roses camp rocking the trailer back and forth, trying to tip it over. They were trying to get back at Kurt for his comments. I started screaming at them, 'The baby's in there, the baby's in there!' They stopped, but it was ugly for a second."[763] In 2010, Duff published an apology to Novoselic in *Seattle Weekly*.[764]

Later that night, Brian May and Roger Taylor from Queen presented Guns with the Michael Jackson Video Vanguard Award. "This announcement gives me more pleasure than I can tell you," May said, adding GNR had "almost singlehandedly put back the passion, and the anger, and the reality into a virtually dormant rock 'n' roll industry. Like the Sex Pistols before them, they rejuvenated the music world." Taylor added, "They're truly the most exciting band in the world, possibly," before rattling off a list of accolades and sales figures. "Their music videos have become short films that are always unique and explosive." Guns strode onstage to collect the prize and kept it short, with Axl thanking a handful of people before adding the award had "nothing to do with Michael Jackson."

To close the show, GNR performed "November Rain," accompanied by a full orchestra. Axl sat at the piano on a custom-made bench that had been designed to resemble a motorcycle seat. Across from Axl, seated at a second piano, was his lifelong musical hero, Elton John. It marked the second time the singer performed with Elton in 1992, but this time they were playing a number written by Axl. The moment instantly became one of Axl's all-time career highlights. "Elton John has always been one of my biggest influences, and if it wasn't for Elton John, this song wouldn't necessarily exist," he said. "So, that was a great honor, to have him play the song. I've never been that nervous, under pressure and also blown away. That's Elton John sitting across playing the song, and he's just into it. He kept teasing me and laughing, and I was trying to keep concentrating. That was the longest version of 'November Rain,' just mentally, to play ever. I was like, 'When is this song gonna end so I can relax?' That was pretty extreme, but that was taking the song to its highest peak for me."[765]

Very, very late

Two days later, Guns were back on the road, this time performing at Foxboro Stadium outside of Boston, one of the dates that had been postponed in July due to Axl's voice issues. Concerned about the recent violence in Montreal and GNR's reputation for going on late, the promoters at Foxboro brought in additional security and insisted the show begin two-and-a-half hours ahead of schedule. Faith No More's would go on at 4:30 p.m., Metallica would perform from 5:45 to 8:00, and Guns would go on around 9:30, wrapping up by midnight.

"The shows have been running very, very late," Brian O'Donovan, general manager of Foxboro Stadium, told *The Boston Globe*. "I certainly think it's unfair to expect the residents to be bombarded after midnight, and the town had the same sentiments. They imposed a curfew of midnight, but they also said you can start two hours earlier."[766]

GNR reluctantly agreed to the revised schedule. Slash disliked being told what time to begin and when to finish. To him, it killed the organic vibe Guns strove to create. "We like to show up, have a good time, and play into the night without worrying about curfews and whatever," the guitarist said. "Concert productions have become too rigid. It's turned into a formula, and we don't come from that side of the fence. I think we'd be fucking the audience more if we adhered to those rules, because we wouldn't be half the band on stage if we didn't do it our way. It's true we've put our audiences through a lot, but it's not that we don't care. Each show is a completely different trip for us, depending on our mental state. We try to approach each one as a unique event – almost like it was our last show. It's hard to regulate something like that. It's hard to say it will start exactly at 9 p.m."[767]

In Boston, however, GNR stuck to the revised schedule and the concert went off as planned. By all accounts, it was a great show. "I wish every night could be this good," Axl told the crowd.

Tour stops in Toronto and Minneapolis followed. Both dates had been postponed – Toronto due to the riot in Montreal and Minneapolis because of Axl's voice issues. To the relief of everyone involved, the Minneapolis stop marked Faith No More's final appearance of the tour – the quintet began playing their own headline dates the following night in Omaha.

Tomahawk

On September 17, the tour stopped at Arrowhead Stadium in
Kansas City, Missouri. The departure of Faith No More meant a
new opening act would need to be brought on board. Axl strongly
advocated for Body Count, a five-piece metal outfit fronted by Los
Angeles rapper Ice-T. Body Count had stirred enormous controversy
for their song "Cop Killer," a first-person account of a man who
murders police due to perceived targeting and brutality. The number
had been issued that spring on Body Count's debut album, mere
weeks before the Los Angeles riots that occurred after the acquittal of
the police who beat Rodney King. "Cop Killer" was denounced by
many, including President George H.W. Bush. Others defended the
incendiary song, including many prominent musicians, who viewed it
through the lens of free speech. Axl thought having Body Count open
for GNR might change the minds of some who had written him off
as racist because of "One in a Million."

"Everybody was really scared about having Body Count on the
tour, which is something we wanted to do for a while now," Axl told
the crowd in Kansas City. "I want to thank you people for proving
everybody that was scared wrong."

For the first part of the show that night, Axl donned a camera
attached to his baseball cap. The "helmet cam" could project video
onto the giant screens on either side of the stage, giving the audience
a view of the performance from Axl's perspective. "In case you might
be curious about what this contraption is on my head, I'm filming a
little video tonight," Axl explained after Guns opened with
"Welcome to the Jungle." "This here is a helmet cam. We've got a
little problem. It doesn't seem to be working quite right because
there's not enough shit inside my head to balance out the weight.
That means every one of you motherfuckers is on this. I may get in a
lot of trouble – people can see what I'm *really* looking at up here."
Some of Axl's helmet cam footage eventually appeared in a 1993
music video for "Dead Horse," although GNR did not play the song
in Kansas City.

Following "Bad Obsession," Guns performed a brief instrumental version of the "Tomahawk Song," which was performed at Kansas City Chiefs football games to pump up the crowd. (The controversial number was featured at Atlanta Braves and Florida Seminoles matches, too.) "They have a problem with this song," Axl said as GNR pounded out the drum-heavy tune behind him. "And they're not gonna be able to play it. That's why we decided to play it. This race war bullshit – they can find something to call racism, everybody is gonna want to use that to make themselves separate. So, we decided to play this for you. A motherfucker who says that this is really because he feels that the white man is making fun of Indians is nothing but a self-glorified double-talking jive motherfucker."

Being back in the Show Me State for GNR's first Missouri appearance since the St. Louis riot, brought out Axl's ire at Arrowhead. His court date to face charges related to the St. Louis riot was only weeks away, and the singer was looking at a potential five-year sentence. He spent several minutes assailing the state's media and politicians and defended the band's decision to leave the stage at the Riverfront. "Hopefully, this is about the closest I'll get to St. Louis, unless they put me away for five years," he said.

The audience booed at the prospect of Axl going to prison. "Slash, why don't you switch guitars," Axl said. "I got a different idea." He called for "Out Ta Get Me," only the eleventh appearance of the *Appetite* deep cut on the Illusion tour. But Axl couldn't let the St. Louis thing go. The instant GNR concluded the song, the singer was back on the subject, ranting about being double-crossed by the prosecutors in St. Louis. "I don't have no respect for the law. All they ever do is lie. It's just like when I was in high school. People wanted to be cops so they could shoot dope smokers and make money selling it themselves. Fuck the law."

Per custom, Guns finished their main set with the singalong "Knockin' on Heaven's Door." As the number concluded and the band departed the stage, Axl couldn't help but to yell, "Thank you – fuck St. Louis!"

GNR returned to play their usual encore, "Paradise City." To introduce it, Slash strummed a few chords on his Les Paul while Axl talked about the importance of not throwing bottles at the stage or fellow concertgoers. As the final song concluded, Axl waved to the masses. "Thank you for being awesome tonight," he said sincerely. "We love you. You're the best."

The singer was less amiable two nights later at Mile High Stadium in Denver, Colorado. Guns had kept 50,000 spectators waiting for nearly two hours before finally coming onstage. Then, halfway through the opening number, Axl threw down his microphone and stormed off. He was having voice problems again. Duff took over and played "So Fine" and "Attitude" before the musicians launched into an instrumental blues jam.

Doug Goldstein followed Axl backstage, where he sat slouched in a waiting limousine. "Everything okay?" he asked the singer. "Yeah, yeah, I'm just pissed off," Axl replied. "I can't sing the way I'd like to; I shouldn't be doing this tour."[768] Promoter Barry Fey threatened to sue the singer if he did not return to the stage. After approximately thirty minutes, Axl was persuaded to go back on, where he told the booing crowd to "shut the fuck up!" Axl continued to complain throughout the rest of the night – the audience was unsympathetic.[769]

"Denver got a lousy show from Guns N' Roses," opined Jennifer Susich, a reporter for a Denver college newspaper. "Everyone in the band had a solo, including Denverite pianist Dizzy Reed. The solos got so long and so dull, many people either left to go home or were in their seats sleeping."[770]

Immediately following the Denver gig, Slash boarded a plane, flying to Oviedo, Spain to guest on Michael Jackson's world tour. The guitarist performed just one song, "Black or White," hammering out its signature riff alongside Jennifer Batten, Jackson's touring guitarist. Slash was adorned head to toe in black leather, replete with top hat, Marlboro dangling from his lips, and a sunburst Les Paul. The guitarist's surprise showing marked the first time he performed in concert with Jackson. "Onstage, his whole professional thing was really where he clicked," Slash recalled[771]

Earlier that day, the guitarist made a much lower-key guest appearance, spontaneously hopping on stage with a local teenage act called Stormy Mondays, who were performing at a street festival. "We were a bunch of seventeen-year-olds, playing outdoors on a dingy stage," singer-guitarist Jorge Otero recalled. "I turned around, and there's this very tall guy with long curly hair covering half of his face, black leather jacket, black jeans, and a top hat. It's Slash. It's 1992, Slash is the world's most famous guitar player. And he's asking to borrow a guitar to play with us."[772] The incredulous young musicians plowed through primitive versions of "Knockin' on Heaven's Door" and "Johnny B. Goode," a memory they would never forget.[773]

Three nights later, Slash was back onstage with Guns at the Oakland Coliseum, a concert that had been rescheduled after the Montreal riot. (In total, eleven of the twenty-four dates on the GNR-Metallica venture were either postponed or cancelled.) Slash had recently announced his engagement to longtime girlfriend Renée Suran, which the guitarist claimed had changed him for the better. Drugs and casual sex with groupies were firmly in the past. "I still drink, but I used to get wasted on stage," Slash told the *L.A. Times* in August. "There were nights when I'd have to start 'Sweet Child O' Mine' four or five times because I was so loaded I couldn't play it. But I got burned out on the whole drug thing and the groupie scene. After a while, you start looking at women like pieces of furniture, something you admire for their lines. And you realize you either keep going on like that forever or you commit to someone you love – and that's what happened to me. I met my fiancée three years ago and I've never been happier."[774]

When Slash and Renée arrived in Oakland, they got into a huge argument over whether to sign a prenuptial agreement. "I went to the gig so angry that I was determined to do what I do when I want to act out: get some smack," Slash recalled. "I got to the show, and I ran into an old friend, a porn star we'll call 'Lucky.' I gave Lucky passes and about seven hundred bucks in cash to get me as much heroin as she could find."[775]

After the concert, where 62,000 fans celebrated their hometown heroes, Metallica, Lucky and her boyfriend arrived at Slash's hotel "with all of this crack and smack. The hours go by, and we are really loaded. Matt calls me sometime in the early morning; he invites me to his room to do some blow. I collapsed like a rag doll in the hallway."[776]

Around 5:30 in the morning, GNR's tour manager, John Reese, got a call from the front desk informing him one of the band members was passed out in a fifth-floor hallway. "I throw on some pants and run out of my room, and Slash is dead. I mean dead, blue dead. He had no pulse," Reese recalled. "Paramedics show up and bump the adrenaline right into his heart."[777]

"My heart stopped for eight minutes," Slash said. "I woke up when the defibrillators sent an electric shock through my chest and stunned my heart into beating again."[778] Two days later, the guitarist was performing before 35,000 at the Los Angeles Memorial Coliseum.

Final four

The appearance at the Coliseum was one of two L.A. stops on GNR's trek with Metallica. The other one was slated to take place six days later at the Rose Bowl. Representatives for the tour tried to book both concerts at the Rose Bowl but officials refused.[779] Local promoters also banned Body Count from performing at all. The city was still rebuilding from the April riots and there were concerns about the controversial "Cop Killer." "I thought it was an inappropriate act, given the circumstances of where our show was taking place," Brian Murphy, the promoter for both venues, told the *L.A. Times*. Murphy was worried that booking Body Count might keep ticket buyers away from a late-night event held in downtown L.A. "I want to keep the perception of our show credible with our audience and reduce any concerns anyone might have about going downtown to the Coliseum."[780] Motörhead would open instead.

Axl told the *Times* that removing Body Count was "shallow-minded. Both Ice and myself are tired of all the racial crap. This was our chance to play together and show people that we're about artistic expression, not violence or prejudice. It comes down to this – freedom of speech is okay, as long as it doesn't piss off some public official."[781]

But Murphy's concern about a low turnout appeared to be well founded – the 72,000-seat Coliseum was less than half full. By all accounts, it was one of the worst gigs of the tour. According to a reviewer, the spectators were "surprisingly subdued. Lemmy grumbled about it, as did Metallica's James Hetfield. Because Metallica's fans are among the most zealous in rock, the relatively subdued reaction seemed to especially distract Hetfield."[782] During GNR's set, Axl called the audience "the most boring crowd that we've played for so far on the face of the earth. Now, we can work together here, and we can continue to stay up here and try to kick some ass. But, if you're tired and it's been a long night and tomorrow is going to be a hard day and you're not really into it, well, we don't have to be either. I'm gonna give what I receive."

The reviews in GNR's hometown papers were as unenthusiastic as the attendees. "Guns N' Roses, complete with the requisite Axl Rose tantrum, have become the pampered, bloated thing they originally rebelled against," the *Los Angeles Daily News* wrote. "There's a cartoonish quality to the once-influential group these days that would have made the members of Spinal Tap proud."[783]

The Guns-Metallica trek limped to Jack Murphy Stadium in San Diego before returning to the Rose Bowl for a second L.A. show. Backstage, Billy Idol, Rick Rubin, Anthrax guitarist Scott Ian, and actor Alex Winter milled about, and foul-mouthed comedian Andrew Dice Clay introduced GNR. Every seat in the 62,000-capacity venue was filled and by all accounts the performance was a 180-degree improvement. "We didn't have such a great experience when we just played the Coliseum," Axl said from the stage that night, sporting a UCLA Bruins jersey. "This makes up for the whole thing. They might even allow us back again." The concert ended with fireworks and Axl passing out roses to the audience.

Despite the improvement, reviewers remained unimpressed. Guns "trundle through their greatest hits with a degree of flatulent self-indulgence rarely seen outside grand opera," the U.K. music publication *New Musical Express* sniffed. "Multiple costume changes, giant inflatables, teams of guest players and absolutely no excitement whatsoever."[784]

But performing at the Rose Bowl meant something to Axl; it had been one of his long-time goals. "Now I feel like I've made it," he said after the show. According to Craig Duswalt, one of Axl's assistants, "Axl, for the first time, seemed extremely proud of his accomplishments. It was the only time I ever saw that in him. We ended up leaving the venue at about 7 a.m."[785] The singer would later reflect on the gig, stating, "Sometimes what you think is going to be that extra special moment isn't quite what you thought it was going to be. When we did the Rose Bowl, that was the dream concert of the whole summer tour, but it didn't feel like that peak moment we thought it would because there was a whole lot more to do."[786]

The GNR-Metallica venture ended on October 6, making up yet another postponement, this one at the Kingdome in Seattle. Motörhead was tapped to open, and Slash joined the venerable metal act for "You Better Run," which he had recorded with them in the spring.

In recent years, Seattle had spawned Nirvana, Pearl Jam, Soundgarden, and Alice in Chains, and was considered the epicenter of grunge at the time. Los Angeles and the Sunset Strip, once seen as ground zero for hard rock, were lampooned by the Seattle acts as passé, a hair-metal joke. A preview of the concert in *The Seattle Times* denounced Guns as "the most self-indulgent, egotistical band in rock."[787]

Still stinging from his backstage encounter with Kurt Cobain at the VMAs, Axl could not resist taking a few shots at Nirvana from the stage. "I'd like to take this time to acknowledge all the great rock 'n' roll that comes out of Seattle," the singer told the audience of 37,000. "To thank Soundgarden, who toured with us and ended up being the coolest people we've ever worked with. Just to make it public, your homeboys Nirvana were just too good to play with us or Metallica. But that's okay. I guess if you wanna sit home, and fuck an ugly bitch, and do heroin instead of out playing rock 'n' roll, that's okay."

Axl's comments were circulated by reporters, who were eager to stoke the feud between the two groups. A few weeks later, Kurt and Courtney responded during an interview. "Did you hear about that show where he got onstage and started saying something like, 'Nirvana's too good to play with us. Kurt would rather be at home with his ugly bitch?'" Courtney Love asked, telling Kurt, "Axl wants to be your friend. Axl thinks that if I wasn't around, you and him could be backstage at arena rock shows fucking self-hating little girls." Cobain laughed and replied sarcastically, "Well, that's always been my goal – to come down to Hollywood and ride motorcycles with Axl on the Strip."788

Back on stage in Seattle, Axl said his goodbyes. "Seeing how this is the last show of this stadium tour, I'd like to thank the crew and every single person that helped make this $10 million monster happen. We did this because we wanted to see a concert like we would've wanted to see when we were fifteen. That goes for us and Metallica, so we sat down and figured out how to do this. And neither band could've done this without about every single person they know's help. So, we'd like to say thank you. And last – but definitely not least – *thank you*."

Initially, the members of GNR and Metallica put a positive spin on their pairing. "We stuck in there and made our points. That was a great achievement as far as I'm concerned," Slash told MTV shortly after the final show in Seattle. Slash had no regrets and said the tour helped GNR bond as a unit. Still, the guitarist conceded, "It was definitely the hardest tour – at least for Guns N' Roses – that we've ever done."789

"We had a blast, man," Dizzy told an interviewer shortly after the trek ended, pointing to the Rose Bowl concert as a particular highlight. "It was one giant party, very fun. It was great doing shows with Metallica."790

But Axl would never forget the difficulties he encountered going on at the end of the night when the audience's energy had waned. "With Metallica playing a full set, and the crowd being really tired by the time they got to us, and so many spectators who really weren't into the music – people who were there just because they wanted to see what everything was about – it was difficult for us," the singer said in a December 1992 interview. "With that many people on the American tour just standing around and not giving us energy back, it was really hard for us to keep up our energy level. You've got people in the front row who are sitting there with their arms crossed and a 'show me something' look on their faces. It's annoying. I don't need people to sit there and 'test' me. I don't need someone sitting there saying 'impress me.' I feel like saying, 'no, you impress me.'"[791]

On December 8, shortly after the tour ended, Metallica released *A Year and a Half in the Life of Metallica,* a documentary that followed the quartet during the recording of the "black" album and subsequent world tour. The film featured their outing with GNR, including footage of the two groups hanging out backstage. Metallica chose to leave in the scene where James Hetfield disparaged Axl's list of pre-show requests.

The Metallica frontman also began firing shots at Axl in the press. "Did I enjoy the tour? It was different," Hetfield said in a *Rolling Stone* cover story that was published in early 1993. "It was a good idea. We really had no idea what was going to come with it. We were out to show people that there was something a little more progressive and hardcore than Guns N' Roses. And to go about it our way. But it was hard going on, dealing with Axl and his attitude. It's not something we'd want to do again."[792]

Metallica's public disparagement of Axl permanently soured relations between the two once-cordial acts. "The Metallica tour was the hardest thing we ever did," Slash said in late 1993. "It turned into such a conflict of interests between the two bands that we're no longer friends anymore. I'm not gonna put blame on anybody, it just turned into something that maybe wasn't such a great idea."[793]

At the time, Guns described the outing with Metallica as the hardest tour they had ever done. As it turned out, the hardest tour they would ever undertake was just about to begin.

Chapter 15

All the World's a Stage

GNR's tour with Metallica destroyed the friendship between the two bands, but it did damage in other ways, too. When the venture was over and the profits and losses were calculated, Guns were shocked to discover after nearly eighteen months on the road, they were practically broke. "We'd barely made any money," said Slash, who married longtime girlfriend Renée Suran on October 10, four days after the trek with Metallica wrapped. "Between the union dues incurred by Axl taking the stage late night after night and the theme parties that bled us dry night after night, we had next to nothing to show for all our hard work. Our profit margin had been eaten up by our excesses."[794]

Axl had a pressing need for cash. On November 9, the singer was found guilty of all five misdemeanor charges against him in St. Louis. The hearing was initially scheduled to take place in October, but it was pushed back after Axl's legal team was able to work out a plea bargain with the prosecutors. The singer was not present for the hearing. Prosecutor Robert McCulloch said holding a jury trial would have "lasted several weeks and turned into something of a circus." Instead, both sides agreed to let Associate Circuit Judge Ellis Gregory make a ruling based on evidence that included police reports and videos of the event.[795] Judge Ellis found Axl guilty of four counts of assault and one count of property damage.

Axl was fined $50,000 and sentenced to two years of probation. Judge Ellis modified the probation terms to allow Axl to travel for work and associate with the known felons in his band. "Does he understand that if he violates probation, I can send him to jail?" Ellis asked Axl's attorney, Arthur Margulis, who confirmed that Axl understood. Ellis noted the $50,000 fine represented a "pittance" of Axl's earnings, but Margulis countered "$50,000 is a lot of money."[796] The fine would be divided evenly among five St. Louis charities, all of which, at Axl's behest, assisted abused children and teenagers. The conviction exposed Axl to civil lawsuits, but he was relieved to be done with the criminal case fifteen months after the St. Louis riot took place.

Between the five-figure court fines, huge attorney fees, and pending civil suits, Axl's bills were stacking up. Guns had just played all over Europe and the US, so the singer looked to generate some cash by venturing to other parts of the world. He ordered Doug Goldstein to set up gigs in any country willing to pay. "So, Doug booked us another year of dates, starting with South America, Japan, and Australia," Slash recalled.[797]

The move had an unexpected upside. GNR's trek across South America in late 1992, followed by concerts in Japan, New Zealand, and Australia in early 1993, forever cemented them as a global act, in the rarified air of the Rolling Stones and U2. A group that had never headlined their own tour prior to *Illusion*, could now play anywhere in the world and pack the house.

Other than the 1991 Rock in Rio appearances, Guns had never played in South America before. There was huge demand for the band, and they were approached by a number of shady, cartel-connected promoters, whose drug money could cover GNR's hefty advances and performance fees. "The hysteria that's going on in South America about us coming over there is sort of apparently unequal," Slash marveled, just after the concerts were announced. "We sold an amazing amount of tickets at an amazingly fast amount of time compared to the acts that usually go over there. That's a whole different country altogether and you want to go and focus on playing. So, we'll see how things develop. I don't know if anybody in the States is gonna hear from us for a while. Everybody's probably sick of us anyway."[798]

Slash may have had a point, judging from the tepid response to "Yesterdays," which GNR released as a single in October. On November 21, the mid-tempo *Illusion* track peaked at number seventy-two on the Billboard Hot 100 chart. Clearly, it was time for Guns to seek fortune outside the US.

Blowing through South America

The next stop on what Dizzy called "the tour that never ends" was Caracas, Venezuela on November 25.[799] GNR's appearance marked the largest concert ever held in the country, and the organizers moved the performance to a makeshift stage that was hastily assembled in the stadium's parking lot to accommodate the 45,000 ticketholders. It was spring in South America and the overall vibe had improved. Guns were relieved to be back to headlining alone, rather than having to compete with Metallica every night. It was nice to play for enthusiastic crowds again, audiences that were dying to see them, rather than Americans with their arms folded.

Following a successful tour launch in Venezuela, there was a military coup just after GNR departed. Some members of the crew and half the group's equipment were left behind. "There were scary moments," Duff recalled a few months after the South American jaunt ended. "We escaped a coup in Caracas by two hours. The airport was bombed two hours after we left."[800]

The next stop was Bogotá, Colombia. By all accounts, GNR's time in Colombia was difficult. The band was hugely popular there – "November Rain" had been number one for an astounding sixty weeks, making it one of the most beloved songs in the nation's history. Five-thousand rabid devotees were waiting for the group at the airport. Upon arrival, Doug Goldstein warned everyone ten American citizens were kidnapped in Bogotá each week. "I want you guys to be careful. We're not going to leave the hotel," the manager told them.[801]

At the airport, each member of the group was assigned to their own SUV and security team. Matt got into the back seat of the vehicle and found himself surrounded by armed guards. "There was one guy on either side of me, each clutching a machine gun," he recalled. "Two guys sat up front, and one of them also had a gun. We even had cops with machine guns riding motorcycles in front, beside, and behind us. When we pulled up outside our hotel, a tank and a load of armed guards were out front."[802]

The exterior of GNR's hotel was mobbed by fans, who swarmed the group members whenever they set foot outside their rooms. They had to be surrounded by gun-packing sentries at all times. "Sometimes I can go out with two security people and have a normal day, just go shopping or look around," Axl said, shortly after the South American tour ended. "In Bogotá it was hectic. You needed two *vans* of security. It was a nightmare. But I went to antique shops because I'm into collecting crucifixes."[803]

Guns were scheduled to play two dates at Bogotá's El Campin stadium, but the delays in getting out of Venezuela meant the two sold-out concerts had to be combined into a single appearance. Thus, El Campin was at double capacity when GNR performed. A surreal event occurred during the show – it began pouring rain just as the band broke into "November Rain." Many in the audience took it as a sign from god – they began crossing themselves, weeping, and praying to the heavens. "The crowd lost their minds," Axl recalled. "That city deserved to have that happen more than any place else in the world. Singing in the rain. It was a very special moment."[804] "That was magical," Roberta Freeman told *Rolling Stone*. "Just to see the fans. Sometimes when you're at a concert and it starts raining, people get bummed out. But it just fueled people and got them going even more. They were *more* excited. It was raining pretty hard. I don't think anyone even cared."[805]

Despite this highlight, Guns barely made it out of Bogotá in one piece. "At some point, I went to leave my hotel room," Duff recalled. "Outside my room stood a machine-gun-toting soldier. He motioned me back inside. We were under house arrest. They were threatening to kidnap Doug, our manager. It was the government, which is scary.

None of the American embassies are very strong down there, so if you really wanted to get out, it would be iffy at best."[806] [807]

During the South American tour, GNR's accountant kept a briefcase full of cash handcuffed to his wrist, money that was used to get out of jams such as this one.[808] Through a series of bargains and bribes, Guns and their entourage managed to escape. "Every country we went to, we were having problems," Matt said.[809]

Next, the group flew the MGM Grand to Santiago, Chile. Matt had a large stash of cocaine leftover from Colombia and snorted it all in the air. "I always did a load of blow on the plane," the drummer recalled. "I had to do it before we landed to avoid being arrested if anyone searched the plane. When we landed in Chile later that day, the government confiscated our plane to see if we had brought any drugs with us from Bogotá. Thankfully they didn't find anything."[810]

As in Colombia, GNR were swarmed everywhere they went. "In Chile, there were 500 kids at the hotel at any given time," Axl recalled.[811] The venue where the band was playing – Estadio Nacional – had been used as a makeshift prison during a political coup in 1973. Upwards of 7,000 men at a time were kidnapped and tortured; many of them did not survive and were allegedly buried at the site. When Axl found out about this, he refused to play, but eventually took the stage two hours late.

It was the largest gig of the South American tour, with 85,000 in attendance. The band was pelted with objects throughout the performance. Less than ten minutes into the appearance, Axl stopped the musicians and, speaking through an interpreter, told the crowd, "If you want to throw another bottle, we will go home." After the concert ended, tragedy struck when a fifteen-year-old female fan was crushed to death outside the venue.

GNR's controversial reputation made the South American excursion challenging for other reasons, too. At every location on the outing, they were accused of carrying drugs and regularly hit up for bribes. Guns and their entourage were constantly stopped, searched, and harassed. In Chile, traces of cocaine were allegedly found on one of the band members' clothing when it was being cleaned by the hotel laundry. The entire group was detained for about nine hours while the MGM Grand was searched. When the police found nothing, Guns were allowed to leave the country.[812]

According to Slash, the difficulties GNR encountered in South America brought them closer together. "We had every obstacle possible befall us, and considering the band's chemistry in the recent past, you would expect that we'd have fallen apart under such duress," the guitarist wrote in his memoir. "But that was the thing about Guns: we'd self-destruct when everything was easy, but in those instances when every single factor seemed to be against us, everyone, Axl included, pulled together to make it happen. Rather than be frustrated by what befell us, in South America, we let the audiences at all those gigs sustain us with their passion and drive us to be our best. Our playing was elevated; it was as intense as the fans were — we were carried away along with them."[813]

Upon departing Chile, GNR flew to Argentina, where they were scheduled to play two shows at River Plate Stadium in Buenos Aires. Stories about their detention in Chile made international headlines, and there was also a wild rumor in the press Axl had burned an Argentinean flag on stage in France. Angry protestors set fire to Guns T-shirts in the streets and attacked fans outside their hotel. "We had all these right-wing skinheads, like Nazis, after us," Duff recalled. "There were hundreds of them, yelling and chanting. It was scary."[814]

In an effort to contain the growing brouhaha, the group, buoyed by Doug Goldstein and the promoter, held a press conference the day before the first concert. "We don't do press conferences," Duff explained through an interpreter. "All these rumors are flying. Where do they come from? Not from us. They come from the press. So, that's why we are here, to clarify a lot of these really ugly, kind of silly and stupid rumors. It makes us sick. We're here to play, we're here to make people happy, and it's really gotten out of hand. We're just a rock 'n' roll band."

"We have been touring for seven years together," Doug Goldstein said. "We've never, ever seen this type of reaction with the press and with the fans. It's more hysteria than we're certainly used to. It gets a little scary."

"In some distorted way, we do appreciate all the attention," Slash added. "We just don't know what to do with it."

Midway through the press conference, Axl arrived, attired in an Argentinean national soccer team's jersey. "In light of the false stories in the papers, I think it's a good gesture for me to wear it," he told the reporters, drawing applause.

Asked about a rumor GNR had gone on stage late in Chile because Axl was drunk or high, the singer responded, "I don't have time to be drunk or drugged before a show, or I couldn't do my show. The truth was that I had strep throat, so I had to do a lot of throat exercises and work with my doctors so that I could do the show, or there wouldn't have *been* a show. People will write anything."

Asked if he was worried about violence at the gig, Axl replied he was concerned about concertgoers' reactions to the false stories about the band. "We're pretty much a target up there," he added. "And we deal with it at every show, 'cause you never know if you're gonna have a crazy that could shoot you when you're up on the stage. But I don't like seeing people in the crowd get hurt. And I'm a little concerned about that. We're gonna try to monitor it the best we can. And if I see anything going on onstage, I stop the show."

After the press conference, Axl sat for an interview that was broadcast on Telefe, a Buenos Aires TV station. He again took pains to quash the rumors swirling around, and assured viewers Guns were there to play the best concerts they could. "I'm wearing this shirt and I'm not a fake," he insisted, pointing to his soccer jersey. "I'm not doing it to just look good. It was given to me and I feel good. I wouldn't wear it as a publicity stunt. I wore the shirt as a gesture of peace, because I really want everything to go well at the shows, and I'm not doing it just so we can play the shows, get paid and leave. And if I had a problem with Argentina, we just wouldn't play here. I'm kind of famous for that."

Axl took the stage in Buenos Aires still wearing the soccer jersey. GNR opened with "Welcome to the Jungle" and brought the house down. Axl wasted little time in addressing the rumors that had been floating around Argentina since the band arrived. Five numbers into the set, speaking through an interpreter named Noelle, Axl told the audience, "There's been a lot of things written in the press, a lot of things about me being anti-Argentinian, that the [promoter] who *didn't* get this concert and *didn't* get to make the money off this concert made up so that he could ruin it for all of us. We'll dedicate this song to that man, and I don't even know his name, 'Double Talkin' Jive' motherfucker.'"

Guns were firing on all cylinders that night, submitting one scorcher after the next. In the stadium, it was pure pandemonium. But when some overexcited spectators began throwing objects at the stage, Axl stopped the musicians midway through "Nightrain" and called for Noelle, the interpreter. "We have some really fucking stupid people here tonight who think that throwing things at the stage will relate into a better show," he said, calm but clearly pissed. "It won't happen that way because we will go home. Don't try me. Now, shall we continue, or shall we go home?" The band picked back up in the middle of "Nightrain," rather than starting it over.

A few songs later, during "You Could Be Mine," it happened again. "Stop," Axl yelled. "Camera on this fucker," he said, holding up a horn-shaped white object about the size of a softball. "Do you think this is funny?" he asked through the interpreter. "If you see somebody beside you throwing something, beat the fucking shit out of them. All they are going to do is rip every one of you off. If one of us gets hit by something like this, or if I see someone in the crowd get hit by something like this, unfortunately the show will be over. We want to have a nice time tonight. We don't want anyone to get hurt – any of you, any of our crew, any of the people working the show, or ourselves. This could hurt someone real fucking bad. This will be the last time I talk about this. We'll try one more time. Thank you." The night ended without further incident.

GNR played a second date in Buenos Aires before the tour moved to Brazil for three final South American appearances, two in São Paulo and one in Rio. Guns had not performed in Brazil since the 1991 Rock in Rio concerts that helped launch the *Illusion* era. As occurred in the previous countries, the band members were mobbed by thousands of rabid fans and effectively trapped in their hotel.

Frustrated, Axl threw a chair at reporters from a hotel window. No one was hurt, but the incident made the news and led to a visit from the local police.[815]

On stage the first night, Axl brought up the furniture-tossing episode. "They made me sign a document saying that I didn't wanna throw that chair. I wanted to throw it, and, if they stop me again, I'll throw however many chairs needed."

As in Argentina, Axl had to halt the performance several times to address objects being thrown at the stage. During the final number, "Paradise City," the singer finally had enough and ended the concert a few minutes early.

Speaking with MTV Brazil, Duff described the issues Guns encountered while touring South America for the first time. "It's very sensationalist and they get the wrong information," he said of the press. "We haven't even left the hotels, and the stories they tell about us get all mixed up and it comes back on us. We're just down here to play rock 'n' roll."

Malibu

GNR's first-ever South American jaunt was a success, but also highly stressful. Now, back home and flush with cash, the group had about a month off before they were due in Japan. Tickets also went on sale for a North American tour that would take place in the winter and spring of 1993. In several cities, fans camped out overnight, waiting in line to snap them up.

Interviewed from Los Angeles during the break, Duff described new material Guns had been writing for the *Illusion* follow-up. "It's even a lot broader now," he said. "The stuff we've been writing at sound check – it's way, way outside. When you're on tour for this long, you kind of lose it a bit so some of the stuff is very heavy, sort of dark. But not in a bad way."[816]

Axl was also interviewed during this time, reporting that Slash was writing riffs to be used for GNR's next album. The singer was unsure what direction it might take. "I'd like the next record to go to farther extremes," he said, adding, "We haven't actually gotten together to collaborate on too many songs. I wrote and recorded a new song that I want to have on the record called 'This I Love,' that's the heaviest thing that I've ever done. But we're not even sure how we're going to go about writing the record this time."[817]

The singer had recently purchased a $4 million mansion in the tawny Point Dume section of Malibu, California. For decades, Malibu has been home to Hollywood A-listers and wealthy industry figures. Even in such gilded company, Axl's new digs stood out, befitting a rock star of world-caliber status. The 4333-square foot, five-bedroom, eight-and-a-half bathroom Mediterranean-style pad was situated on three acres atop a cliff and featured sweeping views of the Pacific Ocean and the city of Malibu. Also on site were a guest house, recording studio, tennis court, swimming pool, hot tub, and a gym.[818][819]

Axl also finally got around to selling the Hollywood Hills residence he'd purchased while battling his next-door neighbor in late 1990. Axl had paid $800,000 for the place and sold it at a loss of more than $100,000.[820] He never spent a single night there.

"I bought a new house, so I guess I'll try to set that up and get some stability in my life," Axl said in mid-December. "I'll be happy doing some domestic things. Stephanie and I have worked very hard to try and have a personal life, but it's not easy. We've tried to stay in touch as much as possible, but our lives are such fast-moving things. Five months for us is like five years for most people."[821]

Axl's new home provided the comfort and security he had long sought. His intention was to live there with Stephanie and her son, Dylan, who had turned two in September. Axl had grown close to Dylan since he and Stephanie began dating. He had a swing set and jungle gym installed in the backyard and had one of the bedrooms filled with toys.

To celebrate the purchase of Axl's new home and mark the turning point in their relationship, Axl and Stephanie hosted a Christmas party that year. Several dozen family and friends attended the soirée, arriving in the late afternoon. Axl and Stephanie had been bickering the entire day. According to Stephanie, "At some point in the middle of the party, Axl entered the house, slammed the door, was obviously very angry, went upstairs and then came downstairs and left the house again. My mother went to speak to him and he began yelling and screaming at her and ultimately told her in no uncertain terms that she was not welcome in his house."[822]

Around midnight, Axl ordered all the guests to leave. Stephanie reportedly called the singer a name, then hit Axl with a chair and punched him in the groin.[823]

Stephanie had a different take on the events that transpired that night. "When I attempted to talk to Axl to address the issues that had upset him, he started yelling and swearing. He then lifted up the kitchen table, knocking off bottles and glasses. I reached for Axl in an attempt to calm him. However, he would not be consoled, and he was clearly out of control."[824] Seymour claimed Axl "attacked her, giving her a black eye and bloody nose. He slapped and punched her and kicked her down a flight of stairs."[825]

"I never saw Axl strike, punch, or slap her," Amy Bailey, Axl's sister, told reporters. "She wants to push things to the edge."[826]

Tokyo in black or white

While Axl and Stephanie were fighting in Malibu, Slash was on a flight to Japan. Upon arrival, the guitarist joined Michael Jackson onstage at the Tokyo Dome on December 30 and 31. Jackson had sold out eight shows at the venue, and invited Slash to perform "Black or White." Although Slash did not appear on the studio track, the public assumed he did. This impression only grew after Slash played the tune with Jackson in Spain that September and for MTV's 10th Anniversary Special a year prior.

In Tokyo, Slash stood aside Jackson, rocking 55,000 devotees. Axl and Slash were international celebrities, instantly recognizable the world over but their stardom was nothing compared to Jackson, who was arguably the most famous person on the planet at the time. The level of hysteria Jackson generated was hard to fathom, even to a seasoned pro like Slash. Performing in concert was perhaps the one time Jackson truly came alive. "I did a couple of shows with Michael in Tokyo and saw how this whole massive thing worked, and he was the center of it," Slash recalled. "The only time he was in any kind of comfort zone was when he was actually onstage. Right after that, Guns came to town and did our shows and our success was massive, but it wasn't as overwhelming as what Michael was going through."[827]

Slash's position near the eye of two separate hurricanes gave him a unique vantage point from which to observe celebrityhood. "I experienced the biggest contrast you can imagine between those two audiences," he said. "I can't think of a more surreal switch than playing one night for Michael Jackson, who was flying around the stage and had kids and toys backstage, to playing with Guns and everything that came with that world – all in the same building."[828] Slash had some downtime between the Michael Jackson and GNR appearances and spent a day visiting Tokyo Disney.

GNR were scheduled to play three concerts at the Tokyo Dome beginning January 12, the second time the Illusion tour stopped there in less than a year. A month earlier, Geffen had released the band's February 22 Tokyo Dome performance as a two-part VHS home video, *Use Your Illusion World Tour – 1992 in Tokyo*. *Entertainment Weekly* reviewed the set, grading it a D and proclaiming it to be both "hysterically indulgent" and "deadly dull."[829] But the tapes proved to be a popular Christmas present, selling more than 500,000 copies worldwide and earning a Gold certification from the RIAA. Doug Goldstein claimed Guns made a fortune from the tapes.[830]

The 1993 Tokyo Dome concerts were among the last GNR would play as a twelve-piece unit. "After we do this Japanese and Australian, New Zealand thing, we're done with that," Duff declared during an interview for Japanese television. "We're stripping back down to a five-piece band again. We've been touring the whole stadium thing, big events on this tour for the past two years, with the real big focus. And I guess it's been, like, 'They're not a rock 'n' roll band anymore.' So we're gonna come back to prove that on any turf, any place, anywhere, we are the same band." At GNR's final Tokyo stop, Rolling Stones guitarist Ron Wood joined for a show-closing rendition of "Knockin' on Heaven's Door."

From Japan, Guns traveled to Sydney, Australia, the first time they had performed there since 1988. Skid Row, who played the first leg of the Illusion trek, returned to open. To keep everyone out of trouble, Skid Row and GNR were booked into separate hotels. "Sebastian is one of my best friends, but once we pair up, all hell breaks loose," Slash explained. "So it's a strategic thing to keep us apart. I can't smoke pot like he does. I just space out too hard."[831]

Also on the bill was Rose Tattoo, a seminal Australian hard-rock outfit whose 1978 tune "Nice Boys" was covered by Guns on the *Live ?!*@ Like a Suicide* EP. Slash described the trip down under as "more of the same – great shows, some drama, plus a lot of expenses go-karting, yachting, and dining."[832]

The Sydney stop was held at the Eastern Creek Raceway and drew roughly 70,000 fans. A few days later, GNR appeared before 75,000 spectators at the Calder Park Raceway in Melbourne. The group was reportedly paid two million dollars for the pair of two-hour performances. "They are the biggest rock 'n' roll band in the world," promoter Michael Gudinski told reporters. "What's in it for us? Well, the bigger the crowd, the more money we'll make. To have the two biggest-grossing concerts in the Southern Hemisphere is a good feeling."[833]

While he was down under, Axl and his entourage visited an animal reserve that was home to kangaroos and wallabies. The singer became enamored with a baby wallaby, which he purchased and named Freddie, a tribute to his hero, Freddie Mercury of Queen. The singer insisted Freddie come on the road with Guns. "Axl built a sling, to mimic the baby wallaby mother's pouch and carried his pet wherever he went," his assistant Craig Duswalt recalled, adding that Axl fed the animal with a baby bottle.[834]

En route to New Zealand, the MGM Grand flew into a monumental storm, hitting severe turbulence and terrifying everyone on board. Earl Gabbidon, Axl's bodyguard, called it the scariest moment in his entire time with GNR. "We all thought for sure we were gonna die. I remember Gilby's wife crying. We really thought it was the end, *La Bamba* style."[835]

Had Guns gone down on that flight, the Illusion trek would have been memorialized as one of rock's most epic tours. As it turned out, life in the GNR camp was about to get far more turbulent as the band rethought their entire operation from the ground up.

Chapter 16

Skin N' Bones

"What you're gonna to see tonight is a lot of shit we've never played live anywhere," Axl told 17,000 concertgoers at the Frank Erwin Center in Austin, Texas. The singer had just finished ranting about Seattle grunge, *Spin* magazine, and GNR's recent ouster from the cool kids' club. "It doesn't matter what we do," he lamented. "They'll always have a problem with us."

Guns' solution was Skin N' Bones, which did away with the trappings of their recent megatours. Gone were the 976 Horns, the backup singers, and Teddy "Zig Zag" Andreadis. The group shelved the massive, multi-leveled WWII bomber stage and the ramps (but kept the trio of video screens). There would be limited lighting and no pyrotechnics of any kind. Even Axl's bicycle shorts and multiple costume changes were excised. For the first time in who knows how long, the singer wore the same outfit the entire night: knee-length, baggy shorts and a sleeveless T-shirt with Charles Manson's face on the front and "Charlie Don't Surf" written on the back – a famous line from the film *Apocalypse Now*.

"There's a lot of bands that go, 'We don't want to be like U2 or Guns N' Roses and do this big theatrical stage show,'" Axl told the crowd in Austin. "Well, we just wanted to see if we could pull off a big show, that was all. And we did – because of you. So now, we're gonna have some fun, try a show we just threw together. We still had no idea what we were doing until last night. So, if you'll bear with our confusion, we'll try to have a good time tonight. And anybody that says we're trying to rip you off or kiss ass or it's contrived, they can suck my dick."

GNR ripped into "Double Talkin' Jive," followed by the first-ever live performance of "The Garden." After the number concluded, Axl said, "I can breathe a little easier. I barely pulled that off. It was a nervous night last night."

Slash was thrilled at the back-to-basics approach. "I couldn't have been happier," he wrote in his memoir. "*Finally*, we were touring as a bare-bones rock-and-roll band again. We got a chance to do the songs scaled back straight up with a band reduced to its normal size. I was *elated*."[836]

The North American leg of Skin N' Bones was mostly stopping in secondary markets Guns had skipped on previous legs of the Illusion tour – the group had played Texas three times in the past two years, but this was their first visit to Austin. The Brian May Band was tapped to open, and tickets were priced at $22.50.

When the Illusion trek began, GNR dug into their new material with excitement. For Skin N' Bones, they were invigorated by deep diving into their catalog, unearthing long-dormant *Lies* tunes and untried *Illusion* material. Instead of "Mr. Brownstone" in its usual second-song position, Guns premiered "Garden of Eden."

Midway through the Austin set, Axl told the crowd, "We're gonna try something here. We've never done this before; we have no idea if you're gonna like it. You make a couple of albums, and you take your time doing it, people think you've been playing for ten years. We're still green."

A team of roadies brought out an old, overstuffed couch, a tall swivel-back chair, and a coffee table and placed them at center stage. Next to this, they set up some congas and a small drum set. A grand piano was wheeled in and positioned behind the couch.

Axl and Slash sat next to each other on the couch, with Gilby to Axl's left on the sofa's arm. Next to Gilby, Duff sat atop the swivel-back chair. Everyone but Axl had an acoustic guitar in hand. Dizzy and Matt took over the percussion instruments. "This couch was my idea," Axl joked to the crowd. "No offense, they're friends of mine,

but I just thought we kinda looked like Tesla without the couch."
The singer was referring to *Five Man Acoustical Jam*, Tesla's hit
"unplugged" album and video from 1990, where the Sacramento
quintet performed cover tunes while seated atop bar stools. "We're
trying to get a coffee-shop vibe going here," Axl continued with a sly
grin. "We're beatniks."

Slash laid his acoustic on his lap and played it with a slide like a
pedal steel, leading the group into "You Ain't the First," which had
only been played half a dozen times at the outset of the Illusion tour
in 1991. Gilby and Duff strummed away at their acoustics, while
Matt applied a soft touch with brushes instead of sticks. Dizzy sang
backup and kept time on a tambourine.

"It's a blast," Dizzy told a reporter later that spring. "When we
first started rehearsals, we brought out all those stools, and we were
sitting there. Axl was like, 'No way, we can't do this. We need a
couch and a coffee table.' It just looks like your living room, like
sitting around in your house jamming. We're trying to portray that to
the audience and make it more real. It's a lot of fun for us."[837]

"You Ain't the First" clattered to a close, and a quartet of topless
"waitresses" strode to the stage toting trays of beer, handing mugs to
everyone in the band. "Isn't that disgusting," Axl joked as the
audience applauded in approval.

Next up was "You're Crazy," which GNR had only played three
times since 1988. On Skin N' Bones, the *Appetite* rocker was slowed
down and performed a la *Lies* – Slash picked away at a Les Paul while
Gilby strummed an acoustic. Duff used an electric bass and Matt
tapped on his small kit with sticks, augmented by Dizzy on congas.

As the number concluded, a man dressed in a Domino's uniform
walked onstage and delivered a couple of hot pizzas to the group.
"Thirty minutes or less," Axl joked, taking a box. The singer handed
it to concertgoers in the front row, who were surprised to discover an
actual pizza inside.

The press was charmed by the Skin N' Bones concept. "It's like a
basement party as done by a guerrilla theater group, with Guns N'
Roses playing the role of the stereo," wrote one reviewer.[838] Another
pronounced, "There was a spirit throughout the evening of a band

that was making it up as it went along, embracing imperfection for the sake of immediacy, doing whatever felt right at the time rather than submitting to any prescriptions."[839]

Axl even called Stephen Thaxton to the stage for an on-the-spot treatment. "I hurt my arm and rather than take the time to worry about it, we're gonna go on with this song while my resident chiropractor, that we found in Dallas, Texas a couple of years ago, works on my arm – live, in Texas. Hit it."

GNR launched into "Used to Love Her," which had remained on ice since August 1991, when Izzy was still in the band. Thaxton adjusted Axl's shoulder while Slash and Gilby hammered away on acoustics. Everyone seemed to be having a great time – the Domino's delivery guy was even playing Dizzy's bongos.

"So, is this working or is this a failure?" Axl asked the Austinites afterward to wild cheers. "Wow," the singer exclaimed. "Now I know what David Lee Roth meant about we don't have fans, we have friends."

Next up was "Patience," another tune from *Lies*. The ballad had been a mainstay of the Illusion tour setlists, but now it was stripped down for the first time, with Slash, Duff, and Gilby on acoustics, Dizzy on piano, and Matt keeping time with a tambourine. Axl could not stay seated for long, rising to move about the stage and better connect with the audience. This was followed by another longtime standard, "Knockin' on Heaven's Door," retooled with Slash and Gilby on acoustics, Duff on bass, Matt on drums, and Dizzy on piano.

"A lot of diehards and metalheads will be like, 'Oh, man, they do a twenty-minute really boring acoustic set,'" Slash told MTV that spring. "But we have a great time doing it and the songs are there. We just do whatever we feel like, which makes it fun for us, and I think people can read that more than when they see a band that's out there doing it like a job and just doing the same ritual routine over and over again."[840]

"November Rain" closed out the acoustic set, with Axl warming up on the piano as the roadies cleared the stage of furniture. "Rain" was reconfigured, too: Axl restored the number's demo roots, playing the entire song largely solo, accompanied by a bit of lilting acoustic guitar from Slash and an occasional "Pat Boone-Debbie Boone" drum fill from Matt. The rest of the musicians joined in for "Rain's" anguished coda. Axl and Stephanie Seymour had broken up recently and the singer threw himself into the number, his beloved ballad never sounding more powerful or exquisite.

"November Rain" concluded, and the roadies swooped in to reset the stage. In keeping with the anything-goes spirit of Skin N' Bones, Axl strapped on an acoustic guitar. "Don't worry, it only gets worse," he quipped. Axl wasn't much of a guitarist and had never played the instrument in concert. For once, the seemingly confident rock star looked almost anxious. "You're gonna witness a first now. Neil Young, watch the fuck out. I'm stalling because I'm real nervous."

GNR had only played "Dead Horse" five times before, and the *Illusion* deep cut was rearranged for Skin N' Bones. Axl played the intro, hacking away gamely at his acoustic as he sang. He removed the instrument as the band joined in. At the end of the number, he strapped on the guitar again and finished the tune solo. The crowd went nuts. "Axl Rose on the acoustic guitar!" Slash proclaimed, as Duff put his arm around the singer in congratulations. Axl looked relieved. "You can see why I don't do that for a living," he joked.

Guns opened the encore with "Nice Boys," a *Live ?!*@ Like a Suicide* rarity they had not played since 1988. They ended, as always, with an anthemic take on "Paradise City."

A review in the *San Antonio Express-News* extolled the Skin N' Bones course correction as a much-need breath of fresh air. GNR put on "an exciting show free of arena-rock clichés and problems that had cropped up at other concerts. They showed a willingness to take chances on unfamiliar material as well as playing the hits. Most of their chances paid off."[841]

Money matters

Everyone in the group seemed relieved to be rid of the twelve-piece setup and stadium-sized production they had been toting around for the past year and a half. "That was shit boring, wasn't it?" Matt told me when I asked him about the big-band era of GNR. "I wanted to kill those girls by the end of that tour. And Axl was doing all these costume changes. I'm like, 'What happened to this fucking band?' So, finally we all agreed to get rid of the horn players. The Skin N' Bones tour was our anti-statement to Axl – 'Let's get rid of these fucking horn players.'"[842]

"I don't think we would have survived much longer doing those big shows," Duff told a Canadian journalist a few weeks after the Austin gig. "We had 140 people working for us. Nineteen semis, nineteen buses, two 747s to take the equipment and another plane for the band. It was too big. When it comes down to it, it's myself, Axl and Slash who have to take care of all the financials. So, here we are being businessmen and trying to rock every night – you've got faxes falling out of your pockets when you're on stage. And the backup singers and the horn players are screaming that they want bigger rooms – it just goes on and on. So, we're back to square one, and it's great."[843]

In Hartford, Connecticut, the group introduced "Sweet Child O' Mine" with a bit of "Since I Don't Have You," a 1958 doo-wop tune Guns would include on their forthcoming covers album. Axl used to sing the song around the house back in GNR's club days, but his breakup with Stephanie Seymour reignited his connection to it.

Skin N' Bones' leaner setup was conceived partly due to financial considerations. It was "aimed at making us money," Slash declared in his memoir.[844] "We lost so much money on the big production tour," Duff conceded. "We had to cart that whole circus all the way through Europe, and then on through Tokyo and Australia and New Zealand."[845]

Skin N' Bones helped financially but it didn't solve the internal problems that plagued GNR. The pared-down lineup only made it through the first two dates before they postponed the next five. At the second show, in Birmingham, Alabama, Axl got frustrated with the sound and left the stage after twenty minutes, letting the musicians jam aimlessly for more than a half an hour before he returned. After that, Axl fired the soundman in front of everybody and proceeded to blow out his voice by singing too hard.[846] "The band still is the same – it's very unpredictable," Gilby sighed. "One day everything's going fine and then it changes."[847]

To make matters worse, Duff began dabbling in heroin. "I was using so much coke by this point that I needed more and more things to counteract it when it was time to take the edge off a coke high," the bassist recalled in his memoir. "One night when I couldn't get my hands on any pills, and someone had some China white – powdered heroin – I snorted that instead. It did the trick: edge dulled. I found that smoking the brown tarlike heroin on tinfoil also did the trick."[848]

Demand for GNR appeared to be waning in some markets. The third Skin N' Bones show was supposed to take place in Cincinnati, Ohio, where ticket sales were modest. "We are not sold out, and we're not going to sell out," declared John Nath, general manager of the Riverfront Coliseum, where Guns had sold 10,000 tickets at a venue that held 16,000. "Maybe the bloom is off this rose. You have to respect the people who are making your fortune for you. You can't make them wait two to three hours in a building. They have lives, too." [849] The gig was postponed to a later date and ultimately cancelled. In other markets, GNR remained as popular as ever. The band's March 17 concert at the Boston Garden was sold out.

In early March, Axl issued a press release announcing his breakup with Stephanie Seymour. "It was fun; I wish Stephanie the best," the singer said, adding he would "hold a casting call to find an actress to replace Seymour in future videos."[850] At GNR's March 6 stop in New Haven the singer dedicated "Estranged" to "someone I used to know," following it with "Since I Don't Have You" by way of introducing "Paradise City."

Guns had a few days off after the Boston date and used the downtime to tape their cover of "Since I Don't Have You" at Sound Techniques, a local hole-in-the-wall recording studio. When Slash called to book the date, the studio's lone employee thought it was a prank. GNR's instruments were packed onto a semi-truck somewhere, so the group grabbed whatever they could find and rented the rest. "We were on the road, we had three days off in Boston, and the song just fit things at the time," Axl explained. "So, we went in and did it without having any clue of what it was gonna sound like musically. Because it's a completely different string arrangement and everything in the original. We went in and just had fun with it."[851] According to Slash, GNR's take on the Skyliners tune "really started to turn this covers thing into an actual album. We did it during off time on the road – that was how badly we wanted to do it."[852]

Around this time, Guns released a music video for "The Garden," a track they performed a couple dozen times on the North American leg of Skin N' Bones and then permanently dropped. Directed by Del James, the video is largely conceptual. The members of GNR only appear briefly, shot separately in black and white in various New York City locations: A forlorn Axl rides a subway, Slash gets wasted in a hotel bed, Duff smokes and spits in a vacant lot, Gilby hangs out in Washington Square Park. This is juxtaposed with color footage exploring the dark underbelly of modern capitalism: strip joints and X-rated theaters in Times Square, garbage strewn sidewalks, brick walls filled with graffiti, pimps, streetwalkers, the National Debt Clock, Grand Central Terminal, and so forth. The inauspicious piece ends with a handwritten note of thanks to Alice Cooper and Shannon Hoon for their vocal contributions.

Trip n' roses

When it was performed, "The Garden" was one of the standout numbers of the Skin N' Bones excursion. As GNR trekked across North America for the umpteenth time, they did not alter the six numbers in the acoustic section of the setlist. The same songs were played in the same order on every stop. Fresh cuts like "Garden of Eden" were performed a couple of times before being permanently dropped. Add in the material Guns played at virtually every concert ("Brownstone," "Attitude," "Jungle," "Sweet Child," "Paradise City"), and Skin N' Bones featured the most predictable setlists of the entire Illusion tour.

Additionally, as delightful as it was to watch GNR sit on a couch and perform acoustically, the contrivance drained some of the vitality that made them famous. "The shows where we did the acoustic set were my least favorite ones," Slash declared later. "They slowed down the show so much and were too choreographed with the sofa and pizza. I like the show to just build and build, not to slow down for long periods of time."[853] "By mid-set, the energy level was obviously lagging," a reviewer wrote of GNR's Portland stop, adding the acoustic set offered the group a breather, but "the expected energy boost never materialized. By the end of the two-plus-hour show, band members looked tired."[854]

The group did their best to keep things interesting and still threw in the occasional surprise. Weary of the long drum and guitar solos, Axl sometimes flipped a coin to determine if Slash or Matt would solo that night. And they continued to work without a setlist, so the running order of the songs changed from night to night.

Following their March 26 gig in Saskatoon, Canada, Slash, Matt, Dizzy, and their respective security teams stopped into Ryly's, a local tavern, where a Montreal bar band named Robin's Trip was on stage. Looking to impress the Gunners, Robin's Trip broke into "Mama Kin," the old Aerosmith tune GNR covered on the *Live ?!*@ Like a Suicide* EP. Between sets, members of both groups sat together and chatted until Robin's Trip got an unexpected offer. "Slash asked if we minded if they got up on stage to jam," bassist Mark Newton recalled. "You'd think these guys would be conceited and arrogant, but they were on our turf, and they acted like they knew it. They got attitude coming out their ears but, one-on-one, they were great guys."[855] The newly formed Trip N' Roses jammed for about thirty minutes, turning in a raucous cover of ZZ Top's "La Grange" and blowing the roof off the tiny venue. "The club was electric, it was jammed with people yelling and screaming," Newton said.

Moreover, despite their obvious exhaustion, GNR continued to perform brilliantly. Night after night, they delivered the goods. For all his petulance, late arrivals, and high-maintenance pain-in-the-ass-ness, Axl remained rock's most compelling frontman. No matter what circumstances he faced, Slash stepped up and played his heart out. Even Duff, besotted by vodka, cocaine, and heroin, never faltered. Matt continued to pound his kit with power and precision.

Gilby and Dizzy were as reliable as the rising sun. Whether they were playing the Boston Garden or the Fargodome, they refused to phone it in.

An issue with Metallica

In December 1992, when Metallica released *A Year and a Half in the Life of Metallica,* the documentary where James Hetfield poked fun of Axl's list of backstage requirements, MTV began airing the clip in its news segments. Hetfield's gleeful dissing of Axl attracted viewers but also generated considerable bad blood between the two groups.

It was the April 3, 1993, issue of *Rolling Stone,* however, that really got Axl's ire. The magazine's cover featured James Hetfield, who spent a good portion of his interview railing against Guns. He blamed Axl for the riot in Montreal and sneered at GNR's internal hierarchy. "They're a different type of band – and I use the word band loosely. It's a guy and some other guys."[856]

Axl felt deeply betrayed. Everyone knew the Guns-Metallica venture was plagued by problems but airing that kind of dirty laundry to the press was beyond disrespectful, totally unprofessional. When the Skin N' Bones tour hit Sacramento, California on April 3, the singer refused to remain silent any longer.

"So, we're around the Bay Area, right?" Axl asked, six songs into GNR's set. The crowd roared in response. "Good. So, we're here on somebody else's turf in a way. Some people we used to like to think that we were homeboys or something. I wanna talk about your good friends Metallica for a minute. Let me tell you a couple of things about Metallica. First off, they do a lot of bitching for a band that got paid about twenty or thirty percent more than what they deserved, because they didn't bring that much."

Axl's comment was met with a mixture of applause and booing.

"Ooh, Axl's talking now," the singer said, mocking Metallica's defenders. "Who does he think he is? I'll tell you who I think I am. I thought I was friends with these people. I don't know how long they were on the road, but there was nobody in their crew that ever got a bonus or paid anything extra for working their ass off and slaving for that band. I watched a lot of people being treated like shit, and it wasn't very enjoyable."

According to one reporter, "The audience, many of whom are fans of both groups, didn't want to hear Rose's angry diatribe, and some even booed, one yelling, 'Shut up and play!'"[857] But Axl was just getting warmed up.

"I watched the man named James prove that – you know, since I'm supposed to be the 'rock racist,' 'cause I used a word once – I watched the man *show me* that he was a motherfucking racist. He had a real big problem with Ice-T and any black man, actually. 'Oh, rap is really terrible. Black men, we can't have them up there.' I watched him be really shitty at black people who worked with us. That wasn't very enjoyable."

The audience was silent now, stunned in disbelief at what they were hearing. Axl continued, ranting about how Metallica blatantly stole ideas from GNR. "I'm gonna dedicate this to people who like to run little videos and say, 'Oh, it was just a joke because we are friends.' You ain't no friend of mine, you stupid little cocksucker. This is for you, Lars, and you, James. This is called 'Double Talkin' Jive' motherfucker."

The second the song was over, Axl started up again. "Now, being here in Sacramento, do you think I would say that shit here of all places if I was afraid of getting called on it? I know that *somebody* here is going to call Metallica and tell them. I personally don't feel like talking to the motherfuckers myself."

Axl was seated on the couch, with the other musicians around him, waiting to begin the acoustic set.

"I ain't telling you not to like their music or them or whatever. But it gets *really* hard when you try to put a show together. We wanted to do a tour with Metallica since the day we started – I remember seeing the band open for Ratt at the Troubadour. We worked real hard to put this thing together. We paid 'em a few million dollars more than any other band shoulda got paid but they wouldn't do it unless they got a certain amount. Okay, fine let's just do the show. We took a loss. We did it because we wanted you to be able to see *that* show. And the only way we could get 'em to do it was to call it co-headlining. So, *fine*, we'll call it co-headlining. But when the shit all went down, they couldn't live with it. 'Oh my God, we're opening for Guns N' Roses. How will we ever live this down?' If that's the way you felt about us, you never shoulda played a show with us to begin with. Just be honest, that's all."

Slash picked a few notes on his slide guitar, dying for Axl to stop. The singer relented and the group played their acoustic set, with Slash mixing bits of The Who's "Pinball Wizard" and John Lennon's "Imagine" into the middle section of "Patience." Teddy Andreadis hopped on stage and joined in for "Knockin' on Heaven's Door," harmonizing on the chorus and adding a harmonica solo. "We miss him," Axl said by way of introduction.

After this, the singer played his acoustic version of "November Rain." As the song reached its conclusion, someone in the audience threw a bottle at the stage, striking Duff. "It came flying out of the top tier," the bassist recalled. "I saw it out of the corner of my eye. It hit Matt's floor tom and careened off. Then everything went black. The bottle had hit me right in the temple and knocked me out. The show ground to a halt. I was rushed to the emergency room."[858]

Moments later, Axl informed the audience the concert was over. "I hate to ruin your fun and our fun, but somebody just hit Duff in the head with a bottle and now he's not able to play. So, we're sorry. Have a good night. And if you find the asshole, kill him." Axl threw down his microphone and stormed off stage.

Confusion ensued. The house lights remained dark, and the audience was uncertain whether to leave. There were boos and calls for an encore. Some chanted the band's name. A few minutes later, a shirtless Slash retook the stage to address the crowd.

"Can I get everybody's attention for a second? This shit happens at a lot of gigs. I know it's not everybody in this building's fault, but some asshole just hit Duff in the head with a bottle of piss. And now he has to go to the hospital. So, it's over. It's just one person that does this stupid fucking conduct at a concert where we're supposed to be having a good time. Does *anybody* understand what I'm saying?"

Yes, the audience replied en masse.

"Anyway, there's no way we can come back on, so this show's over," the guitarist continued. "And if you can do us all a favor and the building a favor and everybody that's working to make this a good time a favor, just leave peacefully. Don't fuck with other people, don't fuck with anything. Just cruise off. And hopefully if we come back to Sacramento, we'll have a full show, and some dickface won't throw shit. For the most part, you guys have been awesome. See ya."

According to a review in the *Sacramento Bee*, "The incident ruined the evening for 16,000 fans, leaving a number of the band's biggest hits unplayed. But it seemed an appropriate conclusion to a show by a band known for its explosive expressions of anger. The music seems purely secondary for Guns N' Roses. Attitude is the thing, and Rose and company have a bad one, clearly missing the apparent connection between the group's rebellion for sale and the flying bottle."[859]

The following week, MTV News dutifully reported the bottle-throwing incident, but spent most of the segment recapping Axl's onstage taunts of Metallica. They replayed the clip of James making fun of Axl and quoted from his *Rolling Stone* interview. Metallica's management sent MTV News a statement: "If James has something to say to Axl, he wouldn't want to say it through the press. He'll say it to his face."[860]

The next night, Duff had sufficiently recovered from the bottle strike to join Guns on stage in Reno, Nevada.

Bee girl

At GNR's April 7 stop in Salt Lake City, Blind Melon joined the Skin N' Bones excursion as an opening act, staying on through June and performing in the U.S., Mexico, and Europe. The quintet's label, Capitol Records, wanted to market Blind Melon as a grunge act, sending the L.A. band to live in Seattle and record with Rick Parashar, who had produced smashes for Pearl Jam, Alice in Chains, and Temple of the Dog.[861] Since issuing their debut in September 1992, Blind Melon had been on the road opening for grunge notables such as Soundgarden and Stone Temple Pilots. The group had released a single and three music videos that garnered little attention. But they built a strong word-of-mouth reputation for their live show and were viewed by industry insiders as a next big thing.

As Blind Melon embarked on the tour with Guns, they were just about to release their second single, "No Rain." The song's accompanying music video featured a young girl tap dancing while dressed in a bumblebee costume and went on to become one of the era's most emblematic videos. Up to this point, however, the quintet had been traveling the U.S. in an RV and were shocked by the excesses of the GNR machine. "We flew on the MGM Grand," Rogers Stevens, guitarist in Blind Melon, recalled. "That was really fun. It was full-on rock star treatment. We went from touring in a van to getting on their plane."[862]

"We would sit on the tarmac and wait for hours for Axl to decide he felt like flying," Mike Osterfeld, Blind Melon's stage manager, added. "We would be on the MGM eating chilled shrimp and drinking whatever we wanted, with the doors open, smoking cigarettes. I would sit in the farthest back seat of the plane, while Shannon and Slash would be up front partying their brains out. Slash's guy had to carry Slash off the plane when we showed up in Guadalajara. They both popped pills, so they passed out on the flight, and they couldn't wake them up. So, he's carrying him out, and I'm carrying Shannon out. They're coming running to the tarmac with wheelchairs for us."[863]

Shortly after GNR's stop in Mexico on April 29, Gilby broke his left wrist while riding a motocross bike. The guitarist had been preparing to participate in a celebrity race that would benefit the TJ Martell Foundation, a charitable organization devoted to leukemia, cancer, and AIDS research. Gilby's accident meant he would not be able to play for several weeks, which led to the cancelling of four East Coast dates that were never made up. It also put GNR's upcoming European trek in jeopardy. The group had a major summer tour booked in massive stadiums across Europe, playing in several countries they had never set foot in. Canceling or postponing the dates would spell financial disaster. The band was desperate to find a replacement to fill in for the first five gigs, until Gilby was healed enough to resume touring.

Guns N' Moses

It was Slash who came up with the idea to call Izzy Stradlin. "I thought it would be interesting," the guitarist said. "Regardless of whatever animosity, it wasn't anything so deep-rooted that it didn't blow over."[864] After Izzy departed in late 1991, he put together a solo act, Izzy Stradlin and the Ju Ju Hounds, and issued a self-titled debut in October 1992. The critically acclaimed release spawned two radio hits – "Shuffle It All" and "Somebody Knockin'" – but did not crack the top 100 in the U.S. It fared slightly better in the U.K., where it reached number 53. Izzy and the Ju Jus promoted the album with a low-key club jaunt in the U.S. and Europe. "I don't have any communication with them," Izzy told *Rolling Stone* when asked about GNR around the time his record was released. "I don't know what they do anymore. Still, I like to think that those guys are all my friends. It's not like I never want to see them again. The channels are very much open."[865]

Axl offered to reach out to Izzy personally about joining Guns for the launch of the European tour. "Axl called me and asked if I would do it," Izzy remembered. "I was home working on my bikes when I got the call. I thought about it for a couple of days, and then said I'd do those five dates. I just saw it as a free holiday, really. I got to go to countries like Israel and Greece where I'd never been before. We never talked about me returning full-time to GNR. And, quite frankly, it wouldn't be something that I'd consider in the slightest."[866]

Izzy used Axl's offer as leverage to get paid some of the money Guns still owed him, and it was soon announced he would fill in for Gilby at gigs in Israel, Greece, Turkey, and the United Kingdom. "We're one of the first stadium bands who's replaced their replacement with the original guitar player," Slash said.[867] Bringing Izzy back on board created some awkwardness for Gilby, who was understandably uncomfortable with the idea.

Izzy met up with GNR in Tel Aviv, Israel to rehearse for a few days before the first gig. The guitarist had not played with Guns since their appearance at Wembley Stadium in London on August 31, 1991, almost two years earlier. According to some accounts, Izzy was underprepared and had to be shown how to play the old material. The tensions between the band and their former guitarist came rushing back. "I really looked forward to playing with him again and hoped that he had changed," Slash recalled. "I booked a place in Tel Aviv to rehearse. But Izzy thought it was unnecessary, that it was just wasted time. He hadn't changed one bit. Izzy simply doesn't like playing rock at the level where we are right now."[868]

Izzy said he felt unwelcome returning to GNR. "Honestly, nothing had changed," he said. "Going back into the band was a strange and uncomfortable experience. It was cool in a way to be able to step back into something I'd left behind and to judge whether anything had improved, but it hadn't. It made me realize why I was glad to get out in the first place."[869]

Izzy had remained sober during his time away from Guns, and he was disappointed the group had not cleaned up their act. If anything, the drinking and drugs were worse than ever. "They were all fucked up," the guitarist recalled. "Duff and these guys, they didn't even recognize me. It was really bizarre. It was like playing with zombies. Ah, man, it was just horrible. Nobody was laughing anymore."[870]

50,000 fans showed up to the first concert, held May 22 at Hayarkon Park in Tel Aviv, eager to see Izzy's return. The band opened with "It's So Easy," with Axl sporting a T-shirt that said Guns N' Moses. Although they were booked to play massive, outdoor stadiums that summer, GNR attempted to retain the spontaneous spirit of Skin N' Bones, bringing the couch and coffee table onstage for the nightly acoustic session. At one point during the show in Tel Aviv, Guns broke into an extemporaneous rendition of "Hava Nagila," a traditional Jewish folk ditty whose title translates to "let us rejoice." Although the fans were thrilled to see Izzy onstage with GNR, even stopping to chant his name at some points, the band sounded unrehearsed and sloppy.

"He's forgotten a few songs, but that's alright," Duff laughed a few days later, during an interview with MTV in Athens, Greece. "People know that he hasn't played with us for over two years, so they're not gonna expect crystal clear, perfect sounds coming off the stage. Because they definitely are not. We've never been perfect."[871] Slash agreed, adding, "We went up there and we played pretty much like a club band. There was a small stage, and we were loose. Izzy hadn't played with us in a long time and had no idea what the set was like – and we didn't know what he was gonna be like. It was all pretty much spontaneous."[872]

After the Athens stop, GNR rented a luxury yacht and spent a day tooling around the Greek islands. That night, the group partied at a local nightclub with a bevy of supermodels that included Claudia Schiffer. Axl never joined the others on these types of excursions. "The band is like two separate things," Gilby explained. "There's the guys, everybody except for Axl, and then there's the band with Axl. When we're on the road, we're always together. We hang out together, just like a band. But that's not including Axl."[873]

Izzy stayed away, too, put off by the excesses of his former group. "The band's egos are way out of control," he said not long after the short-lived reunion. "Axl and Slash had the same attitude toward me as they did before I left, and there is a feeling of unreality about them. They lead isolated lives and don't seem to be in touch anymore with the real world. I spent all my time hanging out with the roadies."[874]

Classic case

Following their time in Greece, GNR performed to 80,000 fans in Istanbul, Turkey. The day before the show, Axl told his assistants he wanted some cans of Coca-Cola Classic in his dressing room before the concert. In 1985, the beverage company had retooled the recipe of its signature soda into a sweeter variation called New Coke. At the time, the original, "classic" version was difficult to find in Istanbul, so Axl's assistants had some six packs flown over from the U.S.[875] These might be the most expensive cans of soda ever consumed.

Izzy took it all in, concluding Axl was worse than ever, perpetually aggrieved about some little thing. The group dynamics hadn't changed much either. Everyone in the organization walked on eggshells, trying to placate the temperamental vocalist and keep the storms at bay. "He was more aggravated when I went in to do their shows than he was when I left the band," Izzy said later that year. "He's just always tense, aggravated, flustered, pissed off or something."[876]

Although Izzy and his former bandmates didn't agree on much during his brief return, his issues with Axl were one area where their opinions converged. The high-maintenance frontman had become increasingly hard to deal with. "Hanging around with Axl was like being in a constant state of chaos with no point to it," Slash declared. "As time wore on, he got more and more out there, and we couldn't argue with him." The singer paid to fly his psychic energy healer Sharon Maynard and her minders to some of the European dates, leading to even more backstage tensions. "It all got out of hand when Yoda and her fucking guards started coming on the road," Slash said.[877]

According to Duff, Maynard inflated Axl's already highly developed ego that much more. "This guru lady would come out on the road with us, and she took Axl for a fucking ride. In France, she would tell him he was Napoleon in a previous life, and in Israel, he was the Roman soldier who stabbed Jesus on the cross. And he believed all this shit. If anything went wrong, it was because there was some intergalactic battle going on out there between past lives or something."

Guns played their final concerts with Izzy on May 29 and 30 in Milton Keynes, England. The Cult, The Brian May Band, Blind Melon, and Minneapolis rockers Soul Asylum were tapped to open. On the second night, Michael Monroe and Ron Wood joined GNR for a show-closing cover of the Rolling Stones' "Honky Tonk Women." Gilby was on hand, too, singing "Dead Flowers," another Stones song, during the acoustic portion of the set.

According to Slash, Izzy demanded a hefty additional payment to play the last concert, threatening to remain backstage if the Guns did not pay. "We hung out, we went shopping in London together, we had fun," Slash recalled. "Then right towards the end, Izzy all of a sudden turned around and stabbed us in the back again, asked for an amazing amount of money to do one show. That's the last time we talked."[878]

For the two Milton Keynes appearances, GNR were ensconced in a luxury hotel in London, chartering a helicopter to get to the gigs. At this point, no one bothered to show up for sound checks anymore, letting members of the crew test out their equipment and adjust the sound levels.[879] Soul Asylum guitarist Dan Murphy couldn't believe how the entire Guns operation centered on Axl – whom he never met during Soul Asylum's stint on Skin N' Bones. "Now that was a band that was decidedly full of themselves," he told the *Indianapolis Star*. "There was a real separation of church and state on that tour. A lot of, 'Don't get too close to that dressing room.'"[880] "It was a lot of waiting for Axl's helicopter to land and we didn't really hang out with them," added Asylum frontman Dave Pirner.[881]

"I hated waiting around for Axl every night," Christopher Thorn, guitarist for Blind Melon, remembered. "I saw what I didn't want to be – that's one thing that tour taught me. People stepping aside because Axl was walking down the hallway. It was so pathetic. We used to have to wait, because he would fly in and out on a helicopter. We weren't flying around with them – we were in a van, trying to keep up with them on tour. There were times when we would want to leave to get to the next show, and we would have to wait for Axl to fly in on the helicopter. It was just always this waiting on Axl thing. It would drive me crazy."[882]

Of course, Soul Asylum and Blind Melon did not have to contend with Axl's level of fame. The singer was swarmed by fans everywhere he went; traveling by car could be difficult, time consuming, and even dangerous. A simple limo ride from the hotel to the gig might require hours of coordination, the hiring of additional security on the fly, and renting decoy vehicles to throw the devotees off his trail.[883] Getting to the gig by helicopter was an immense relief to Axl, one less thing to deal with.

The acts Axl invited to open described him as being out of touch, but if the singer tried to interact with them, they acted awkward and weird, daunted by his enormous celebrity. When Axl walked into a dressing room backstage, all conversations stopped, and everyone froze and stared at him. If Axl made even a minor joke, the room would erupt in peals of laughter. "It's hard, because everybody wants to talk to you," the singer confessed. "It's especially annoying when people are really drunk and talk for half-an-hour to an hour about something you're really not interested in, just because they're having their chance to talk to somebody they are into. You don't want to hurt their feelings, but at the same time you wanted to have a good time and, instead, all of your time is taken up. It's kind of weird to know where your responsibilities end and where they begin."[884] The singer endured this for half a decade, and eventually decided it was easier to simply keep to himself. Yes, fame changed Axl, but it changed everyone around him even more.

Axl's bandmates resented the singer and envied his position atop GNR's hierarchy, but they responded by getting wasted every night. Axl, stone cold sober for the past two years, was still the one holding it all together, still delivering monumental performances at every show. "He is one of the greatest frontmen of all time," Teddy Andreadis marveled. "As quirky and as asshole as he was, nobody could do what he did."[885]

After five appearances, Izzy's return came to an end. His worst fears realized, GNR's founding guitarist was happy to be done with his former group once and for all. The feelings were mutual. "Never again," Axl said after the tour was over. "We really don't wanna have anything to do with Izzy."[886]

Mood swings

Following the shows in England, Skin N' Bones crisscrossed Europe, making stops in Austria, the Netherlands, Denmark, Norway, and Sweden. "I've given up on itineraries," Duff told a reporter. "I just get on the plane and go."[887] Asked about new material that was being written, Duff was noncommittal. "GNR always jams new stuff at soundcheck – when we do soundchecks," he said. "We have some cool riffs already but it's going to be a while before our next official record comes out."[888]

On the European leg of the Skin N' Bones tour, interaction among the group members was at an all-time low. Axl, Slash, and Duff sometimes stayed in separate countries, flying in for gigs and then splitting immediately after.[889] Axl was harder to deal with than ever. "If Axl's in a good mood, us others in the band don't have to think about what he's doing and why," Slash told a reporter in Stockholm. "But if he's in a worse mood, we have to spend a big part of the show not making him more pissed off or irritated and therefore screw the show even more. Axl will absolutely not do anything he doesn't feel like, and I respect that. Of course, it happens that a show doesn't fully work due to his mood-swings. But he can't pretend."[890]

On June 26, GNR played the massive Olympiastadion in Munich, Germany. Footage from the concert would ultimately be used in the "Estranged" music video. A few days later, they rendezvoused at the Estadi Olimpic in Barcelona, Spain. Axl arrived from Venice; Duff flew in from Ibiza.[891]

Axl had been deeply concerned for some time about Slash and Duff, his founding bandmates. The recent hassles with Izzy only stoked the singer's trepidation. Slash's overdose and near-death experience in San Francisco was the final straw. Axl fretted that if Slash died, control of GNR's name would revert to Slash's wife or someone else. The singer had similar apprehensions about Duff, who was lost in a haze of vodka, cocaine, and heroin.

Just before the show in Spain, through one of his managers, Axl presented Slash and Duff with a contract stating he would retain all rights to the name Guns N' Roses in the event one or both of them died or departed the group. Signing the agreement meant Axl alone would control GNR's name. Duff leafed through the papers, stunned.

"What the fuck?" the bassist said, incredulous. At Axl's insistence, the trio had recently renegotiated GNR's royalties, with the singer getting a larger percentage than the other two.

"The truth is, you guys are not in good shape – you know that yourselves," the manager told them, holding out a pen. "If one of you dies, nobody wants to have to spend years in court battling your families or whatever."[892]

Outside, the stadium was already filled with people, chanting the group's name. The manager implied Axl would not go onstage unless Slash and Duff signed the contract. Feeling as if they had no choice, they signed. They no longer had any rights to the Guns N' Roses name. GNR was becoming less of a democratic band and more of an Axl Rose project. All of this set the stage for transformations to come.

On July 13, Guns played their last European date at the Palais Omnisports de Bercy in Paris. The next day they flew to Argentina for the final two shows of the longest tour in rock history.

The last two

Guns returned to Buenos Aires for two concerts, which took place on July 16 and 17 at the River Plate Stadium, where the group had performed the previous December. Like their earlier visit to Argentina, GNR ran into trouble almost as soon as they set foot in the country.

The band members were holed up at the Park Hyatt Hotel, which was mobbed by reporters, photographers, and 3,000 fans gathered outside. The devotees sang, cried, waved banners, and did everything they could to breach the hotel's front doors. A former state intelligence agent alleged someone in the Guns organization purchased fifty grams of cocaine upon arriving in Argentina. A few hours before GNR's first concert was scheduled to begin, a federal judge ordered a search of all the band's equipment, backstage areas, and hotel rooms.[893]

Four dozen narcotics officers descended on the Park Hyatt to search for drugs. The chief of police demanded to see Axl's room. "Axl had no idea what was going on," Craig Duswalt, one of Axl's assistants, recalled. "He was eating dinner inside his room, while Steve was taping his ankles for the show."[894]

The police squad drew their guns and forced their way into Axl's suite, on the top floor of the hotel. They overturned the singer's room and assumed they had struck gold after finding five plastic baggies full of white powder – Axl's bath salts. The situation became incredibly tense, with the adrenalized, gun-toting officers screaming and menacing Axl and his team. "Somehow, they ran tests and determined that we were telling the truth. No cocaine," Duswalt said.[895]

Just as the officers were preparing to leave Axl's room, the chief of police turned to the singer and asked for an autograph. "Happened all the time," Duswalt remembered. "Give Axl, or members of the band, crap for a few hours, accuse them of something illegal, threaten them, and once nothing is found instantly turn into best friends and expect an autograph. Incredible."[896] Axl signed.

Shortly afterward, the singer held an impromptu press conference at the hotel. "The whole thing seems like a joke to me," he said, adding, "I love coming to Argentina, but I'm worried about the fans and what happens at the show; I am also concerned about what this has to do with freedom."[897] That night, Axl ordered GNR's walk-on music be changed to Stealers Wheel's "Stuck in the Middle With You," with its pointed lyrics about being surrounded by clowns and jokers.

55,000 fans were on hand each night, as GNR delivered Illusion's final two concerts. At the previous Argentina stops, Guns were a twelve-piece band, with the horn section and backup singers. On this night, they brought the couch and coffee table, opening the acoustic sets with "Dead Flowers" by the Rolling Stones. Slash incorporated bits of John Lennon's "Imagine" and Kansas's "Dust in the Wind" into the introduction to "Patience."

The final show was broadcast live on television in Argentina and Uruguay. It was winter in Argentina and Axl took the stage sporting a flannel shirt over his black Charles Manson T-shirt and shorts. "I was trying to make a statement," Axl would later say about the Manson T-shirt, which he donned at nearly every gig on the Skin N' Bones tour. "I wore it because a lot of people enjoy playing me as the bad guy and the crazy. Sorry, I'm not that guy. I'm nothing like Manson. That's what I'm saying. Plus, I like the black humor of the 'Charlie Don't Surf' line for the movie *Apocalypse Now*."[898]

The singer donned the Argentinian national soccer team's jersey later in the night. In a rare change of attire, Slash wore the same blue-and-white striped soccer shirt throughout the concert. Axl called for a translator, dedicating "Double Talkin' Jive" to "the man who made the false report on us, the judge who issued the order, and sixty stupid police."

The last show ended as the Illusion concerts always did, with a rousing rendition of "Paradise City." For the final time, GNR gathered at the front of the stage to take a bow. Afterward, Axl heaved bouquets of red roses into the enraptured audience. The singer then sought out Slash, wrapping the guitarist in a bear hug. The pair held each other for a moment, an acknowledgement of all they had accomplished together. They took one final bow before departing the stage arm in arm. "Amid all of the high and low points, we did some amazing performances that rival all of the bands I looked up to as a kid," Slash wrote in his memoir. "We had a very established chemistry and a dynamic that was priceless. We made history."[899] Nearly nineteen years would elapse before Guns N' Roses would play another concert.

Around 2:00 a.m., GNR and their entourage took over the bar at the Park Hyatt, with Axl playing the grand piano into the wee hours. The party broke up sometime around six in the morning. There was nothing to do now except say farewell and return home.

"I walked down to Axl's room and said goodbye," Stephen Thaxton, Axl's chiropractor, recalled. He had been on the road as part of Axl's inner circle for more than two years. "In the last scenes of *Dances with Wolves*, there's the Native American on top of the mountain screaming how much he respects and loves his friend. I remember Axl and I both kind of felt that same way. That's probably the most special memory I have from that whole tour – knowing how much you care about somebody, and they care the same about you. You can't buy that kind of love for one another."[900]

Gilby's final encounter with Axl was less sentimental. "Axl came up to me at the last GNR show in Argentina and said it was nice knowing you," the guitarist recalled.[901]

"The tour was awesome," Matt enthused. "We did two-and-a-half years, we had our private jet, and we flew home in '93. We landed on our own private air strip in L.A., and the limos pulled up. There were thirty-five people in the entourage on the airplane – the bodyguards, an accountant, a masseuse, a chiropractor, two private photographers, and a publicist. We got off the airplane and Axl looked over at me and said, 'Hey Matt, I'll see you in a couple of years.' So, it was like, okay, we're going to take a break. I got into my own private limo, and everyone drove off in their separate directions."[902]

"I've got a lot of stamina, but that entire tour, it was such an endurance thing," Slash recalled. "That was a hell of a long tour. A lot of stuff went on. Nine kids were born, a dozen people got divorced, a dozen people got married. I got married. All this stuff went on while we were still doing the tour. It was like watching real life going down in this mad environment."[903] GNR's diehard road dog added, "When it was over I was fried, and as hard as it was for me to admit it, I was glad to be home for the first time in my life."[904]

After two-and-a-half years, the Illusion trek was officially over, but Axl wasn't done just yet. The Illusion era did not end on a stage in Buenos Aires. It concluded the following month with the most ambitious creative project the singer ever dreamed up.

Chapter 17

Estranged

Slash encountered post-road depression as soon as the Illusion tour was over. Historically, the guitarist responded to the condition in one of two ways: Dive headlong into drugs and alcohol or get busy working. This time, for the most part, he chose the latter. The guitarist occupied himself by finishing GNR's long-in-the-works covers album, putting last-minute touches on a few of the tracks and then mixing the entire release. Slash also built a home studio and started working up material for the next Guns record. "Trying to keep the band together as a cohesive unit so we don't splinter off," as he put it.[905]

There were plans to create a documentary from the footage captured by the two-man camera crew who followed GNR for the entirety of the Illusion tour. "We'd like to make a movie," Axl said. "We filmed everything that we did on the road for the last few years, and we'd like to make a documentary movie and put out a soundtrack to that."[906] Slash added that no one had tried to hide anything from the film crew, that they had witnessed every ribald incident that took place onstage and backstage. "We really let them in, and they got it all," he said. "They captured the kind of history that anyone aside from the members of the band would never see. That footage is the Holy Grail of Guns N' Roses."[907]

There was also another music video to complete, one that would officially close out the Illusion era. Clocking in at nearly nine-and-a-

half minutes, "Estranged" was the second-longest track on the twin
Illusion records – only "Coma" was longer. "Estranged" was distinct,
even among GNR's lengthiest and most ambitious pieces. It featured
no chorus and was built around half a dozen musical movements.
The number began with Axl almost whispering in a haunted voice,
accompanied only by his forlorn piano, building over time to an
immense climax featuring the entire band.

"Estranged" was among Axl's most personal works. "It's about
not wanting something to die, caring about another person and not
wanting them to destroy themselves – and there's not a goddamn
thing you can do about it," the singer explained. "The song can be
applied to Steven Adler; the song can be applied to members of my
family; it can be applied to the relationship I had with Erin, to the
relationship with Stephanie. To me, this and 'Coma' are the two
heaviest songs I've ever written."[908]

Axl believed the video for "Estranged" needed to convey the
number's deep sense of emotion. Nothing less than a visual
masterpiece would suffice. He insisted that Andy Morahan, who
helmed "Don't Cry" and "November Rain" – as well as
"Yesterdays" and "Garden of Eden" – be brought on board to direct.
"I've worked with Andy a lot, and there's a lot of trust involved," the
singer explained. Morahan added, "We try to make videos that excite
people. The best thing you can do when it comes to expectations is to
throw people off. If they expect the answer, then give them
something else. It's too easy to give people the answer – and there are
no answers with this band."[909]

Axl wrote the song "Estranged" in response to the ending of his
relationship with Erin Everly. Its accompanying music video would
be the singer's response to the demise of his relationship with
Stephanie Seymour.

Axl had originally envisioned "Estranged" to be the final act in
the trilogy that began with "Don't Cry" and "November Rain."
According to Andy Morahan, "There was pressure to come up with
part three of the trilogy. Why did Steph die, which was the big
question."[910] Seymour had played a central role in the first two
videos, but now that she and Axl were split, the trilogy's plot had to

be rewritten. Del James' short story "Without You" was tossed and the creative team worked to develop a new concept.

"We had intended to make the sequel or the follow-up and the conclusion of 'November Rain,'" Axl explained.[911] "Two thirds into the project, real life changed all the plans – something we had worked on for five years had to be rewritten. As an artist, I had to figure out how to rise above my own creation. I was stopped dead in my tracks and had to write a whole new thing that I liked even more. 'Estranged' isn't a part of the trilogy, it's more like part four. So, it's a video about transcendence of a real life situation and didn't have a lot to do with the story that was intended."[912]

Axl was determined to create the most incredible music video of all time, proving to Stephanie her presence on screen was not needed, that he could develop something even more spectacular without her. The singer spared no expense. With a final price tag of about $4 million (about $11 million today), "Estranged" would be the priciest video of the Illusion era. To this day, it remains one of the five most expensive music videos ever produced, with a budget that topped all but one of Michael Jackson's famed celluloid extravaganzas. "There was a desire to make it wondrous and fantastic and surreal," Andy Morahan recalled. "Axl drove a lot of that; he wanted to be as mysterious and surreal as possible. He realized it made the enigma more powerful."[913]

Like "Don't Cry" and "November Rain," the "Estranged" video was filled with psychedelic images, changing scenery, and a large cast. The video begins with two brief shots of empty children's play equipment – a tire swing, a swing set – followed by a scene where dozens of police officers and emergency workers descend upon Axl's Malibu mansion at night. A helicopter flies overhead, shining its searchlight down as the officers – weapons drawn and flashlights in hand – breach the front door and comb through the property. Axl, dozing and out of sight in a nursery, barely wakes and then falls back to sleep. This is followed by footage of GNR rocking 75,000 fans in a massive outdoor stadium.

"Don't Cry" captured Guns performing live atop a skyscraper in Los Angeles, and "November Rain" shot the twelve-piece band accompanied by an orchestra in an ornate theater. "Estranged" relied upon live footage videotaped at the Olympiastadion in Munich, Germany on the Skin N' Bones tour, along with closeups shot on a soundstage at Long Beach Arena. In both settings, Axl wore his black Charles Manson T-shirt and baggy black shorts.

The live footage is followed by clips of GNR hanging out backstage, recovering from the concert. Axl lies on a red sofa, eventually rising and stepping into a shower where he closes his eyes and lets the water pour over him. After more footage of Guns performing live, the video cuts back to a daylight scene at Axl's mansion, high on a hilltop in Malibu and overlooking the ocean. Police officers and emergency workers, including Axl's brother Stuart Bailey – all wearing white uniforms – begin to vacate the premises. In the back yard, a group of children, also dressed in white, play on a swing set and jungle gym. We see a brief shot of a stuffed elephant – a gift Axl had given to Stephanie. We cut to Axl's living room, where a life-sized crucifix hangs on one wall. Axl and his bodyguard Earl stride through the house, both dressed in white. Axl's T-shirt contains a single word: "deep."

"It's really wild to be doing this video in my home with my family," Axl said during the production. "It would have been nice if it would have happened with Stephanie and I, but the woman continually worked very subtly at destroying that and trying to keep me from being here, for whatever reason."[914]

In the video, Axl then steps into a white limousine, which makes its way off the property and onto the winding hilltop road that surrounded the singer's mansion. GNR are seen boarding the belly of a jumbo jet, followed by a scene where Axl walks by himself down a completely empty Sunset Boulevard at night. Dolphins swim through the streets, which are flooded like a flowing river. Afterward, Slash appears to float down the same street, wailing away at a Les Paul. To get these shots, the group paid to shut down Sunset Boulevard, capturing footage outside the Rainbow, the Roxy, and other iconic venues. To give the impression Slash was floating, the guitarist mimed his solo while standing on a small, wheeled platform that rolled on a track.

The video cuts to Axl walking, this time atop a Titanic-sized oil tanker. He strides straight to the railing, climbs it, and leaps five stories into the water below. From the deck of the oil tanker, Gilby throws Axl a life preserver, but the singer casts it aside. These scenes were shot by a 35-man crew aboard the Judith Prosperity, a supertanker located off the southern coast of Texas, about ten miles into the Gulf of Mexico.[915]

In the video, Duff rows by in a lifeboat, trying to rescue Axl. But the singer closes his eyes and sinks into the sea. A wave pool in San Diego was hired out to capture these scenes. "I went into the water for about eight hours or so, freezing water," Axl said on the set. "It's more mentally exhausting than physically exhausting."[916]

In "Estranged's" most memorable sequence, a pod of dolphins appears out of nowhere, circling the drowning singer. Axl – eyes open – grabs one of their fins and is pulled to the surface. "The music in the song always reminded us of whales at that particular point," Axl explained. "Dolphins showed up and it kind of brings all that together."[917] Axl later added that the scene was "my way of giving something back to the dolphin, which are endangered and threatened with extinction."[918] According to Andy Morahan, Axl told him, "I don't want any more beautiful girls in my videos; I'd rather have a dolphin."[919]

Axl, Morahan, and the crew captured these scenes in the Bahamas at Dolphin Cay, which offers visitors an opportunity to swim and interact closely with the sea mammals. The dolphins received a lot of attention from viewers and reviewers. "The dolphins were a metaphor," Morahan explained. "He had the opportunity to be saved three times. He rejects every opportunity to be saved, and then he's not saved, because he's asking God to save him, and God said, 'Well, you had three opportunities.' You think it's all over, it's death, and he sinks underneath, but finds this new heaven in the abyss. It's a kind of a rebirth image; in this way he finds his nirvana, his heavenly kind of state of grace."[920]

After Axl is resurrected by the dolphins, the video moves to a scene where Slash plays a second solo, this time standing atop the ocean's surface. To achieve the effect, Slash was taped on a makeshift platform in the Pacific Ocean, wearing a wet suit beneath his jeans and T-shirt.

Following Slash's solo, a rescue helicopter flies overhead, with Matt peering out the window, searching for Axl. The drowning singer is spotted and a frogman dives into the ocean, pulling Axl up to safety with a cable. As "Estranged" concludes, the singer's red-and-white Converse "Axl" shoe sinks to the sea floor. The final shot consists of a soaking wet Axl in a white robe, smiling as he sits next to an animatronic dolphin, which wears one of the singer's red flannel shirts. The handwritten words "Lose Your Illusions, Love Axl" appear as the screen fades to black.

"It's not obvious what it's all about," Duff said on the set. "It'll keep you guessing forever. Nobody's ever gonna actually come out and say, 'This is exactly what this means here.' It's up to the viewer."[921]

"This is gonna blow people away," Andy Morahan enthused. He and Axl were deliberately trying to create mystery and intrigue. "It's not a narrative thing, it's really surreal. This will probably be the most emotive video because there'll be a lot of things that will touch chords in people that they haven't expected. I'm trying to make this more spiritual. This is gonna be the deepest one in a weird way."[922]

Slash appreciated "Estranged's" relatively lighthearted tone, compared to the more serious mood of the first two videos, pointing out no one died in this one. "'Estranged' ended everything with *Use Your Illusion* that we went through on an emotional level and everything about our existence in general. It's basically cleaning the slate. Those two records, the videos, the tours; that whole thing."[923]

Lawyers, guns, and money

The September 1993 issue of *Forbes* magazine ranked GNR the world's highest-earning musical act, reportedly raking in $53 million in the previous year, roughly $125 million in today's dollars. Some of the proceeds were being used to cover the band's legal fees.

In mid-August, Axl testified in the wrongful termination lawsuit filed by ex-drummer Steven Adler. Sporting the same light green

Versace suit he wore to court in St. Louis, Axl recounted how everyone in Guns besides him was having drug problems when they opened for the Rolling Stones in 1989 and how Adler was put on probation. Slash, Duff, and Doug Goldstein also testified. Adler appeared in court, too, nodding out at times due to his continued heroin use.

In September, just before the case went to trial, attorneys on both sides reached a settlement where Adler was paid $2.5 million plus 15% of his pre-termination royalties. Afterward, GNR issued a brief statement to the press: "We're not thrilled about having to pay Steven Adler more money than we already were paying him, and we continue to believe in the defense we asserted in the lawsuit. But we are certainly glad to have the dispute behind us."[924]

Toward the end of August, shortly after he testified in the Steven Adler lawsuit, Axl filed a lawsuit of his own in Los Angeles Superior Court. The singer sued ex-girlfriend Stephanie Seymour for "assault, battery and the recovery of more than $100,000 worth of jewelry, including a diamond, gold and turquoise necklace and a 4.5-carat diamond engagement ring." Axl's sister, Amy Bailey, told *People* magazine, "He wants them returned. Rather than keep them as a sad and sorry reminder, he wants to give them to a child-abuse charity."[925] Axl's assault accusations stemmed from the ill-fated Christmas party at his Malibu mansion the previous December.[926]

Stephanie had quickly moved on from Axl after the couple split the previous February, hooking up with a married father of five named Peter Brant and becoming pregnant. The former supermodel immediately countersued Axl, claiming he was physically abusive and had refused to return some clothing that belonged to her son, Dylan.[927] "I strongly disagree with Mr. Rose's version of these matters," she told reporters. "I was never engaged to Mr. Rose. I have gone on with my life, and I hope that he can do so as well."[928]

"Deep inside, underneath all the varying emotions, I do love this person and care about what happens to them," Axl admitted around the time he filed the lawsuit against Stephanie. "But not at the point of being a martyr or hurting anyone that's in my life."[929]

Axl and Stephanie's lawsuits were eventually settled out of court. "Both parties agreed to dismiss their claims against each other. The litigation has been resolved," Axl's legal team told the press in 1995.[930]

In mid-September, Duff's years-in-the-making solo debut, *Believe in Me*, was released by Geffen. Despite an all-star roster that included Lenny Kravitz, Jeff Beck, and Sebastian Bach, *Believe* stalled out at number one-hundred-thirty-seven on the Billboard album chart. Ignoring this tepid reaction, Duff cobbled together a band that included Teddy Andreadis on keyboards and harmonica. Toward the end of the month, Duff's group appeared at small venues in San Francisco and New York before embarking on a two-month tour of Europe, opening for the Scorpions. Dates in Japan and Australia followed. "We played some inspired shows, but there were also times when I shouldn't have been up there, times when I let it go too far and my performance suffered," the bassist admitted. "There I was in huge venues, playing with my own band, under my own name, not bringing my A-game."[931]

Meanwhile, Slash continued to fight post-tour depression in his home studio, where he was working on demos for the next GNR release. "Me, Axl, Duff, Matt and Gilby are writing some awesome tunes. We're eight songs into the next record already," the guitarist enthused, adding that tour dates were already being discussed. "Me and Axl are talking about going in to record a new album in February, so I'm hoping to be on the road by the summer. With this one right now, everyone is really happy, even though we're dealing with court cases and lawsuits. The grooves on this record are great. I don't know what the finished product will sound like or how it will be received, but we're all very happy and that's all I care about."[932]

Passion and spontaneity

The Spaghetti Incident, GNR's covers album, was released on November 23, 1993. Asked about the title, Slash explained it was "an inside joke, an actual incident when we were trying to get it together to write the *Illusion* records in Chicago."[933] Guns originally conceived of

Spaghetti as an EP consisting of punk tunes the band blasted out live during the initial *Illusion* sessions in 1990. Over time, the concept evolved into a full-blown album of not-necessarily-punk songs. *Spaghetti* opened with "Since I Don't Have You," the 1958 Skyliners ballad Axl insisted GNR record to help process his breakup with Stephanie Seymour. Duff featured heavily on *Spaghetti*, handling lead vocals on three tracks, including the Misfits' "Attitude," which Guns had played frequently on the Illusion tour. Duff's cover of Johnny Thunders' "You Can't Put Your Arms Around a Memory," an outtake from his solo effort, was recorded without the other members of GNR.

Slash even took a turn on lead vocals for the first time, duetting with Axl on T. Rex's "Buick Makane," which Guns paired with a brief take on Soundgarden's "Big Dumb Sex." Slash did not enjoy the experience, claiming he only agreed to sing lead because he wanted the tune to be included on *Spaghetti*. "The song wasn't quite right for Axl's voice, so he asked me to sing it," Slash said. "But beyond that, I'm not the singing type. It's probably my first and probably my last time singing. It came out okay, it's just I hated doing it."[934]

Ultimately, *Spaghetti* highlighted GNR's varied influences, from 1970s Scottish hard rockers such as Nazareth to 1980s L.A. punk heroes like Fear. "It's really not a punk record anymore," Slash explained. "The first couple of songs we were jamming on were definitely punk, but as we got into it, it evolved into a Guns N' Roses cover record. You can't really say Nazareth are a punk band, can you? There was no master plan to it"[935 936]

Spaghetti began as a way for the musicians to blow off steam during the high-pressure sessions for *Illusion*, where every track was being heavily scrutinized by producers, managers, and Geffen staff. There was little thought the cover tunes would be used for anything other than B-sides or possibly an EP, so no one paid much attention to them. "We started it just to alleviate all the pressure of doing the *Use Your Illusion* records," Slash explained. "We'd just jam on songs that we grew up with, off the top of our heads. They were a lot of fun to do and nobody in the business took it all that seriously so there was none of this outside business bullshit going on. It was a relief, and it was also very grounding when the stress seemed so unbearable."[937]

During the never-ending Illusion tour, GNR enjoyed popping into an obscure studio in a random city and laying down a track in a single session. "It was a real bonding thing for the guys in the band just to book a studio without asking anybody for the money or anything," Slash said. "I'd call up some studio and just go, 'Yeah, this is Slash from Guns N' Roses and can we book the studio from such and such a time to such and such a time and record a song.' And then we'd all show up with borrowed gear. It was probably one of the things that was most instrumental in keeping us going."[938]

In Slash's mind, this off-the-cuff approach gave *Spaghetti* a looseness sometimes missing from the heavily produced and overthought *Illusion* sessions. "It's not so serious but it's real honest. It's live and haphazard, just us hanging out. It's not making any particular statement; it's just about passion and spontaneity."[939]

Axl, Slash, and the others hoped their covers would lead listeners to the native versions. The band included a note in the CD booklet advising, "A great song can be found anywhere. Do yourself a favor and go find the originals." Axl explained each number was chosen for personal reasons. These were "historical and musical gems that may have been overlooked. In Indiana, I was ridiculed and physically attacked for my musical tastes, tastes that I never made any effort to hide. I thought it would be interesting for the so-called mainstream and the people who were against this material when I was a teenager to actually hear these songs."[940]

Perhaps more importantly, *Spaghetti* would give GNR fans something to listen to until the band released their next album. "God knows when that'll be," Slash said.[941]

Manson

Spaghetti received the most notoriety for its thirteenth number, a hidden track not listed anywhere on the record, mentioned in Geffen's pre-release publicity materials, or included on advance copies sent to reviewers. "Look at Your Game, Girl" was written by

Dennis Wilson, a founding member of the Beach Boys, who drowned in 1983 at the age of 39.

In the late 1960s, Wilson had befriended a hippie drifter and aspiring musician named Charlies Manson. Looking to break into the music industry, Manson recorded a fourteen-track demo that included a cover of Wilson's "Look at Your Game, Girl." Manson's showbiz career did not pan out, but he gained infamy for founding a cult whose members went on a killing spree in August 1969 that led to the gruesome murders of seven people, including pregnant actress Sharon Tate. Manson was convicted and had been in prison ever since. His demo continued to circulate on the bootleg market, a pop-culture curiosity for those trying to make sense of his descent into crime. Groups such as the Lemonheads and Red Kross had covered Manson's songs, and Nine Inch Nails leader Trent Reznor famously moved into the house where the Manson murders took place to record NIN's acclaimed sophomore effort, *The Downward Spiral.*

According to Doug Goldstein, Stuart Bailey played a demo of "Look at Your Game, Girl" to Axl, who promptly "went nuts over it."[942] The tune's lyrical reference to "illusions" and a woman who plays mind games were primary draws. Like "Since I Don't Have You," Axl thought it would be another perfect kiss-off to Stephanie Seymour. He recorded the track without the other members of the band, accompanied by Carlos Booey on acoustic guitar and a bit of percussion courtesy Dizzy Reed. "I like the lyrics of the song," Axl explained. "It was something that people hadn't heard and was a missing part of the puzzle. Almost everything about Charles Manson has been public, but this was something that wasn't public on a big scale, and I just thought that people would be interested in hearing it."[943]

Slash agreed the number possessed a certain morbid humor – a folksy ditty sung by a psychopath, not completely unlike GNR's chipper murder ballad "Used to Love Her." The guitarist grew up around the music industry in L.A. and recalled the Manson murders from his childhood. "Even though I was only four in 1969, I remember what a shock it was to my hippie parents that there would be someone like Manson out there. It was one of those 'wake up and smell the roses' things that signaled the end of the whole love era."[944]

"Game, Girl" became a source of friction within GNR, whose members were reluctant to include anything associated with Manson on *The Spaghetti Incident*. "Axl was talking about it and me and Slash were cringing, going, 'No! Please! It's a nice album,'" Duff recalled.[945] "We were a little bit shy about doing it, because we didn't want anybody to pin us on a Manson thing," Slash added. "We did it anyway, but we didn't want to put its title and Charlie Manson's name on the record. We didn't want to give him the credit."[946]

As soon as word got out, "Game, Girl" generated enormous controversy, particularly in L.A. where the shock and pain of Manson's killing spree had not subsided much over the years. "Doesn't Axl Rose realize what this man did to my family?" Sharon Tate's sister Patti Tate told the *Los Angeles Times*. "It really hurts and angers me that Guns N' Roses would exploit the murders of my sister and others for capital gain."[947] Vincent Bugliosi, who prosecuted the Manson Family and penned the 1974 best-seller *Helter Skelter* about the case, was appalled. "It's a sad commentary on justice in America that a murderer who was supposed to receive the death penalty ends up having his song appear on a hit rock album. From a moral standpoint, it's truly distasteful."[948] The California Board of Corrections denounced GNR, and a police union in Connecticut issued a public statement warning parents about the track.[949] [950]

Axl said he thought the number had been written by Dennis Wilson, but Geffen publicist Bryn Bridenthal admitted, "There is a copyright in the name of Charles Manson. We don't know it to be a fact that the royalty payments would go to Manson, and that's something we're investigating."[951] Songwriting royalties for the number would total more than $60,000 per million units sold.

David Geffen, head of GNR's record label, was vacationing in Barbados when he learned about the kerfuffle on CNN.[952] Geffen personally knew two of Manson's victims and was mortified to be associated with the track. The entertainment mogul was deeply embarrassed but also outraged Manson might somehow profit from *The Spaghetti Incident*. "I would hope that if Axl Rose had realized how offensive people would find this, he would not have ever recorded this song in the first place," Geffen told the *Los Angeles Times*. "The issue is not the song itself. The fact that Charles Manson would be earning money based on the fame he derived committing one of the most horrific crimes of the 20th Century is unthinkable to me."[953]

Geffen Records President Ed Rosenblatt also weighed in. "We would have preferred the song wasn't on the album. We genuinely regret the distress this situation has caused. It is certainly not our intent or desire to glorify or enrich anyone who commits heinous and violent crimes."[954] [955] Asked for comment, Doug Goldstein replied, "Axl wants the song to speak for itself. It wasn't done for the critics or anybody else. It was a bonus for the fans."[956]

There were calls for Geffen to remove the offensive track, but David Geffen said doing so was contractually impossible. "The band has complete control of its material," he explained. "People at my company, as well as the other members of the band, had urged Axl to eliminate the song from the record, but he wouldn't. It related in a meaningful way to a relationship that was important to him."[957]

As the controversy continued to unfurl, Axl tried to explain himself in a statement to the press: "Personally, I liked the lyrics and the melody of the song," he said. "Hearing it shocked me, and I thought there might be other people who would like to hear it. The song talks about how the girl is insane and playing a mad game. I felt that it was ironic that such a song was recorded by Charles Manson, someone who should know the inner intricacies of madness. Manson is a dark part of American culture and history. He's the subject of fear and fascination through books, movies and the interviews he's done. Most people hadn't heard anything Charles Manson recorded."[958]

Axl vowed to donate his royalties from the track to an environmental organization, but added, "The media are enjoying making a big deal out of Guns N' Roses covering a song that Charles Manson recorded, but if another band had recorded that song, it probably wouldn't have been of interest. The media need their 'bad guys' to guarantee some ratings, so they use Manson's name coupled with mine to promo their news programs."[959] Axl complained that his good deeds were rarely written about in the press.

Bryn Bridenthal, the Geffen publicist, added, "If anybody had any idea of what this was going to become, it would have been a very different thing. The truth is, they don't go looking for trouble. It just happens to them." [960]

Ultimately, it was decided GNR's proceeds from the tune would be donated to the son of one of Manson's victims.[961] Slash issued a mea culpa on behalf of the band. "We naively thought there was a certain dark humor in Manson singing these love song lyrics, but now I find the word 'humor' doesn't fit into the equation. Especially when we think about the families of his victims and how this makes them feel. There are no words to describe him as a human being. He's the epitome of what's wrong with human existence and we don't want to glorify Manson in any way. But rather than pull the track it seems like we could at least help out a kid who lost his dad."[962] Slash would later declare the situation "got blown way out of proportion."[963]

A joyful racket

The Spaghetti Incident was released on November 23, 1993, entering the Billboard album chart at number four. It was certified Platinum in January 1994, denoting sales of one million in the U.S. The brouhaha over "Game, Girl" overshadowed the discussion of *Spaghetti*'s merits, which were not found in the punk numbers, but in oddities such as "Since I Don't Have You" and the band's raucous take on Nazareth's "Hair of the Dog," which highlighted the influence of vocalist Dan McCafferty on Axl.

Famously cranky *Village Voice* music critic Robert Christgau graded *Spaghetti* an A-, writing he was "impressed," marveling that Axl outdid New York Dolls singer David Johansen on "Human Being."[964] Industry journal *Music Week* awarded *Spaghetti* their rock "pick of the week" and predicted it would "dominate the charts until Christmas at least."[965] *Entertainment Weekly* gave *Spaghetti* an A- and a backhanded compliment, asserting it proved GNR "doesn't need two padded CDs, a horn section and a bevy of backup singers to make a joyful racket."[966]

Many reviewers took the release as an opportunity to beat up on GNR. *Rolling Stone* scored it 3.5 out of five stars, opining Guns "had grown to represent this generation's ultimate in bloated rock excess."[967] British music magazine *Select* ranked it two out of five stars, describing how the band chose punk tunes and "gave them 'the old GNR treatment.' You wouldn't wish 'the old GNR treatment' on your worst enemy."[968] Others made much ado about *Spaghetti* selling *only* a million units, as if cover-song albums ever generate big sales.

A sharper critique was that GNR were trying to latch onto the mainstream popularity of alternative rock and claim punk bona fides they did not truly possess. "Guns N' Roses reassert their roots in hard-edged rock & roll the way that U2 tried to with *Rattle and Hum* when their 'authenticity' had become suspect," wrote *Rolling Stone*, which added, "Axl doesn't quite connect to the punk-rock material on *Spaghetti* as anything but a conduit for pure aggression."[969]

Simply, GNR were never a punk band. The covers by Aerosmith, Rose Tattoo, Bob Dylan, and Wings that appeared on previous Guns releases more accurately reflected their influences, as did the many classic and hard-rock numbers they interpolated on the Illusion tour: "Wild Horses" by the Rolling Stones, "It's Alright" by Black Sabbath, "Only Women Bleed" By Alice Cooper, and "Hotel California" by the Eagles. There were also passages from numerous Beatles tunes GNR quoted in their Illusion-era concerts, including "Lucy in the Sky with Diamonds," "Happiness Is a Warm Gun," "I Want You (She's So Heavy)," and John Lennon's "Imagine."

Attempting to quell the controversy surrounding "Look at Your Game, Girl," in early December, Guns released "Estranged" as *Illusion's* final single. Concurrently, MTV premiered the song's accompanying megabudget video, shot in August and September. "We planned to make that video for a long time. We got it done and we wanted to put it out, and we also had *Spaghetti Incident*," Axl explained, joking, "It's confusing for us, and we wanted everybody else to celebrate and join in the confusion."[970] "Estranged" garnered considerable radio airplay, peaking at number sixteen on the Billboard Album Rock Tracks chart in mid-January 1994.

In late January, GNR issued "Since I Don't Have You" as a single. A writeup in *Billboard* magazine noted, "Here to compete with the successful 'Estranged' (taken from the *Use Your Illusion* opus) is this swaying cover of the Skyliners pop classic. Guns N' Roses, with its own inimitable slash-and-burn delivery, leaves its marks all over it."[971] The song peaked at number sixty-nine on the Billboard singles chart in March, driven in part by a music video that premiered on MTV in late February.

The video for "Since I Don't Have You" was directed by Sante D'Orazio and featured a series of surreal scenes shot in slow motion. Axl, dressed in white, makes out with an attractive blonde on a hotel bed. In another scene, the singer is bound with ropes and gagged with a black bandana. The singer rides in the passenger seat of a convertible, driven by a demon, portrayed by actor Gary Oldman, who was friends with Slash at the time. The group, minus Slash and Axl, chill around a fire at a beach party, flanked by palm trees and bikini-clad supermodels. Matt paddles around on a surfboard wearing sunglasses and red leather pants, while Duff lazes in a hammock. The demon appears there, too, cackling wildly as he stokes the fire. Slash appears only briefly, mostly shot in a studio, playing his Les Paul while standing in front of a green screen. In another scene, he plays while being paddled in a boat by the demon. The video ends with Axl and the car sinking into a pool of water. The video for "Since I Don't Have You" marked the final appearance of the Illusion-era band.

Looking to the future

The end of the Illusion era found GNR looking ahead, thinking about a new album, one that would top the twin *Illusion* discs. "Slash has been working with a lot of riffs, and I've been working out where my head's at about things," Axl said. "I'd like the next record to go to farther extremes. If I'm expressing anger, I'd like to take that farther; if I'm expressing happiness and joy, I'd like to take that farther."[972]

Axl was insistent the next album would be more futuristic, melding syncopated beats and elements of electronic music to the classic Guns sound. The singer cited "My World" as a primary example of the direction he intended to take. "I'm interested in the fusion of what GNR has with that futuristic style. If it was taken seriously and patiently, that combination could be amazing. It would be a much fuller thing than anybody's ever heard."[973] The singer added that Guns had focused on making traditional rock music thus far, but now it was time to take it to the next level. "I'd like to see if we could add anything to GNR, possibly bring in a new element that hasn't been there before," he said. "When I did 'My World,' everyone dug it. By the next record I think we can branch out a lot further."[974]

A tour was in the early planning stages, too, according to Axl. "We're aiming at '96, and we'll probably be doing a lot of recording between now and then. We're still trying to move ahead."[975]

Slash had a similar story, telling the press Guns was already well into their next release, writing an entirely new set of material – no covers, no leftovers from the old days. "We're working on the next record now. I've been doing the demos with the other guys at my house," he told a reporter in early 1994.[976] "So far, we've done fourteen songs. It shouldn't take as long for the next album to come out."[977]

Asked to describe the new material, Slash joked, "We have a new fusion jazz approach. We've been listening to Yes a lot lately."[978] Getting serious, the guitarist explained, "Most of it's really slinky groove things, but real mean. They're sort of like dirty sex, and there are some that are just fast and hard. There's a lot of really brash stuff that we've finished already that's really killer. What I want to do is get between eight and twelve songs done, get in and record them real simply and quick. I can't wait."[979]

But by the spring of 1994, it was clear everything had changed. Axl did not approve of the demos Slash and the band had been recording, finding the material too traditional for his liking. "There is no next GNR album," Gilby told a reporter. "We started working on one, and it got canned. It's an Axl thing. He just wasn't into what we were doing, so he's kind of rethinking what he wants to do. He threw a wrench into everything. So, nothing's happening right now. We're not gonna do anything. We were gonna do a lot of shows, but we're not gonna do 'em now. Nobody's really getting along right now. Everybody just called everything off."[980]

The Illusion era was officially over. The Guns N' Roses of that time had become permanently estranged.

Nothing Lasts Forever

When the Illusion era began in the summer of 1989, Guns N' Roses were mired in controversy over "One in a Million." As the Illusion era wound down at the end of 1993, GNR were embroiled in controversy over "Look at Your Game, Girl." In between, the band arguably accomplished more than they had during any other period of their career.

At the outset of the Illusion era, the group embarked on a mission to surpass the impact of *Appetite for Destruction*. In many regards, they succeeded. *Use Your Illusion I* and *II* shattered sales records, topped the charts in multiple countries, and were bestowed with numerous accolades. GNR were the first musical act in history to issue two entirely new records on the same day. *Illusion I* and *II* debuted in the first and second positions on the Billboard album chart and both releases remained on that chart for more than two years. *Illusion* spawned generation-defining singles such as "Don't Cry," "November Rain," "You Could Be Mine," and "Civil War." Five *Illusion* singles landed on the Billboard Hot 100 chart, including two top-ten hits.

The *Illusion* albums were nominated for a slew of honors, including two Grammys, three American Music Awards, and a Brit Award. Due to the success of the *Illusion* records, GNR won an American Music Award for best hard-rock group in 1992 and a 1993 World Music Award for being the best-selling hard-rock act on the planet. To date, the twin *Illusion* records have sold about 35 million units worldwide.

"We're very proud of what we've done for ourselves," Axl said about *Use Your Illusion*, toward the end of the Illusion tour. "We still feel it's the best thing we could have done. If we didn't outdo *Appetite*, it was going to take away from our success and the amount of power we had gained to do what we wanted. We got all the material out of our systems, and commercially it's been a major success."[981]

The nine pioneering music videos from *Illusion* received critical praise and cemented GNR's reputation as one of rock's most visually creative and ambitious artists. Guns were nominated for five MTV Video Music Awards for their *Illusion* videos, winning twice. In the age of streaming, "Welcome to the Jungle" remains GNR's most popular song, but "November Rain" is the group's most enduring video – the first by a hard-rock act to reach a billion views on YouTube.[982] "You can have a great band, a great video or a great song, but you kind of need all three for anything to be lasting and iconic," said Andy Morahan, who directed most of *Illusion's* celebrated visual works. "As a combination of music, video and that moment in time, they're very poignant to where the band were in that time and the cultural history of music videos."[983]

The Illusion world tour was the longest in rock history, with 192 concerts that took place over two-and-a-half years in 28 countries. More than seven million people attended.[984] Axl's iconic wardrobe and signature stage moves remain instantly recognizable the world over. The Illusion concert captured on *Use Your Illusion World Tour – 1992 in Tokyo I* and *II* was a runaway bestseller on home video, earning Silver, Gold, or Platinum certifications in nine countries. "Now that the tour is over, I can reflect, and I'll see if I've really achieved my goals," Axl said at the time. "I can sit back and go 'ahhh.'"[985]

Slash, too, looked back on this epoch with a sense of wonder and amazement. "The *Use Your Illusion* records, if anybody knew the whole story of what we were going through, they'd realize how important those records are to us and why they took so long – but you had to be there," he said in early 1994, near the end of the

Illusion era. "We had every reason to split up before those albums, as far as the obstacles we had to face. And then being able to pull off that tour, with Izzy leaving in the middle of it. And then being able to go back into the studio and do *The Spaghetti Incident*."[986]

The Illusion era was also beset by controversies and challenges. Despite the commercial success of the *Illusion* albums and the millions of tickets sold for the tour, GNR did not earn much money during this time. The profits were consumed by union fees, curfew violation fines, attorneys, bodyguards, $100,000 afterparties, a huge crew, and an enormous entourage that traveled by private jet and stayed in luxury hotels. "We also had a very temperamental singer who would show up four hours late to Madison Square Garden, which is a union building," Duff recalled in 2004. "So, you're paying quadruple overtime – you're paying to play. We played Lausanne in Switzerland, where people take trains to go to the concert. We had to pay to keep the train station open."[987]

During this period, GNR also contended with record-company battles, bad press, medical issues, riots, arrests, lawsuits, substance abuse, and the tribulations of megastardom. "The thing I can't stand is I cannot get into my car and go to local clubs I used to hang out at," Slash griped in early 1994, summarizing his life at the end of the Illusion era. "I can't go to the local store or market without feeling everybody's staring at me. People see you like you're a cartoon character, like you're Bugs Bunny walking down the street. That gets to be a drag."[988]

Ultimately, the Illusion era proved to be the end of Guns N' Roses as we knew them. GNR's five original members were on hand in Chicago at the outset, but only three were there at the end. The democratic band of brothers who produced *Appetite for Destruction* was ultimately replaced by the Axl Rose Project. "It's Axl's band, and he runs it the way he wants," Gilby complained in early 1994, not long after the Illusion era wrapped. "Whatever he wants to do is gonna happen. I have been fired a few times, and it was for nothing that I did. You don't know what's going to happen in GNR. I don't know if I'm going to be around for the next album. I don't know who's going to be around."[989] Axl fired Gilby later that year.

"The bottom line is that nothing can come between Slash and I," the singer said around this time. "We're like each other's balance and counterpart. As long as we have that bond, we still have Guns N' Roses."[990] But Slash would eventually depart, too, as would Duff, leaving Dizzy Reed as the last man standing. Axl began anew, finally issuing a new GNR album in 2008. The singer could never escape the legacy of *Use Your Illusion*, reuniting with Slash and Duff in 2016, returning to the road to play all those great, old songs again. But some things only come around once, and, as Slash said, you had to be there. From 1991 to 1993, when Guns dropped *Illusion* and toured the world, it generated an excitement that can never be recaptured.

In the end, the music has endured. The magic, power, and mystery of the Illusion era can still be found in the thirty songs captured on those two records, where the group swung for the fences and knocked it out the park. The artistry and audacity of the Illusion era can still be found in those nine incredible videos, too, harkening back to a time when everything seemed possible, and the only limits were those of the imagination. And it's still there in the live concerts, where the world's most dangerous band gave their all every night on a tour that seemed like it would never end. We didn't want it to end, but nothing lasts forever. So, we relisten and rewatch, looking back and remembering all that was and all that was lost. And even if we will never again have GNR as they were in the Illusion era, they gave us something that can never be taken away. Thanks to Axl, Slash, Izzy, Duff, Matt, Dizzy, and Gilby, we will always have the music.

Appendix

Researching and Writing
Estranged

I must have been one of the first people in Lawrence, Kansas to purchase *Appetite for Destruction* when it was released in late July 1987. I was a teenage hard-rock guitarist with long hair and an affinity for groups like Hanoi Rocks and Metallica. My bandmates and I would sift through the latest issues of *Hit Parader* and *Circus*, reading up on our favorite artists. Mötley Crüe bassist Nikki Sixx regularly touted an up-and-coming Hollywood act known as Guns N' Roses. That cool name plus Nikki's endorsement was enough for us, and the second I saw a cassette tape of GNR's debut in a downtown Lawrence record store, I snapped it up.

My bandmates and I fell passionately in love with *Appetite*, fully recognizing its greatness and significance from the first listen. This was not just another band; this was our generation's Led Zeppelin. We professed *Appetite's* greatness to everyone we knew, making converts out of many. All anyone had to do was listen to grasp how great it was. We were stunned when GNR didn't take off immediately but vindicated when the world eventually caught on.

Inspired in no small part by Axl and Izzy's pilgrimage from the Midwest to Hollywood, my band and I moved to L.A. in the fall of 1988. We figured if they could do it, why not us? The following year, when the Rolling Stones announced Guns as openers for their shows at the L.A. Coliseum, we snapped up tickets. Little did I know my first GNR concert would be one of the most notorious shows in the band's history.

In writing this book, I drew upon my personal recollection of that performance, as well as two other concerts I attended on the Illusion tour. The second was held at the Great Western Forum in Los Angeles on July 29, 1991, prior to the release of the *Illusion* albums, when Izzy was still with the band. The third concert, which featured Body Count and Metallica, was held September 30, 1992, at Jack Murphy Stadium in San Diego. At that point, GNR featured a twelve-musician lineup, including Izzy's replacement, Gilby Clarke. Witnessing these three incredible Illusion-era concerts forever cemented my fandom of one of rock's all-time great bands.

Estranged is a work of rock history and I approached the researching and writing as a historian might. In 2001, while working as a music journalist, I interviewed Matt Sorum, who drummed on the *Illusion* albums and tour.[991] I retained a copy of our conversation and drew upon it in writing this book. Matt, Slash, Duff, and Steven have all released memoirs, which served as primary sources for this book.

Estranged is written from a chronological, real-time perspective and relies largely on news sources, reviews, and interviews published from 1989 to 1994. I lightly edited some material for the sake of clarity. To research *Estranged*, I scoured the internet for every magazine article, interview, CD review, and concert write-up of GNR during the *Illusion* era. Immense credit goes to the website Appetite for Discussion: For Guns N' Roses - Past and Present (a-4-d.com). The site editors have done an incredible job of exhaustively cataloging virtually everything that has ever been published about GNR. When I set out to begin researching the Illusion era, it did not take me long to find this extraordinary resource, without which this book would not have been possible.

I also want to give a special mention to the Appetite for Distortion podcast, whose genial host Brando Weissler has spent the better part of a decade tracking down anyone and everyone who ever crossed paths with GNR (afdpod.com). Brando's 500+ interviews with band members, managers, video directors, close collaborators such as Alice Cooper, and many more provided insights to the Illusion era that enhanced every page of this book.

In researching *Estranged*, I also conducted a close analysis of the music, including multiple listens to each *Illusion*-era studio album, outtake, B-side, demo, and rare recording. There were also the nine official music videos created for *Illusion* and three "making of" home-video releases, *Makin' F@*!ing Videos*. Finally, I did a deep dive into the live history of *Illusion*, including scrutinizing official in-concert releases as well as the hundreds of amateur videos posted online.

A number of dedicated YouTubers have curated and compiled these videos online, providing more critical source material for this book. These include but are not limited to the YouTube sites Guns N' Roses Live Era Photography, Guns N' Roses Argentina, Rod N' Rhiad, GnR Brazil, Guns N' Roses Unofficial, Rhiad N' Roses, Fans & Roses, Rock N' Roll True Stories 2, Dust N' Roses, GnR Legacy, WTF Music, and many more. Drawing upon these and other sites, during the more than three years I spent researching *Estranged*, I compiled a chronological playlist of more than 300 official and unofficial Illusion-era videos, which can be found at youtube.com/@GHArchives/playlists.

Ultimately, my goal in writing *Estranged* was to do away with the myths of the Illusion era and reveal its truths: How the songs were written and recorded, the logistics of a three-year world-spanning tour, and how the magnitude of the Illusion era changed all parties involved. For those seeking sex and drugs, there is plenty in this story, but *Estranged* is not only about debauchery and largesse. It is about aiming to achieve greatness under intense scrutiny and keeping a disparate team functioning under massive pressure. Ultimately, I hope this book serves as a celebration of and conversation starter about GNR's most ambitious and artistic era.

Estranged is intended to provide an in-depth account of the Illusion era, but it is not exhaustive or encyclopedic. I thank you for reading and welcome your comments and corrections.

Notes

[1] Robert Hilburn. 1991. "Run N' Gun." *Los Angeles Times*, July 21.

[2] Robert Hilburn. 1989. "Showdown at the Coliseum." *Los Angeles Times*, October 15.

[3] Robert Hilburn. 1988. "Taste Makers: Axl Rose." *Los Angeles Times*, December 25.

[4] Patrick Goldstein. 1989. "Behind the Guns N' Roses Racism Furor." *Los Angeles Times*, October 15.

[5] Jon Parales. 1989. "There's a New Sound in Pop Music: Bigotry." *The New York Times*, September 10.

[6] Nick Kent. 1989. "Daze of Guns N' Roses." *The Face*, October.

[7] Juan Williams. 1989. "Fighting Words: Speaking Out Against Racism, Sexism, and Gay-Bashing in Pop." *The Washington Post*, October 15.

[8] Patrick Goldstein. 1989. "Behind the Guns N' Roses Racism Furor." *Los Angeles Times*, October 15.

[9] Nick Kent. 1991. "Welcome to My Nightmare." *Vox*, October.

[10] Robert Hilburn. 1989. "Still the Greatest." *Los Angeles Times*, October 20.

[11] Steven Adler with Lawrence J. Spagnola. 2010. *My Appetite for Destruction*. HarperCollins Publishers.

[12] Duff McKagan. 2011. *It's So Easy (and Other Lies)*. Orion.

[13] Robert Hilburn. 1991. "Run N' Gun." *Los Angeles Times*, July 21.

[14] Steven Adler with Lawrence J. Spagnola. 2010. *My Appetite for Destruction: Sex & Drugs & Guns N' Roses*. HarperCollins Publishers.

[15] Steven Adler with Lawrence J. Spagnola. 2010. *My Appetite for Destruction: Sex & Drugs & Guns N' Roses*. HarperCollins Publishers.

[16] Slash with Anthony Bozza. 2008. *Slash*. Harper Entertainment.

[17] Robert Hilburn. 1989. "Still the Greatest." *Los Angeles Times*, October 20.

[18] Duff McKagan. 2011. *It's So Easy (and Other Lies)*. Orion.

[19] Richard Cromelin. 1989. "Guns N' Roses Show Some Mettle." *Los Angeles Times*, October 21.

[20] Doug Simmons. 1989. "Rolling Stones/Guns N' Roses: Stoned in L.A." *Village Voice*, October 31.

[21] Jonathan Gold. 1989. "No Surprises in Third Night of Stone N' Roses." *Los Angeles Times*, October 23.

[22] Steve Sutherland. 1991. "White Riot." *Melody Maker*, August 3.

[23] Joe Bosso. 1989. "Agony N' Excesses." *Guitar World*, March.

[24] "Interview with Axl Rose." *Popular 1*, April 1988.

[25] Fabio Testa. 1988. "Hollywood Street Kings." *Concert Shots*, January.

[26] Del James. 1989 "The World According to W. Axl Rose." *RIP*, April.

[27] Arlett Vereecke. 1989. "Man with a Sweet Child in his Eyes." *Kerrang*, June 10.

[28] Arlett Vereecke. 1989. "Man with a Sweet Child in his Eyes." *Kerrang*, June 10.

[29] Steven Adler with Lawrence J. Spagnola. 2010. *My Appetite for Destruction: Sex & Drugs & Guns N' Roses*. HarperCollins Publishers.

[30] Slash with Anthony Bozza. 2008. *Slash*. Harper Entertainment.

[31] Kori Rumore. 2016. "The Time Guns N' Roses Squatted in Chicago." *Chicago Tribune*, July 1.

[32] Malcom Dome. 1989. "Mad, Bad, and Dangerous to Know." *Raw*, July 28.

[33] Oliver Klemm. 1989. "Revolution Calling." *Metal Hammer*, September.

[34] Del James. 1989 "The World According to W. Axl Rose." *RIP*, April.

[35] Duff McKagen. 2011. *It's So Easy and Other Lies*. Touchstone.

[36] Greg Kot. 1991. "Guns N' Roses Reborn." *Chicago Tribune*, May 19.

[37] Kori Rumore. 2016. "The Time Guns N' Roses Squatted in Chicago." *Chicago Tribune*, July 1.

[38] Hal Dardick. 2019. "John P Kelly, firefighter and popular Lincoln Park bar Owner Dies." Chicago Tribune, February 15.

[39] David Silverman. 1989. "Psssssssst . . . If You See Guns N' Roses in Chicago, Just Remember: You Didn't." *Chicago Tribune*, June 26.

[40] Duff McKagen. 2011. *It's So Easy and Other Lies*. Touchstone.

[41] Louis Marciano, dir. 1993. *Makin' F@*!ing Videos Part II*. Geffen Home Video.

[42] Louis Marciano, dir. 1993. *Makin' F@*!ing Videos Part II*. Geffen Home Video.

[43] Arlett Vereecke. 1989. "Man with a Sweet Child in his Eyes." *Kerrang*, June 10.

[44] Slash with Anthony Bozza. 2008. *Slash*. Harper Entertainment.

[45] Mick Wall. 1990. "Stick to Your Guns." *Kerrang*, April 21.

[46] Slash with Anthony Bozza. 2008. *Slash*. Harper Entertainment.

[47] Slash with Anthony Bozza. 2008. *Slash*. Harper Entertainment.

[48] Mick Wall. 1990. "Stick to Your Guns." *Kerrang*, April 21.

[49] Duff McKagen. 2011. *It's So Easy and Other Lies*. Touchstone.

[50] Lonn M. Friend. 1990. "Slash: Under the Black Hat." *RIP*, February.

[51] Arlett Vereecke. 1989. "Man with a Sweet Child in his Eyes." *Kerrang*, June 10.

[52] Axl Rose interview. July 1989. MTV Networks.

53 Axl Rose interview. July 1989. MTV Networks.

54 Axl Rose interview. July 1989. MTV Networks.

55 Axl Rose interview. July 1989. MTV Networks.

56 Mick Wall. 2016. "Izzy Stradlin: Life and Death and Guns N' Roses." *Classic Rock*, November 7.

57 Nick Kent. 1991. "Welcome to My Nightmare." *Vox*, October.

58 Bill Flanagan. 1990. "The Heartbreakers Highway." *Musician*, April.

59 The Associated Press. 1989. "Rock Guitar Player Freed on Bail After Incident on Jetliner." *Arizona Daily Star*, August 31.

60 The Associated Press. 1989. "Rock Guitar Player Freed on Bail After Incident on Jetliner." *Arizona Daily Star*, August 31.

61 The Associated Press. 1989. "Rock Guitar Player Freed on Bail After Incident on Jetliner." *Arizona Daily Star*, August 31.

62 "First Off." 1989. *Los Angeles Times*, September 1.

63 The Associated Press. 1989. "Rock Guitar Player Freed on Bail After Incident on Jetliner." *Arizona Daily Star*, August 31.

64 "First Off." 1989. *Los Angeles Times*, September 1.

65 Art Tavana. 2016. "Where's Izzy?" *L.A. Weekly*, October 22.

66 The Associated Press. 1989. "Guns N' Roses Player Arrested at Sky Harbor." *Arizona Daily Star*, August 31.

67 The Associated Press. 1989. "Guns N' Roses Player Arrested at Sky Harbor." *Arizona Daily Star*, August 31.

68 "Izzy Stradlin." 2006. TuneCore Podcast, November 12.

69 Bill Flanagan. 1990. "The Heartbreakers Highway." *Musician*, April.

70 United Press International. 1989. "Top MTV Honors to Young." *Dixon Telegraph*, September 8.

71 Steve Hochman. 1989. "Feud Between Rockers Boils Over Backstage at MTV Awards." *Los Angeles Times*, September 8.

72 Bill Flanagan. 1990. "The Heartbreakers Highway." *Musician*, April.

73 Mick Wall. 2016. "Life and Death, Sex and Drugs, and Guns N' Roses." *Classic Rock*, November 7.

74 Charles M. Young. 1992. "Izzy Stradlin's Side of the Story." *Musician*, November.

75 Jonathan Gold. 1989. "Guns N' Roses Lets 'er Rip in Stones Warmup." *Los Angeles Times*, October 16.

76 Liz Scarlett. 2023. "The Strange Story Behind Axl Rose Allegedly Getting into a Fight with David Bowie." Classic Rock, August 23.

77 Jonathan Gold. 1989. "Guns N' Roses Lets 'er Rip in Stones Warmup." *Los Angeles Times*, October 16.

78 "Gunner Gets His Day in Court." *Arizona Republic*, October 18, 1989.

79 "Gunner Gets His Day in Court." *Arizona Republic*, October 18, 1989.

80 Mick Wall. 2016. "Life and Death, Sex and Drugs, and Guns N' Roses." *Classic Rock*, November 7.

81 Del James. 1991. "Here Today, Gone to Hell (And Lovin' It)." *Rip*, September.

82 Matt Sorum with Leif Eriksson and Martin Svensson. 2022. *Double Talkin' Jive: True Rock 'n' Roll Stories from the Drummer of Guns N' Roses, The Cult, and Velvet Revolver.* Rare Bird Books.

83 Mick Wall. 2016. "Life and Death, Sex and Drugs, and Guns N' Roses." *Classic Rock*, November 7.

84 Andy Widders-Ellis. 1991. "The Hands Behind the Hype." *Guitar Player*, December.

85 Nick Kent. 1989. "The Daze of Guns N' Roses." *The Face*, October 13.

86 John Stix. 1992. "Slash: No Illusions." *Guitar for the Practicing Musician*, April.

87 Mark Rowland. 1990. "Appetite for Reconstruction." *Musician*, December.

88 Lonn M. Friend. 1990. "Slash: Under the Black Hat." *RIP*, February.

89 "Famous Last Words." 1990. MTV, August 31.

90 Ingrid Sischy. 1992. "Axl Rose." *Interview*, May.

91 "Famous Last Words." 1990. MTV, August 31.

92 Henry Yates. 2011. "Double Vision." *Total Guitar*, July.

93 Joe Logan. 1989. "Rolling to a Stop." *Philadelphia Inquirer*, December 18.

94 Joe Logan. 1989. "Rolling to a Stop." *Philadelphia Inquirer*, December 18.

95 Nick Kent. 1991. "Welcome to My Nightmare." *Vox*, October.

96 Nick Kent. 1991. "Welcome to My Nightmare." *Vox*, October.

97 Joe Logan. 1989. "Rolling to a Stop." *Philadelphia Inquirer*, December 18.

98 Mick Wall. 2016. "Life and Death, Sex and Drugs, and Guns N' Roses." *Classic Rock*, November 7.

99 Duff McKagen. 2011. *It's So Easy and Other Lies*. Touchstone.

100 "Wearing Flippers in the Sand." 1990. *Raw*, April 18.

101 "Guns N' Roses Update." 1990. *Blast*, May.

102 "Wearing Flippers in the Sand." 1990. *Raw*, April 18.

103 Mick Wall. 1990. "Stick to Your Guns (Pt. 2)." *Kerrang*, April 28.

104 Lonn M. Friend. 1990. "Slash: Under the Black Hat." *RIP*, February.

105 Jeff Kaye. 1990. "G N' R Language on ABC Draws Heat. *Los Angeles Times*, January 24.

106 "Wearing Flippers in the Sand." 1990. *Raw*, April 18.

107 Lonn M. Friend. 1990. "Slash: Under the Black Hat." *Rip*, February.

108 Patrick MacDonald. 1991. "The Adventure of Duff and His Guns." *Circus*, November 30.

109 Emilio J. Rondeau. 1991. "War of the Roses." *Vox*, January.

110 Mick Wall. 1990. "Stick to Your Guns (Pt. 2)." *Kerrang*, April 28.

111 Mick Wall. 1990. "Stick to Your Guns (Pt. 2)." *Kerrang*, April 28.

112 Mick Wall. 1990. "Stick to Your Guns (Pt. 2)." *Kerrang*, April 28.

113 Mick Wall. 1990. "Stick to Your Guns (Pt. 2)." *Kerrang*, April 28.

114 Mick Wall. 1990. "Stick to Your Guns (Pt. 2)." *Kerrang*, April 28.

115 Mick Wall. 1990. "Stick to Your Guns (Pt. 1)." *Kerrang*, April 21.

116 Ian Fortnam. 2023. "Once You're My Age, Every Day Has to Carry Some Risk." *Classic Rock*, February 22.

117 Sylvie Simmons. 1991. "Tears Before Bedtime." *Q*, July.

118 Jeffrey Ressner and Lonn M. Friend. 1991. "Slash: The Rolling Stone Interview." *Rolling Stone*, January 24.

119 Andy Widders-Ellis. 1991. "The Hands Behind the Hype." *Guitar Player*, December.

120 Jeffrey Ressner and Lonn M. Friend. 1991. "Slash: The Rolling Stone Interview." *Rolling Stone*, January 24.

121 Steve Morse. 1991. "A Slashing Defense of Guns N' Roses." *The Boston Globe*, December 5.

122 Andy Widders-Ellis. 1991. "The Hands Behind the Hype." *Guitar Player*, December.

123 Adam Sweeting. 1991. "The Heavy Petals." *The Guardian*, September 12.

124 Michael Hann. 2019. "Slash on His Greatest Hits." *The Guardian*, February 14.

125 Andy Widders-Ellis. 1991. "The Hands Behind the Hype." *Guitar Player*, December.

126 Jeffrey Ressner and Lonn M. Friend. 1991. "Slash: The Rolling Stone Interview." *Rolling Stone*, January 24.

127 Matt Sorum with Leif Eriksson and Martin Svensson. 2022. *Double Talkin' Jive: True Rock 'n' Roll Stories from the Drummer of Guns N' Roses, The Cult, and Velvet Revolver*. Rare Bird Books.

128 "Axl Rose Seeks Erin Everly Split." *Los Angeles Times*, May 25.

129 Rockline. 1994. "Interview with Axl and Slash." January 3.

130 John Stix. 1992. "Slash: No Illusions." *Guitar for the Practicing Musician*, April.

131 Duff McKagen. 2011. *It's So Easy and Other Lies*. Touchstone.

132 "Famous Last Words." 1990. MTV Networks, August 31.

133 "Dizzy Reed, Body Count, and Gotthard." 2014. One on One with Mitch LaFon, Episode 30, July 21.

134 Alan di Perna. 1992. "Smoking Gun" *Guitar World*, February.

135 "Interview with Dizzy." 2018. GN'R Central, February 20.

136 Alan di Perna. 1992. "Smoking Gun" *Guitar World*, February.

137 Mark Rowland. 1990. "Appetite for Reconstruction." *Musician*, December.

138 Alan di Perna. 1992. "Smoking Gun" *Guitar World*, February.

139 Alan di Perna. 1992. "Smoking Gun" *Guitar World*, February.

140 John Stix. 1992. "Duff: Bionic Bass." *Guitar for the Practicing Musician*, April.

141 Matt Sorum with Leif Eriksson and Martin Svensson. 2022. *Double Talkin' Jive: True Rock 'n' Roll Stories from the Drummer of Guns N' Roses, The Cult, and Velvet Revolver.* Rare Bird Books.

142 Robert Hilburn. 1991. "Run N' Gun." *Los Angeles Times*, July 21.

143 Patrick MacDonald. 1991. "The Adventure of Duff and His Guns." *Circus*, November 30.

144 "In Conversation with Matt Sorum." 2016. Spitfire Audio, January 25.

145 John Stix. 1992. "Duff: Bionic Bass." *Guitar for the Practicing Musician*, April.

146 Mick Wall. 1990. "Stick to Your Guns (Pt. 1)." *Kerrang*, April 21.

147 John Stix. 1992. "Duff: Bionic Bass." *Guitar for the Practicing Musician*, April.

148 Robyn Flans. 1991. "Matt Sorum: Guns N' Roses New Stickman." *Modern Drummer*, June.

149 Slash with Anthony Bozza. 2008. *Slash.* Harper Entertainment.

150 "In Conversation with Matt Sorum." 2016. Spitfire Audio, January 25.

151 Robyn Flans. 1991. "Matt Sorum: Guns N' Roses New Stickman." *Modern Drummer*, June.

152 Alan di Perna. 1992. "Smoking Gun" *Guitar World*, February.

153 Nick Kent. 1991. "Welcome to My Nightmare." *Vox*, October.

154 Alan di Perna. 1992. "Smoking Gun" *Guitar World*, February.

155 Robyn Flans. 1991. "Matt Sorum: Guns N' Roses New Stickman." *Modern Drummer*, June.

156 Duff McKagen. 2011. *It's So Easy and Other Lies.* Touchstone.

157 Edgar Klusener. 1992. "Hound Dog." *Rock World*, November.

158 Bill Flanagan. 1992. "Shadowboxing with Axl Rose." *Musician*, June.

159 Doug Newcomb. 1990. "Axl Rose's BMW 325i." *Car Audio Electronics*, August.

160 Interview with Axl Rose. 1991. Rockline, November 27.

161 Dafne Castronovo. 2014. "Interview with Mark Kostabi." ShahrazadArt, December 3.

162 Matt Sorum with Leif Eriksson and Martin Svensson. 2022. *Double Talkin' Jive: True Rock 'n' Roll Stories from the Drummer of Guns N' Roses, The Cult, and Velvet Revolver*. Rare Bird Books.

163 Castro, Peter. 1990. "A Thorn in Rose's Side." *People*, August 27.

164 Robyn Flans. 1991. "Matt Sorum: Guns N' Roses New Stickman." *Modern Drummer*, June.

165 "Famous Last Words." 1990. MTV Networks, August 31.

166 Andy Widders-Ellis. 1991. "The Hands Behind the Hype." *Guitar Player*, December.

167 John Stix. 1992. "Slash: No Illusions." *Guitar for the Practicing Musician*, April.

168 Alan di Perna. 1992. "Smoking Gun" *Guitar World*, February.

169 John Stix. 1992. "Slash: No Illusions." *Guitar for the Practicing Musician*, April.

170 Andy Widders-Ellis. 1991. "The Hands Behind the Hype." *Guitar Player*, December.

171 John Stix. 1992. "Slash: No Illusions." *Guitar for the Practicing Musician*, April.

172 Slash with Anthony Bozza. 2008. *Slash*. Harper Entertainment.

173 John Stix. 1992. "Slash: No Illusions." *Guitar for the Practicing Musician*, April.

174 John Stix. 1992. "Slash: No Illusions." *Guitar for the Practicing Musician*, April.

175 Jamie Dickson. 2019. "Lenny Kravitz." *Music Radar*, March 12.

176 Mark McStea. 2024. "Lenny Kravitz Breaks Down 5 of His Classic Songs." *Guitar Player*, March 20.

177 Jamie Dickson. 2019. "Lenny Kravitz." *Music Radar*, March 12.

178 Mark Rowland. 1990. "Appetite for Reconstruction." *Musician*, December.

179 Interview with Slash. 2018. Triple M Brisbane, September 25.

180 Interview with Slash and Eric Dover. 1995. Triple M Radio, February.

181 Kory Grow. 2018. "Lenny Kravitz: My Life in 15 Songs." *Rolling Stone*, October 9.

182 Jamie Dickson. 2019. "Lenny Kravitz." *Music Radar*, March 12.

183 Mark McStea. 2024. "Lenny Kravitz Breaks Down 5 of His Classic Songs." *Guitar Player*, March 20.

184 Jeffrey Ressner and Lonn M. Friend. 1991. "Slash: The Rolling Stone Interview." *Rolling Stone*, January 24.

185 Andy Widders-Ellis. 1991. "The Hands Behind the Hype." *Guitar Player*, December.

186 Slash with Anthony Bozza. 2008. *Slash*. Harper Entertainment.

187 Joseph Vogel. 2019. *Man in the Music: The Creative and Work Life of Michael Jackson.*

188 Sylvie Simmons. 1991. "Tears Before Bedtime." *Q*, July.

189 Jeffrey Ressner and Lonn M. Friend. 1991. "Slash: The Rolling Stone Interview." *Rolling Stone*, January 24.

190 James Muretich. 1994. "Slash." *The Calgary Herald*, January 29.

191 Mark Rowland. 1990. "Appetite for Reconstruction." *Musician*, December.

192 Sylvie Simmons. 1991. "Tears Before Bedtime." *Q*, July.

193 Jeffrey Ressner and Lonn M. Friend. 1991. "Slash: The Rolling Stone Interview." *Rolling Stone*, January 24.

194 Andy Widders-Ellis. 1991. "The Hands Behind the Hype." *Guitar Player*, December.

195 "Interview with Dizzy." 2018. GN'R Central, February 20.

196 John Stix. 1992. "Slash: No Illusions." *Guitar for the Practicing Musician*, April.

197 "Famous Last Words." 1990. MTV Networks, August 31.

198 Jeffrey Ressner and Lonn M. Friend. 1991. "Slash: The Rolling Stone Interview." *Rolling Stone*, January 24.

199 John H. Lee. 1990. "Singer Axl Rose Accused of Assault." *Los Angeles Times*, October 31.

200 "Axl Rose Urges a Test of Truth." *Los Angeles Times*, November 27.

201 "Axl Rose of Guns N' Roses - 1990 Arrest." *Moto Stringer*. YouTube, August 7, 2023.

202 "Axl Rose of Guns N' Roses - 1990 Arrest." *Moto Stringer*. YouTube, August 7, 2023.

203 "Axl Rose Arrested." 1990. MTV News, October 30.

204 Ruth Ryon. "Rocker Axl Rose Heads for the Hills." *Los Angeles Times*, November 25.

205 Martin Gould. 2017. "Rock Photographer Tells the Stories Behind Music's Most Iconic Pictures". *Daily Mail*, October 17.

206 "A Neighbor Says Axl Rose Hit Her with a Wine Bottle, and He Says She's Got a Corkscrew Loose."1990. *People*, November 19.

207 "A Neighbor Says Axl Rose Hit Her with a Wine Bottle, and He Says She's Got a Corkscrew Loose."1990. *People*, November 19.

[208] "Axl Rose Wins Restraining Order." 1990. *Los Angeles Times*, November 21.

[209] "A Neighbor Says Axl Rose Hit Her with a Wine Bottle, and He Says She's Got a Corkscrew Loose."1990. *People*, November 19.

[210] "Axl Rose Urges a Test of Truth." *Los Angeles Times*, November 27.

[211] "A Neighbor Says Axl Rose Hit Her with a Wine Bottle, and He Says She's Got a Corkscrew Loose."1990. *People*, November 19.

[212] Josh Meyer and John Kendall. 1990. "D.A. Won't Prosecute Singer Rose." Los Angeles Times, November 29.

[213] "A Neighbor Says Axl Rose Hit Her with a Wine Bottle, and He Says She's Got a Corkscrew Loose."1990. *People*, November 19.

[214] Jeffrey Ressner and Lonn M. Friend. 1991. "Slash: The Rolling Stone Interview." *Rolling Stone*, January 24.

[215] "Scenes from a Marriage." 1991. United Press International, January 28.

[216] "Scenes from a Marriage." 1991. United Press International, January 28.

[217] Greg Prato. 2008. *An Angel on One Shoulder, A Devil on the Other: The Story of Shannon Hoon and Blind Melon.* Greg Prato.

[218] Greg Prato. 2008. *An Angel on One Shoulder, A Devil on the Other: The Story of Shannon Hoon and Blind Melon.* Greg Prato.

[219] Greg Prato. 2008. *An Angel on One Shoulder, A Devil on the Other: The Story of Shannon Hoon and Blind Melon.* Greg Prato.

[220] Greg Prato. 2008. *An Angel on One Shoulder, A Devil on the Other: The Story of Shannon Hoon and Blind Melon.* Greg Prato.

[221] Del James. 1992. "I, Axl." *Rip*, October 11.

[222] Josh Meyer. 1991. "Song's Over for Storied Rock Studio." *Los Angeles Times*, February 28.

[223] Del James. 1992. "I, Axl." *Rip*, October 11.

[224] Jean Marie Laskas. 1992. "On the Road with Guns N' Roses." *Life*, December 1.

[225] Del James. 1992. "I, Axl." *Rip*, October 11.

[226] Greg Prato. 2008. *An Angel on One Shoulder, A Devil on the Other: The Story of Shannon Hoon and Blind Melon.* Greg Prato.

[227] Ingrid Sischy. 1992. "Axl Rose." *Interview*, May.

[228] Mick Wall. 1990. "Stick to Your Guns (Pt. 2)." *Kerrang*, April 28.

[229] Scott Rowley. 2018. "Chinese Whispers." *Classic Rock*, March.

[230] Matt Sorum with Leif Eriksson and Martin Svensson. 2022. *Double Talkin' Jive: True Rock 'n' Roll Stories from the Drummer of Guns N' Roses, The Cult, and Velvet Revolver.* Rare Bird Books.

[231] "Axl Gets in the Ring." 1992. *Metallix*, December 5.

232 "Axl Gets in the Ring." 1992. *Metallix*, December 5.

233 Kory Grow. 2016. "Inside Guns N' Roses' History-Making *Use Your Illusion* Albums." *Rolling Stone*, September 16.

234 Marc Spitz. 1999. "Appetite for Self Destruction." *Spin*, July 1.

235 David Fricke. "Life After Guns N' Roses." *Rolling Stone*, October 29.

236 Slash with Anthony Bozza. 2008. *Slash*. Harper Entertainment.

237 Mick Wall. 1990. "Stick to Your Guns (Pt. 2)." *Kerrang*, April 28.

238 Louis Marciano, dir. 1993. *Makin' F@*!ing Videos Part II*. Geffen Home Video.

239 Louis Marciano, dir. 1993. *Makin' F@*!ing Videos Part II*. Geffen Home Video.

240 Slash with Anthony Bozza. 2008. *Slash*. Harper Entertainment.

241 Random Notes. 1991. *Rolling Stone*, May 16.

242 Doug Newcomb. 1990. "Axl Rose's BMW 325i." *Car Audio Electronics*, August.

243 Bill Flanagan. 1992. "Shadow Boxing with Axl Rose." *Musician*, June.

244 "An Appetite for Construction – The Axl Interview." 1993. *Raw Magazine*, November 11.

245 Andy Secher. 1993. "Axl Speaks Out." *Hit Parader*, June.

246 Donna Yuzwalk. 1991. "Slash." *Rip It Up*, September.

247 Matt Sorum with Leif Eriksson and Martin Svensson. 2022. *Double Talkin' Jive: True Rock 'n' Roll Stories from the Drummer of Guns N' Roses, The Cult, and Velvet Revolver*. Rare Bird Books.

248 "The Way the Music Died. 2004. PBS Frontline, May 27.

249 Slash with Anthony Bozza. 2008. *Slash*. Harper Entertainment.

250 "Rock in Rio." 1991. *The Week in Rock*. MTV Networks.

251 Duff McKagen. 2011. *It's So Easy and Other Lies*. Touchstone.

252 Slash with Anthony Bozza. 2008. *Slash*. Harper Entertainment.

253 "Rock in Rio." 1991. *The Week in Rock*. MTV Networks.

254 *Hard 'N' Heavy Volume 13*. 1991. Warner Music Vision.

255 *Hard 'N' Heavy Volume 13*. 1991. Warner Music Vision.

256 Mark Rowland. 1990. "Appetite for Reconstruction." *Musician*, December.

257 Ingrid Sischy. 1992. "Axl Rose." *Interview*, May.

258 Marc Spitz. 1999. "Appetite for Self Destruction." *Spin*, July 1.

259 Robert Hilburn. 1991. "Run N' Gun." *Los Angeles Times*, July 21.

260 Bill Flanagan. 1992. "Shadow Boxing with Axl Rose." *Musician*, June.

261 Kim Neely. 1992. "Axl Rose: The Rolling Stone Interview." *Rolling Stone*, April 2.

262 Ingrid Sischy. 1992. "Axl Rose." *Interview*, May.

263 Kim Neely. 1992. "Axl Rose: The Rolling Stone Interview." *Rolling Stone*, April 2.

264 Kim Neely. 1992. "Axl Rose: The Rolling Stone Interview." *Rolling Stone*, April 2.

265 Ingrid Sischy. 1992. "Axl Rose." *Interview*, May.

266 Dave DiMartino. 1991. "Guns N' Roses: Out of Control." *Entertainment Weekly*, August 9.

267 Dave DiMartino. 1991. "Guns N' Roses: Out of Control." *Entertainment Weekly*, August 9.

268 Dave DiMartino. 1991. "Guns N' Roses: Out of Control." *Entertainment Weekly*, August 9.

269 Alan di Perna. 1992. "Smoking Gun" *Guitar World*, February.

270 Chris Mitchie. 2000. "The Bill Price Interview." *Mix*, November 1.

271 Chris Mitchie. 2000. "The Bill Price Interview." *Mix*, November 1.

272 John Stix. 1992. "Slash: No Illusions." *Guitar for the Practicing Musician*, April.

273 Dave DiMartino. 1991. "Guns N' Roses: Out of Control." *Entertainment Weekly*, August 9.

274 Philippe Manoeuvre. 1992. "Interview with Izzy." *Rock & Folk*, September.

275 Nick Kent. 1991. "Welcome to My Nightmare." *Vox*, October.

276 "Guns N' Roses Tour '91." MTV Networks, May 25, 1991.

277 "Guns N' Roses Tour '91." MTV Networks, May 25, 1991.

278 Robert Hilburn. 1991. "Guns N' Roses: The Shape of Things to Come." *Los Angeles Times*, May 13.

279 Del James. "Here Today, Gone to Hell (And Lovin' It)." *Rip*, September.

280 "Guns N' Roses Tour '91." MTV Networks, May 25, 1991.

281 Ingrid Sischy. 1992. "Axl Rose." *Interview*, May.

282 Curt Gooch and Jeff Suhs. 2018. "When Crüe Ruled the World." *Rock Candy*, December/January

283 Adrienne Stone. 1990. "Wowing the World at Farm Aid IV." *Circus*, June 30.

284 Ingrid Sischy. 1992. "Axl Rose." *Interview*, May.

285 "Guns N' Roses Tour '91." MTV Networks, May 25, 1991.

286 Andy Widders-Ellis. 1991. "The Hands Behind the Hype." *Guitar Player*, December.

287 "Guns N' Roses Tour '91." MTV Networks, May 25, 1991.

288 "Guns N' Roses Tour '91." MTV Networks, May 25, 1991.

289 "Guns N' Roses Tour '91." MTV Networks, May 25, 1991.

[290] "Guns N' Roses Tour '91." MTV Networks, May 25, 1991.

[291] "Axl Rose Sings Tunes by Teleprompter." 1991. *New York*, June.

[292] Del James. 1991. "Here Today, Gone to Hell (And Lovin' It)." *Rip*, September.

[293] "Backstage: Guns N' Roses. 1991. *Performance*, August 2.

[294] *Guns N' Roses Use Your Illusion*. 1991 tour program.

[295] *Guns N' Roses Australian Tour Special.* January 1993.

[296] Matt Sorum with Leif Eriksson and Martin Svensson. 2022. *Double Talkin' Jive: True Rock 'n' Roll Stories from the Drummer of Guns N' Roses, The Cult, and Velvet Revolver.* Rare Bird Books.

[297] "Guns N' Roses Tour '91." MTV Networks, May 25, 1991.

[298] "Guns N' Roses Tour '91." MTV Networks, May 25, 1991.

[299] "Guns N' Roses Tour '91." MTV Networks, May 25, 1991.

[300] "Guns N' Roses Tour '91." MTV Networks, May 25, 1991.

[301] "Guns N' Roses Tour '91." MTV Networks, May 25, 1991.

[302] "Guns N' Roses Tour '91." MTV Networks, May 25, 1991.

[303] "Guns N' Roses Tour '91." MTV Networks, May 25, 1991.

[304] Kim Neely. 1991. "Guns N' Roses." *Rolling Stone*, September 5.

[305] "Guns N' Roses Tour '91." MTV Networks, May 25, 1991.

[306] Kim Neely. 1991. "Guns N' Roses." *Rolling Stone*, September 5.

[307] Mick Wall. 1990. "Stick to Your Guns (Pt. 1)." *Kerrang*, April 21.

[308] Kim Neely. 1991. "Guns N' Roses." *Rolling Stone*, September 5.

[309] Robert Hilburn. 1988. "Taste Makers: Axl Rose." *Los Angeles Times*, December 25.

[310] Mick Wall. 1990. "Stick to Your Guns (Pt. 1)." *Kerrang*, April 21.

[311] Interview with Arlett Vereecke. 2017. GN'R Central, December 10.

[312] Bessel van der Kolk. 2014. *The Body Keeps the Score*. Viking.

[313] "Guns N' Roses Tour '91." MTV Networks, May 25, 1991.

[314] Mark D. Allan. 1993. "No Stradlin' For Izzy." *The Indianapolis Star*, February 21.

[315] Mark D. Allan, 1991. "Guns N' Roses: Great Rock, Too Much Talk." *The Indianapolis Star,* May 29,

[316] Mike Redmond. 1991. "All GNR Fans Needed Was a Little Patience." *The Indianapolis News*, May 29.

[317] Gregg Montgomery. 1991. "Police Estimate 100 Arrested at Concert." *Noblesville Ledger*, May 29.

[318] Robert Hilburn. 1991. "Run N' Gun." *Los Angeles Times*, July 21.

[319] Kim Neely. 1991. "Guns N' Roses." *Rolling Stone*, September 5.

[320] "Rose Exercises Right." 1991. *Ottumwa Courier*, June 3.

[321] "Guns N' Roses Tour '91." MTV Networks, May 25, 1991.

322 Dave Larsen. 1991. "Guns N' Roses Performance Simply Superb." *Dayton Daily News*, June 3.

323 "Roses Rock 30,000 in Toledo." 1991. *Detroit Free Press*, June 4

324 "Guns N' Roses Rocks Coliseum and Fans with a Wall of Noise." *Beacon Journal*, June 5.

325 Chris Mitchie. 2000. "The Bill Price Interview." *Mix*, November 1.

326 Chris Mitchie. 2000. "The Bill Price Interview." *Mix*, November 1.

327 Robert Hilburn. 1991. "Run N' Gun." *Los Angeles Times*, July 21.

328 Robert Hilburn. 1991. "Run N' Gun." *Los Angeles Times*, July 21.

329 Robert G. Waldvogel. 2023. "MGM Grand Air: Airline or Corporate Jet?" *Metropolitan Airport News*, December 12.

330 David Konow. 2002. *Bang Your Head: The Rise and Fall of Heavy Metal.* Three River Press.

331 Malcolm Dome. 2020. "Slash: The Lost Interview." *Rock Candy*, February,

332 "Guns N' Roses Tour '91." MTV Networks, May 25, 1991.

333 Matt Sorum with Leif Eriksson and Martin Svensson. 2022. *Double Talkin' Jive: True Rock 'n' Roll Stories from the Drummer of Guns N' Roses, The Cult, and Velvet Revolver.* Rarc Bird Books.

334 Kim Neely. 1991. "Guns N' Roses." *Rolling Stone*, September 5.

335 Nick Kent. 1991. "Welcome to My Nightmare." *Vox*, October.

336 Kim Neely. 1991. "Guns N' Roses." *Rolling Stone*, September 5.

337 Kim Neely. 1991. "Guns N' Roses." *Rolling Stone*, September 5.

338 Robert Hilburn. 1991. "Run N' Gun." *Los Angeles Times*, July 21.

339 Interview with Arlett Vereecke. 2017. GN'R Central, December 10.

340 Jim Farber. 1991. "Gunning for Trouble?" *New York Daily News*, June 19.

341 "Interview with Axl Rose and Sebastian Bach." 2006. *Eddie Trunk's Friday Night Rocks*, May 5.

342 "Stadium Rock." 2000. Top Ten S2.E5, February 19.

343 Jim Farber. 1991. "Gunning for Trouble?" *New York Daily News*, June 19.

344 Peter Watrous, 1991. "Guns N' Roses and Personal Thorns." *The New York Times*, June 19.

345 Matt Sorum with Leif Eriksson and Martin Svensson. 2022. *Double Talkin' Jive: True Rock 'n' Roll Stories from the Drummer of Guns N' Roses, The Cult, and Velvet Revolver.* Rare Bird Books.

346 Kim Neely. 1991. "Fans Riot at Guns Show." *Rolling Stone*, August 22.

347 Kim Neely. 1991. "Fans Riot at Guns Show." *Rolling Stone*, August 22.

348 Kim Neely. 1991. "Fans Riot at Guns Show." *Rolling Stone*, August 22.

349 Matt Sorum with Leif Eriksson and Martin Svensson. 2022. *Double Talkin' Jive: True Rock 'n' Roll Stories from the Drummer of Guns N' Roses, The Cult, and Velvet Revolver*. Rare Bird Books.

350 Christian Schaeffer. 2016. "Riverport Riot: An Oral History of the Guns N' Roses Show That Sated St. Louis' Appetite for Destruction." *Riverfront Times*, June 29.

351 Kim Neely. 1991. "Fans Riot at Guns Show." *Rolling Stone*, August 22.

352 Christian Schaeffer. 2016. "Riverport Riot: An Oral History of the Guns N' Roses Show That Sated St. Louis' Appetite for Destruction." *Riverfront Times*, June 29.

353 Andy Widders-Ellis. 1991. "The Hands Behind the Hype." *Guitar Player*, December.

354 Kim Neely. 1991. "Fans Riot at Guns Show." *Rolling Stone*, August 22.

355 Kim Neely. 1991. "Fans Riot at Guns Show." *Rolling Stone*, August 22.

356 Durchholz, David. 1991. "Appetite for Destruction: Inside the Guns N' Roses Riot." *Riverfront Times*, July 10.

357 Andy Widders-Ellis. 1991. "The Hands Behind the Hype." *Guitar Player*, December.

358 Malcolm Dome. 1991. "Delusions and Illusions." *Metal Hammer*, September.

359 Kim Neely. 1991. "Fans Riot at Guns Show." *Rolling Stone*, August 22.

360 Kim Neely. 1991. "Fans Riot at Guns Show." *Rolling Stone*, August 22.

361 Robert Hilburn and Chuck Philips. 1991. "Axl Blames Lax Security for Melee." *Los Angeles Times*, July 5.

362 Andy Widders-Ellis. 1991. "The Hands Behind the Hype." *Guitar Player*, December.

363 Christian Schaeffer. 2016. "Riverport Riot: An Oral History of the Guns N' Roses Show That Sated St. Louis' Appetite for Destruction." *Riverfront Times*, June 29.

364 Matt Sorum with Leif Eriksson and Martin Svensson. 2022. *Double Talkin' Jive: True Rock 'n' Roll Stories from the Drummer of Guns N' Roses, The Cult, and Velvet Revolver*. Rare Bird Books.

365 Chuck Philips. 1991. "GNR Tour Disrupted After Melee." *Los Angeles Times*, July 4.

366 Durchholz, David. 1991. "Appetite for Destruction: Inside the Guns N' Roses Riot." *Riverfront Times*, July 10.

367 Chuck Philips. 1991. "GNR Tour Disrupted After Melee." *Los Angeles Times*, July 4.

368 Durchholz, David. 1991. "Appetite for Destruction: Inside the Guns N' Roses Riot." *Riverfront Times*, July 10.

369 Kim Neely. 1991. "Fans Riot at Guns Show." *Rolling Stone*, August 22.

370 Chuck Philips. 1991. "GNR Tour Disrupted After Melee." *Los Angeles Times*, July 4.

371 Kim Neely. 1991. "Fans Riot at Guns Show." *Rolling Stone*, August 22.

372 Chuck Philips. 1991. "GNR Tour Disrupted After Melee." *Los Angeles Times*, July 4.

373 Vince Horiuchi. 1991. "Safety Concerns Prompt County to Review Concert." *Salt Lake City Tribune*, July 6.

374 Harry Sumrall. 1991. "Guns for Hire." *The Mercury News*, July 19.

375 Andy Widders-Ellis. 1991. "The Hands Behind the Hype." *Guitar Player*, December.

376 Malcolm Dome. 1991. "Delusions and Illusions." *Metal Hammer*, September.

377 "Guns' Texas Show Quiet." 1991. Associated Press, July 8.

378 Duff McKagan. 2011. *It's So Easy (and Other Lies)*. Orion.

379 Dave DiMartino. 1991. "Guns N' Roses: Out of Control." *Entertainment Weekly*, August 9.

380 Malcolm Dome. 1991. "Delusions and Illusions." *Metal Hammer*, September.

381 Malcolm Dome. 1991. "Delusions and Illusions." *Metal Hammer*, September.

382 Robert Hilburn. 1991. "Run N' Gun." *Los Angeles Times*, July 21.

383 Matt Sorum with Leif Eriksson and Martin Svensson. 2022. *Double Talkin' Jive: True Rock 'n' Roll Stories from the Drummer of Guns N' Roses, The Cult, and Velvet Revolver*. Rare Bird Books.

384 "Doug Goldstein and Dr. Stephen Thaxton Talk UYI Tour and GNR Chiropractics." 2019. Appetite for Distortion: Episode 101, January 30.

385 Ingrid Sischy. 1992. "Axl Rose." *Interview*, May.

386 "Ohio College Senior Wins Axl Rose's Condo." 1991. *Orlando Sentinel*, August 27.

387 Knight Ridder Newspapers. 1991. "Akron College Student Wins Right to Evict Rocker Axl Rose." *Muncie Evening Press*, August 27.

388 Lori Buttars. 1991. "Security Strategy Planned for Guns N' Roses Concert." *Salt Lake City Tribune*, July 12.

389 Lori Buttars. 1991. "Guns N' Roses Goes Off Unexplosively." *Salt Lake City Tribune*, July 12.

390 Lori Buttars. 1991. "Guns N' Roses Goes Off Unexplosively." *Salt Lake City Tribune*, July 12.

391 Andy Secher. 1993. "Axl Speaks Out." *Hit Parader*, June.

392 Patrick Macdonald. 1991. "Seattle Concert a Homecoming for Guns Bassist." *The Seattle Times*, July 12.

393 Robert Hilburn and Chuck Philips. 1991. "Axl Blames Lax Security for Melee." *Los Angeles Times*, July 5.

394 Patrick Macdonald. 1991. "Energetic Guns N' Roses Leaves Fans with Many Sound Memories." *The Seattle Times*, July 17.

395 Steve Sutherland. "White Riot! On the Road with Guns N' Roses." *Melody Maker*, August 3.

396 Malcolm Dome. 1991. "Delusions and Illusions." *Metal Hammer*, September.

397 Nick Kent. 1991. "Welcome to My Nightmare." *Vox*, October.

398 Nick Kent. 1991. "Welcome to My Nightmare." *Vox*, October.

399 Nick Kent. 1991. "Welcome to My Nightmare." *Vox*, October.

400 Nick Kent. 1991. "Welcome to My Nightmare." *Vox*, October.

401 Barry Walters. 1991. "Guns N' Roses Without Violence." *San Francisco Examiner*, June 21.

402 Steve Sutherland. "Rising from the Ruins." *Melody Maker*, August 10.

403 Nick Kent. 1991. "Welcome to My Nightmare." *Vox*, October.

404 Nick Kent. 1991. "Welcome to My Nightmare." *Vox*, October.

405 Robert Hilburn. 1991. "Stop the Presses! Axl's Upset Again." *Los Angeles Times*, July 27.

406 Dave Wielenga. 1991. "More Guns Than Roses." *The Press-Telegram*, July 27.

407 Robert Hilburn. 1991. "Stop the Presses! Axl's Upset Again." *Los Angeles Times*, July 27.

408 Marc Lacey. 1991. "Inglewood to Cite Axl Rose's Driver." *Los Angeles Times*, August 8.

409 Marc Lacey. 1991. "Police Face Axl Rose Tantrum, Take Back Ticket." *Los Angeles Times*, August 1.

410 Marc Lacey. 1991. "Inglewood to Cite Axl Rose's Driver." *Los Angeles Times*, August 8.

411 Matt Sorum with Leif Eriksson and Martin Svensson. 2022. *Double Talkin' Jive: True Rock 'n' Roll Stories from the Drummer of Guns N' Roses, The Cult, and Velvet Revolver*. Rare Bird Books.

412 Robert Hilburn. 1991. "A Blistering L.A. Finale by Guns N' Roses." *Los Angeles Times*, August 5.

413 "Ex-Drummer Says Guns Shot Him Up with Drugs, Dropped Him." 1991. *Deseret News*, July 21.

414 Kim Neely. 1992. "Axl Rose: The Rolling Stone Interview." *Rolling Stone*, April 2.

415 David Fricke. "Life After Guns N' Roses." *Rolling Stone*, October 29.

416 Duff McKagan. 2012. *It's So Easy and Other Lies*. Touchstone/Simon & Schuster.

417 Slash with Anthony Bozza. 2008. *Slash*. Harper Entertainment.

418 Duff McKagan. 2012. *It's So Easy and Other Lies*. Touchstone/Simon & Schuster.

419 Duff McKagan. 2012. *It's So Easy and Other Lies*. Touchstone/Simon & Schuster.

420 Michael Goldberg. 1992. "The Making of the King of Pop." *Rolling Stone*, January 9.

421 Andy Widders-Ellis. 1991. "The Hands Behind the Hype." *Guitar Player*, December.

422 Slash with Anthony Bozza. 2008. *Slash*. Harper Entertainment.

423 Slash with Anthony Bozza. 2008. *Slash*. Harper Entertainment.

424 Dean Delray. 2021. Episode #590. Let There Be Rock Podcast, May 10.

425 Louis Marciano, dir. 1993. *Makin' F@*!ing Videos Part II*. Geffen Home Video.

426 Del James. 1995. "Without You" in *The Language of Fear*. Dell Books/Doubleday.

427 Dean Delray. 2021. Episode #590. Let There Be Rock Podcast, May 10.

428 Jean Marie Laskas. 1992. "On the Road with Guns N' Roses." *Life*, December 1.

429 "Axl Gets in the Ring." 1992. *Metallix*, December 5.

430 "Axl Gets in the Ring." 1992. *Metallix*, December 5.

431 "Axl Gets in the Ring." 1992. *Metallix*, December 5.

432 "Axl Gets in the Ring." 1992. *Metallix*, December 5.

433 Sam Coare. 2020. "It Was All Falling Apart at the Seams." *Kerrang*, September 17.

434 Mark Racco, dir. 1993. *Makin' F@*!ing Videos Part I*. Geffen Home Video.

435 Dean Delray. 2021. Episode #590. Let There Be Rock Podcast, May 10.

436 Sam Coare. 2020. "It Was All Falling Apart at the Seams." *Kerrang*, September 17.

437 Dean Delray. 2021. Episode #590. Let There Be Rock Podcast, May 10.

438 Dwight Loop. 1991. "Guns N' Roses Picks Work by Local Artist for New CD Cover." *Santa Fe New Mexican*, December 20.

439 Peter Wilkinson. 2000. "Axl Rose: The Lost Years." *Rolling Stone*, May 11.

440 Scott Rowley. 2018. "Chinese Whispers." *Classic Rock*, March.

[441] David Konow. 2002. *Bang Your Head: The Rise and Fall of Heavy Metal.* Three River Press.

[442] Steve Hochman. 1991. "Marketing Triumph for Guns N' Roses." *Los Angeles Times*, September 18.

[443] Chris Morris. 1991. "GN'R Sets Spark 'Illusion' Of Grandeur." *Billboard*, August 24.

[444] Steve Hochman. 1991. "Marketing Triumph for Guns N' Roses." *Los Angeles Times*, September 18.

[445] Chris Morris. 1991. "GN'R Sets Spark 'Illusion' Of Grandeur." *Billboard*, August 24.

[446] Katy Hasty. 2008. "Kanye Edges GNR, Ludacris for No. 1 Debut." *Billboard*, December 3.

[447] Chris Morris. 1991. "GN'R Shoots to No 1 - and No. 2." *Billboard*, October 5.

[448] Recording Industry Association of America. 2025. Gold & Platinum. RIAA.com.

[449] Bill Flanagan. 1992. "Shadow Boxing with Axl Rose." *Musician*, June.

[450] Stefan Chirazi. 1994. "Get Outta the Ring!" *Kerrang*, January 8.

[451] Philippe Manoeuvre. 1992. "Interview with Izzy." *Rock & Folk*, September.

[452] "Axl Gets in the Ring." 1992. *Metallix*, December 5.

[453] Janiss Garza. 1991. "*Use Your Illusion I.*" *Entertainment Weekly*, September 20.

[454] Paul Eliott. 1991. "*Use Your Illusion I/II.*" *Kerrang*, September 21.

[455] David Fricke. 1991. "*Use Your Illusion I.*" *Rolling Stone*, October 17.

[456] Robert Hilburn. 1991. "Guns N' Roses' Double-Barreled *Illusion.*" *Los Angeles Times*, September 15.

[457] R.J. Smith. 1991. "The Last Angry White Man." *LA Weekly*, October 4-10.

[458] Paul Elliott. 1991. "Use Your Illusion I/II." *Vox*, October.

[459] Joe Queenan. 1991. "Misfit Metalheads." *Time*, September 30.

[460] Patrick Goldstein. 1991. "Ring Side." *Los Angeles Times*, September 15.

[461] Chris Morris. 1991. "Rumors Persist: Izzy or Isn't He Leaving GN'R?" *Billboard*, October 5.

[462] Philippe Lageat. 2001. "Izzy Stradlin Recounts the Birth of Guns N' Roses." *Rock Hard*, April.

[463] Paul Elliott. 1992. "The Man Who Quit Guns N' Roses." *Kerrang*, September 5.

[464] Kim Neely. 1992. "Axl Rose: The Rolling Stone Interview." *Rolling Stone*, April 2.

465 Kim Neely. 1992. "Axl Rose: The Rolling Stone Interview." *Rolling Stone*, April 2.

466 Murray Engleheart. 1993. "Single Gun Theory." *Rip*, April.

467 Tom Moon. 1991. "A More In-Control Guns N' Roses?" *The Philadelphia Inquirer*, December 16.

468 Kim Neely. 1992. "Axl Rose: The Rolling Stone Interview." *Rolling Stone*, April 2.

469 Author interview with Matt Sorum. June 8, 2001.

470 Interview with Slash. 1991. *Countdown*. Reelin' In the Years Productions, May.

471 Alan di Perna. 1992. "Smoking Gun" *Guitar World*, February.

472 "Lisa Maxwell Talks 976 Horns." 2021. Appetite for Distortion, Episode 252, March 8.

473 "Roberta Freeman talks One in a Million, Race, and James Hetfield." 2020. Appetite for Distortion, Episode 201, September 14.

474 Andy Greene. 2020. "Veteran Backup Singer Roberta Freeman Talks Life on the Road with Guns N' Roses, Pink Floyd." *Rolling Stone*, June 24.

475 Andy Greene. 2020. "Veteran Backup Singer Roberta Freeman Talks Life on the Road with Guns N' Roses, Pink Floyd." *Rolling Stone*, June 24.

476 "Roberta Freeman talks One in a Million, Race, and James Hetfield." 2020. Appetite for Distortion, Episode 201, September 14.

477 "Black or White." *Wikipedia, The Free Encyclopedia.*

478 Slash with Anthony Bozza. 2008. *Slash.* Harper Entertainment.

479 Steve Morse. 1991. "A Slashing Defense of Guns N' Roses." *The Boston Globe*, December 5.

480 James Muretich. 1994. "Slash." *The Calgary Herald*, January 29.

481 Steve Morse. 1991. "A Slashing Defense of Guns N' Roses." *The Boston Globe*, December 5.

482 Matt Allen. 2021. "Guns N' Roses Were a Gang." *Kerrang*, July 23.

483 Mike Boehm. 1991. "O.C. Guitarist to Join Rock's Black Crowes." *Los Angeles Times*, November 16.

484 "Gilby Clarke – Ex Guns N' Roses Rocks Indiepower." 2018. Indiepower TV, October 24.

485 Louis Marciano, dir. 1993. *Makin' F@*!ing Videos Part II*. Geffen Home Video.

486 Louis Marciano, dir. 1993. *Makin' F@*!ing Videos Part II*. Geffen Home Video.

487 Andrew Daly. 2024. "Gilby Clarke Survived a Baptism by Fire in Guns N' Roses." *Guitar World*, March 18.

[488] Marc D. Allan. 1992. "Rockin' Hard at the Dome." *The Indianapolis Star*, July 21.

[489] "Guns N' Roses: Back to Basics." 1993. *Hartford Courant*, March 4.

[490] Del James. 1992. "I, Axl." *Rip*, September.

[491] Jon Parales. 1991. "Guns N' Roses Brings New Lineup to the Garden." *The New York Times*, December 11.

[492] David Fricke. 1991. "Guns N' Roses." *Rolling Stone*, December 12-26.

[493] Steve Morse. 1991. "Guns' Blast-Off Wasn't Worth the Wait." *The Boston Globe*, 12.6.91

[494] Roger Catlin. 1991. "Guns N' Roses in Concert at Last: New Arrangement of an Old Band." *Hartford Courant*, December 7.

[495] "Lisa Maxwell Talks 976 Horns." 2021. Appetite for Distortion, Episode 252, March 8.

[496] "Lisa Maxwell Talks 976 Horns." 2021. Appetite for Distortion, Episode 252, March 8.

[497] Dean Delray. 2021. Let There Be Rock Podcast, Episode #590, May 10.

[498] Louis Marciano, dir. 1993. *Makin' F@*!ing Videos Part II*. Geffen Home Video.

[499] Meredith Blake. 2022. "The 'November Rain' Music Video Defined a Generation." *Los Angeles Times*, June 7.

[500] Meredith Blake. 2022. "The 'November Rain' Music Video Defined a Generation." *Los Angeles Times*, June 7.

[501] Louis Marciano, dir. 1993. *Makin' F@*!ing Videos Part II*. Geffen Home Video.

[502] Alex Scordelis. 2022. "The Untold Story of Some Guy Plowing into a Wedding Cake in a Guns 'N Roses Music Video." *Vice*, February 18.

[503] Meredith Blake. 2022. "The 'November Rain' Music Video Defined a Generation." *Los Angeles Times*, June 7.

[504] Alex Scordelis. 2022. "The Untold Story of Some Guy Plowing into a Wedding Cake in a Guns 'N Roses Music Video." *Vice*, February 18.

[505] Sam Coare. 2020. "It Was All Falling Apart at the Seams." *Kerrang*, September 17.

[506] "Slash Answers Questions." 2001. Snakepit.org, April 13.

[507] Louis Marciano, dir. 1993. *Makin' F@*!ing Videos Part II*. Geffen Home Video.

[508] Sam Coare. 2020. "It Was All Falling Apart at the Seams." *Kerrang*, September 17.

[509] Meredith Blake. 2022. "The 'November Rain' Music Video Defined a Generation." *Los Angeles Times*, June 7.

510 Del James. 1989. "Axl Rose: The Rolling Stone Interview." *Rolling Stone*, August 10.

511 Lisa Ladouceur. 2003. Interview with Dave Navarro. *The Toronto Eye*, September 29.

512 Eric Snider. 1991. "Rock's Big Guns on Target." *St. Petersburg Times*, December 29.

513 Steffan Chirazi. 1992. "Gardener's World." *Kerrang*, April 4.

514 Steve Kandell 2005. "Dear Superstar." *Blender*, July.

515 Nisha Gopalan. 2012. "Chris Cornell on Soundgarden's New Album, the Queen of England, and Axl Rose." *Vulture*, November 13.

516 Bill Flanagan. 1992. "Shadow Boxing with Axl Rose." *Musician*, June.

517 Marc Spitz. 1999. "Appetite for Self Destruction." *Spin*, July 1.

518 GNREvolution.com. "Memories of the Use Your Illusion Tour: An Interview with Tracey Amos."

519 David Wild. 2000. "Axl Speaks." *Rolling Stone*, February 3.

520 Del James. 1995. "Without You" in *The Language of Fear*. Dell Books/Doubleday.

521 Craig Duswalt. 2014. *Welcome to My Jungle*. Benbella Books.

522 Del James. 1992. "I, Axl." *Rip*, October.

523 Larsen, Dave. 1991. "Guns N' Roses Arrives Late and Doesn't Deliver." *Dayton Daily News*, January 14.

524 Larsen, Dave. 1991. "Rose's Injury Puts Thorn in Guns' 2nd Concert." *Dayton Daily News*, January 15.

525 Del James. 1992. "I, Axl." *Rip*, October.

526 Del James. 1992. "I, Axl." *Rip*, September.

527 Phil Alexander. 1992. "Shattering Your Illusions." *Raw*, March 4-17.

528 Bill Flanagan. 1992. "Shadow Boxing with Axl Rose." *Musician*, June.

529 Craig Duswalt. 2014. *Welcome to My Jungle*. Benbella Books.

530 Kim Neely. 1992. "Axl Rose." *Rolling Stone*, October 15.

531 Kim Neely. 1992. "Axl Rose: The Rolling Stone Interview." *Rolling Stone*, April 2.

532 Kim Neely. 1992. "Axl Rose." *Rolling Stone*, October 15.

533 Katherine Turman. 1987. "Tattooed Love Boys Take a Shot in the Dark." *Music Connection*, November 30 - December 13.

534 Nick Gillespie. 1988. "Shooting from the Lip with Guns N' Roses." *Smash Hits*, November.

535 Marc Spitz. 1999. "Appetite for Self Destruction." *Spin*, July 1.

536 Gary Graff. 1992. "Guns and Metallica Stage Metal Assault." *The Detroit Free Press*, July 19.

[537] Marc Spitz. 1999. "Appetite for Self Destruction." *Spin*, July 1.

[538] Robert Hilburn. 1992. "Rock's Dream Team." *Los Angeles Times*, August 9.

[539] Bill Flanagan. 1992. "Shadow Boxing with Axl Rose." *Musician*, June.

[540] Bill Flanagan. 1992. "Shadow Boxing with Axl Rose." *Musician*, June.

[541] Phil Alexander. 1992. "Shattering Your Illusions." *Raw*, March 4-17.

[542] Bill Flanagan. 1992. "Shadow Boxing with Axl Rose." *Musician*, June.

[543] Matt Resnicoff. 1992. "Slash Shows His Face." *Musician*, June.

[544] Author interview with Matt Sorum. June 8, 2001.

[545] "Lisa Maxwell Talks 976 Horns." 2021. *Appetite for Distortion*, Episode 252, March 8.

[546] Peter Wilkinson. 2000. "Axl Rose: The Lost Years." *Rolling Stone*, May 11.

[547] Andrew DiCecco. 2022. "An Interview with Former Guns N' Roses Manager Alan Niven." *VW Music*, September 10.

[548] David Konow. 2002. *Bang Your Head: The Rise and Fall of Heavy Metal*, Three River Press.

[549] Bill Flanagan. 1992. "Shadow Boxing with Axl Rose." *Musician*, June.

[550] Bill Flanagan. 1992. "Shadow Boxing with Axl Rose." *Musician*, June.

[551] "Slash the Last Romantic. 1992. *People*, April 27.

[552] *Headbangers Ball*. 1992. MTV Networks, May.

[553] "The Smashing Pumpkins 1992-04-06." SPCodex.wiki

[554] Kim Neely. 1992. "Axl Rose." *Rolling Stone*, October 15.

[555] Bill Flanagan. 1992. "Shadow Boxing with Axl Rose." *Musician*, June.

[556] Greg Kot. 1992. "An Arena Full of Rock N' Roses." *Chicago Tribune*, April 12.

[557] Greg Kot. 1992. "An Arena Full of Rock N' Roses." *Chicago Tribune*, April 12.

[558] "Axl Gets in the Ring." 1992. *Metallix*, December 5.

[559] "Don't Look for W. Axl Rose and Guns N' Roses in Concert Again Anytime Soon." *Chicago Tribune*, April 16.

[560] Kim Bell. 1992. "Dodging County Is Costing Axl Rose." *St. Louis Post-Dispatch*, April 15.

[561] Michael Gougis. 1992. "Guns N' Roses Puts on a Real Showstopper." The Associated Press, April 11.

[562] "Don't Look for W. Axl Rose and Guns N' Roses in Concert Again Anytime Soon." *Chicago Tribune*, April 16.

[563] Michael Gougis. 1992. "Guns N' Roses Puts on a Real Showstopper." The Associated Press, April 11.

[564] Michael Kates. 1992. "Guns N' Roses Cancels Show After Lead Singer Skips Town." *Chicago Tribune*, April 11.

[565] Michael Gougis. 1992. "Guns N' Roses Puts on a Real Showstopper." The Associated Press, April 11.

[566] Michael Kates. 1992. "Guns N' Roses Cancels Show After Lead Singer Skips Town." *Chicago Tribune*, April 11.

[567] Jae-Ha Kim and Scott Fornek. 1992. "Axl Rose a Fugitive After Show Cancelled." *Chicago Sun-Times*, April 12.

[568] Michael Kates. 1992. "Guns N' Roses Cancels Show After Lead Singer Skips Town." *Chicago Tribune*, April 11.

[569] Michael Gougis. 1992. "Guns N' Roses Puts on a Real Showstopper." The Associated Press, April 11.

[570] "Don't look for W. Axl Rose and Guns N' Roses in concert again anytime soon." *Chicago Tribune*, April 16.

[571] Fred W. Lindecke. 1992. "Rock Star Evades Long Arm of Law." *St. Louis Post-Dispatch*, April 12.

[572] The Associated Press. "Concert Is Canceled After Band's Singer Flees to Avoid Arrest." 1992. *The New York Times*, April 12.

[573] Fred W. Lindecke. 1992. "Rock Star Evades Long Arm of Law." *St. Louis Post-Dispatch*, April 12.

[574] Jae-Ha Kim and Scott Fornek. 1992. "Axl Rose a Fugitive After Show Cancelled." *Chicago Sun-Times*, April 12.

[575] Duff McKagan. 2011. *It's So Easy (and Other Lies)*. Orion.

[576] *Headbangers Ball*. 1992. MTV Networks, May.

[577] *Headbangers Ball*. 1992. MTV Networks, May.

[578] *Headbangers Ball*. 1992. MTV Networks, May.

[579] Chris Roberts. 1992. "Guns N' Roses: Knockin' On Britain's Door." *Melody Maker*, May 30.

[580] Gary Graff. 1992. "Guns and Metallica Stage Metal Assault." *The Detroit Free Press*, July 19.

[581] *Headbangers Ball*. 1992. MTV Networks, May.

[582] "Rock Star Axl Rose to Confront Charges." *St. Louis Post-Dispatch*, June 4, 1992:

[583] "Rock Star Axl Rose to Confront Charges." *St. Louis Post-Dispatch*, June 4, 1992:

[584] Interview with Slash. 1991. *Countdown*. Reelin' In the Years Productions, May.

[585] Duff McKagan. 2011. *It's So Easy (and Other Lies)*. Orion.

[586] Ronan McGreevy. 2017. "Mountcharles Not Fearing 'Typhoon of Chaos' as Guns N' Roses Head for Slane." *The Irish Times*, May 27.
[587] Interview with Slash. 1991. *Countdown*. Reelin' In the Years Productions, May.
[588] Del James. 1992. "I, Axl." *Rip*, November.,
[589] Duff McKagan. 2011. *It's So Easy (and Other Lies)*. Orion.
[590] Duff McKagan. 2011. *It's So Easy (and Other Lies)*. Orion.
[591] "Guns N' Roses Invaded Paris!" 1992. Press Release from Polygram Diversified Entertainment, April 29.
[592] "Beck Drops Out." 1992. MTV Networks.
[593] "Beck Drops Out." 1992. MTV Networks.
[594] "Beck Drops Out." 1992. MTV Networks.
[595] "Beck Drops Out." 1992. MTV Networks.
[596] Josh Jones. 2010. "Jeff Beck's Music Business Lessons." *Clash*, April 27.
[597] "Beck Drops Out." 1992. MTV Networks.
[598] Matt Sorum with Leif Eriksson and Martin Svensson. 2022. *Double Talkin' Jive: True Rock 'n' Roll Stories from the Drummer of Guns N' Roses, The Cult, and Velvet Revolver*. Rare Bird Books.
[599] Kate Meyers and Benjamin Svetkey. 1991. "Warren Beatty's Relationships." *Entertainment Weekly*, August 2.
[600] Steve Hochman. 1992. "Vintage Guns N' Roses." *Los Angeles Times*, June 8.
[601] Author interview with Matt Sorum. June 8, 2001.
[602] David Fricke. 1992. "Izzy Stradlin." *Rolling Stone*, October 29.
[603] Rachel Halliwell. 1992. "Band Pulls Plug on Gig Leaving Mersey Fans Disappointed." *The Liverpool Echo*, June 9.
[604] Slash with Anthony Bozza. 2008. *Slash*. Harper Entertainment.
[605] Duff McKagan. 2011. *It's So Easy (and Other Lies)*. Orion.
[606] John Stix. 1992. "Slash: Guitar from the Gut." *Guitar for the Practicing Musician*, November.
[607] Mary Anne Hobbs. 1992. "Dude's Corner." *New Musical Express*, June 20.
[608] "Guns N' Roses in Athens." 1993. The O-Zone, May 31.
[609] Peter Wilkinson. 2000. "Axl Rose: The Lost Years." *Rolling Stone*, May 11.
[610] Bill Flanagan. 1992. "Shadowboxing with Axl Rose." *Musician*, June.
[611] "Sperm and Cuddly Toys." *OOR*, August 8.
[612] Mark Putterford. 1992. "Real Ugly Experience." *Select*, August.
[613] Mark Putterford. 1992. "Real Ugly Experience." *Select*, August.
[614] Mark Putterford. 1992. "Real Ugly Experience." *Select*, August.
[615] Mark Putterford. 1992. "Real Ugly Experience." *Select*, August.

[616] William Shaw. 1992. "Twist of Fate." *Details*, September.

[617] Mark Putterford. 1992. "Real Ugly Experience." *Select*, August.

[618] Brad Tolinski. 1992. "Trial by Fire." *Guitar World*, November.

[619] Brad Tolinski. 1992. "Trial by Fire." *Guitar World*, November.

[620] Kurt Loder interview with Axl Rose. 1992. MTV News, July 12.

[621] Duff McKagan. 2011. *It's So Easy (and Other Lies)*. Orion.

[622] Mike Wake. 2020. "The Secrets of GNR's Overlooked Albums." *Guitar World*, July 25.

[623] Lisa Johnson. 1994. "War of the Roses." *Kerrang*, May 14.

[624] Robert Hilburn. 1992. "Rock's Dream Team." *Los Angeles Times*, August 9.

[625] Nikhil Deogun. 1992. Axl Rose Arrested In NY; Extradition Sought." *St. Louis Post-Dispatch*, July 13.

[626] Robert Hilburn. 1992. "Rock's Dream Team." *Los Angeles Times*, August 9.

[627] Nikhil Deogun. 1992. "Axl Rose Arrested In NY; Extradition Sought." *St. Louis Post-Dispatch*, July 13.

[628] Robert Hilburn. 1992. "Rock's Dream Team." *Los Angeles Times*, August 9.

[629] Kurt Loder interview with Axl Rose. 1992. MTV News, July 12.

[630] Mandulo, Rhea. 1992. "Guns N' Roses Singer Arrested at Airport." UPI, July 12.

[631] Nikhil Deogun. 1992. "Axl Rose Arrested In NY; Extradition Sought." *St. Louis Post-Dispatch*, July 13.

[632] Nikhil Deogun. 1992. "Axl Rose Arrested In NY; Extradition Sought." *St. Louis Post-Dispatch*, July 13.

[633] Kurt Loder interview with Axl Rose. 1992. MTV News, July 12.

[634] Kurt Loder interview with Axl Rose. 1992. MTV News, July 12.

[635] Kurt Loder interview with Axl Rose. 1992. MTV News, July 12.

[636] William C. Lhotka and Virgil Tipton. 1992. "Axl Rose Expected Here Today." *St. Louis Post-Dispatch*, July 14.

[637] William C. Lhotka and Virgil Tipton. 1992. "Axl Rose Denies Guilt; Trial Set for October." *St. Louis Post-Dispatch*, July 15.

[638] William C. Lhotka. 1992. "Axl Rose Found Guilty, Faces Civil Suits." *St. Louis Post-Dispatch*, November 11.

[639] William C. Lhotka and Virgil Tipton. 1992. "Axl Rose Denies Guilt; Trial Set for October." *St. Louis Post-Dispatch*, July 15.

[640] William C. Lhotka and Virgil Tipton. 1992. "Axl Rose Denies Guilt; Trial Set for October." *St. Louis Post-Dispatch*, July 15.

[641] Kurt Loder interview with Slash. 1992. MTV News, July 14.

[642] Press Release. June 1992. "Guns N' Roses Invite Charities & Activists to Set Up Booths at Summer Stadium Shows." Geffen Records.

[643] Robert Hilburn. 1992. "Rock's Dream Team." *Los Angeles Times*, August 9.

[644] Robert Hilburn. 1992. "Rock's Dream Team." *Los Angeles Times*, August 9.

[645] Gary Graff. 1992. "Guns and Metallica Stage Metal Assault." *The Detroit Free Press*, July 19.

[646] Interview with Slash and Lars Ulrich. 1992. Rockline, July 13.

[647] Jon Bream. 1992. "Guns N' Roses and Metallica Bring Different Worldviews to Their Monstrous Summer Tour." *Star Tribune*, August 4.

[648] Matt Sorum with Leif Eriksson and Martin Svensson. 2022. *Double Talkin' Jive: True Rock 'n' Roll Stories from the Drummer of Guns N' Roses, The Cult, and Velvet Revolver.* Rare Bird Books.

[649] Gary Graff. 1992. "Guns and Metallica Stage Metal Assault." *The Detroit Free Press*, July 19.

[650] Jim Sullivan. 1992. "Testing Their Metal." *The Boston Globe*, July 27.

[651] "Guns N' Metallica – Unleashing the Monster." 1992. MTV Networks.

[652] Interview with Slash and Lars Ulrich. 1992. Rockline, July 13.

[653] Interview with Slash and Lars Ulrich. 1992. Rockline, July 13.

[654] Gary Graff. 1992. "Guns and Metallica Stage Metal Assault." *The Detroit Free Press*, July 19.

[655] Gary Graff. 1992. "Guns and Metallica Stage Metal Assault." *The Detroit Free Press*, July 19.

[656] Brad Tolinski. 1992. "Trial by Fire." *Guitar World*, November.

[657] Gary Graff. 1992. "Guns and Metallica Stage Metal Assault." *The Detroit Free Press*, July 19.

[658] Interview with Slash and Lars Ulrich. 1992. Rockline, July 13.

[659] Robert Hilburn. 1992. "Rock's Dream Team." *Los Angeles Times*, August 9.

[660] Marc D. Allan. 1992. "Rockin' Hard at the Dome." *The Indianapolis Star*, July 21.

[661] Robert Hilburn. 1992. "Rock's Dream Team." *Los Angeles Times*, August 9.

[662] Peter Wilkinson. 2000. "Axl Rose: The Lost Years." *Rolling Stone*, May 11.

[663] "Guns N' Minneapolis." 1992. *Star Tribune*, June 26.

[664] Interview with Slash and Lars Ulrich. 1992. Rockline, July 13.

665 Jon Bream. 1992. "Guns N' Roses and Metallica Bring Different Worldviews to Their Monstrous Summer Tour." *Star Tribune*, August 4.

666 Interview with Slash. 1992. MTV Networks, July 20.

667 Bruce Britt. 1992. "No Bed of Roses." *Los Angeles Daily News*, July 21, 1992.

668 Robert Hilburn. 1992. "Rock's Dream Team." *Los Angeles Times*, August 9.

669 Interview with Slash. 1992. MTV Networks, July 20.

670 Jon Parales. 1992. "A Battle of 2 Headliner Bands." *Los Angeles Times*, July 20.

671 Matty Karas. 1992. "Guns Fail to Come Up Smelling Like Roses." *Asbury Park Press*, July 20.

672 Bruce Britt. 1992. "Guns N' Roses Fires Mostly Blanks on Tour." *Observer-Reporter*, July 24.

673 Barbara Jaeger. 1992. "Guns N' Roses Misfires." *The Record*, July 20.

674 Tom Sinclair. 1992. *Rolling Stone*.

675 Matt Sorum with Leif Eriksson and Martin Svensson. 2022. *Double Talkin' Jive: True Rock 'n' Roll Stories from the Drummer of Guns N' Roses, The Cult, and Velvet Revolver*. Rarc Bird Books.

676 Robert Hilburn. 1992. "Views from Inside Rock's Dream Team." *Los Angeles Times*, August 9.

677 Matt Sorum with Leif Eriksson and Martin Svensson. 2022. *Double Talkin' Jive: True Rock 'n' Roll Stories from the Drummer of Guns N' Roses, The Cult, and Velvet Revolver*. Rare Bird Books.

678 Matt Sorum with Leif Eriksson and Martin Svensson. 2022. *Double Talkin' Jive: True Rock 'n' Roll Stories from the Drummer of Guns N' Roses, The Cult, and Velvet Revolver*. Rare Bird Books.

679 Interview with Dizzy Reed. 2020. GN'R Central, February 20.

680 Drew Masters. 1992. "Guns N' Roses: The Dirt on Montreal, Axl, and More." M.E.A.T., September.

681 Slash with Anthony Bozza. 2008. *Slash*. Harper Entertainment.

682 Jon Bream. 1992. "Guns N' Roses and Metallica Bring Different Worldviews to Their Monstrous Summer Tour." *Star Tribune*, August 4.

683 Bob Dillier. 1992. "200 Fans Arrested at Heavy Metal Concert." *Daily Journal* July 23.

684 Bob Dillier. 1992. "200 Fans Arrested at Heavy Metal Concert." *Daily Journal* July 23.

685 Peter Agostinelli. 1992. "Axl's Unrestrained Ego Bigger Than Hoosier Dome." *Journal and Courier*, July 24.

[686] Mike Redmond. 1992. "Rose's Music Hath More Charm Than He." *The Indianapolis News*, July 23.

[687] Marc D. Allan. 1992. "Guns More Mouth Than Music." *The Indianapolis Star*, July 24.

[688] Axl Rose. 1992. Letter to Marc D. Allan, July 24.

[689] Axl Rose. 1992. Letter to Marc D. Allan, July 24.

[690] D. Carol Kribel and Paula Jarrett. 1992. "Axl at Arni's: Fans eat it up." *Journal and Courier*, July 25.

[691] Robert Hilburn. 1992. "Views from Inside Rock's Dream Team." *Los Angeles Times*, August 9.

[692] Russ DeVault. 1992. "Guns N' Bruises." *The Atlanta Constitution*, July 31.

[693] Jon Bream. 1992. "Guns N' Roses and Metallica Bring Different Worldviews to Their Monstrous Summer Tour." *Star Tribune*, August 4.

[694] Jon Bream. 1992. "Guns N' Roses and Metallica Bring Different Worldviews to Their Monstrous Summer Tour." *Star Tribune*, August 4.

[695] Michael McGovern. 1992. "Homestead Act of '92." *New York Daily News*, July 30.

[696] Robert Hilburn. 1992. "Views from Inside Rock's Dream Team." *Los Angeles Times*, August 9.

[697] Robert Hilburn. 1992. "Views from Inside Rock's Dream Team." *Los Angeles Times*, August 9.

[698] *A Year and a Half in the Life of Metallica* (Adam Dubin, director). 1992. Elektra Entertainment.

[699] David Fricke. 1993. "Don't Tread on Me." *Rolling Stone*, April 3.

[700] Interview with Doug Goldstein. 2015. One on One with Mitch Lafon, Episode 100, April 5.

[701] *GN'R & Metallica: Live & Loud*. 1992. MTV Networks, September.

[702] Matt Sorum with Leif Eriksson and Martin Svensson. 2022. *Double Talkin' Jive: True Rock 'n' Roll Stories from the Drummer of Guns N' Roses, The Cult, and Velvet Revolver*. Rare Bird Books.

[703] Matt Sorum with Leif Eriksson and Martin Svensson. 2022. *Double Talkin' Jive: True Rock 'n' Roll Stories from the Drummer of Guns N' Roses, The Cult, and Velvet Revolver*. Rare Bird Books.

[704] Duff McKagan. 2011. *It's So Easy (and Other Lies)*. Orion.

[705] *GN'R & Metallica: Live & Loud*. 1992. MTV Networks, September.

[706] *GN'R & Metallica: Live & Loud*. 1992. MTV Networks, September.

[707] *GN'R & Metallica: Live & Loud*. 1992. MTV Networks, September.

[708] *GN'R & Metallica: Live & Loud*. 1992. MTV Networks, September.

[709] "12 Heavy Metal Fans Face Charges for Riot." 1992. *Vancouver Sun*, August 10.

710 Kate Dunn and Ann McLaughlin. 1992. "Heavy Mess." *The Gazette,* August 10.

711 "Angry Rock Fans riot in Montreal." 1992. Associated Press, August 10.

712 Duff McKagan. 2011. *It's So Easy (and Other Lies).* Orion.

713 David Fricke. 1993. "Don't Tread on Me." Rolling Stone, April 3.

714 Mark Lepage. 1992. "Dynamite Concert Turns into a Dud." *Montreal Gazette,* August 15.

715 Michael McNamara, dir. 1998. *Metallica: Behind the Music.* VH-1 Productions.

716 David Fricke. 1993. "Don't Tread on Me." Rolling Stone, April 3.

717 Duff McKagan. 2011. *It's So Easy (and Other Lies).* Orion.

718 Slash with Anthony Bozza. 2008. *Slash.* Harper Entertainment.

719 *GN'R & Metallica: Live & Loud.* 1992. MTV Networks, September.

720 Mark Lepage. 1992. "Other Stadiums to Hear OIB's Version of Riot at Rock Concert." *Montreal Gazette,* August 15.

721 Brad Tolinski. 1992. "Trial by Fire." *Guitar World,* November.

722 Brad Tolinski. 1992. "Trial by Fire." *Guitar World,* November.

723 "Andy Morahan Talks Directing Guns N' Roses Music Videos." 2020. Appetite For Distortion: Episode 187. April 21.

724 "Andy Morahan Talks Directing Guns N' Roses Music Videos." 2020. Appetite For Distortion: Episode 187. April 21.

725 "Guns N' Roses in Athens." 1993. MTV Networks, May.

726 "Andy Morahan Talks Directing Guns N' Roses Music Videos." 2020. Appetite For Distortion: Episode 187. April 21.

727 "Andy Morahan Talks Directing Guns N' Roses Music Videos." 2020. Appetite For Distortion: Episode 187. April 21.

728 Drew Masters. 1992. "Guns N' Roses: The Dirt on Montreal, Axl, and More." *M.E.A.T.,* September.

729 "Guns N' Roses in Athens." 1993. MTV Networks, May.

730 Mary Anne Hobbs. 1992. "Dude's Corner." *New Musical Express,* June 20.

731 Matt Smith. 1992. "Violence is Golden." *Melody Maker,* August 8.

732 William Shaw. 1992. "Twist of Fate." *Details,* September.

733 Robert Nelson. 1992. "Have Faith." *El Paso Times,* August 7.

734 Drew Masters. 1992. "Guns N' Roses: The Dirt on Montreal, Axl, and More." *M.E.A.T.,* September.

735 Slash with Anthony Bozza. 2008. *Slash.* Harper Entertainment.

736 Enric Volante. 1992. "Swollen River Turns Rock Concert into Nightmare for Some." *The Arizona Daily Star.*

737 Jean Marie Laskas. 1992. "On the Road with Guns N' Roses." *Life*, December 1.

738 Bill Flanagan. 1992. "Shadowboxing with Axl Rose." *Musician*, June.

739 Brad Tolinski. 1992. "Trial by Fire." *Guitar World*, November.

740 "Doug Goldstein and Dr. Stephen Thaxton Talk UYI Tour and GNR Chiropractics." 2019. Appetite For Distortion: Episode 101, January 30.

741 Drew Masters. 1992. "Guns N' Roses: The Dirt on Montreal, Axl, and More." *M.E.A.T.*, September.

742 Jean Marie Laskas. 1992. "On the Road with Guns N' Roses." *Life*, December 1.

743 Jean Marie Laskas. 1992. "On the Road with Guns N' Roses." *Life*, December 1.

744 Bill Flanagan. 1992. "Shadowboxing with Axl Rose." *Musician*, June.

745 Robert Hilburn. 1992. "Views from Inside Rock's Dream Team." *Los Angeles Times*, August 9.

746 Lynn Hirshberg. 1992. "Strange Love: The Story of Kurt Cobain and Courtney Love." *Vanity Fair*, September.

747 Bob Cannon. 1992. "Nirvana Bashing." *Entertainment Weekly*, September 25.

748 Philip Booth. 1992. "Roses' Concert Has Its Thorns." *The Tampa Tribune*, September 4.

749 Mike Oliver. 1992. "Some Sound Off Over Nudity at Concert" *Orlando Sentinel*, September 4.

750 Mike Oliver. 1992. "Some Sound Off Over Nudity at Concert" *Orlando Sentinel*, September 4.

751 Mike Oliver. 1992. "Some Sound Off Over Nudity at Concert" *Orlando Sentinel*, September 4.

752 Philip Booth. 1992. "Roses' Concert Has Its Thorns." *The Tampa Tribune*, September 4.

753 *GN'R & Metallica: Live & Loud*. 1992. MTV Networks, September.

754 *GN'R & Metallica: Live & Loud*. 1992. MTV Networks, September.

755 Jean Marie Laskas. 1992. "On the Road with Guns N' Roses." *Life*, December 1.

756 Jean Marie Laskas. 1992. "On the Road with Guns N' Roses." *Life*, December 1.

757 Del James. 1992. "I, Axl." *Rip*, September 19.

758 Alisa Valdes. 1992. "Lisa Maxwell: From Berklee to Guns N' Roses." *The Boston Globe*, July 31.

759 Craig Marks and Rob Tannenbaum. 2011. *I Want My MTV: The Uncensored Story of the Music Video Revolution*. Plume.

760 Bob Cannon. 1992. "Nirvana Bashing." *Entertainment Weekly*, September 25.

761 Craig Marks and Rob Tannenbaum. 2011. *I Want My MTV: The Uncensored Story of the Music Video Revolution*. Plume.

762 Interview with Nirvana. 1992. MTV Networks, September 11.

763 Craig Marks and Rob Tannenbaum. 2011. *I Want My MTV: The Uncensored Story of the Music Video Revolution*. Plume.

764 Duff McKagan. 2010. "All Apologies." *Seattle Weekly*, February 11.

765 Louis Marciano, dir. 1993. *Makin' F@*!ing Videos Part II*. Geffen Home Video.

766 Jim Sullivan. 1992. "Guns N' Roses Roll in to Foxboro Stadium." *The Boston Globe*, September 10.

767 Brad Tolinski. 1992. "Trial By Fire." *Guitar World*, November.

768 Interview with Doug Goldstein. 2015. One on One with Mitch Lafon, Episode 100, April 5.

769 Rick Roddam. 2016. "The Night Guns N' Roses Almost Started a Riot in Denver." King FM, December 5.

770 Jennifer Susich. 1992. "Big Bash at Mile High Stadium." *Highlander*, September 24.

771 Matt Allen. 2021. "Guns N' Roses Were a Gang." *Kerrang*, July 23.

772 "From Woodstock to Springsteen." 2016. Pop Dose, February 18.

773 "Woodstock '99 and Jamming with Slash in '92." Stormymondays.com.

774 Robert Hilburn. 1992. "Views from Inside Rock's Dream Team." *Los Angeles Times*, August 9.

775 Slash with Anthony Bozza. 2008. *Slash*. Harper Entertainment.

776 Slash with Anthony Bozza. 2008. *Slash*. Harper Entertainment.

777 *Guns N' Roses: Behind the Music*. 2004. VH-1 Productions.

778 Slash with Anthony Bozza. 2008. *Slash*. Harper Entertainment.

779 Robert Hilburn. 1992. "Rock's Dream Team." *Los Angeles Times*, August 9.

780 Steve Hochman. 1992. "Ice-T Is 'Vetoed' From 2 Guns Shows." *Los Angeles Times*, September 24.

781 Steve Hochman. 1992. "Ice-T Is 'Vetoed' From 2 Guns Shows." *Los Angeles Times*, September 24.

782 Robert Hilburn. 1992. "For Guns, No Night of Dreams." *Los Angeles Times*, September 29.

783 Fred Shuster. 1992. "Metal Giants Falter in Stadium Slugfest." *Los Angeles Daily News*, September 29.

[784] Stephen Dalton. 1992. "Metallica: High on Iron Scion." *New Musical Express*, October 24.

[785] Craig Duswalt. 2014. *Welcome to My Jungle*. Benbella Books.

[786] "An Appetite for Construction – The Axl Interview." 1993. *Raw Magazine*, November 11.

[787] Patrick Macdonald. 1992. "Testing Their Metal." *The Seattle Times*, October 2.

[788] Everett True. 1992. "All You Need is Love." *Melody Maker*, December 19-26.

[789] Interview with Slash. 1992. MTV Networks, October.

[790] Interview with Dizzy Reed. 1992. In Your Face, October.

[791] "An Appetite For Construction – The Axl Interview." 1993. *Raw Magazine*, November 11.

[792] David Fricke. 1993. "Don't Tread on Me." *Rolling Stone*, April 3.

[793] Steffan Chirazi. 1994. "Get Outta the Ring." *Kerrang*, January 8.

[794] Slash with Anthony Bozza. 2008. *Slash*. Harper Entertainment.

[795] Associated Press. 1992. "Axl Rose Convicted of Assault." *Variety*, November 10.

[796] William C. Lhotka. 1992. "Plea Bargain For Axl Rose Has A Twist." *St. Louis Post-Dispatch*, November 10.

[797] Slash with Anthony Bozza. 2008. *Slash*. Harper Entertainment.

[798] Interview with Slash. 1992. MTV Networks, October.

[799] Interview with Dizzy Reed. 1992. In Your Face, October.

[800] Steve Morse. 1993. "The Rude N' Rowdy Guns Tour." *The Boston Globe*, March 12.

[801] Matt Sorum with Leif Eriksson and Martin Svensson. 2022. *Double Talkin' Jive: True Rock 'n' Roll Stories from the Drummer of Guns N' Roses, The Cult, and Velvet Revolver*. Rare Bird Books.

[802] Matt Sorum with Leif Eriksson and Martin Svensson. 2022. *Double Talkin' Jive: True Rock 'n' Roll Stories from the Drummer of Guns N' Roses, The Cult, and Velvet Revolver*. Rare Bird Books.

[803] "An Appetite for Construction – The Axl Interview." 1993. *Raw Magazine*, November 11.

[804] "An Appetite for Construction – The Axl Interview." 1993. *Raw Magazine*, November 11.

[805] Andy Greene. 2020. "Veteran Backup Singer Roberta Freeman Talks Life on the Road With Guns N' Roses, Pink Floyd." *Rolling Stone*, June 24.

[806] Duff McKagan. 2011. *It's So Easy (and Other Lies)*. Orion.

[807] Finlay McDonald. "Axl Was a Girl." 1993. *Kerrang*, April 17.

808 Matt Sorum with Leif Eriksson and Martin Svensson. 2022. *Double Talkin' Jive: True Rock 'n' Roll Stories from the Drummer of Guns N' Roses, The Cult, and Velvet Revolver.* Rare Bird Books.

809 Interview with Duff and Matt. 1992. MTV Brazil, December 11.

810 Matt Sorum with Leif Eriksson and Martin Svensson. 2022. *Double Talkin' Jive: True Rock 'n' Roll Stories from the Drummer of Guns N' Roses, The Cult, and Velvet Revolver.* Rare Bird Books.

811 "An Appetite for Construction – The Axl Interview." 1993. *Raw Magazine*, November 11.

812 Reuter. 1992. "Guns N' Roses Cleared in Chilean Drug Search." *The San Francisco Examiner*, December 4.

813 Slash with Anthony Bozza. 2008. *Slash.* Harper Entertainment.

814 Steve Morse. 1993. "The Rude N' Rowdy Guns Tour." *The Boston Globe*, March 12.

815 Associated Press 1992. "Police Charge Rose with Endangering Lives." The Pantagraph, December 11.

816 Donna Yuzwalk. 1993. "It's Duff at the Top." *Rip It Up*, January.

817 "An Appetite for Construction – The Axl Interview." 1993. *Raw Magazine*, November 11.

818 Ruth Ryon. 1993. "Rocker Buys $3.95-Million Beach House." *Tampa Bay Times*, January 3.

819 Emma Richardson. 2024. "Axl Rose House: 4.2 Million." Gigwise, July 1.

820 Ruth Ryon. 1993. "Rocker Buys $3.95-Million Beach House." *Tampa Bay Times*, January 3.

821 "Axl Speaks." 1993. *Hit Parader*, June.

822 Marc Spitz. 1999. "The Unbelievable Truth." *Spin*, July.

823 People Staff. "Axl's Christmas Surprise." 1993. *People*, September 13.

824 Marc Spitz. 1999. "The Unbelievable Truth." *Spin*, July.

825 "Stephanie's Secret: Axl's No Rose." 1994. *People*, July 18.

826 People Staff. "Axl's Christmas Surprise." 1993. *People*, September 13.

827 Matt Allen. 2021. "Guns N' Roses Were a Gang." *Kerrang*, July 23.

828 Slash with Anthony Bozza. 2008. *Slash.* Harper Entertainment.

829 Glenn Kenny. 1993. *"Use Your Illusion I & II: World Tour 1992 in Tokyo." Entertainment Weekly*, February 5.

830 Interview with Doug Goldstein. 2015. One on One with Mitch Lafon, Episode 100, April 5.

831 Steve Braunias. 1993. "We're Still Turned On By One Another." *Raw*, June 23-July 6.

[832] Slash with Anthony Bozza. 2008. *Slash*. Harper Entertainment.

[833] Muriel Reddy. 1993. "The Big Gigs." *The Age*, January 24

[834] Craig Duswalt. 2014. *Welcome to My Jungle*. Benbella Books.

[835] Interview with Earl Gabbidon. 2002. Metal Sludge, December 17.

[836] Slash with Anthony Bozza. 2008. *Slash*. Harper Entertainment.

[837] "Guns N' Roses in Athens." 1993. MTV Networks, May.

[838] Patrick Beach. 1993. "Party Time for Guns N' Roses." *Des Moines Register*, March 14.

[839] Don McLeese. 1993. "Axl Leads Polite Guns Assault." *Austin American-Statesman*, February 25.

[840] "Guns N' Roses in Athens." 1993. MTV Networks, May.

[841] Robert Johnson. 1993. "Rested Guns N' Roses Puts on Exciting Show." *San Antonio Express-News*, February 25.

[842] Author interview with Matt Sorum. June 8, 2001.

[843] David Howell. 1993. "Illusions Aside, it's a Whole New, Back-to-Basics Show from the World's Most Notorious Rockers." *Edmonton Journal*, March 26.

[844] Slash with Anthony Bozza. 2008. *Slash*. Harper Entertainment.

[845] Steve Morse. 1993. "The Rude N' Rowdy Guns Tour." *The Boston Globe*, March 12.

[846] Steve Morse. 1993. "The Rude N' Rowdy Guns Tour." *The Boston Globe*, March 12.

[847] Roger Catlin. 1993. "Guns N' Roses, Back to Basics." *Hartford Courant*, March 4.

[848] Duff McKagan. 2011. *It's So Easy (and Other Lies)*. Orion.

[849] Cliff Radel. 1993. "Staying Out Late with the Bad Boys," *The Cincinnati Enquirer*, February 26.

[850] "Axl Rose Cancels Girlfriend, Postpones Concerts." 1993. *The Atlanta Constitution*, March 3.

[851] Interview with Axl and Slash. 1994. Rockline, January 3.

[852] Interview with Axl and Slash. 1994. Rockline, January 3.

[853] Fan Questions/Slash Answers. 2000. Snakepit.org, May.

[854] J. Michael Stockman. 1993. "Members of Guns N' Roses Need to Stop, Catch Their Breath." *The Statesman Journal*, April 3.

[855] Terry Craig. 1993. "Gunners Impress Band at Ryly's." *The Star Phoenix*, March 29.

[856] David Fricke. 1993. "Don't Tread on Me." *Rolling Stone*, April 3.

[857] David Barton. 1993. "Guns N' Roses Gets a Jarring Reception." *Sacramento Bee*, April 5.

[858] Duff McKagan. 2011. *It's So Easy (and Other Lies)*. Orion.

[859] David Barton. 1993. "Guns N' Roses Gets a Jarring Reception." *Sacramento Bee*, April 5.

[860] MTV News. 1993. MTV Networks, April 11.

[861] Greg Prato. 2008. *An Angel on One Shoulder, A Devil on the Other: The Story of Shannon Hoon and Blind Melon*. Greg Prato.

[862] Greg Prato. 2008. *An Angel on One Shoulder, A Devil on the Other: The Story of Shannon Hoon and Blind Melon*. Greg Prato.

[863] Greg Prato. 2008. *An Angel on One Shoulder, A Devil on the Other: The Story of Shannon Hoon and Blind Melon*. Greg Prato.

[864] Sylvie Simmons. 1994. "Home Sweet Home." *Kerrang*, March 12.

[865] David Fricke. 1992. "Life After Guns N' Roses." *Rolling Stone*, October 29.

[866] "Izzy Stradlin." 1993. *Metal CD*, volume 1, number 12.

[867] "Guns N' Roses in Athens." 1993. The O-Zone, May 31.

[868] "We're Just a Rock 'n' Roll Band." 1993. *Metal Zone*, December.

[869] "Izzy Stradlin." 1993. *Metal CD*, volume 1, number 12.

[870] "Mavericks: Izzy Stradlin." 2001. Classic Rock, June.

[871] "Guns N' Roses in Athens." 1993. MTV Networks, May.

[872] "Guns N' Roses in Athens." 1993. The O-Zone, May 31.

[873] Lisa Johnson. 1994. "War of the Roses." *Kerrang*, May 14.

[874] "Izzy Stradlin." 1993. *Metal CD*, volume 1, number 12.

[875] Craig Duswalt. 2014. *Welcome to My Jungle*. Benbella Books.

[876] Osamu Masaui & Steve Harris. 1993. Interview with Izzy, September 22.

[877] Interview with Slash and Duff. 2004. *Nuts*, October.

[878] Sylvie Simmons. 1994. "Home Sweet Home." *Kerrang*, March 12.

[879] Duff McKagan. 2011. *It's So Easy (and Other Lies)*. Orion.

[880] Dave Lindquist. 1998. "High-Achieving Soul Asylum is Cool Opening for Newcomers." *Indianapolis Star*, August 16.

[881] "Dave Pirner Talks New Soul Asylum, Prince, and Jay & Silent Bob." 2019. Appetite For Distortion, Episode 125, June 10,

[882] Greg Prato. 2008. *An Angel on One Shoulder, A Devil on the Other: The Story of Shannon Hoon and Blind Melon*. Greg Prato.

[883] Craig Duswalt. 2014. *Welcome to My Jungle*. Benbella Books.

[884] Arlett Vereecke. 1989. "Man with a Sweet Child in his Eyes." *Kerrang*, June 10.

[885] "Roberta Freeman Wishes You Were Here." 2021. Appetite for Distortion, Episode 302, September 8.

[886] Interview with Axl and Slash. 1994. Rockline, January 3.

887 Steve Morse. 1993. "The Rude N' Rowdy Guns Tour." *The Boston Globe*, March 12.

888 Del James. 1993. "Gunnin' Solo." *Rip*, November.

889 Duff McKagan. 2011. *It's So Easy (and Other Lies)*. Orion.

890 "We're Just a Rock 'n' Roll Band." 1993. Metal Zone, December.

891 Duff McKagan. 2011. *It's So Easy (and Other Lies)*. Orion.

892 Duff McKagan. 2011. *It's So Easy (and Other Lies)*. Orion.

893 "Guns 'N' Roses Escape Charges in Argentina." 1993. *The Windsor Star*, July 19.

894 Craig Duswalt. 2014. *Welcome to My Jungle*. Benbella Books.

895 Craig Duswalt. 2014. *Welcome to My Jungle*. Benbella Books.

896 Craig Duswalt. 2014. *Welcome to My Jungle*. Benbella Books.

897 "Guns N' Roses in Argentina." 1993. *Vos En Todas*, July 21.

898 Press Release. November 30, 1993. "Axl on 'Look at Your Game, Girl.'" Geffen Records.

899 Slash with Anthony Bozza. 2008. *Slash*. Harper Entertainment.

900 "Doug Goldstein and Dr. Stephen Thaxton Talk UYI tour and GNR Chiropractics." 2019. Appetite For Distortion, Episode 101, January 30.

901 Q&A with Gilby. 2009. Gilby Clarke Forum, February 1.

902 Robyn Flans. 2001. "Matt Sorum: Surviving Super Stardom." *Modern Drummer*, September.

903 Sylvie Simmons. 1994. "Home Sweet Home." *Kerrang*, March 12.

904 Slash with Anthony Bozza. 2008. *Slash*. Harper Entertainment.

905 Sylvie Simmons. 1994. "Home Sweet Home." *Kerrang*, March 12.

906 Interview with Axl and Slash. 1994. Rockline, January 3.

907 Slash with Anthony Bozza. 2008. *Slash*. Harper Entertainment.

908 Agust Jakobsson (director). 1994. *The Making of Estranged: Part IV of the Trilogy*. Geffen Home Video.

909 Agust Jakobsson (director). 1994. *The Making of Estranged: Part IV of the Trilogy*. Geffen Home Video.

910 Agust Jakobsson (director). 1994. *The Making of Estranged: Part IV of the Trilogy*. Geffen Home Video.

911 Agust Jakobsson (director). 1994. *The Making of Estranged: Part IV of the Trilogy*. Geffen Home Video.

912 Interview with Axl and Slash. 1994. Rockline, January 3.

913 Sam Coare. 2020. "It Was All Falling Apart at the Seams." *Kerrang*, September 17.

914 Agust Jakobsson (director). 1994. *The Making of Estranged: Part IV of the Trilogy*. Geffen Home Video.

915 David Glessner. 1993. "Guns N' Roses Video Filmed in Gulf." *The Galveston Daily News*, September 2.

916 David Glessner. 1993. "Guns N' Roses Video Filmed in Gulf." *The Galveston Daily News*, September 2.

917 Agust Jakobsson (director). 1994. *The Making of Estranged: Part IV of the Trilogy*. Geffen Home Video.

918 Press Release. November 30, 1993. "Axl on 'Look at Your Game, Girl.'" Geffen Records.

919 Sam Coare. 2020. "It Was All Falling Apart at the Seams." *Kerrang*, September 17.

920 Agust Jakobsson (director). 1994. *The Making of Estranged: Part IV of the Trilogy*. Geffen Home Video.

921 Agust Jakobsson (director). 1994. *The Making of Estranged: Part IV of the Trilogy*. Geffen Home Video.

922 Agust Jakobsson (director). 1994. *The Making of Estranged: Part IV of the Trilogy*. Geffen Home Video.

923 Steffan Chirazi. 1994. "All Guns Blazing." *Kerrang*, January 15.

924 Melinda Newman. 1993. "Guns N' Roses Moves on After Drummer's Lawsuit." *Tampa Bay Times*, October 4

925 People Staff. 1993. "Axl's Christmas Surprise." *People*, September 13.

926 "Stephanie's Secret: Axl's No Rose." 1994. *People*, July 18.

927 Associated Press. 1993. "Axl Rose, Former Fiancée Trade Assault Charges From 1992 Fight." *Logansport Pharos Tribune*, November 11.

928 "Axl's Christmas Surprise." 1993. *People*, September 13.

929 Agust Jakobsson (director). 1994. *The Making of Estranged: Part IV of the Trilogy*. Geffen Home Video.

930 Q&A, 1995. *Parade*, May 14.

931 Duff McKagan. 2011. *It's So Easy (and Other Lies)*. Orion.

932 Steffan Chirazi. 1994. "All Guns Blazing." *Kerrang*, January 15.

933 Jim Sullivan. 1993. "Guns N' Roses Dips into History." *The Boston Globe*, November 26.

934 Mike Roberts. 1994. "Slash Quakes in Snowstorm." *The Province*, February 2.

935 Chris Gill. 1994. "Punk Days Revisited: Slash Returns to His Roots." *Guitar Player*, January.

936 Sylvie Simmons. 1994. "Home Sweet Home." *Kerrang*, March 12.

937 James Muretich. 1994. "Slash." *The Calgary Herald*, January 29.

938 James Muretich. 1994. "Slash." *The Calgary Herald*, January 29.

[939] Press Release, November 23, 1993. "The Spaghetti Incident." Geffen Records.

[940] Press Release. November 30, 1993. "Axl on 'Look at Your Game, Girl.'" Geffen Records.

[941] Press Release, November 23, 1993. "The Spaghetti Incident." Geffen Records.

[942] "The Gunners and Charles." 1994. *Hot Metal*, January.

[943] Interview with Axl and Slash. 1994. Rockline, January 3.

[944] Press Release. December 8, 1993. "Guns N' Roses Leave Manson Track on Album So Murder Victim's Son Can Collect Royalties." Geffen Records.

[945] "The Gunners and Charles." 1994. *Hot Metal*, January.

[946] Chris Gill. 1994. "Punk Days Revisited: Slash Returns to His Roots." *Guitar Player*, January.

[947] Chuck Phillips. 1993. "Manson Song May Be Removed from Album." *Los Angeles Times*, December 1.

[948] Chuck Phillips. 1993. "Manson Song May Be Removed from Album." *Los Angeles Times*, December 1.

[949] J.D. Considine. 1993. "Guns N' Roses Under Fire for Manson 'Bonus' Song." *The Baltimore Sun*, December 3.

[950] "Beach Boys Were the First to Record Manson Song." 1993. *Hartford Courant*, December 8.

[951] J.D. Considine. 1993. "Guns N' Roses Under Fire for Manson 'Bonus' Song." *The Baltimore Sun*, December 3.

[952] "Playboy Interview: David Geffen." 1994. Playboy, September.

[953] Chuck Phillips. 1993. "Manson Song May Be Removed from Album." *Los Angeles Times*, December 1.

[954] Press Release. December 8, 1993. "Guns N' Roses Leave Manson Track on Album So Murder Victim's Son Can Collect Royalties." Geffen Records.

[955] "Beach Boys Were the First to Record Manson Song." 1993. *Hartford Courant*, December 8.

[956] Steve Hochman. 1993. "It's No Illusion: Guns N' Roses Does Charles Manson." *Los Angeles Times*, November 21.

[957] "Playboy Interview: David Geffen." 1994. Playboy, September.

[958] Chuck Phillips. 1993. "Manson Song May Be Removed from Album." *Los Angeles Times*, December 1.

[959] Press Release. November 30, 1993. "Axl on 'Look at Your Game, Girl.'" Geffen Records.

[960] J.D. Considine. 1993. "Guns N' Roses Under Fire for Manson 'Bonus' Song." *The Baltimore Sun*, December 3.

961 Press Release. December 8, 1993. "Guns N' Roses Leave Manson Track on Album So Murder Victim's Son Can Collect Royalties." Geffen Records.
962 Press Release. December 8, 1993. "Guns N' Roses Leave Manson Track on Album So Murder Victim's Son Can Collect Royalties." Geffen Records.
963 Mike Roberts. 1994. "Slash Quakes in Snowstorm." *The Province*, February 2.
964 Robert Christgau. 1994. "The Consumer Guide." *Village Voice*, January 18.
965 Andy Martin. 1993. "Market Preview." *Music Week*, November 27.
966 "Review: The Spaghetti Incident?" 1993. *Entertainment Weekly*, November 26.
967 Jonathan Gold. 1993. "The Spaghetti Incident." *Rolling Stone*, December 9.
968 Clark Collis. 1994. "Punk's Dead … Not!" *Select*, January.
969 Jonathan Gold. 1993. "The Spaghetti Incident." *Rolling Stone*, December 9.
970 Interview with Axl and Slash. 1994. Rockline, January 3.
971 Larry Flick. 1994. Single Reviews. *Billboard*, January 22.
972 "An Appetite for Construction – The Axl Interview." 1993. *Raw Magazine*, November 11.
973 "An Appetite for Construction – The Axl Interview." 1993. *Raw Magazine*, November 11.
974 Del James. 1992. "I, Axl." *Rip*, October 11.
975 Interview with Axl and Slash. 1994. Rockline, January 3.
976 Mike Roberts. 1994. "Slash Quakes in Snowstorm." *The Province*, February 2.
977 James Muretich. 1994. "Slash." *The Calgary Herald*, January 29.
978 James Muretich. 1994. "Slash." *The Calgary Herald*, January 29.
979 Sylvie Simmons. 1994. "Home Sweet Home." *Kerrang*, March 12.
980 Lisa Johnson. 1994. "War of the Roses." *Kerrang*, May 14.
981 "An Appetite for Construction – The Axl Interview." 1993. *Raw Magazine*, November 11.
982 Peter Suciu. 2023. "Guns N' Roses 'November Rain' Has Become the First Hard-Rock Video To Be Viewed Two Billion Times On YouTube." *Forbes*, February 20.
983 Sam Coare. 2020. "It Was All Falling Apart at the Seams." *Kerrang*, September 17.
984 Press Release, November 23, 1993. "The Spaghetti Incident." Geffen Records.

[985] "An Appetite for Construction – The Axl Interview." 1993. *Raw Magazine*, November 11.

[986] James Muretich. 1994. "Slash." *The Calgary Herald*, January 29.

[987] "The Way the Music Died." 2004. PBS Frontline, May 27.

[988] Steffan Chirazi. 1994. "Get Outta the Ring." *Kerrang*, January 8.

[989] Lisa Johnson. 1994. "War of the Roses." *Kerrang*, May 14.

[990] "An Appetite for Construction – The Axl Interview." 1993. *Raw Magazine*, November 11.

[991] See: Geoff Harkness. 2001. "Seven Questions with Matt Sorum." *Lawrence Journal-World*, June 28.

www.ingramcontent.com/pod-product-compliance
Lightning Source LLC
Chambersburg PA
CBHW051209130726
47988CB00001B/37